To Mildred

Harriet
Christmas 1984

CARAVAN ACROSS CHINA

An American Geologist Explores the Northwest, 1937-1938

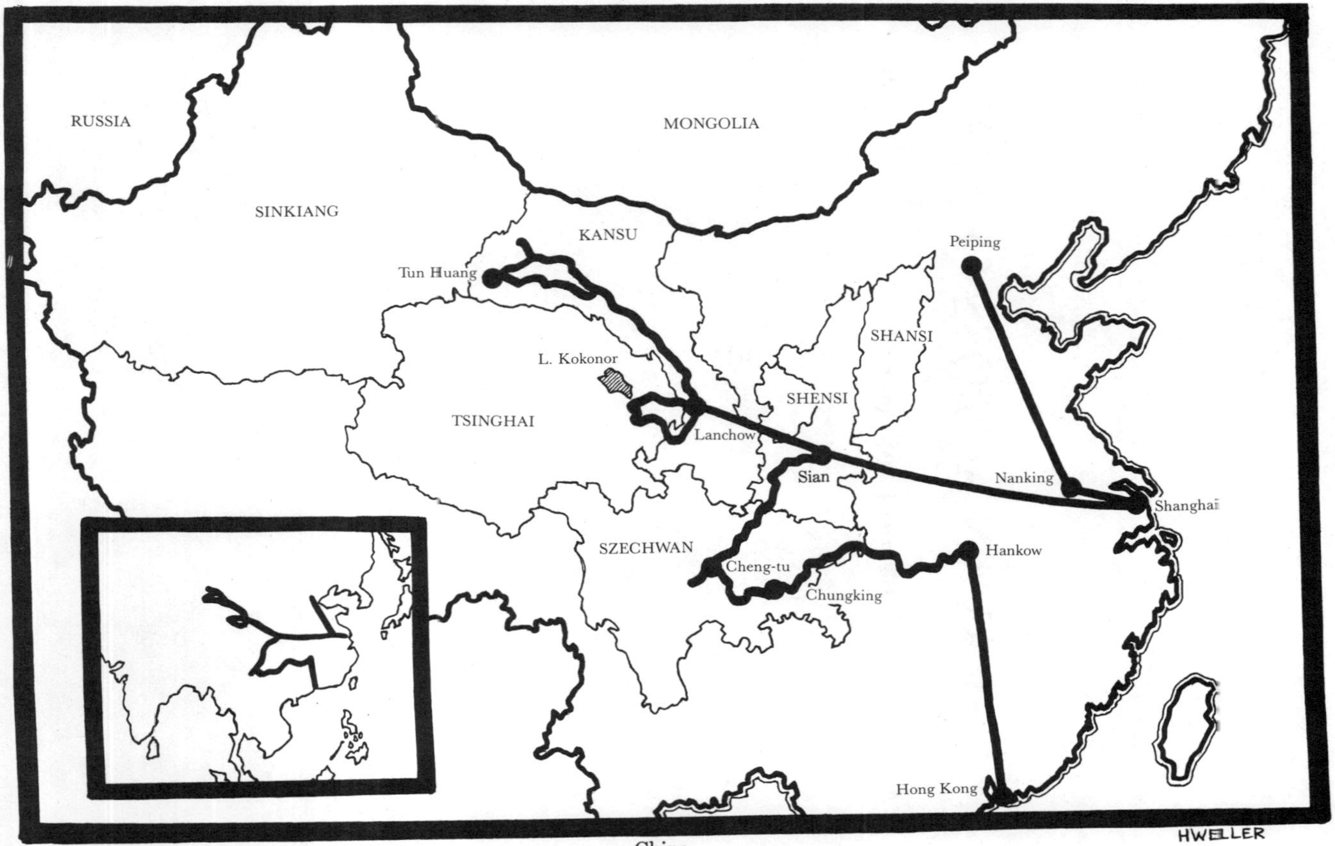
RUSSIA
MONGOLIA
SINKIANG
KANSU
Peiping
Tun Huang
SHANSI
L. Kokonor
SHENSI
TSINGHAI
Lanchow
Sian
Nanking
Shanghai
SZECHWAN
Hankow
Cheng-tu
Chungking
Hong Kong
HWELLER

MAP I

China

CARAVAN ACROSS CHINA

An American Geologist Explores the Northwest, 1937-1938

J. Marvin Weller

Edited by Harriet Weller

March Hare Publishing
1251 Dolores Street
San Francisco, CA 94110

Published by:

March Hare Publishing
1251 Dolores Street
San Francisco, CA 94110
(415) 826-5609

Printed in the United States of America

Library of Congress Cataloging in Publication Data

Weller, J. Marvin (James Marvin), 1899-
Caravan across China.

1. China, Northwest--Description and travel.
2. Petroleum--Geology--China. 3. Weller, J. Marvin
(James Marvin), 1899- . I. Weller, Harriet.
II. Title.
DS793.N6W45 1984 915.1'40442 84-23367
ISBN 0-918295-00-9

This is published in memory of my father

who had the strength and courage to embark on this adventure,

and is dedicated to the strength and courage of my mother

who stayed at home.

Table of Contents

List of Illustrations

Maps

Photographs (following page 204)

Acknowledgements

I could not have produced this book without a lot of help. Of primary importance are the meticulous characters of both my parents which resulted in the various papers concerning the trip being in order and readily available to me. I thank Arthur Anderson, Bob Lebow, Katherine Lawson, and Bill McIndoe, from a winter evening on Stanyan Street, for planting the seed of a possible book in my mind. My mother, Phyllis Gothwaite Weller, strongly supported the project, continually giving me much needed confidence, while the spirit of my father, I'm sure, hovered close by. Betty Shor, a writer from San Diego, was invaluable to me from the very beginning, first by giving her helpful suggestions on procedure, second by reading and commenting on one of the later versions of the manuscript, and all along, by offering necessary encouragement from a professional to an amateur.

I had much needed editorial assistance from many sources, starting with Peggy Northrup, who made some corrections as she did the second draft typing job. Emmy Lou Hansen of Sacramento, who was fighting a losing battle with cancer, really took me to task as she whacked her tenacious way through the manuscript, taking it into its third draft. Cheyney Johansen helped to coordinate the revisions in her word processor and was instrumental as the idea of a manuscript began to develop into a book with a future. Finally, Hilary Pritchard read the material and, with a few last-minute corrections, pronounced it ready for an audience. From that point on, I was guided by Lowell Moss, who saw to the production of the finished product.

I thank all of the above as well as the unnamed others who listened, read, and advised as I wended my way through five years of action and periods of inactivity. Here is our mutual adventure.

Harriet Weller
San Francisco, California
Spring 1984

Introduction

This book is the result of a pre-Christmas evening on Stanyan Street in 1977 when a small group of friends followed dinner with brandys in front of a golden fire. Among the group was a photojournalist and a book distributor whose territory was practically the whole of Asia and, naturally, we soon got into adventure stories from distant lands. For myself, I told what I could of my father's experiences as an oil geologist in the northwest provinces of China in 1937-38 when I was only a child in grade school. The magic of this particular evening and the interest shown by my friends in the story fanned an enthusiasm in me to further investigate my father's old adventure.

In the late 1970s, China was beginning to reopen its doors to the western world, American interest in sinology was becoming widespread, and tour groups were starting to venture into the Middle Kingdom. Suggestions from my friends that there might be a market for a book about my father's trip started to converge with my own realization that the material contained both the intrigue of a secret mission and a partial history of the inside of a war, as well as descriptions of a remote and seldom traveled part of the world. I began to reread the family's collection of my father's letters from China and leafed through his diary, field reports, and official correspondence. I spent many hours sitting on the floor in dark stacks of the main public library looking through books written by others who had traveled along the Silk Road of northwestern China in the 1920s and '30s. I was inspired by adventure and bored with my job. The following spring I took a short leave of absence from my work, purchased an electric typewriter, several reams of cheap paper, by chance located a 1974 edition of *The Times Atlas of China* in a second-hand bookstore, and settled into a challenging new task.

It was my intention from the very start of the project that this was to be my father's book as he might have written it. I started by carefully organizing the family letters and, interweaving this material with his other papers and reports, compiled a chronological and comprehensive rendition of the expedition. Without a doubt, I had stepped back some forty-five years to a very different conception of time, values, social consciousness, and political thought. I did not want to change my father's observations and expressions, and I did not, which may result in the material being dated and sometimes sounding biased. At that time, however, the American people were strongly in support of Chiang Kai-shek and his Nationalist government as it struggled against aggressions by Japan and threatening actions by Chinese communists. On the other side of the world, Europe was headed toward World War II. As these conflicts had not yet become irreparable, however, it was with a false sense of security that my thirty-seven-year-old father pushed off into the interior of Asia on the very eve of the Japanese invasion of China's east coast.

The advance preparations my father was able to make before the trip were practically nil, as he had less than a month from the time he received the proposal to his agreeing to go, and then only two weeks to get proper inoculations, passport papers, shop, pack, and meet his departure date. During this period of time, his principal mental preoccupation was to familiarize himself as much as possible with information available about the knowns and unknowns of geology in the areas of China he was to investigate. It is, indeed, unfortunate that he did not have the time to also gain a better background in Chinese history and culture that would have enabled him to view the sights he was to see with more knowledge and rendered his accounts more sophisticated. He had, however, the scientist's power of observation and a naturalist's love of the physical world around him, as well as a deep-seated curiosity to learn what he could from his native companions. The impressions he presents, therefore, tend toward a kind of country folksiness, and his existence during that year seems somehow very honest, if perhaps somewhat naive.

The letters, that had started as ordinary correspondence, developed into a journal format as he traveled westward from Sian and began to serve several purposes. He realized that he was embarking on a unique experience and that, unless he kept a careful written account, much of what he saw and did would soon fade from memory. He began to write longer letters to describe everything that interested him and soon found it difficult to keep his account up to date. The activity then took on the additional function of a catharsis against the discomforts, loneliness, and irritations of the journey which could easily be magnified to make life under those conditions unbearable. Although he felt that Sutton and Sun were good companions, he attributed his general contentment to never being at a loss for something to do, such as add to the letter that was never finished.

It is interesting to note that none of his letters was censored by the Chinese and that all of them arrived at their destinations, intact, which speaks highly of the Chinese postal service operating under primitive and confused conditions.

I do not know the details as to why my father was selected to be sent on this journey. I can only surmise that his two-year involvement as a young oil geologist in northwestern India between 1920-22 played a role, in that he had prior experience doing fieldwork in the backwaters of Asia. Memories of India were apparently stirred by some of the sights in China, as he makes note of comparisons some fifteen years later in these letters.

Again, because this is my father's book, and in order to be consistent and in tune with the time-frame of the story, I have used the older, previously-accepted westernized spellings of Chinese cities rather than the new pinyin system. Therefore Beijing (once Peking) is spelled "Peiping" as my father wrote it in the late 1930s. In many cases, the towns he traveled through were far too small to be noted in my large Atlas, and my father's phonetic spellings must stand as written. There are references in the manuscript that I question, not so much as to truth as to meaning. However, my father is not here to explain, and I have left the words much as they were written. Some of these instances are inconsistencies relative to monetary values and measurements, which are sometimes written in terms of Chinese equivalencies and at other times as his English-speaking mind must have thought of them at the time. They are not always identified as one or the other, and the reader will have to be unconcerned as to exact translation.

Incredibly, I found that my father's mode of travel and his observations of life in central China in 1937 were not far different from the experiences of those who traversed the area before him in the early 1900s: the archeologists, Sir Aurel Stein and Langdon Warner, to name two. In turn, their accounts are not so far removed from experiences related by the original travelers as they inched along the caravan routes 200 to 2,000 years ago. If there is any message here at all, it is that modern China is unbelievably young and that, unfortunately or not, it took the harrowing conditions of war to stimulate her out of obsolescence into the world of today.

CARAVAN ACROSS CHINA

PART I

Invitation to an Adventure

Urbana, Illinois
January 8, 1937

A week ago Thursday I received a long distance call from C.E. Bowen of Standard Vacuum Oil Company in New York asking me to come out there to discuss a proposal. I left Urbana on Sunday, arrived in New York at 9:30 Monday morning, and went directly to his office. He told me that a group of wealthy Chinese, headed by Dr. Wellington Koo (formerly ambassador to the United States, now ambassador to France), has an oil concession covering several provinces in northwestern China. Chiang Kai-shek is also supposedly in on it. Last year they had an exploring party in the area, consisting of some Chinese and a Russian, and another geological party is scheduled to go back in the spring. A Canadian who is acting as agent for the Chinese has approached Standard Vacuum in New York about joining them in the development of oil resources in the region. Since Standard knows nothing about the promise of the area they want a first hand report before committing themselves to a deal, and arrangements are being made to have two Standard geologists accompany the return party. I have been asked to take a leave from the Illinois Geological Survey to be one of them. I was told that, if I accept, I will travel immediately to The Hague where I will meet the Canadian, continue on to Paris for consultation with Koo, and then proceed to China. Because of the international rivalry over oil, Standard is very anxious that its name be kept out of the picture, so tell no one. Also, at this time it is not to be known that Koo is a principal. I will be an employee of Standard Vacuum and will be paid by them, although I am to say that I am employed directly by the Chinese. That is all I actually know about the deal at this time, and I can learn little more until I reach Europe. Standard officials apparently don't know much more.

My salary will be $12,000 plus expenses for one year. I was offered $10,000, but held out for a larger sum and got it. I also demanded $50,000 in insurance and finally, after a lot of argument, succeeded in being placed on the same basis as other Standard employees, which amounts to one year's salary in case of natural death and another $10,000 for accidental. This was the best I could do, and I had to fight for it.

Before reaching an agreement on terms I called on Dr. H.F. Bain, former Illinois State Geologist who has been all over China. Of course I could not tell him all I knew and, of course, under those circumstances he seemed somewhat hesitant to give advice. In any case, he gave me a letter of introduction to a Dr. Wong who is head of the Chinese Geological Survey in Nanking, as well as a secretary to Chiang Kai-shek. He said that I could rely upon what Wong could tell me of conditions in the country, as well as about the competence of the Chinese who would lead the expedition. Bain also gave me a card introducing me to T.K. Li, head of an import-export company in New York, who has frequently acted as an agent for the Chinese government in the U.S. He knows all of the big Chinese and practically assured me that, if the expedition had the backing of the Chinese government, it would be adequately protected.

There is to be another American geologist on the trip. His name is Fred Sutton, and he has worked for the last ten or fifteen years in South America. I am assured that he is a man who knows his way around and can take care of himself. He is about five years older than I and has a wife and family in Salt Lake City. I have not met him, but am told that he has a good disposition and is easy to get along with.

After returning to Urbana I went to the doctor who pronounced me fit, and I am now taking all the shots we can think of. Yesterday morning I sent Standard a wire confirming my acceptance. I sail from New York for Europe on February 3rd and will probably reach China in the middle of April.

S.S. *Bremen*, at sea
February 7, 1937

It is now 10:00 A.M., and only a short while ago I pulled myself out of bed. You, at home and presumably on the usual schedule, may find this slothful, but when I went to breakfast I was only the second passenger to present himself. (Yesterday I didn't get up until noon.)

Our ship left New York at midnight on February 2nd, rather than on the following day as expected. That, plus the fact that my train into New York was late, cut back on some of the time I had planned for errands and visits. In any case, directly upon my arrival in New York on Monday the 31st, I proceeded to the Standard Vacuum offices. Fred Sutton was already there; a stocky, sandy-haired fellow with a crooked smile, he seems exceedingly quiet and, while I don't think he will prove to be a voluble man, he will certainly be the type who is easy to travel with. And, surely, he must be a good geologist or he would not have obtained this assignment. As I already knew, he is recently up from Argentina where, by the way, he knew Ruthven Pike (who is now working along the Arabian side of the Red Sea). He also knew Ted Link in Colombia.

What was left of my morning was taken up with various bits of business around the office. After lunch I called on Bain's friend, Mr. Li, who promised me some letters of introduction, which were duly delivered to the boat. I was able to spend some time at Columbia University talking with Dr. Charles Berkey and had the opportunity to investigate written reports from the American Museum's Central Asiatic Expedition. I tried to meet with Walter Granger, the paleontologist of that trip, but my timing was unsuccessful. I had a good visit with Ben Cox (who was responsible for my hooking up with Standard for this expedition) and met a few other geologists who warm office chairs there. I did some last minute shopping and found a place to buy film at a discount. It was a hectic two days, during which I rode in more taxis than I ever have in all of my past life, and then some.

The *Bremen* is a wonderful ship in every way, although I do not think it can have nearly its full capacity of passengers. Fred and I have adjoining staterooms with bath, which are most comfortable. They are on the outside, so I can look out of my porthole and see the waves—which I don't often want to do. The seas have been rather rough, bad enough to make us about six hours late in crossing. The first day out I was terribly sick, and I stayed in bed all of the second. I have gradually become used to the motion, but traveling on a boat has never been fun for me.

We are due to reach Cherbourg tomorrow about noon. We will not go to The Hague as I had previously thought, but will proceed directly to Paris on the boat train.

Genoa, Italy
February 11, 1937

We are in Italy, preparatory to taking to sea again tomorrow on the Dutch steamer, *Christian Huygens,* just as I am getting accustomed to being on land again; I would really like to stay motionless a while longer. This time we will be on board for about twenty days and should reach Singapore on or about March 2nd, where we change to another boat. It was originally planned that we would take a faster boat, which would have allowed more time in Paris, but because two other Standard men had already arranged passage on her and it was thought that four of us being together might create suspicion, we leave on this earlier ship. I think it is to stop in Colombo, Belawan, and possibly one other Dutch Indies port on the way to Singapore.

But to get on with the record of our past activities. The *Bremen* reached Cherbourg close to noon on February 8th, where we went ashore via tender. Customs took over an hour, during which only our hand baggage was inspected; our trunks went straight through to Paris. The boat train consisted mostly of modern cars where first class was comparable to our parlor car, and lunch was served at our seats. The countryside we saw before dark fell was very pretty but terribly wet. Apparently Europe has also been having heavy rains and streams were lapping at the edges of their banks, with some areas badly flooded. It was rolling landscape, carefully kept, with little fields and orchards separated by hedges and neat rows of trees. The land was all green and, except for the leafless trees, it was hard to realize that it was winter.

We were in total darkness before arrival in Paris at 6:30 P.M., and it was raining hard. We taxied directly to our hotel and planned to return to the station the next day for our trunks, but while we were eating dinner the company's chief geologist from The Hague arrived with the information that we were to sail again, sooner than expected. We gave up the idea of getting the trunks through French customs, and I have been wearing the same shirt ever since disembarking at Cherbourg.

Tuesday morning we went to the Chinese Embassy to check in with Dr. Wellington Koo. Our conversation with him was most interesting, although it was soon apparent that he had little conception of what a field party could or should do. He had taken it for granted that we would work in comparatively small areas, but was easily convinced that it would be best for us to cover as large a territory as possible. At this time we also learned that we are to be the principle part of the expedition; the Chinese participants are solely to take responsibility for our care and proceed us into the field to make advance arrangements. Plans for conducting the work will be done by consultation between us and the Chinese assigned to us; we are to determine what we want to do, and they are to make certain that it is both possible and safe. We shall probably be granted the right to use maps and have other liberties that few foreigners have been allowed in China. It is apparent that the oil syndicate is really a private one, but that it has the full approval and support of the government. I think that we will be touring areas and seeing sights where few travelers have been before and, altogether, the proposition looks good to us.

The afternoon was far gone when we broke away. We hired a car with an English-speaking driver to see what we could of Paris before dark. That night we went to the *Folies Bergère*, which is something like an American burlesque show but much more elegantly staged. The star, Josephine Baker, the Harlem girl written up in *Time* magazine last year, is immensely popular in Paris. It is easy to see that the French have no color prejudice. She was really good.

All of Wednesday morning was consumed in getting our trunks

bonded through France, a task we could not have accomplished without the able assistance of an American Express official. That noon Dr. Koo sent his big Packard for us, and we went to his home for a Chinese dinner. The food was interesting as well as excellent, and I am pleased that my experiences with chopsticks at Dr. Garrett's home in Urbana stood me in good stead; I was able to feed myself without seeming a total fool. We learned that Madam Koo had left Paris that very morning on a flight to China bearing letters relative to our plans, so we are being preceded by a very important advance agent. She will make the trip in only ten days, whereas it will take us at least a month. It has also become obvious that the Canadian who is acting as liaison is not an ordinary promoter, as I had thought, but a prominent architect responsible for the most modern and extensive hospital in all of China.

After a whirlwind short stay, during which we saw very little of Paris, we left on the 10:20 train for Italy. Although Fred and I each had separate compartments for the night, I found it much less comfortable than an American Pullman berth. Upon awakening in the morning, we were in the French Alps near the border, traveling along a narrow valley. The air was foggy, but I could see snow at the tops of the very steep mountains on either side. We were eating a terrible breakfast when we crossed the border. While there were many formalities about passports, baggage in bond, steamer tickets, and money, our hand bags were not examined. We progressed through the mountains a long while, and after many tunnels we gradually came down into vineyard-covered foothills and eventually onto a broad green plain of farmland. The train system in Italy is completely electrified and runs smoothly with little of the chattering clickity-clack we are accustomed to.

We arrived in Genoa in the early afternoon, where it was one hour later than in France. The city, larger than I had expected, is built on several spurs of mountains which run down to the sea. The ridges rise to over 1,500 feet; a number of them are crowned by forts built by the French kings who at one time held this part of Italy. After checking into our hotel we took a ride on a "rubberneck" bus from which we saw the city and all of its architectural stages, from the very ancient to the ultra-modern. Judging by the emphasis placed on it by the guide, however, most of the tourists were expected to be primarily interested in a large Catholic cemetery. To my mind, it was one of the most hideous and grotesque places I have ever seen, filled with costly and showy tombs and sentimental statuary. The principal motif was that of life-sized and realistic representations of family members gathered in positions of grief and bereavement.

Although the architecture here is quite different from that of Paris, the houses still conform with one another and are built close and tall. In the old part of the city the streets are so narrow that the opposite houses are almost within touching distance, and there is no way that light or air can ever penetrate them. After living in such places even the slums of New York City must seem like heaven. The Italians appear to greatly enjoy displaying their laundry out of windows; necessary, I suppose, because of minimal space. Even the most respectable structures are decorated from top to bottom with flapping, drying garments.

The army is much in evidence, more so than in France, and the soldiers are better dressed and set a smarter style. The present government seems to have done a great deal in public works; the most conspicuous are the series of tunnels built under the town's ridges. These must be a great convenience.

Tomorrow morning we must see to getting our belongings onto the boat. We sail at 2:00 in the afternoon.

S.S. *Christian Huygens,* at sea
February 15, 1937

This is a Dutch boat and, of course, is much smaller than the *Bremen.* Most of the work is done by Javanese boys who understand nothing but their own language, and the ship's officers do not speak anything but Dutch very well. My cabin is a comfortable one, but neither the food nor the service compares with that of the *Bremen.* That was a really grand ship, even though the Germans, anxious for U.S. money, stubbornly insisted on dollars in payment although everything was priced in marks.

We sailed out of Genoa on a lovely sunshiny day. Late in the afternoon we saw the tip of Corsica off to the west and passed St. Helena during the night. The following afternoon we saw Stromboli's volcano with its thin plume of smoke. We were in the Straits of Messina at dusk, which presented us with a double row of almost continuous lights twinkling along the shores of both Italy and Sicily. We have passed Crete and continue southeast across the Mediterranean Sea to Port Said where we land tomorrow and I can mail this short note.

S.S. *Christian Huygens,* at sea
February 24, 1937

Tomorrow we reach Colombo. It has been a pleasant trip with unusually smooth seas, although the deisel motor which powers the ship vibrates badly most of the time.

We went ashore at Port Said, but stayed only half an hour. There is nothing to do or see there, and on the streets we were hounded by dirty natives who haggled with us to buy things we could not possibly want or need.

The last time I passed by this way, in 1920, we started south into the Suez Canal at midnight so I saw only the lower part, but this time we entered at noon and I was able to see the northern section before darkness fell. We emerged from the southern end at 2:00 A.M. They have built a fine paved road which parallels the Canal where before there were only a few earthworks and barbed wire entanglements remaining from the war.

Since leaving the Suez we have followed a route much more to the south of the one I previously sailed on the way to Bombay and have passed several groups of islands. Those nearer the African coast are volcanic, capped by lava flows, and look both desolate and uninhabited. Further southeast they seem to be coral atolls, lying low in the water, covered with palm trees. The Minicoy Lighthouse appeared as a slender white spire above the palms and looked quite pretty from a distance.

As I get better acquainted with Fred Sutton I like him more and more. At first I think he rather resented having someone from outside the company placed over him in charge of the work. But the fact that he has spoken to me about it in the way he did makes me feel everything is alright and that we will get along pleasantly.

Here I have been gone less than a month and already it seems like a long and lonesome time. Actually, I have been spending a large part of my waking hours reading up on the geology of China and am nearly through all of my books, some of which are quite sizeable. I'll soon have to find something else to keep me occupied.

S.S. *Christian Huygens,* at sea
February 28, 1937

We are certainly in the tropics now, gradually drawing nearer to the equator; in Singapore, the day after tomorrow, we will be just one and a half degrees to the north of it. It has been warm ever since we entered the Red Sea and has been growing steadily more humid and sticky. I find it hard to believe that you are still having winter weather at home.

We arrived in Colombo February 25th, where we had a very short stopover. It is an attractive city, reasonably clean and well-kept, with only a moderate amount of smells in the bazaars. The streets were alive with people and funny little oxen no bigger than Shetland ponies which are the motor power for the local carts. I presume their main advantage is that, because of their size, they cannot eat very much. Many of the men here grow their hair long and tie it up on the back of their heads in buns. Perhaps the most interesting thing to me was the lovely public park in an area called "Cinnamon Gardens", where I saw some of the world's most exotic tropical vegetation: the vanilla vine, cocoa tree, and fly-catching flowers intermingled with the usual rubber, coconut, and banana trees. The local zoo, although not large, was particularly intriguing because of its collection of tropical and Asian birds and animals. Among its attractions is the daily showing of a team of performing elephants.

We next stopped at Sabang, a very small island off the northwestern tip of Sumatra. It was our first taste of what is called "The Indies" and is a beautiful place with steep hills rising directly from the sea, profusely covered with palms and other colorful trees, shrubs, and vines. The town is a free port where cargo is transshipped all over the area. At least half of the population appears to be Chinese, which well illustrates the penetration of that race throughout this part of the world. It is also the first place I have seen in the Orient where there are no beggars.

The next morning we were in Belawan, the port which serves Medan. Here we lost one pair of what had become our special boat friends. Fox works for Standard Oil of California and has come out here to get a seismograph outfit operating under the very difficult conditions offered by the jungle.

We arrive in Singapore tomorrow.

S.S. *Scharnhorst,* at sea
March 8, 1937

We landed in Singapore on March 2nd after lunch. Fred and I had some difficulties because our passports had no British visas and the British are very touchy in Singapore, I suppose because of the great naval base they are building there. Our passports were taken from us, and we were forced to report to the immigration officer on the dock and wait several hours to go through the formality of paying $2.00 (Straits) to get them back, duly stamped. Although we had been told by both the steamship line's agent and the American Express in Paris that we would not need visas to stop over between boats, and the ship's purser had concurred, they were all wrong. After settling ourselves at a Dutch pension in town, we arranged for our continuing steamship tickets to China.

I don't have a very clear recollection of my visit to Singapore fifteen years ago, but what I saw this time is nothing like what I remember. Before, there were very few motor cars, and we rode around in rickshaws exclusively. Today it is larger and busier, and although the rickshaws are still in great abundance, they are far outnumbered by autos. The guidebook says the city has over 600,000 inhabitants, mostly Chinese. Port Said was once the place to see a wild mixture of races and nationalities, but it cannot compare with modern Singapore. Sprinkled among the Chinese are Malays, Indians of all kinds (Hindu, Mohammedan, Sikh), and Javanese. Again, I was surprised to see no beggars and to find the place relatively clean. Of course the native quarters had their smells, but the streets were comparatively wide and free of refuse. The Chinese, on the whole, appear to be clean people; the women and children are particularly tidy. The little girls are very attractive in their brightly colored "pajamas", and I did not see a single one that was really dirty. (In fact, most of them were cleaner than our daughter is sometimes.)

Aside from its Oriental atmosphere, there is nothing particularly intriguing about Singapore, and I would certainly hate to live there. While the sun shines most of the time, there are showers almost every day and heavy downpours sometimes at night, with a resulting high humidity which makes the fairly moderate temperature quite oppressive.

We visited the Botanical Gardens, which are truly beautiful, and hired a car to tour the island through its cover of palm trees and the rubber and pineapple plantations.

Our ship, the *Scharnhorst*, had docked in the morning and, as we were losing interest in Singapore's sightseeing properties, we boarded her after lunch even though she was not due to leave until the next day. Although she is less than half the size of the *Bremen* and much better fitted out and better served than the *Huygens*, she is certainly not built for tropical service. The electric fans in the dining room are totally inadequate, forcing us to leave the table immediately upon completing our meals. Furthermore, the deck space is small and relatively enclosed, allowing for little breeze.

Tomorrow morning we reach Manila, where we will be for twelve hours. The seas have been smooth as a pond, with so little motion one doesn't realize one is moving at all. I have read two of the ship's library books and am well into a third.

S.S. *Scharnhorst,* at sea
March 10, 1937

I airmailed my last letter from Manila; however, as it just missed one of the Clippers it must wait over a week for the next one.

We arrived in Manila early, and everyone was routed out at 6:00 A.M. for a most perfunctory quarantine inspection before disembarking. All we did was walk past a table and drop off a yellow card that had been handed out at dinner the night before.

Once ashore, Fred and I passed an enormous and incongruous Ford garage on our way to the old walled city of Spanish times. This is an interesting place, very crowded inside the walls which may have provided protection once but don't look like much now, although they have been kept in good repair. The streets are narrow, sidewalks almost nonexistent, and the old gates are just wide enough to allow the passage of a car or cart one at a time. Traffic is congested, caused mostly by innumerable slow moving two-wheeled carriages which are ornately decorated with hammered brass and drawn by tiny ponies.

The natives of Manila make a decidedly better appearance than other Orientals I have seen. The men all wear European trousers, and almost everybody has shoes. It seems to be a prosperous place, and I was most impressed by the many large and fine looking schools. We passed some of the high schools as the young students were leaving and, if one were to forget the dark faces, one might think one was in an American city, their clothes and behavior are so like our own.

We spent quite a long time at the post office buying stamps from two young clerks. They were very friendly and talkative, and we all had a jolly time; I would talk with them in English and Fred would go after them in Spanish, which seemed to tickle them greatly.

While having a drink at the Manila Hotel we ran into Bain (who I last saw in New York and with whom I discussed the possibilities of this trip). We had a nice visit, during which he informed me that, while meeting a co-worker who had been traveling on our ship, he had seen some of my baggage on the customs house pier. I hurriedly returned to the ship and, sure enough, the bag containing my bedding had been put off in error. I got the attention of the baggage master and, looking around, I also found one of Fred's bags. We got them both back on board just in time to sail.

We eat at a table with an entertaining couple from Philadelphia. They are in their early forties and have just come from a tour through India. It is apparent that they have lots of money and go somewhere exotic every year. Last year they went big game hunting in Africa, and this year he wanted to bag a Bengal tiger.

Next stop, Hong Kong.

Shanghai
March 14, 1937

Unfortunately, our Hong Kong stopover was under adverse conditions. The day was misty with continuous drizzle, the visibility was bad, and the hilltops totally obscured from view. Even so, it was obvious that the harbor is truly beautiful, with mountains rising directly out of the sea. We spent some time wandering aimlessly about the native quarters of the city, but the weather dampened our spirits considerably.

Before the ship sailed out of Hong Kong at about 5:00 P.M., some seventy Australian Rotary Club members straggled aboard with their wives and children. Apparently they had been on some sort of cruise from Australia on a small ship which had passed through a terrific storm and had to lay-to for several days. They had an awful time; the captain didn't know where they were, and I guess they were all scared to bits. Three of them had fallen and broken arms and legs. They certainly looked frazzled.

After boarding the *Scharnhorst* we learned how to best finance our stay on a German vessel. We found that we could buy marks on shore for about half their supposed value on the international market. So we went to the American Express Office in Hong Kong and acquired the marks with which we paid our ship's bills. In addition, I bought a Leica camera for about half the cost in the United States. I have wanted one for years, but the high price has kept me from seriously considering ownership. Now that I have one I anticipate some quality photographs of the trip.

We awoke on the morning of March 8th in the middle of the muddy Yellow Sea. The water was so shallow that several times the ship scraped against the bottom, and the laboring of the engine caused great vibrations. We picked up our pilot while still out of sight of land, but after a time we saw the low-lying coast of China and, as it closed in on us from both sides, realized that we were in the river. The fields gradually gave way to buildings, which became more numerous until their crowding indicated that we were indeed in Shanghai. The ship proceeded some distance further, then turned around in mid-channel and backed to the dock. We were met by Mr. Hussey, the Canadian architect, and Mr. Irving Suez. They saw us through customs, cutting through all the red tape, and helped us check into the Park Hotel, Shanghai's newest and best.

That evening we were invited to dinner at the home of Dr. U.Y. Yen, along with Hussey, Suez, and Mr. Chow Tso-ming, one of the biggest Chinese bankers in Shanghai. Unfortunately, the latter spoke no English. Yen is Wellington Koo's brother-in-law. He was educated in England and has an honorary degree from a California university. A very wealthy man, he lives in the top two floors of a tall new apartment in the French Concession, which is attractively fitted out in modern Chinese style. We were served a Chinese dinner of shark's fins, preserved eggs, and I don't know what all, which was eaten with chopsticks and washed down with such quantities of warm rice wine, I fancied I was floating. After dinner we visited and talked a little business and, about midnight, were ushered out to a Chinese dancing club, where we had a drink and watched the proceedings. The orchestra was entirely composed of American Negroes playing American music. The dance floor was surrounded by chairs occupied between dances by taxi dancers. These were all young Chinese girls, most of them attractive in their bright dresses cut straight to the floor, with high collars, no sleeves, and slits up each side to the knee. They all wore their hair curled, and I have nowhere seen shoes with higher heels.

Harry Hussey is a very friendly man, probably in his late fifties, who has lived in China for over twenty-five years and seems to know everyone here of any consequence. His home is in Peiping. He appears to be a man of considerable importance and has acted for the Chinese government on various occasions. For instance, he was a Chinese representative of the Lytton Commission, which investigated and reported upon the Japanese seizure of Manchuria. He has long been interested in the oil resources of northwestern China and has apparently spent a considerable amount of his own money gathering information about it.

Suez is Chinese, probably in his fifties, who speaks perfect English, but dresses in the long gown and cloth shoes of the conservative middle and upper classes. Not only has he been the Chinese Consul General in New York, he has served in a similar capacity in Mexico and Peru, and has been some kind of government official in Tibet. He is to be our agent and will accompany us to make all of the official arrangements. It is incredible to me that a man of this stature would be willing to undertake such duties. We are also to be furnished with a "No. 1" and a "No. 2 boy" and a cook, all of whom are known to be reliable men. There will be a Chinese engineer and junior geologist in attendance. Other men to make up our party will be obtained in the northwest.

Uncertain conditions in the northwest seem to have been adjusted, and there appears to be no reason why we cannot proceed peacefully with our work. The missionaries are all at their posts out there and more are going in, which is apparently an indication of stability. Tomorrow we are to interview a man who is particularly well-informed about that part of the country, and we will surely get the latest dope from him. Altogether, everything appears in good order, and Fred and I are both enthusiastic about the prospects.

PART II

Preparation for the Unknown

Shanghai
March 20, 1937

We have been here a week, and I am beginning to feel much at home. This is the longest we have spent in any one place in well over a month.

The men here are very pleasant and helpful. Our principal contact is, of course, Hussey who designed and built the big Rockefeller Hospital in Peiping. He is a close friend of Wellington Koo and is at present assisting Madam Koo in purchasing fittings for the new Chinese Embassy in Paris. He certainly has some intriguing tales to tell of his experiences of over twenty-five years in China.

The Chinese with whom we have become best acquainted is Dr. U.K. Yen. We have been to his home twice for excellent Chinese dinners, during which we learned quite a bit about him. His wife is a full sister of Madam Koo. His father-in-law was quite a man. He started out with a small stake in a Javanese sugar plantation from which he branched out into everything imaginable, leaving many millions of dollars to between twenty and forty children by a number of wives. Hussey says there are half-brothers and sisters all over China. Yen, in his own right, is an exceedingly wealthy man who makes fortunes by playing the stock or exchange markets of London, New York, and Shanghai, working against the different closing times of the markets around the world. He makes investment speculation seem easy work.

Mr. Chow is president of the biggest Chinese bank. He was educated in Japan and does not speak English. He is, I think, the man at the head of the syndicate.

Our basic servants have been engaged for us, and we are now

having tents made as well as arranging for the purchase of our other pieces of equipment. This is the current activity of Mr. Suez.

The trouble in northwest China seems to have pretty well evaporated. According to accounts here it has not been serious as far as Europeans are concerned. One of the high military commanders in the northwest has, at the request of our group, inquired about local conditions in all of the districts. The wires have been coming in for the last day or two, and so far reports are favorable for our departure.

I now have a Chinese name which sounds as much like "Weller" as possible, "Way-loo". The first written character means "forearmed", the second, a "two-storied building". The whole might be translated as "castle" or "guardtower".

Tonight we plan to go to Nanking to call upon Dr. Wong, who is the principal secretary in the executive branch of the government, as well as the head of the Chinese Geological Survey. He has been out in the country where we are going, and I hope he can give us some information with which we can begin to plot our work. We are extremely fortunate in having obtained copies of military maps as well as permission to use them. These cover large areas of the northwest including all of Kansu Province, where we plan to do much of our work. These maps will save us a great deal of effort.

Sutton is a nice fellow, easy to get along with, and apparently an excellent geologist. I am very pleased.

Shanghai
March 22, 1937

The Nanking trip has been cancelled several times for different reasons. It is necessary to have a letter of introduction from Mr. Chow, but he has been tied up as head of the Chinese delegation to a Chinese-Japanese Economic Conference and seemingly has been unable to find the time to sign it. After the letter finally materialized we bought train tickets, only to learn that Dr. Wong was arriving in Shanghai that same night. The result was that we did not go to Nanking at all, but met with Wong here for a short time yesterday. Arrangements have been made for us to visit the Survey in Nanking on Wednesday, so we shall take the train tomorrow night unless, of course, something else develops. Anyway, we are being initiated into Oriental ways. The Chinese are by no means as busy as they let on, nor are they as busy as they probably think they are.

These days have been hectic ones for us. We have met and consulted repeatedly with the men here, have been to the doctor, shopped, and seen something of the city. The group evidently has little knowledge of what our work should consist of, which in retrospect is good in that it leaves us with a fairly free rein to do what we want. Hussey is very enthusiastic, and full of stories of lakes of oil as told by some Russian adventurer whom he has grubstaked in the past. He is, I feel, perhaps too optimistic. We have become pretty well acquainted with Mr. Suez, who appears to be a good man and practically perfect for the job as far as we're concerned. We have only seen our "No. 1 boy", but he, at least, is pleasant and alert. Our tents are being made to order at less than half their cost in the U.S., and they are probably better tents at that. I bought a sheepskin coat made in Minneapolis and paid no more for it than it would have cost in Urbana. We have purchased most of our traveling needs at a large local department store that carries everything imaginable, and the articles comprising our camping gear pile up in our rooms like junk heaps. I am buying first class cigarettes made in China by an English firm for twelve cents per can of fifty. Our hotel, the best in town, costs $4.50 (U.S.) per day for a room with bath and meals.

Shanghai is not a particularly interesting city. It is too modern, with fine new buildings of fifteen stories or higher, to look like what I expected. However, most of the streets are narrow and congested with Chinese pulling rickshaws and carts, pushing wheelbarrows, carrying bundles on poles over their shoulders, all of them hawking, spitting, and blowing their noses indiscriminately. Add all the autos, buses, and street cars and it makes getting around a slow process.

Our permanent address is c/o Yen in the Continental Bank Building. All mail addressed to us there will be forwarded wherever we are, into the interior as far as possible. Do not, however, send packages. And do not expect packages from me. My one attempt to mail a parcel from the general post office took an entire afternoon. I had a terrible time, reporting to at least sixteen different people without being able to find adequate directions, all in the very midst of swarms of Chinese burdened with string-tied bundles of all sizes. It was a terrible mess.

Shanghai
March 28, 1937

We went to Nanking on Tuesday night and returned Friday afternoon. It is only 103 miles west of Shanghai, but the train takes six hours at the very fastest to make the trip. Our train left at 11:00 P.M. and arrived at 7:00 A.M., eight hours later. The cars are of European design with compartments, one of which Sutton and I shared. I had the lower berth that extended crosswise, and Sutton took the upper which ran lengthwise, At Nanking we found the recommended hotels full and finally succeeded in getting a room at the third one we called upon. This, the Nanking Hotel, probably had an international clientele at one time, but is now run by and for the Chinese, and we were the only Caucasians staying there. We got a large single room and had a second bed moved in. Suez managed to get a small room that was vacated later in the afternoon. There was no heat in the radiators and it snowed all day, it was not exactly clean but probably not as dirty as it looked and, finally, the meals were most ordinary. This has convinced us to switch to ordering Chinese food, which is much better than European style, and has made us decide that we had best take a good Chinese-style cook with us into the field. I am sure that such a man will be easier to obtain than a passable western-style one.

After breakfast we visited the Geological Survey. Director Wong was preparing to leave for England as a member of the Chinese delegation to the coronation of King George, so we consulted with Assistant Director Huang. We also purchased some of their publications. The Survey has a staff of fifteen which is contained in two new buildings, one a museum and one with offices and a laboratory. The floors were cement and, as the buildings were totally without heat, we nearly froze to death. Sutton has caught a nice cold which he is still enjoying. That night we simply went to bed just to try to get warm.

The sun shone the next day, but it was still cold. We returned to the Survey and talked (through Suez in Chinese) with C.C. Sun, a geologist who has worked in Kansu Province. We hope we can get him to accompany us, as we were able to get from him our first real information about what that part of the country is actually like.

In the afternoon we drove around the city. Although Nanking was once one of the classical capitols of China, it has been destroyed so many times that about all that remains of its ancient glory is the great city wall which is thirty-two miles long, between thirty and fifty feet high, and is still mostly in good repair. Nanking was reestablished as the capitol ten years ago, and the present goverment has done much to widen the principal streets and build numerous large government buildings. Some of them are strictly old Chinese in style, many of them are quite modern with great green tile roofs which are lovely, while others of western design look quite incongruous. With time, Nanking will probably become just another big modern city.

We visited the Museum of Antiquities, which is more of a storehouse than a museum, very small with old dusty objects either poorly arranged or not arranged at all. It is located on the site of the old Ming Palace, which has unfortunately been demolished. From there we drove out of the city to Sun Yat-sen's tomb, which can be seen from quite a distance. It is built on the side of a low, but steep mountain with a fine road leading to it and beyond. The tomb is a long and comparatively narrow rectangle with stairs up the middle and terraces along either side, the whole enclosed by a low wall. One enters at the bottom through a great gate and proceeds upward by I don't know how many hundreds of steps through several ornamental buildings to the tomb itself at the top. The buildings and stairs are a light grey granite, the roofs a vivid blue. It is extremely beautiful and much larger than one realizes until one has climbed all the steps . . . a fitting monument to a great man. The view from the top is magnificent, with low mountains outlined by the newly fallen snow rising irregularly from the level fields.

Next we toured through a small park on an island in a lake just outside Nanking's walls. In the summer the lake is said to be filled with pink lotus and must be quite pleasant to view. Now, of course, there are no signs of them, and it was so cold that we did not linger.

We paid another visit to Huang at the Survey the next morning and had lunch at the hotel with Suez and his son, Robert. He has been schooled in the U.S., a graduate from Michigan, and is now an officer in the Chinese Army, teaching in the School of Motor Transport. He is a nice young fellow, in his twenties and quite American in manner. Suez said that when Robert was a small boy in the U.S. he had to send him back to China to relearn Chinese.

Soldiers are much in evidence in China. They are all over the railroad stations as well as in each of the railroad cars. Nanking has a number of large military schools for both officers and enlisted men where much is being done to uplift army standards. Most of the soldiers we saw in Nanking were good-looking and well-uniformed; these, however, are not typical of the regular Chinese army. In any case, the improved condition of the military seems to be having its results, as shown by the present attitude of the Japanese.

Our train started back in mid-afternoon, and I eagerly stared out of the window until it was totally dark. For a long way the railroad skirts the edge of a group of hills on the south side of the Yangtze, and we caught several glimpses of the great river. All of the lower land is farmed, divided into small fields by ridges of earth and terraced to slightly different levels. Little attempt, however, appears to have been made to cultivate the slopes, although some of them have recently been laid out and planted with mulberry trees for silkworms. Many other kinds of trees are being planted, and the country we saw is not the treeless China I had been led to expect from my reading. Domestic animals seem scarce; a few donkeys, water buffalo, and pigs. I saw no goats, although I would think they would have loved these hillsides.

One prominent feature of the Chinese countryside, and evidence of the land's great age, is the number of graves. They are mostly low mounds of earth, though some of the more important ones are surrounded by incomplete circular ridges. They are everywhere; in some parts as much as a quarter of the land is occupied by them and therefore remains uncultivated. Most of the houses are wretched affairs of bamboo or cane lattice, plastered with mud and thatched with straw. The common people are terribly dirty, clothed in ragged padded cotton garments from which the stuffing oozes at every rent, but they seem to be a cheerful lot and always ready to smile or laugh.

Shanghai is upon occasion overrun with tourists. The *Empress of Britain* was in port a week ago, and another round-the-world boat is here now. The travelers are mostly an odd looking bunch; many of them are old and, I suspect, from small towns. Some of the men look as though they had just removed their overalls and had dressed up for Sunday. Our *Scharenhorst* friends, the Laws from Philadelphia, are in town now, just back from Peiping. They leave tomorrow for Japan. The Schoefields, with whom we traveled on the *Christian Huygens*, are also here for a couple of weeks. It is interesting how shipboard friendships take hold.

Shanghai
April 5, 1937

Last Wednesday the mail boat, *President Jackson*, came in, but we were not able to get our mail from the American Express until Friday. This is a good example of how things move in the Orient . . . very slowly.

We still do not know the exact details of the arrangements between the Chinese and the company. We do know that we shall start work in Kansu Province, but just how this will be done cannot be determined until we are there on the ground. We have information of somewhat doubtful authenticity of an extremely large oil seepage on the border between Kansu and Tsinghai near Lake Kokonor. If the reports are true (they come by way of Russians), this is probably the biggest seepage in the world. It is said to cover an area of 250 square miles, half of which is supposed to be an actual lake of oil with fumes so strong and suffocating that, when the Russians first found it, they were afraid to approach it "for fear of being overcome". The trouble with this story is that the Chinese know nothing of such a place, and none of the explorers of that region have ever mentioned it.

At present we are just sitting and waiting. We cannot move until Chinese passports for the interior are granted and, although these were applied for long ago, there seems to be much red tape, and Orientals do seem to have a total indifference to time. Originally, I had hoped we could start inland two or three weeks after arrival. After experiencing local tactics I then expected the delay to extend a month. Now it looks like it might be much longer.

I have been trying to study a little Chinese. Part of the language is simple, and yet it proves so very difficult in other ways.

Shanghai
April 8, 1937

Still nothing has happened. We are having our saddles made and continue to wait for our Chinese passports. Presumably the passport delay is related to a change in the administration in Kansu Province. About the time we reached China the governor there resigned or was transferred, and some time passed before his successor was named. He has not yet taken over his duties there, and now rumors are that he has declined his appointment. We had a letter of introduction from Dr. Koo to the old governor. It is useless now, so I have opened it to see what it looks like. Here it is . . . an authentic letter from a Chinese ambassador to a Chinese potentate. Don't let it get into the hands of anyone who reads Chinese as I don't have the slightest idea what it says.

Meanwhile I continue to learn more about our people here. For instance, I have become aware that Hussey does not get on too well with some of our Chinese. I have also learned that he dearly loves to talk and that not everything he says can be relied upon. I don't mean to imply that he falsifies, only that he tends to run off at the mouth and that he colors what he says according to his whim of the moment. He is a great admirer of the Chinese and in some ways seems more Chinese than the Chinese do. At the same time, Dr. Koo has told us that Hussey is one of his oldest friends and that he has perfect confidence in him. He has also been most helpful and friendly to us.

Dr. Yen is apparently typical of the modern city Chinese. He is both excitable and timid. The other evening he came up to see me and, as he stepped out of the elevator, he slipped and sat down, plop, on the newly polished floor. He told me about the episode in great detail as he entered my room. When I asked him if he had hurt himself I quite expected him to demure with a "No", but his answer was, "Yes, very much", in spite of little evidence of harm.

Yen's reactions and Hussey's (always optimistic) are often opposed, so things don't get decided. Chow, who appears to be head man, is difficult to reach, either because he is very busy or because he is so important that he must act so. The result of all this is too many cooks in the kitchen and no one to stir the broth, and the situation is annoying. Once we get to work we will be out from under and can do as we please. In the meantime, one of the urgent things that needs to be decided is, how do we go to Lanchow? The most direct way would be by rail to Sian and from there either by motor or plane, but the vicinity of Sian has been quite unsettled, so it might be unsafe to send our supplies via that route. The other way is to go by way of Peiping and fly in from there, sending our supplies by truck over a northern road. This route is farther and would take more time.

We have been variously advised about carrying arms in the field. Some have said "by all means", while others have said "by no means". We have decided to take them in any case. The Chinese government does not allow the import of pistols or rifles, so they are not for sale in the stores. I tried at first to borrow them from the U.S. Marines, but when I went to the American Consulate I found there was too much red tape involved to seriously consider it. Although we have been promised the loan of a rifle, I was stumped on how to get a revolver. Today I put ads in the newspapers and have learned of a collection of confiscated revolvers for sale by the municipal police. Fred and I will investigate that possibility. In the meantime, all of our camping equipment is gathered together and ready to go, and only our provisions remain to be purchased.

One of the principal problems currently causing our delay is that there is famine in the northwest and a consequent uneasiness among the agricultural communities. Relief measures are only beginning to be taken, partially, I think, because troop movements have so tied up the railroad that food could not be sent in. It is hoped that when the new provincial governor takes over his duties, these conditions will clear up.

It is a fact that the country is much more firmly united and under control by the central government than at any time since the revolution against the "war lords". The Communist group so strongly entrenched in northwestern China seems to have been successfully brought back into the fold, and the bandit gangs still at large seem not to be the "desperados" they are imagined to be. Persons who have come in contact with them say they are more or less good-natured farmers who have fallen on hard times and that they resort to violence only when provoked. It seems that accounts of famine and violence are always exaggerated, presumably because they make good newspaper stories. This sentiment is echoed by Dr. Miller, who has inoculated us against everything possible in preparation for our travels and has been particularly kind about furnishing us with information, letters of introduction, and giving us advice about various drugs and how to use them if necessary.

Shanghai
April 21, 1937

We are still here, and our moment of departure seems as far away as ever. It rained all day yesterday, and I just sat and read. My most strenuous occupation on the day before that was the purchase of a screw-driver and file. Today Fred and I went around to the central police station to look at their collection of confiscated pistols, which were mostly in pretty bad shape and without ammunition. Time and talk, however, uncovered a good rifle and a .45 revolver with accompanying ammunition, both of which we bought. My newspaper ads resulted in the acquisition of another rifle and a .38 revolver. We have obtained the proper permits from the U.S. Marshal here and now must get carrying licenses from the Chinese authorities.

Northwestern China is apparently full of all kinds of game. Sutton knew someone in New York who was over here in 1914-15 for the oil company, and all he could talk about was the fine hunting. If we ever get away from here we should have some good chances to hunt. Fresh meat will most likely be very welcome.

Although there is nothing particularly beautiful about Shanghai, it is well cared for. There are practically no flies and not many beggars. There is one little girl I have noticed begging along the streets near the hotel who has been taught an appeal in English that she does not understand, but repeats endlessly. It goes, "No mama, no papa, no money, no chow, no whiskey-soda." Hussey says that he pays a few of the beggars ten cents a week "salary" to keep the other beggars from bothering him.

There has been a bit of excitement locally because two prominent Chinese bankers have been kidnapped from their car along the highway between here and Nanking. Wealthy men are apparently always in danger of kidnap here. In fact, like Chicago, Shanghai has a reputation as a crime center. It doesn't seem so bad to me, considering its large population and the poverty of most of the people.

Although at first I thought I would try to learn some Chinese, I have just about forsaken the idea. Now that I know something about the language, it seems hopeless to accomplish much in a short time without a good deal of hard work. There are only 400 different syllables in the entire language, and each of these may be spoken in four different ways, making a total of only 1600 different words. With this small number there are, of course, innumerable homonyms. It is possible to say a sentence quite correctly and no one would understand what you meant because they didn't know what you were talking about. I have a Chinese-English dictionary in which I can look up the meanings of 10,000 characters (there are 50,000 altogether). It lists 101 different characters all pronounced "e", each meaning something different.

The characters are very interesting, and I am sure it would be easier to learn to read Chinese than to speak it. There are 214 radicals and 888 phonetics. In general, the radicals give some clue as to the meaning of the characters, and the phonetics commonly suggest the sounds. Of course the characters were originally pictorial, but they have been greatly conventionalized. Some are very appropriate and therefore easy to remember.

For instance, 木 is "wood", 林 is "forest", and 森 is "dense forest" or "jungle". 女 is "woman". Woman with a roof over her is "peaceful": 安. "Child" is 子. Combine woman and child and you have "good": 好. Put a roof over a child and you have "words": 字. A roof over a pig is "home": 家.

I have just finished reading *The Travels of Marco Polo* for the second time. He certainly had a great adventure and mostly relates things very vividly, although parts of his book are rather tedious. Thirteenth century China was probably superior to Europe relative to the size of its cities and greater wealth; however, current conditions of living do not measure up to escalated western standards.

A great deal of space in the newspapers is being devoted to Japan. It is hard for me to understand their attitude toward the Chinese when obviously it is in their interest to be friendly with China. They are neither big enough nor rich enough to dominate China, but they seem to pay no heed to these factors. Someday Japanese arrogance will cause them to blow up and burst. Meanwhile, China is steadily and quietly strengthening herself and is developing into a country with a future. Japan is not, and I feel that the outcome of a war now is questionable.

Shanghai
April 12, 1937

Airmail service is being started between China and the United States, so I am sending this letter off as sort of a souvenir. My last letter went out on the *President Taft*, so you should receive this one first.

According to the schedule, this letter will leave here on Tuesday morning by Chinese airmail bound for Hong Kong. There it will be picked up by the *China Clipper*, carried to Manila and then, by way of Guam and Hawaii, to San Francisco. From there it will go by ordinary U.S. mail. The actual flight from Shanghai to San Francisco should take just one week, so you ought to receive this in about twelve days. Think of it!

We are still being held up for lack of Chinese passports. Apparently the authorities wish to make very sure that we will not get into trouble; they seem more concerned about our safety than we are. Our Chinese friends do not seem to mind the tedious wait and appear confident that the difficulties will iron themselves out given the necessary time. I guess we are being treated to a good example of Oriental patience. Fred and I certainly are being well paid to do nothing, but we are also losing the best time of the year for field work in the northwest. A little longer and it will be hot and rainy there.

Mr. K.C. Li, the Chinese I met in New York City through an introduction from Dr. Bain, is here in our hotel. He has been made President of the China Trust Company, which is some kind of semi-official government agency. I went to call on him this morning, but he has gone to Nanking for several days.

Shanghai
April 29, 1937

I have just learned that our friends here have known all along that we could not possibly leave for the interior before now because there has been a government order forbidding the granting of passports to Kansu before April 26th. They didn't tell us because they apparently did not want us to become discouraged. However, the newly appointed governor of Kansu is expected to take up his duties within a week or two, so perhaps we can begin to feel positive about our position.

We have been running about recently with Lt. Commander and Mrs. Ihrig of the U.S. Navy. They are both from Salt Lake City, old schoolmates of Fred's whom he has not seen in twenty years. The

Commander serves aboard the U.S.S. *Augusta,* the flagship of the Asiatic Fleet which arrived from Manila last week. We all had a late dinner together on the hotel's fourteenth floor, which has an orchestra for dancing and a small floor show. We left there about 1:00 A.M. for a tour of the night clubs. First we went to the Tower Room in the Cathay Hotel where we had pointed out to us "Two-Gun" Cohen, originally a Canadian prizefighter and for many years Sun Yat-sen's bodyguard. He is now supposedly selling munitions and is said to be a general in the Chinese Army. (This title is bandied about with a frequency that makes me think there must be as many Chinese generals as Mexican ones.) We left the Tower at 3:00 and proceeded briefly to The Lido, a Chinese cabaret, and on to St. George's, run by an ex-U.S. soldier. There were many sailors from the fleet there, having a good time dancing with the Chinese and Russian taxi girls. Finally, we went to Del Monte's, which is mostly patronized by the British, and I got home to my hotel bed about 5:30 in the morning. Although the evening was interesting, I would not care to do it again; I was somewhat disappointed that Shanghai night life is not nearly as wicked as I had supposed.

The Ihrigs invited us for dinner on the flagship on Tuesday evening. The ship is anchored in the river about two miles downstream from the main part of town. We caught the steam tender at the Bund at 5:00 and reached the *Augusta* at 5:30. Ihrig showed us all over and explained the workings of a battleship. She is one of the first of the 10,000 ton treaty cruisers, now about ten years old, and is equipped with three batteries of six- or eight-inch guns. They will shoot sixteen miles and can fire forty shells a minute. She also carries four airplanes on deck which can be shot off from catapults. With the fighting equipment, officers, 600 men, and a detachment of Marines on board, it is all pretty well crowded and without any signs of luxuries. As both the Admiral and the Captain were ashore, Ihrig was in command, and every few minutes a batch of radio messages would be brought to him for review. I was particularly interested in the navigational instruments and was amazed at what Ihrig told us about the accuracy of modern day navigation. We had a plain but good dinner, after which we watched an open-air movie up on deck. It was rather chilly.

Tonight Sutton and I are leaving for Peiping. We shall be gone about a week.

Peiping
May 3, 1937

We have been in Peiping for two days now, and without any doubt this is the most interesting city I have ever seen. None of the other Oriental cities can compare with its barbaric splendor, even though it is quite dilapidated and much the worse for wear.

Our trip here by train occupied one and a half days and two nights and was rather tiresome. The cars were of the old European compartment type, and the train rattled and lurched along quite slowly most of the time. The first day, north of Nanking, we passed through a green countryside of little terraced fields. During the second night we went through what I have been told is one of the prettiest parts of China, the western section of Shantung Province, but of course we could not see it. The second day we were in the vast delta area of the Yellow River, flat plains of dusty brown, newly plowed earth. The little villages were made up of small brown mud houses, and the train was filled with dust. We reached Peiping about 2:00 P.M. and went directly to our hotel which is inside the Tartar City facing the Legation Quarter. Sutton and I went for a walk up on the city wall, but a bad dust storm blew up and beat us back to the hotel.

Peiping probably covers more area than Shanghai, but is not so congested; the streets are laid out in orderly east-west, north-south patterns, with the old Chinese City to the south and the old Tartar City to the north. Each is surrounded by a great wall about fifty feet high and twenty-five feet thick, each about sixteen miles in extent, In the center of the Tartar City is the Imperial City, surrounded by its own wall, and inside that is the Forbidden City, which is also walled. (The Chinese certainly went in for wall building with enthusiasm.) These walls are built of large bricks; the places from which the earth was dug to make the bricks now form a series of lakes within the old Imperial City.

Whereas Shanghai is predominantly a commercial city, Peiping is for tourists during "the season", which is now about over. The climate is different from Shanghai's; it is very dry, and the curse of the place is the clouds of dust raised by every breeze or passing vehicle.

We brought Suez with us as this is his home, and his wife, according to reports, has not been well for some time. He has taken us around to see the sights and to visit the geologists here. (On the whole, Chinese geologists impress me unfavorably.)

We started with the Temple of Heaven, which we probably should have saved for last. The temple itself is only one and not the largest of several buildings occupying a large walled enclosure within the Chinese City. It is perfectly gorgeous, and I can find no words to do it justice. The graceful form of the buildings and their vivid but harmonious coloring is unlike anything that one can imagine. The heavy tiled roofs are dark blue and green, adorned with dragons. The pillars are bright vermillion, and only after seeing them can one truly appreciate the term "chinese red". The other parts are mainly blue and green, with much gilding in the form of dragons and various designs. Around the buildings are terraces with marble stairs and carved balustrades.

We went next to the Temple of Confucius and the Buddhists, which are typical Chinese style with heavy tiled roofs above wood constructions. Lack of care has rendered them quite disreputable. (This was perhaps emphasized by the fact that the Temple of Heaven had recently been renovated.) The Temple of Confucius, used several times a year, contains the paraphernalia for sacrifice, musical instruments, and lamps, but no figures of any sort. In smaller buildings surrounding the main temple there are great blocks of stone supported by giant marble turtles on which are engraved the eulogies on Confucius written by various emperors. There are other great stones and tablets in the courtyards, engraved with the names of scholars and some of the classical writings, which are badly weathered and dirty from the ink used to make rubbings. Although the architecture of the Lama, or Buddhist, Temples is much the same as the Confucius Temple, the atmosphere is very different. There are innumerable gilded grotesque statues of Buddha, one nearly fifty feet high, as well as unlife-like statues of his twelve disciples. There are also many religious paintings on the walls, lending a distinctly Indian touch. The interiors of the buildings are so dark that it is hard to see what they contain, but the main temple is noticeably occupied and in use. Most of the resident priests are boys badly in need of baths, wearing robes that are far from clean. The services seem to consist of monotonous chants, ringing of bells, changing of robes, putting on and taking off of hats, and bowing to statues; on the whole, a great waste of time in idolatry.

Next we went to a garden in the corner of the Imperial City where there is a large lagoon below a steep hill, crowned on the top by a large Buddhist stupa, or solid pagoda. The view from the hilltop is a splendid survey of the entire Forbidden City with its multitude of golden yellow tiled roofs.

This afternoon we drove to the Summer Palace of the old Dowager Empress, about six miles outside the city on the edge of the western hills overlooking a lake. The old Summer Palace was burned by the British in the latter part of the last century, and this one is said to have been built by the Empress with funds raised for the purpose of acquiring a Chinese Navy. Perhaps it is just as well, for had the money been spent for a navy there would be nothing left now to show for it. The buildings of the Summer Palace form a labyrinth and include innumerable courts. Some of the structures contain their original furniture, which may be partly seen by squinting through dirty windows, while other buildings are currently in use, rented out to various people as summer cottages. Most of them are in disrepair and much in need of paint. It all seems in bad taste because they are so tightly crowded, even though a few of the buildings are set off to advantage and are quite impressive, at least from a little distance. The most outlandish structure is the marble pavilion in the shape of a paddle-wheeled boat. I guess one could say it was the only boat built for the Navy. To me the most interesting feature of the Summer Palace complex is a group of beautiful bronze animals which depict not only the conventional lion, crane, and deer, but also many fanciful mythical dragons.

Yesterday Suez took us to lunch at a local Chinese restaurant which is famous for its roast duck. The ducks are fattened until they actually cannot move and then roasted whole on an open fire made of some special kind of wood. We reached the restaurant by passing along an alley, three feet wide and very dirty, and through a kitchen dark with the smoke of the ages. We climbed up a steep and narrow flight of stairs to a room over-looking the dark grey tiled roofs of the neighboring houses. The table cloth had been washed without the aid of soap and contained an impressive collection of grease spots. We were joined by Mrs. Suez and a daughter, an attractive girl in her twenties, and another girl of similar age. The meal was quite good, and Mrs. Suez, like her husband, spoke remarkably creditable English.

Last evening we had dinner at Suez's home. Again, it was reached by a narrow, dirty alleyway and through a red gate in a high wall. Behind the wall was a garden and a very comfortable house furnished in European style, with Chinese decorations. Dinner was served in his study because Suez said the proper dining room was filled with books. The study was also filled with books, and I couldn't see how the dining room could be any fuller. As I have said before, we are very fond of Suez. He is a real Chinese gentleman, nearly sixty years old (although he doesn't look it), speaks perfect English, and has a nice sense of humor. Judging from Mrs. Suez's wedding ring, I gather they are Christian.

Shanghai
May 9, 1937

To continue with my report on Peiping, Tuesday morning we went through the southern half of the Forbidden City. This area contains a series of great audience halls and courts surrounded by smaller chambers, remarkable for their golden tile roofs (gold was the imperial color) which glow in the sunshine with indescribable richness. The buildings are all in a more or less derelict state, with faded, peeling paint, but when viewed from across a court they are still quite impressive. They are mostly elevated, surrounded by terraces paved with large grey bricks, and guarded by beautifully carved white marble balustrades. The designs are of dragons and phoenixes, and around the edge of each terrace is a series of beastly gargoyles. The courts are unkempt, with grass and weeds sprouting up between the bricks. Building entrances are usually guarded by fanciful lions of marble or bronze, but there are a variety of other bronze animals about, some realistic, some mythical, and all of them show particularly fine workmanship. There are many great cauldron-like vessels, mostly of bronze or iron, that apparently were kept filled with water for use in case of fire . . . a real hazard to be considered in such a series of connected wooden buildings. Many of the vessels and some of the animals had at one time been covered with gold leaf, but most of this has been scraped off by vandals, who have done further damage by breaking off pieces of the tile work.

The precincts of the Forbidden City are now deserted except for the occasional tourist and the soldier guards; still, it is easy to imagine the glittering pageant that must have been made by the royal family, the imperial statesmen, and the hordes of soldiers and servants who lived and died here when the place was alive.

Our afternoon was devoted to a series of parks west of the Forbidden City, but within the confines of the Imperial City. The Chinese have a penchant for fanciful and flowery names, and the large lagoons are known as the high-sounding North, Middle, and South Seas. One of the most remarkable items here is the Nine Dragon Screen, a section of wall about forty feet long and ten feet high, with relief tile work depicting nine dragons on each side, all in different colors, forms, and positions.

The next morning we returned to the Forbidden City and toured the north half which was used as living quarters by the imperial family. It is so extensive that only one-third of it is open at a time; I have been told that it would take three whole days to see it all. Again, it is a labyrinth of buildings, passageways, small courts, and gardens, and I wondered if the Emperor himself ever needed a guide or a map to take him to his various concubines. By this time we were becoming rather tired of Chinese buildings for, no matter how magnificent, there is a monotonous sameness to them all, and most of them are in considerable disrepair. There are so many old public buildings and grounds in Peiping that it would cost a fortune to keep them up. I think it would be best for the government to renovate only a selection of the best and let the rest go to wrack and ruin, which many of them are rapidly doing.

We spent the afternoon seeing the wholesale shops and market area. We saw rugs ranging in price from $1.00 to over $3.00 (U.S.) per square foot. They are fine, thick rugs, but to me they somehow lack the charm of the Persian and Turkoman carpets with their characteristic designs. There is a great variety of knicknacks in cloisonne, pottery, glass, and carved materials such as can be seen in most Chinese shops in America. Linen is quite cheap, with rather fine cross-stitching and applique work. The native bazaar was a maze of tiny shops selling everything imaginable.

We had dinner at Suez's, where we acquired more practice with our chopsticks. The two girls were missing this time and in their place was a young man who, unfortunately, spoke Russian rather than English.

Fred and I were on our own the following day, so in the morning I took a rickshaw to Coal Hill in the center of the Tartar City. This is a steep hill about a block long and 150 feet high which is said to be made of coal piled there by the emperor in Marco Polo's time to insure a fuel supply in case of siege. It is now overgrown with trees and crowned by five graceful pavilions, one of which contains a large figure of Buddha. The view from the top encompasses the shimmering golden roofs of the Forbidden City to the south, the great Drum and Bell Tower to the north, and two hills capped by Buddhist pagodas to the west, all merged with the city's low, one-storied grey tiled houses separated by narrow, dusty alleys. Far away in all directions rise the great guard houses that surmount the wall of the Tartar City and mark the positions of its gates. I sat on the hill and enjoyed the vista for quite a while.

Fred joined me in the afternoon when we took rickshaws to the old Mongol Observatory on the east wall of the city. The observatory consists of nearly a dozen great instruments, built by the early Jesuits to make astronomical measurements. Cast in bronze with marvelous workmanship and ornamental dragon designs, they have stood there exposed to the elements for centuries and, aside from worn gold leaf and a few rusty iron parts, they appear to remain in good condition. Some of the instruments were stolen by German troops at the time of the Boxer Uprising. One of the peace treaty clauses after the Great War provided for the return from Berlin of the instruments, practically the only reward that poor China obtained for its participation with the Allies.

We returned to Shanghai on May 8th, and I am glad to be back in my old hotel room here, which is much more comfortable than that at the Grand Hotel de Pekin, in spite of its elegant sounding name. Also, Shanghai is not so dirty and dusty.

Shanghai
May 14, 1937

Our affairs here have at last reached a stage where some motion is discernible. I don't recall how much I have written about the political situation we have been up against, but anyhow, I understand it much better now, so here goes.

The political and military control exercised by the Central Government in Nanking over the rest of China has, until recently, varied pretty much depending upon distance. Last year Nanking had no practical control in the faraway northwestern provinces, and the army of "Young Marshal" Chang Hsueh-liang, which had been driven out of Manchuria by the Japanese, had control over the large area centering around Sian. Last December Chang's army there was supposedly fighting the Communists who had been driven up into Shensi Province from the southeastern coast. The fighting was nominal, however, and some kind of deal was made whereby they should join forces against the Japanese, leading China into war with Japan. Chiang Kai-shek, who unlike many of the other generals here has, I believe, the welfare of China deeply at heart, realized that a successful war against Japan could not be waged at this time. He felt that this was a potentially dangerous situation and, against the advice of other members of the government, he went to Sian to try to straighten things out. He was taken prisoner by the "Young Marshal's" forces on December 16th. The resulting furor raised throughout the length and breadth of China demonstrated conclusively for the first time the nationwide backing that Chiang Kai-shek possessed. He was eventually released and Chang surrendered, was tried, found guilty, sentenced to punishment, and then pardoned, but he is now, according to Yen, actually a closely guarded prisoner on Chiang's country estate. The whole affair greatly enhanced the prestige of Chiang Kai-shek and his government, and Nanking has now come to be the actual Central Government of China to an extent never before realized. Since December the "Young Marshal's" troops have been moved out of the northwest, split up, and incorporated into Central Government forces in many different places. It is hoped that they will be subjected to strict discipline and that their previous unruly influence will be negligible. At present, I am told, there are only a few detachments of his cavalry still in Shensi, and the area has been taken over by loyal and better-trained Central Government forces. This precedent has been applied to some of the other outlying provinces, where similar substitutions of troops have or are being effected. Also, the new provincial authorities are being appointed directly from Nanking and are not, as often in the past, unscrupulous men who had obtained high positions for themselves which were confirmed by the government only because it could do nothing else without provoking civil war. (It seems one principle of Chinese statesmanship is to avoid fighting at all costs and to accomplish one's aims by means which we might ordinarily consider corrupt. At the same time, it does seem more civilized than fighting and is probably just as effective, as well as cheaper, in the long run. It takes more time, but these people have infinite patience.)

Anyway, as a result of the kidnapping in Sian and the unsettled conditions thereabouts, the government on December 26th decreed that no passports would be issued for the northwest for a period of three months. Before this time was up it was extended for another month, so from the very start there was no possibility of beginning our work there before late April. Another difficulty involves the governorship of Kansu. Shortly before our arrival in China the governor resigned or was transferred. The man appointed to succeed him had been involved with the Sian affair in some way and was wounded. Scared of returning to that area, he pleaded illness as an excuse to postpone taking office. The Central Government, understanding the circumstances, waited long enough for him to "save face" and then appointed another man, Ho Yao-tzu, a Mohammedan Chinese, formerly minister to Turkey, to take his place. Ho has already gone to Sian and is expected to take up his duties shortly. Since the displacement of the last actual Kansu governor, until now there has been no one in supreme control of the province who could take responsibility for our safety and, consequently, the government has been unwilling to grant us passports.

A few hours before we left for Peiping we received word that General Ku Cho-tung, Director of the Generalissimo's Provisional Headquarters in Sian, who is at present in command of all troops in the northwest, had granted permission for us to receive our Kansu passports in Sian. As soon as we returned to Shanghai I called at the passport office here to request visas for Sian, only to be informed that such permits could only be obtained from the Ministry of Foreign Affairs in Nanking and only after satisfactory reasons for making such a trip were presented. I reported this to Yen who has wired Nanking. Now I have just heard that our Tsinghai passports are on the way to us.

All of this has alerted me to possible problems should other provincial governors leave their posts, and I am now insisting that, before we leave Lanchow for the interior, we be furnished with a complete set of passports from the Central Government in Nanking, one for the entire party and one for each of us individually. My feeling is that, although Nanking passports may not be much use by themselves in the provinces without the supplementary local papers, I am unwilling to trust solely in the passports issued by the local authorities. Should those be unrecognized by successors, our Nanking passports would be our only protection. I think they can be obtained and sent to us as soon as Ho arranges for our Kansu passports.

When we first arrived here I had hoped to get away for the field in early April. This unexpected long delay has seriously cut into our field season just at the time of year that would have been most pleasant for working. Now by the time we get out there it will be hot, and the rainy season will have started. We don't know how late we can work into the fall, but we shall take in supplies to last six months.

I think I am beginning to understand the Chinese system. It is primarily characterized by "buck-passing", and the final results depend considerably on the extent of one's influential connections with high officials. Most of the people here give the impression of being extremely busy, but I am coming more and more to believe that this is largely a pose and a means of avoiding unpleasant or unwanted duties and responsibilities. Office clerks appear to devote a great deal of time to reading newspapers or loafing about, and their masters are so occupied with social functions that a large part of their daytime hours must be employed in recuperation. It is not surprising that everything not of the most immediate importance is postponed for as long as possible. There does not seem to be any way to beat the system.

Shanghai
May 16, 1937

There has been much excitement here with the touted British Coronation Celebration which has resulted in decorations and lights and the closing of most of the foreign businesses since May 12th. One would think we were part of the British Empire. The main event was a "Tattoo" held in the Race Course Park, right across from our hotel, which I witnessed from my window. I didn't think much of it . . . it seemed to me that planning a two-hour performance such as that must have taxed the minds of those responsible. There was lot of marching under floodlights before a backdrop resembling a castle. Most of the marchers were the local British troops, sailors from the fleet, and a regiment of Russian municipal guards. They were in regular uniforms, fancy-dress uniforms, kilts, and track suits. There were a lot of salutes fired, and someone even skipped rope. Beforehand there was a street parade, which attracted some ruffians prepared for trouble. They threw rocks, and the police charged the crowd, breaking heads right and left. I later read that fifty people ended up in the hospital. The next night the police came with bigger clubs and there was another riot, but not so violent.

The city has also been celebrating its annual "Basket Fair", commemorating the birth of Buddha. For blocks around the Temple the sidewalks are filled with small mat booths selling everything and anything. It is said to be an outgrowth of a country fair dating back to the days before Shanghai became a great city. There were shoving crowds of Chinese looking over the merchandise on display, but few foreigners. There were certainly few things that a foreigner might need or want to buy.

Shanghai
May 23, 1937

We have at last received our passports for Tsinghai. These will get us to Sian, where General Ku is expecting us, and further on to Lanchow, where Governor Ho is now established. How our actual plans will go from there depends upon the receptions these gentlemen give us, along with information about conditions in the country around there.

Licensing our firearms is our current activity. Applications were first made out, entirely in Chinese, of course. That took one day. These were properly endorsed by the American Consulate. This took another day. Then we took them to the police headquarters, and the actual licenses were promised in a week's time. When I asked if the process could be speeded up a bit I was told that it was not at all possible, that granting them in one week was very fast work indeed.

Arrangements have been made for one of the Chinese geologists from the Survey to accompany us into the northwest. We were going to meet him at Suez's house for dinner tonight, but he did not come down from Nanking as expected, so Fred and I dined with Suez alone. It was a good Chinese dinner. Toward the end of the meal Suez apologized for not having a dessert. (The Chinese don't serve dessert, and Fred has quite a weakness in that direction.) And then, after all the bowls had been cleared from the table, surprise . . . along came an enormous platter of strawberries. They were delicious.

We have been having some hot and humid weather, 94 degrees plus. When the sun shines it is quite uncomfortable. For some reason, on the very hottest day of all I took a notion to visit the Chinese City, which is the old city antedating the foreign settlements and outgrowth into the Chinese territories that has developed today. It was once surrounded by the usual wall, which is all gone now; inside, however, it has probably not changed much, with twisting, winding, narrow streets which must take people years to know. There are many shops devoted to the tourist trade, but the most interesting part is the Chinese quarter, and the most impressive place of all is the bird market where thousands of cages contain birds of every description, all singing and warbling and making a terrible commotion. Included for good measure are cages of rats, mice, chipmunks, guinea pigs, turtles, toads, and doubtless other kinds of beasts that I overlooked.

Running through the city there is a canal filled with sluggish, green, and filthy-looking water which, oddly enough, doesn't smell as bad as it looks. The canal is crossed by numerous plain but gracefully arched bridges, and at one place a bridge expands to encompass a tea house said to be 400 years old. Its blackened condition leads me to believe it. Here the water is filled with goldfish and turtles, all swimming about together.

Although one coming here directly from the West might think Chinese cities dirty, I am constantly surprised that they are so clean. The people live in the greatest possible congestion, there is no sanitation, and some of their habits are disgusting. In spite of this the smells are not of filth, but are the natural smells of people and their food. Chinese cities are certainly much cleaner than those of India.

Shanghai
May 28, 1937

We are finally in the midst of last-minute activities for we leave here on June 2nd for Sian. Our Tsinghai passports took two weeks to reach us after having been authorized by Nanking. Then Yen dilly-dallied so long in closing the deal with the Survey for the loan of one of their geologists that we have had to wait even longer, but it is settled now, and C.C. Sun will join us in Sian on June 5th. At present we are sitting around waiting because we can get no berths on the train before next Wednesday. Apparently they never heard of adding another car to a train or running another section when traffic is heavy .

Today we had tea at the home of Mr. Chow, the chief man of the Chinese syndicate. Also present were Suez and Yen, another bank president, and a Chinese we have not met before. "Tea" consisted of soup, three kinds of dumplings containing meat, vegetables, and candied fruit, steamed sweet bread and, of course, the warm Chinese rice brandy they call wine. Most of the time they talked Chinese among themselves, as only Suez and Yen spoke English. I guess it was a sort of farewell party for us.

In the morning I called on Mr. Twogood, the head of Standard Vacuum here. It was the first time I had met with him; I just wanted to get acquainted in case we should have to call on him in an emergency.

We shall have to spend several days in Sian, which is where we leave the railroad. General Ku is the military commander in charge of the Generalissimo's northwestern headquarters and one of the men who accompanied Madam Chiang when she joined her husband, Chiang Kai-shek, when he was held prisoner by Chang Hsueh-liang last December. It was a very daring act, and they all risked their lives. General Ku has already promised us his assistance in our work. From Sian we will go to Lanchow where Governor Ho now officiates (he is a good friend of one of our bank presidents), and then we shall proceed to Sining in Tsinghai, the headquarters of General Ma Pu-fang, one of the few remaining real "war lords" in China. I expect that from now on it will be prudent for me to leave many things unsaid in my letters, for they might be opened. Also, the mail service may not be too good, so don't worry if you don't hear from me regularly as we may be out for a considerable period when we cannot send letters at all.

Shanghai
June 5, 1937

Again my premonitions of leave-taking were premature. We are, however, leaving tonight, and our baggage has already gone.

We had our tickets for the 2nd, but had to postpone departure when we discovered that a release from Chinese customs was necessary in order to ship goods out of the city. We finally got it, but several days were required.

The latest is that our alidades are technically "instruments of war" because they have stadia attachments. This required a permit from the Ministry within China. Initially we got them in because our friends' influence made it unnecessary for our baggage to be examined. We are now applying for the proper permits and trust that they will catch up with us before we are asked to show them. Otherwise the instruments may be impounded or confiscated.

Our train leaves at midnight tonight for Nanking, where we ferry across the Yangtze and begin travel in a northerly direction. We change at Suchow to a train that runs west from Shantung Province to Sian. This is Saturday; I suspect we will reach Sian Monday afternoon or evening. I have no way of knowing how long we will be there, but assume from the way things get accomplished around here that it will take a week or so to get matters straightened out there so that we can move on to the next step in Lanchow.

I have taken most of my clothes around to a cold storage place where they will be kept until our return. I have left myself one suit which I will get out of tomorrow on the train and into my working khakis. It would really appear that at last we are off.

PART III

The Push Off Into the Northwest

Sian
June 8, 1937

Greetings from Sian, the "Northwestern Capital of China". Finally we are away from Shanghai and its miserable climate. Our last day there was unbearably hot and humid, so that the slightest exertion resulted in violent perspiration. Here it is dry; although it is hotter at midday, one does not feel it so much, and the nights are cool with nice breezes.

We left Shanghai Saturday night on the Peiping Express and traveled to Suchow which we reached about 5:30 P.M. on Sunday. There we changed to the Lunghai Railroad which delivered us to Sian on Monday evening. This latter train was excellent, perhaps as good as any in the world, and since we were the only ones traveling first class we had the whole car to ourselves, each of us in our separate compartments.

Monday we passed through interesting country, a great loess region. Part of the time we were among great gullied hills, all terraced, where the people lived in caves dug back into the perpendicular walls of loess. Further on we came to the Yellow River, now in its low water stage and looking very small and rather insignificant in its wide valley of sand banks. We finally left the river and followed a broad alluvial cultivated valley with mountains rising up into the clouds on both sides. Much of the country is very dry, and the early crops seem unusually poor. Recent rains, however, make the farmers' prospects look brighter. Nearer to Sian there is considerable irrigation, and the crops look generally better.

Sian is an important city with over 200,000 people enclosed in its great wall. As I have said, practically every city is walled; even the country villages and individual farm dwellings are surrounded by walls of mud. Sian's wall, however, is in better repair than any we have seen thus far; in fact, it does not appear to be very old. The railroad station is north of the city and, since the railroad has only recently been completed this far west, the station is quite new. After our passports were properly examined, we got into the car sent for us by the bank and were driven to our hotel, which is only about a year old. I have a large room with bath for $2.00 (U.S.) per day, the comfort of which I certainly did not expect to find here. The hotel manager is a nice young man who speaks quite good English, having spent several years in Manila.

The city is much like Peiping, except for the lack of tourists and tourist-catering businesses, and it is not nearly as dusty. The buildings are mostly one storied, made of grey bricks or mud, their drab appearance relieved only by tree tops that rise up here and there from within walled gardens.

This morning we reported in to the Sian branch of the Kincheng Bank. We passed through the main office, an unprepossessing room filled with clerks, through several back rooms, across a narrow alleyway, and finally into a small sitting room whose chief virtue was that it was cool. The springs had broken loose from several of the chairs, but I finally found one that was not too uncomfortable. The most conspicuous objects in the room were several large silver plaques and a number of silver loving cups commemorating the twentieth anniversary of the bank, which apparently had just been celebrated. We were served tea while Fred and I listened to an interminable but animated conversation in Chinese between Suez, Sun, and two members of the bank's staff.

When we left the bank we were driven to the Confucian Temple which is now being extensively renovated, although it was difficult to see it as it will be. There is an important collection of engraved stone tablets scattered about, some properly set up, but most of them lying piled high in great confusion. The caligraphy work is beautifully done, and I was told that stone rubbings of a classical or historical nature are used extensively as copy books in the Chinese schools. I bought several rubbings from a shop just outside the temple area.

This evening we picked up the bank manager and went to call on General Ku. His house is the former residence of the general associated with the "Young Marshal" at the time of the kidnapping affair last December. Ku, at forty, seems to be a very young man to have eighty-seven divisions, or nearly a million men, under his command. Although he spoke only Chinese, he seemed pleasant and unassuming. Again, Fred and I were only spectators as he asked about our plans and told something about the conditions in Kansu. He has promised to telegraph instructions for his subordinates to look after us.

This visit was followed by a dinner party in our honor, given by the bank manager at the hotel. Including the four of us, there were twelve people in all. The manager spoke no English, but all of the rest did; one was a graduate of the University of Wisconsin, another of Johns Hopkins. One of the men, an old friend of Suez's, is director of the Bureau of Forestry here. I had an interesting conversation with him during which I told him about Maxwell Dorsey's request for peach seeds. He seemed particularly anxious to introduce American apples into China and, as it seemed that he and Dorsey could help one another out, I took his name and address and gave him Dorsey's. His name is Mr. Han and, although he is a funny-looking little moth-eaten man with a very red nose I enjoyed talking with him immensely.

During dinner our friends tried to carry on their conversation in English so as to include us, but from time to time the strain would become too much and they would lapse into Chinese. We are getting quite expert at pretending to listen with great interest to long conversations in which we can only pick up a very rare word now and then. Chinese, as it is spoken, seems to be a relatively characterless language, and it is difficult to make out the various sounds.

Sian
June 9, 1937

This morning we took a car and drove to Hua Tsing Chi, a warm spring about twenty miles east of Sian near the town of Ling Tung Hsien. It was here that Generalissimo Chiang Kai-shek was staying when he was taken prisoner. The story goes that he was surprised in the early hours of the morning and a brisk fight ensued, resulting in the deaths of some ten or twelve soldiers. Chiang got out of bed, climbed through a back window, over a wall, and fled up the hillside. He fell into a hole among the rocks about halfway up and was too exhausted to clamber out. There he was found. The scars made by the bullets are plainly visible on the mud walls of his house, and bullet holes pierce many of the windows.

The springs issue from the foot of a high and steep hill on the south side of the valley that the railroad follows into Sian. The mineralized water is about the right temperature for a comfortable hot bath, and the place has been famous in the past as a resort. More recently it was known as the favorite retreat of a beautiful concubine of one of the Chinese emperors. The water is pristine clear and is led from the principal spring into a series of tile baths which are much frequented by all sorts of people because the water is supposed to be particularly good for skin troubles. We were invited to bathe, but politely declined. From the baths the water passes into small canals and is finally led off the mountain and used for irrigation of the nearby land. A group of small buildings occupies the immediate area around the spring; among them many trees and shrubs have been planted in a rather ill-kept attempt at a series of gardens which are surrounded by a mud wall. The buildings are dingy and have the dilapidated appearance characteristic of most Chinese places that have not been recently restored.

I walked up the pathway of rough steps that has been built into the hillside where Chiang was captured. It is very steep and such a stiff climb that I was completely out of breath, with my legs about ready to give way beneath me, when I finally got there. A space about the rocks has been cleared away and great characters have been carved in them and painted red, presumably telling the story of what happened here. This place will probably become a national shrine, and the memory of the beautiful imperial concubine will be eclipsed.

When Fred and I returned to the car we found that the driver was taking a bath, so we walked through a nearby country market and wandered into a small temple where several women with tiny bound feet were lighting joss sticks before the image of a deity who, it happens, was also the early emperor who initiated flood control works in China.

The walls outside the temple gate were painted with fierce-looking figures bearing drawn swords — the guardians of the gate.

Pomegranates are raised here, and the small trees are now in full bloom with beautiful red flowers. The wheat is ripe and being harvested by hand with a sickle. The thrashing is accomplished by spreading the cut grain out on a thrashing floor and then pulling a heavy stone roller around and around over it. The straw is raked off, and what remains is tossed up in the air which blows the chaff away, leaving the wheat grain behind.

While passing through the country we saw a number of brick kilns in operation, mainly mounds of earth with thin curls of smoke issuing from them. The Chinese have developed a method of burning bricks with a minimum of fuel; they are only half burned and then doused with water. The product is the peculiar greyish brick so much in evidence here and, although they certainly are not the best bricks made, they seem to suit the local purposes. However, most of the ordinary houses here are made of simple mud or adobe.

This noon we met the only American currently living in Sian, a young man who is the representative of the Texas Company. His name is Fitch, and he is the third generation of his family to live in China. Suez knew his grandfather well, and his aunt played the organ at Suez's wedding. Fitch has only been in Sian for seven months, long enough to witness the revolt and also, I would think, long enough to be sick of it. Although Sian is an important city, I should certainly hate to be stuck away here by myself for very long.

Sian
June 10, 1937

Our boxes have not yet arrived from Shanghai. That means that we shall not be able to leave here before next Tuesday at the very earliest.

Today we were invited out to lunch by Mr. Han. Again, there were about twelve of us, and we met at a Chinese restaurant near the center of the city. We went in through a shop that looked something like a drug store, into a back room where some men were painting signs, and then upstairs to the second floor. The room there overlooked the street and had a floor made from the most uneven and warped boards I have ever stumbled across. We sat around drinking tea and eating peanuts and watermelon seeds until all the guests arrived; then we seated ourselves at a large circular table and pitched into the typical classy Chinese meal of many courses, all served in bowls set in the center of the table. One helps oneself with chopsticks from the common dishes. With such a meal it is hard to keep from eating too much, for if one eats more than two or three bites from each course he is full long before the meal is over.

After luncheon two car loads of us drove out to Han's experimental garden, a mile or so west of the city. It is a large enclosure surrounded by a wall, and he has planted many varieties of fruit trees and grapes there, as well as vegetables and flowers. Most of the fruit trees are yet too young to bear, although there were some grapes and peaches, unripe, of course, at this time of year. Altogether the place looked inadequate, but it is the only thing of this sort in this part of China and is at least a start.

Tonight the local Rotary Club, all Chinese, met at the hotel for dinner. There were twelve of them, all but two of whom we had met either at luncheon today or at the dinner just after our arrival. Apparently we have met all of the elite among the modern Chinese here.

In the evening Fred, Suez, Sun, and myself congregated in my room and started talking about how rubbings are made from the engraved stone tablets that are so common all over China. We examined the ones I bought the other day, and Suez translated some of the inscriptions and explained the history and mythology represented in the pictures. From this, our talk drifted into the subject of Chinese literature and education. A young Chinese, the hotel accountant, joined us, and after the others left I had a long chat with him. He is very anxious to come with us into the interior, but of course I have no use for him under the present circumstances. However, if Suez should decide not to stay with us we would certainly need someone who can speak English fairly well. Suez is pretty old to go on a rough trip such as this, and he is not particularly enthusiastic about doing so. Our geologist, Sun, does not speak or understand English adequately enough to act as our interpreter. As this young fellow is a very likeable chap and speaks

English reasonably well, perhaps I should keep him in mind.

Sian
June 11, 1937

It rained lightly last night, and this morning it is comfortably cool. The latest Shanghai papers report 97 degrees, the hottest day of the year thus far. Late this afternoon the atmosphere cleared and we got our first real view of the mountains south of the city. The high tops were still wreathed in clouds, and banks of soft white mist filled the deeper valleys, a really very pretty sight.

After lunch Suez and I hired a couple of rickshaws, equipped with the characteristic long awnings which protect both the occupant and the puller from the sun and rain, and we sloshed off through the mud back to the Confucian Temple. We wanted to see the famous old stone that records the history of the Nestorian Christian Church in China. We had walked right by it when we were there before, but like many of the other stones it was covered with a mat due to the renovation work being done. We had hoped to get a man from one of the rubbing shops to come with us and make a rubbing while we watched, but we could not find one who would do it. The stones are being catalogued, and taking rubbings would apparently interfere.

Sian is, after all, a very drab place. The city space enclosed by the wall is large, but built up solidly only to the south and west of the belltower that marks the city's center. Mr. Han told me that only in these parts can good water wells be dug. Water is carried in large wooden buckets via wheelbarrows by coolies who must struggle desperately to keep the barrows up and moving. It must be a terribly hard life to be poor here.

Sian
June 12, 1937

My pen ran dry last night, hence the sudden stop.

This morning we went to the bank to arrange for our funds to be transferred to Lanchow. I forgot to duck for the doorway as I was coming out and gave myself an awful knock. No one here is expected to be as tall as I am, and many of the doors are exceptionally low.

After lunch we took a car and drove south out of town to two pagodas known as the Large and the Small Swan Towers; they are some 1,300 to 1,400 years old. The Large Tower is the older and located about two miles farther out. It is in a vast enclosure that also includes a number of Buddhist shrines of rather ordinary nature. These are typical Chinese buildings with the usual life-sized and fierce-looking stone figures of the twelve apostles or "lohens", I think they are called. Only two priests were in evidence in one of the buildings, whose lower floor had several old scroll paintings on the wall and some carved stone images stacked in the corner. There were also two enormous baskets filled with unhulled rice lying there. On the second level of this building there was a gilt Buddha, and a hole had been cut into the floor so it could be viewed conveniently from the ground. The tower itself is a massive structure with thick brick walls. A series of stairs runs up the center from one platform to the next, from which window-like openings look out in each direction. I don't know exactly how tall the tower is, but it was a good stiff climb to the top. Gaudily painted plaster gods lurk in niches at each level; one of them was a many-armed Hindu-like diety. A particularly large niche on the ground level was being used to store straw, and the heads of several gods poked up above the stalks almost as if they were trying to hide there. Stone tablets were set into the mud-plastered walls, and parts of the wall were papered — why, I cannot imagine — with newspapers, the most conspicuous of which were advertising sheets from several California cities pricing groceries and auto accessories. The view from the top of the tower was quite a vista of the surrounding countryside with Sian in the distance. Just below and outside the wall enclosing the tower was a small village at whose edge was the thrashing floor where reaped wheat lay spread to be thrashed by a stone dragged round by an ox or mule.

On the way to the second tower we stopped at a private garden that is much admired locally. It is about a city block in extent and surrounded by the inevitable wall about ten feet high. Around the inside edge were planted several rows of tall, straight poplars, encompassing other trees, bushes, and bamboo in considerable profusion and variety. It was pleasing in contrast to the rather bleak surrounding countryside, but the Chinese do seem to lack an appreciation of open space and grass, which made it less than attractive to me.

The Small Swan Tower was being used by the military as a munitions storehouse, but we thought we would try to visit it anyway. The wall surrounding the tower and its accompanying buildings was mud, with battlements, loopholes, and bastions. We were stopped at the gate by two soldiers with packs on their backs and armed with bayonetted rifles. One wore a steel helmet of distinctly German design. Suez talked with them and handed out his card which one helmeted soldier took to his officer, returning in about fifteen minutes with approval for us to enter. Most of the buildings here are being used as barracks, and we passed through groups of soldiers in all possible stages of undress. Close by one of the buildings was a large cast-iron bell which, according to legend, if struck by one whose relative is absent or unaccounted for, will cause the missing party to write if he still lives or to manifest himself in a dream if he is dead. The tower here is quite different from the other in shape and shows a distinct Hindu influence. It is in precarious condition as it is practically split in half from top to bottom. Tradition has it that it was split apart by one earthquake and put back together by another, but this is obviously not the whole truth as the cracks are plainly due to serious structural failure of the arches above the windows on the north and south sides. We did not go inside as it is said that the tower can no longer be ascended, which I can well believe from its appearance. Its top now seems to be the home of innumerable swallows which were flying above us in the clouds in search of their late afternoon snack of insects.

We were told that the Buddhist temples surrounding these two towers are where the Buddhist classics brought overland from India along the Silk Road were first translated into Chinese.

A striking feature of this part of China are the walls, which are often loopholed and battlemented in mute testimony to the unsettled conditions that have long existed here. Right now, however, everything is quite serene and peaceful and everyone, including the soldiers, goes about his business confident and unmolested.

We were not permitted to dine at the hotel tonight because of a big banquet, so we went out to a Ningpo restaurant for dinner, up the usual steep stairway and into a heavily beamed room with a very low ceiling. I was much amused at the food Suez ordered. He complains that western meals include too much meat and yet tonight we had: first course, pork; second course, duck; third course, chicken; fourth course, cauliflower; fifth course, fish; sixth course, fish; and seventh course, rice. There was a noisy crowd in the booth next to us. At first I thought they were practicing college yells, but Suez told me that they were only playing the "finger counting" game. This is a popular pastime around here where, amidst much shrieking, people try to guess the total number of fingers to be held up at one time by the group. It was apparent that they were having a wonderful time. When we got back to the hotel the tables were still set up for the banquet and waiting. I don't think the dinner guests ever showed up.

Sian
June 16, 1937

Sunday was the day of the Dragon Boat Festival but, as there is no body of water around here, nothing happened. We have had, however, a more or less steady drizzle of rain for the past four or five days. Yesterday, twelve days after having been "express shipped" from Shanghai, our camp equipment and provisions arrived. Ordinarily a truck caravan leaves here each odd numbered day for Lanchow, and we had planned to get our things off at the first opportunity, but because of the rains the unpaved roads are a mess and the trucks must wait for them to dry up. We shall just have to be patient again. It's getting to be quite a habit with us; soon we will be unable to hurry at anything. Suez's astrologer in Peiping has forecast that we will not reach our destination before August, so it appears that we are fated to be delayed.

Today, during an interval between showers, we visited the local museum where we found the marble and bronze statuary of Buddhas and other gods most inadequately housed and displayed. The only items of particular interest to me were four horses in bas-relief, somewhat less than natural size. These and two others were recovered from the tomb of an emperor hereabouts. The story is that they were stolen by the father of one of the former governors of the province and sold to a Japanese. Because they were too large for easy transportation, they were broken up into moderately sized pieces. The theft was discovered, and these four were salvaged. The other two are now probably somewhere in Japan.

The streets are all decorated with Chinese flags today, but I have been unable to find anyone who knows why.

There are currently four other Americans at the hotel; one is a man named Latimor who lives in Peiping and has done some exploratory travel in Chinese Turkistan. The others are tourists who have come to climb a sacred mountain in a range nearby, but like us are marooned in their rooms by the rain.

Dr. Koo told us in Paris that there was nothing particularly secret about our business here, but Dr. Yen in Shanghai is very suspicious and has insisted upon making a deep mystery of our doings. Therefore we have all had a big laugh over a paragraph or two that appeared in the local Chinese newspaper yesterday. It told all about us, who we are and what we intend to do, as well as stating that we are working for Dr. Koo and Company. Apparently it was a copy of the formal notice about us sent out by the Nanking government to the officials throughout the northwest. Yen may be disturbed about it, but because it wasn't a result of our actions we can be amused.

Sian
June 18, 1937

Our business is progressing again. Yesterday the rain stopped and today the sun once more ruled the sky. Our outfit, weighing well over four tons, has been loaded onto the trucks, and early tomorrow our servants will be on their way with it to Lanchow. Trucks are very scarce here now because those that have gone inland have been prevented by the weather from returning. Through our "pull", however, we managed to get two government trucks assigned to us (two-tonners of German make with diesel motors). Each carries two drivers and our servants, who will have to burrow in amongst the load. I fear they will have a rough journey. One of the drivers told Suez that when the road is good the 300-mile-plus trip can be made in three days, but I suspect it will take them at least four or five days, unless there is more rain, and then Lord knows how long it will take them to get there. I heard of one man who was on the road for forty days! By mule carts, which can travel in all kinds of weather, the journey takes eighteen days, and until three or four years ago that was the way everyone traveled up to Lanchow. The customs stations and guards along the road have been instructed to let our things through without examination or payment of tolls; we are indeed privileged persons. We, ourselves, will go up on the plane next Tuesday. The flight takes a little over two hours. We are allowed only thirty-five pounds of baggage, so have retained only our most essential belongings. We are now in the last hotel in this part of China. Arrangements have been made for our accommodations in Lanchow at a sort of officers' club . . . what it will be like is quite beyond my imagination.

Since the rains started the city has been one continuous puddle, so I have not done much wandering about. Yesterday, however, I did take a long walk from the hotel in the northeastern part of the city, south to the main street, west to the bell tower in the center, and then on almost to the west gate. I didn't see one single foreigner until I returned to the hotel. Everyone stared at me and I stared right back, as well as rubbered into many of the shops along the way. There were a few modern-looking stores selling things like clocks, phonographs, silk, etc., but most of the shops were open-fronted with all their stock exposed in baskets and on a few shelves. One of the most impressive buildings I saw was the public bath house, but I have no idea what it is like on the inside.

The spectacles that the men wear here are most amusing. The lenses are round, at least two inches in diameter, and the bows, instead of hooking over the ears, end in a pair of clips that grasp the head firmly above and in back of the ears. They give the wearers a very solemn and owl-like appearance. Next to the glasses in curious interest come the straw hats which exist in every conceivable size and shape, from imitations of our western models to great flopping structures that stick out at least a foot in all directions. Most of the men have shaved heads, although one sees an occasional western-style haircut or a queue wound around the head. Women do not wear either glasses or hats. Their hair is simply drawn back quite tightly, knotted at the back of the head, and enclosed in a sort of hair net. Some of the children have their heads partially shaved in odd patterns. There are no diapers in China. The system consists of making children's pants open between the legs and behind so it is only necessary to squat for elimination purposes while otherwise a more or less respectable appearance is presented, although bare and rather dirty bottoms are not an unusual sight. Some of the children run about quite naked.

Our hotel is on the street that leads from the railway station outside the north wall to the main part of town, and there is a constant procession of carts and wheelbarrows. I am awakened every morning by the complaining squeak of hundreds of wheels which no amount of grease seems to help. Since most of the carts are equipped with automobile wheels and tires, I would think that this part of the country would be an excellent market for American rubber tires.

Many soldiers have been marching by, either to or from the station, each with a rifle almost as big as he is (I think they are old Russian rifles similar to those we drilled with in S.A.T.C.), and each has a pack on his back. These are neatly made on bamboo frames and covered by a coolie hat woven of split bamboo. At each belt swings an enamelled cup. Actually, they don't look too bad. A field kitchen brings up the rear of each company, consisting of old gasoline cans and a few large iron kettles swinging from shoulder poles. Individual soldiers roaming the streets don't look as impressive as they do on the march; their uniforms are cotton, badly fitted, usually much-worn khaki or a greyish blue. I don't know what the distinction is — there may be none — as sometimes part of a man's uniform is one color and part another. Their carriage is not what we expect of our soldiers, and most of them look like what they probably are — poor farm men and boys. The most incongruous feature is their footwear. Leather shoes are rarely seen;

most of them wear the cheapest sort of black canvas and rubber-soled tennis shoes. Some wear Chinese cloth shoes, some wear rubbers, and some, boots of a curious native make. The officers look much like the men and have no noticeable distinguishing badges of office except their Sam Brown belts and brass-handled short swords.

There are numbers of maimed men, without arms and legs, on the streets. I presume they are discharged soldiers from the numerous civil wars.

But, to a more cheerful subject. Last night we dined at the home of Mr. Liu, the local manager of the Kincheng Bank, a man in his thirties (although it is difficult to judge people's ages here), very nice-looking and intelligent. Unfortunately he does not speak English. He lives in the far part of the city and we drove there by car, first down the main streets, which are paved beneath their top surface of mud or dust, and off onto unpaved and very narrow muddy alleys. We stopped at his gate, a double one with two sets of heavy doors capable of cutting the courtyard off from the outer world. The court was rather dismal-looking, despite its trees and flowering shrubs, because the lack of grass and a damp yellow-brown soil dominated the scene. We were shown into a room overlooking the court and served tea while we were carefully inspected by several children peeking at us through the windows. The room was high-ceilinged, lit by an ornate old-fashioned electric chandelier whose globes had probably never been emptied of dead bugs since its installation. The walls and ceilings were untidily papered with common white Chinese paper, and the walls were hung with several scrolls of large Chinese characters and a few pictures. Although these were all probably quite old they seemed unattractive to me, with the exception of one drawing in subdued colors of three men tasting vinegar from a jar held by a servant boy. Suez said that it was probably over 200 years old and evidently had been done by a real master. The furniture was cheap and the chairs uncomfortable; a bed stood in one corner of the room and a big pile of books in another. The floor was brick, with two gaudy and very dirty rugs under a table in the center of the room. Before dinner Liu showed us his small collection of jade pieces and other highly polished carved stones. Like most Chinese, he has a real passion for such things and some of them were quite beautiful. The dinner was a nice Chinese one — the only new dish we had was a sweet soup, made from a fungus that grows on oak trees in Szechuan, which tastes oddly like tapioca. The Chinese are great for liquor after dinner, so we finished off with neat whiskey and something else so strong that the first sip took my breath away.

This noon Suez and I had a Chinese lunch; first course, ham; second course, fried pork; third course, chicken and bean curd; fourth course, eels; and fifth course, dumplings. (Too much meat!) The ham was cured without salt and was quite good. It appeared in rectangular pieces with the skin still on and, although the hairs had been shaved off, the lower portions were plainly visible in the semi-transparent skin.

Sian
June 20, 1937

Today we took rickshaws downtown to the street where most of the curio shops are located. Much of the stuff was junk not worth carrying off, but there were some interesting pieces recovered from old graves, mostly bronze objects ranging from coins and spear points to Buddhas, baked clay figures, polished stones, etc. Nearby, a public park was planted with small trees and shrubs. The pomegranates were in blossom but, as usual, there was no grass. Pinned up along a wall was a series of paintings, mostly black and white and mostly semi-cartoons relating to politics. The draftsmanship was quite inferior. At the back of the garden was a tiny ill-kept zoo with a porcupine, a wolf, foxes, eagles, owls, a deer, and bear cubs, all of them very moth-eaten and unhappy-looking.

At lunch Suez and I were joined by Fitch, who invited us to accompany him and two Germans for a drive to the mountains south of the city. We went. The Germans have a three-and-one-half-ton diesel truck that they are demonstrating around China, so the five of us plus five Chinese climbed aboard for our journey. We left the city south along the main road, past the Swan Towers, and turned off onto a carttrack that led through a number of small villages and, after about twenty miles, to the foot of the mountains where a stream flows out onto the plain. The mountains here are mostly granite with very steep slopes. We left the truck and hiked along a trail for about half a mile up the stream to a beautiful pool where we shed our clothes and went swimming. It was wonderfully clear and cool, with the stream tumbling down among the boulders in a series of little waterfalls. It was lots of fun. We were, of course, of great interest to the nearby villagers, many of whom lined the bank to watch us. Fitch says this valley runs back to an important pass through the mountains which is used by coolies running packs through here to Szechuan. Near the mouth of the valley is an imposing small mud fort with high walls and battlemented towers which has been newly repaired. The nearby plain is mostly rice paddies full of standing water, and the very narrow road that threads through is raised barely above the water level. It is certainly not intended for trucks, and the driver had a difficult time navigating some of the tight corners. Further on the rice gives way to other crops, one of which is wheat, now harvested and being thrashed. The villages are surrounded by high mud walls, mostly in disrepair, which seems to indicate that at present they are not needed. These people are obviously very poor and the children are never washed; they are either naked or covered only by raggedy shirts. And everywhere the cur dogs — the driver was continually having to stop sharply to avoid running over them. Actually, he did run over two; one was probably killed and the other more scared than hurt, I think. These country dogs, however, look healthier and better fed than the equally numerous city dogs. (I have never seen more sad and mangy specimens than some of these.)

After our swimming venture we returned to the hotel and sat around drinking beer. Two other Germans joined us. Flyers for the Eurasia Airline, we learned that they are the pilots of the plane we are taking to Lanchow tomorrow. Another American arrived at the hotel today who is said to be traveling for National Geographic Magazine. The son of the Swedish missionary who accompanied Sven Hedin on his last trip has also been here recently. He had some hair-raising adventures, if Hedin's last book is to be believed. They got caught in the midst of a local war in Chinese Turkistan and were apparently captured successively by each side.

I am certainly glad to be away from Shanghai and its vile climate. Here it may be quite warm during the day, but it cools off quickly after the sun goes down, and there is usually a nice breeze coming through my window. My next letter will be from Lanchow. The altitude there is considerably higher than here, so the nights may be cold. By the time we reach Tsinghai Province, which is at 10,000 feet, sheepskin coats may be in order. I imagine that my next letter will take somewhat longer to reach you because it will be coming out of one of the most remote parts of China. Do not worry about my safety; the government is looking out for us in every way, and our two Chinese companions think enough of their own skins to veto any proposals we might make that would be particularly risky.

Lanchow
June 23, 1937

Yesterday was the big day of my first airplane ride. We had an early lunch before driving out to the airport west of town, arriving half an hour before the plane was scheduled to leave. As it happened, we had to then wait an extra hour because the incoming plane from Shanghai was late. Planes operated by the Eurasia Company (a Chinese-German outfit) are all metal three-motor monoplanes seating seventeen passengers. Our plane had been standing in the sun all day and was stifling when we climbed in, but as soon as the motors started up ventilation was furnished by individual air hoses with nozzles at the end. This at least kept the perspiration from rolling. The seats were comfortable but, as usual in any kind of vehicle, they were set too close together for my long legs, and I was jammed into a bolt-upright position and could not lean my head back and go to sleep as the others did. The ride was not as exciting as I had anticipated, nor did I experience the sensation of great speed that I expected. In spite of this, we made the long trip in two and a half hours. Because I am not a good sailor I thought I might be air sick, but our passage was not rough and, when mountainous air currents did jerk us about, the motion was not the even roll of a ship but spasmodic and unexpected. Altogether it was not half bad, and certainly it is the way to travel in a hurry. I would not like, however, very much of such travel for long hours at a time.

Sian is located in the midst of a large alluvial valley between mountains on the north and south. This region is flat with only a slightly rolling topography approaching the mountains. It is almost all under cultivation and, as the plane gradually climbed to 2,500 meters (over 7,500 feet), we looked down on a patchwork of small fields and farmsteads. Soon it became apparent that this surface was rising as there began to appear long, narrow, and almost straight gullies cutting into the loessal soil, which increased in number and depth while the flat surface gave way to rolling topography with terraced slopes. Looking down upon this maze of terraced fields gives one the impression of actually looking at a topographical map, as the edges of the terraces follow along the outlines of the hillsides, delineating all the details of their changing slopes. Presently there arose above the terraces steep, high hills covered by soft green vegetation. They were the summits of a low range of mountains composed of old hard rocks almost completely buried beneath the loess. We followed the edge of these hills for some distance with steeper hills rising to the north, and then the plane began to climb again as we started over the Lu Pan Shan range of mountains. Soon the plane was flying at 2,900 meters (about 10,000 feet) and was only a few hundred feet above the highest summits. This was the most beautiful part of the whole flight, as cultivated fields were replaced by steep slopes clothed with dense trees and open valleys with low growing plants. From our height the forests looked like deep green blankets of moss and the intervening valleys like velvet of a somewhat lighter shade of green. The atmosphere over Sian had been clear with some haze, but now dense clouds hung over the mountains, and we flew just beneath their lower surfaces. Rain was falling in patches here and there, and the plane dodged in and out between the showers. After passing over the mountains, we came down again to about 2,500 meters. The country here was quite different from any we had seen before, a great loess plateau almost completely eroded into steep rounded hills where no flat areas remained and the surfaces were terraced. It was very arid, and the green of the growing crops was neither as deep nor as continuous as near Sian. I noted many peculiar depressions on the lower parts of the hillsides and thought at first that they marked the locations of collapsed cave dwellings. Further study made me realize that they were too large for that explanation, and I finally decided that they were probably sinkholes caused by the solution of gypsum beds included in the red bed series. I was watching for evidence of landslides and, although I saw a few small ones, I didn't recognize any features that might have been associated with the great earthquake that hit this part of the country in, I think, 1921, when several hundred people were said to have been killed and whole villages buried. As we neared the Yellow River, on whose south bank Lanchow is located, some of the valleys became larger with very distinct evidence (by way of terraces) of three or four periods of down-cutting by the river. I asked Sun if any work had been done on the physiography of the Huang Ho Valley, but his answer was no. Already I have seen some interesting geological aspects and, although I don't quite understand them at this point, it is apparent to me that there are a number of intriguing problems present. Unquestionably this region presents opportunities for some entrancing exploration, but I am afraid that we shall be able to do only such superficial work here that explanations will be suggestions without proof. Lanchow's airport is located southeast of the city, and the plane swooped down, banked in a steep turn, and came to earth without passing over any part of the city's environs.

We were met at the airport by a representative of Governor Ho and, after passport formalities, boarded a bus for a very bumpy ride to our present stopping place. Before the mutiny last fall this was a sort of Y.M.C.A.-type hotel, "The Officers' Moral Endeavor League" headquarters. It is now a cross between an officers' club and a hotel. From the outside it is a pleasant-looking two-story building, but inside it is quite bare and dilapidated, in spite of being only two years old and probably the newest building in town. They say that it was much better before all the trouble swept through this part of the country last year and that there are plans to put it back in shape with a foreign-style cook and the works, but we are here betwixt and between. At present the hotel part is nearly empty. My room is fairly large with a high ceiling and, although adequately furnished with local furniture that looks a little amateurish, it seems rather barren. My bed has an unyielding set of springs and a thin bat of cotton for a mattress, covered by a cloth spread with a printed blue border. The remainder of the bedding consists of a silk-covered quilt folded in such a way so as to become a kind of sleeping bag. The pillow is filled with chaff and isn't very soft. However, hardships are not unexpected, and we find these to be better accommodations than we had any reason to anticipate.

Governor Ho has only been here about a month and apparently has been unable to find suitable living quarters for himself and his family. His wife and two-year-old son, who flew up with us, are all ensconced in one half of our building, which is therefore very closely guarded. We have to pass through two gates, each guarded by a policeman armed with a rifle and fixed bayonet, and at the door is a third policeman with a Mauser pistol. I hope they get to recognize us soon as it is a bother getting in and out of our quarters, what with the identification and language problems. I think the police are a special branch of the army here as they are scattered about everywhere. There are even traffic policemen on most of the corners of the very narrow streets of this primitive city. This is such an out-of-the-way place that only two years ago, we are told, European dress had never been seen here. Arrival of new officials and others from the eastern provinces, however, is changing many things.

Lanchow
June 24, 1937

Lanchow is the last city of more than local importance in China and is the capital of Kansu Province. It has a population of about 100,000 and is growing fast. It is located at an elevation of about 1,500 meters on the south bank of the Yellow River (here called the Huang Ho), in a valley which is about one and one-half miles wide and bordered on either side by great barren hills a thousand feet or so high, deeply eroded with very steep slopes. It is, of course, walled, and I can look out of my window over a few grey tiled roofs to the north wall, only about fifty yards away. Immediately below and on the other side of the wall is the river. The main part of the city is very congested, with narrow unpaved streets lined by a continuous string of pitiful little shops. Few of the buildings are more than one story and, as mud is the favorite building material for both walls and roofs, it is all very drab. Some of the more pretentious places are made of common grey Chinese brick with tiled roofs. There is no water supply here other than the river, so a constant procession of coolies parades the streets carrying river water in wooden buckets bouncing from the ends of shoulder poles. Electricity was brought in a year ago, but the current is weak, the light feeble. It is turned on only at night. The generator parts had to be carted in over rough roads for over 500 miles or brought up the river against strong currents for an even greater distance, so the dim night light is truly an important accomplishment. Coal used for fuel is hauled into the city by mule carts from mines about fifteen miles away. There are said to be about forty Europeans now living in or near the city — mostly missionaries. Yesterday we ran into Mr. Davies, a Seventh Day Adventist whom we met last month on the train to Sian. He was in a mule cart and as we were passing by in rickshaws we could only wave and say hello.

Shortly after arriving at the Officers' Club on Tuesday evening, we were met by Dr. Han, the head of the Government Health Service to whom one of our Sian friends had written concerning our arrival. As no meals are currently being served at the Club and the local restaurants are reputably bad, he had kindly invited us to take our meals with him. He received his training at the Rockefeller Hospital in Peiping and speaks English quite well in spite of little practice in recent years. Probably in his forties, he is not only a very pleasant but also a most remarkable man. Starting from nothing, in two years he has built a medical center consisting of a fifty-bed hospital, an out-patient clinic which treats over one hundred patients a day, and a training school for doctors and nurses. He has little money with which to work and has had to do everything himself, from planning the buildings to supervising their construction. He showed us through his hospital and the other buildings, apologizing profusely for the lack of conveniences and the makeshift nature of everything, although he needn't have done so. The whole place looked well-kept and even better planned than some hospitals I have seen in the States and, needless to say, it was far beyond the expectations for any institution that one might expect to find in this far corner of the world. He presently has a staff of six Chinese doctors, two of whom are women, and an equal number of trained nurses. Most, if not all of them, are Christians, and if this is an example of what missionary work can accomplish in producing competent and public-spirited Chinese, I shall have to revise some of my opinions about the men of God who go off into the wild to convert the heathen.

Dr. Han's residence, a number of small rooms opening onto a brick court, is reached through a doorway between two small shops on one of the main streets just outside of the west gate to the main city. Not married, he has turned his home into a kind of club for the doctors and nurses, several of whom eat with him. There were eight of us for dinner that night, and we had what I thought was a better Chinese meal than we have had since the dinner at Dr. Yen's home in Shanghai, perhaps because it was simpler. I would say that the Chinese method of preparing vegetables is superior to ours, but I like our meats better.

Next morning Dr. Han sent one of his boys over here to get our breakfast for us. He had to shop for food first, so there was quite a delay before we were finally satisfied with boiled eggs, coffee, and rolls.

We had hoped that our trucks, which left Sian four days ahead of us, would reach here the same day as ourselves, but they have not come. (I just heard that the passenger bus that left here Sunday bound for Sian was held up and robbed on the Shensi border.) Since we can do little business until our possessions arrive, after breakfast we took rickshaws southeast of the city about a mile or so to Wu Chuan Shan, or Five Spring Hill. The rickshaw pullers had a hard time of it because the road was rough and slightly uphill most of the way. At the foot of the hill bordering the valley, we got out and walked through a large gateway to a group of buildings surrounding irregularly arranged courts which extended up the hillside for some distance. Most of these buildings were vacant except for a few images and tablets, but several refreshment establishments were located along the way. We walked to the top to see some relatively unimpressive springs and a Taoist shrine featuring a group of Buddhas, and stopped for lunch midpoint on the hillside at a restaurant with an open covered balcony fitted out with tables and stools and some rather uncomfortable reclining couches. Here we spent almost half of the afternoon enjoying the lovely view across the valley, out over the tops of the lower buildings' elaborately tiled roofs. These roofs, some of the most intricate we have seen, have dragons at the gables, ridges full-to-overflowing with other figures, and complicated spires moulded of mud which is baked like brick. Now that I am becoming more familiar with Chinese buildings, I am beginning to realize the almost unbelievable lengths these people go to in matters of ornamentation, while the really important structural features are carelessly accomplished.

The valley spread out before us, and the irrigation patterns showed up plainly as green patches against a desolate background. Large areas are not cultivated and seem to be given over to old graveyards marked by tall slender monuments surmounted by lions and more or less ruined ceremonial archways. The quality of the light at this altitude in this dry air gave the distant hills an unreal appearance, and we were mesmerized for several hours. Many of the hilltops are crowned with earthworks and small fortifications, which made me think of Foreign Legion movies more than anything else, although they are also similar to structures I saw in the Northwest Frontier Province of India.

After we bestirred ourselves from our reverie, we took the rickshaws back to town and to the truck office to inquire about our trucks (no news) and then to the river. Some of the streets are paved with large stones that have worn so unevenly that the jolting and jostling was most unpleasant. We really should have walked rather than ridden. The Huang Ho, or Yellow River, is a pretty respectable river here considering that we are so far from the sea. It is not as wide as the Mississippi, even in its high stage at this time of year, but it is just as muddy and much swifter. We saw some of the peculiar local rafts which are made of inflated sheep skins bound to wooden frames. They are light and buoyant and are used to float local produce downstream, where they are then deflated and carried back on land for a repeat performance. Upriver from the city are several enormously high water wheels driven by river current to raise water for irrigation. The river is crossed by a four-span iron bridge, made in America and erected in 1927. It is one of the wonders of the world in this region, even though it doesn't look like much to us. There is a suburb on the north side of the river to match the walled suburbs spreading out to the east, south, and west.

The people here are much like Chinese elsewhere except that the children are dirtier, if that is possible. Lower-class women also have no aversion to dirt, although the younger ones are not bad looking. The men, unless engaged in dirty occupations, seem to take more pride in cleanliness. It is obvious that upper-class men consider themselves superior to all the others by their haughty strut and attitude. For the first time we see the Mohammedans standing out from the rest of the population. They are distinctly Chinese in type, but show their mixture of western blood in more aquiline features and heavier beard growth.

The climate here is pleasant, as summer days should be. Midday is hot, but not oppressive, and the nights cool off comfortably. The locals say that very warm weather for several days at a stretch like this will bring rain. The effect of the altitude is plainly shown by the crops, which are not as far along here as at Sian, and the wheat is not yet ripe.

I'll send this letter off before it gets too heavy for air mail. If left to ordinary mail, it might be held up for weeks by bad roads.

Lanchow
June 25, 1937

We checked at the Central Bank and found that our money has been transferred satisfactorily, and this morning one of our trucks pulled in, along with three of our servants. It was held up less than ten miles outside of Sian because the bridge over the Kei Ho had washed out and all vehicles had to be ferried across. This truck was the last one over that night and, because it was too dark to ferry the others, our second truck was left behind. The following morning the river level had become too low for the ferry to operate and, as there was still too much water to ford, our other vehicle has to wait for more rain to cause the river to rise. By then, of course, the roads will be in bad shape and it will have to wait some more until the ground dries up. Ah well, such is travel in China.

Shortly after our arrival Suez and Sun called upon Governor Ho, and we were all pleasantly surprised to learn that northwest Kansu is open to us whenever we wish to start out in that direction. Although we have been hearing that conditions there are again unsettled, apparently the reports have been much exaggerated. We now propose to first make a shorter trip to Sining in Tsinghai and back into the Kokonor region to get our outfit in good working order before setting out on the long trek to the northwest. These places in northeastern Tibet are ruled by General Ma, who is something of an autocrat and quite independent of the central government. Although he made no objection to the initial issuance of our Tsinghai passports, we have been a bit apprehensive about our actual reception there. Ma has a representative here now, and we will be put in touch with him soon, so perhaps very shortly, and finally, we may be at work.

The matter of "face" enters into everything. Yesterday when Suez and I were talking about uncertainties regarding Ma's reception, I suggested that we wire him ourselves of our proposal to enter his domain within a few days. Suez said not, that it would be embarrassing to both him and us should Ma wish to deny our entry. It would be much better to proceed in a roundabout way. So Suez and Sun have arranged an introduction to Ma's representative here with the intention of having him wire Ma of our intentions and then again wire Ma when we leave.

The initial novelty of Chinese food has worn off somewhat, and I am finding that too much meat and all that rice is no substitute for potatoes and bread. The Chinese have very few of what one might call table manners and, although each meal is a somewhat lengthy and formal ceremony (most meals take at least two hours), almost any behavior is permitted. The first thing that appears at the table is a number of small towels wrung out in steaming hot water for wiping the face and hands. They may reappear at any time during and after the meal, which is all very well except that fresh ones are not always used, and it can only be hoped that the boiling water sterilizes them even though previous dirt is not removed. Then comes weak green tea which is drunk without anything in it to give it flavor; I suppose it serves its purpose because unboiled water cannot be trusted, and the slight tea flavor at least takes away the flat taste of hot water. Tea is served everywhere and at any time as a mark of courtesy, usually accompanied with saucers of dried roasted pumpkin and watermelon seeds to be consumed leisurely while the food is being cooked. Obviously this is a lengthy process because good restaurants have no prepared meals; all dishes are cooked to order, and there are long consultations and directions given concerning the way each item should be prepared. The first dish eventually appears and is plopped in the center of the table where all can reach it with their chopsticks. Other dishes arrive at intervals until the table is very crowded. Eating is quite spasmodic and may be interrupted at any time to smoke a cigarette, and now and then someone leaves the table to hawk and spit at the ever-present spittoon. The last courses are the soup and rice which, to me, have little appeal when my hunger has been pretty well abated. There are no napkins, but small squares of paper are furnished to wipe off the dishes and eating implements, which are invariably greasy. Fred and I are not totally satisfied with this, however, and always order a bowl of boiling water in which to sterilize them. The restaurants are terribly noisy and although the premises are always small, the waiters and cooks shout back and forth at one another at the tops of their voices which, from constant abuse, have become very harsh.

Lanchow
June 27, 1937

Fred and I have checked over the supplies that were unloaded from the first truck into a storeroom at Dr. Han's hospital, and yesterday our own cook started to cook for us from some of the canned goods we brought. A lunch of Campbell's soup, corned beef with corn, beans, mashed potatoes, and bread and butter (the first good butter we have had since Shanghai) really tasted swell to us. However, since our supplies are not sufficient for two big meals a day, he will prepare mostly Chinese food from local sources. We took a tin of California pears over to dinner at Dr. Han's the other evening, but since the Chinese are not partial to sweet things, I don't know what was thought of them.

We had the rain that was predicted after the hot spell; the evenings and early mornings have been quite cool. I have been glad for my leather horsehide jacket, purchased in Shanghai for less than $10.00 (U.S.).

Suez has received word that our second truck is one stage out of Lanchow, but muddy roads have prevented it from proceeding on into the city. We hope it gets here by tomorrow as it has already been nine days since it left Sian.

Transportation to this place is so costly that everything that has to be brought in is very expensive. Gasoline is $3.00 per gallon and kerosene is $2.00. (These are Chinese dollars; to get an approximate U.S. equivalent, divide by three.) Local products are almost unreasonably cheap. For instance, I bought some nice small brass candlestick holders for fifteen cents each that have been made from old melted-down Chinese coins that went out of circulation some ten years ago; the amount of copper in each holder is surely worth more than the fifteen cents it costs. Also, we have bought a number of grain sacks that farmers use here. They are about five feet long and twelve to fourteen inches in diameter, strongly made of goat or yak hair, the yarn spun by hand and woven on hand looms. These were less than fifty cents each and will be just right for our future collection of geologic specimens.

When I was in China in the '20s the money in circulation was almost entirely silver. Now all silver has been called in by the government. In Shanghai new nickel coins of five, ten, and twenty cents are in use, but elsewhere there is only paper money and copper coins. Paper "shinplasters" in denominations of less than a dollar are the principal medium of exchange for ordinary people and are unutterably filthy. They seem never to be recalled by the banks, circulating instead until they disintegrate into shreds. Here there is paper money down to five cents and in Peiping down to two and a half cents (Chinese). There are recently minted copper one cent coins, but most of the copper coins are older and in higher denominations. The actual value of these coins seems to vary in different parts of the country. In Shanghai $1.00 is equal to 300 coppers, here it is 400, and in Peiping, 520. It seems crazy, but that is the way it is. Paper money exists in almost endless variety. There are notes issued by different branches of the several government banks that are generally accepted anywhere, and there are also notes issued by provincial banks which are no good outside their respective provinces. It is therefore essential that one carefully watches the money one is given in change.

So far I have not noticed a great variety of birds. There are the ubiquitous English sparrows, of course, as well as clouds of swallows in the morning and evening skies searching out their meals of insects. Most conspicuous are the big black and white magpies and doves very much like our mourning doves, both in looks and in their long, low, sorrowful cooing. I have seen blackbirds much larger than ours, and eagles are abundant. In fact, just now one is sitting on a telegraph pole outside my window.

I am surprised by the absence of obnoxious flies here. Screens are almost unknown, even on the best of buildings, but in spite of the quantities of dirt about, flies are not much in evidence. There are probably only twenty of them in my room right now. They look like the common housefly but act much differently, hovering around in bunches in the room, chasing one another, but they do not settle or crawl on or even show any attraction for food. This is lucky because the toilet is just outside my window. It is a two-story structure with the second floor divided into six stalls without seats, only a board missing in the center of the floor of each stall through which everything drops to the ground below where a dog or two is always on the prowl.

But to a more pleasant subject. Many of the trees here are the same or similar to ours. Probably the most common are willows and black locusts. There are the "Trees of Heaven", which have been introduced into America, and the elms and cedars, the last of which are favorite trees in temple grounds. In Peiping there are very old and distorted specimens. Cedars also furnish wood that is highly esteemed for coffins because of its lasting qualities. Of course there are many trees I have not seen before. One of the prettiest is the mimosa, with tiny divided leaves and pink feathery flowers. And the mulberry. A large one grows in the court of the next compound where children run in and out, picking up berries from the ground and eating them, while a policeman with a bayonetted rifle tries to rout them out.

This afternoon we walked out to Wu Chuan Shan again to take some pictures. Between the city and the hill south of the valley there are continuous terraced fields irrigated from the springs. Although they are now planted in wheat and vegetables, Sun told me that two years ago there was nothing but opium poppies growing here. I recalled stories told by Mr. Davies, the local missionary we met on the Sian train, about the farmers south of Lanchow who used to grow nothing but poppies, extracting the opium from the growing plants, chopping up the stalks to feed the animals, and lastly, grinding up the pods to make their bread. Certainly conditions here are much improved. Probably no one who has not been here can know how bad things once were. The opium suppression campaign of the government is not the joke that some of our magazines and newspapers make it out to be. At present all opium shops are licensed and all opium smokers must register for permits to buy amounts that are gradually cut down. Younger addicts are admitted to hospitals as vacancies occur in order to be cured of the habit. The only ones actually executed are those without permits caught stealing drugs or those who reacquire the habit after having been "cured". Further cultivation of poppies is being prohibited in everwidening areas, and it is now only in the remoter provinces like Kansu where any poppies are allowed. It has taken great courage on the part of the authorities to push the suppression campaign because an enormous revenue was once derived from the opium traffic which is now lost and must be made up in other ways.

I saw my first yaks this afternoon. They are curious-looking animals very like small cows, and at first I thought that's what they were. These yaks are not as hairy as I expected, although perhaps in the Tibetan highlands they will be more hirsute. Their legs are disproportionately short for their bodies, and they are so low to the ground that I could almost step right over them. Their colors range from all black to spots and patches to all white. Also for the first time I saw children gathering mule droppings from the road. This was a common sight in India which I have not seen here before now.

Today is Sunday and the streets are swarming with people togged out in their best silk gowns. Since this is not a Christian place I am surprised at this response to a Christian holy day. I have also leaned that some of the better-class children, whom I had previously taken for girls because of elaborate hair ribbons and pigtails, are actually little boys. Their appearance certainly seems incongruous.

Lanchow
June 29, 1937

We are still taking shots. A package arrived yesterday from Peiping containing vials of "Typhus Vaccine Peiping", which is the only place in the world where it is produced. It is made there by German Catholic missionaires from lice fed on beggars and is supplied by them to their various missionary stations throughout north China and Mongolia where typhus is ever present. They have not lost a brother from the disease since they started the program. The vaccine consists of three shots; we will get our first at Dr. Han's hospital tomorrow. Since we expect to be leaving soon, we will have to give the other weekly shots to ourselves in the field. By that time I will have been vaccinated against smallpox, tetanus, typhoid, diptheria, bubonic plague, cholera, and typhus. There is no malaria in this part of the country, for which I am thankful, so the only thing to fear now is dysentery, which we will try to guard against by being careful about our food and drink.

Our servants have had to obey orders to be vaccinated, but neither Suez nor Sun would have anything to do with the procedure. The Chinese, at least the upper-class ones, seem awfully afraid of being hurt and would apparently rather run the risk of getting sick than submit to a mildly painful precaution. When they are sick, however, or imagine themselves so, they will undertake all kinds of heroic but useless treatment. One of their favorites is cauterization, and one sees people with numerous scars acquired in that fashion. Suez has big scars on his jaw just under both ears, one on the top of his head, and quite a series of them on his back and belly, even though he is a highly educated, intelligent man. Another form of treatment formerly in favor, although now dying out, is the sticking of long pins into various parts of the anatomy. It is probably for the good of all that this practice is rapidly assuming the status of a "lost art".

Our second truck came in today. Not only was it held up in crossing the river outside of Sian but it later broke down on the road, where it stood until some part was replaced by a new piece sent out from town. Motor vehicles are terribly abused here. Trucks are invariably overloaded with freight and then, to add insult to injury, as many passengers as possible clamber aboard. Apparently the living load is not possessed of any weight.

Fred and I spent the morning going over our equipment which has been unloaded at the hospital and have selected most of the items we plan to take on our first trip out. We have nearly twice as much as we will need, but felt it better to have duplicates than to be held up or inconvenienced by loss or damage. We also assembled our saddles which were made in Shanghai and tried one out on one of Dr. Han's mules. They are not as good as I had thought and promise to be rather uncomfortable.

Now that everything is here we will soon be starting out in earnest. We propose first to make a trip of several weeks duration through eastern Tsinghai (the most northeastern province of Tibet). There is a good road between here and Sining, its capital, which is passable by motor, usually in one and a half days; however, we are going by horseback and mule train in order to study the geology along the way, which will take us a week or so. We made a bargain for mules today, and I hope we can start out on July 1st or 2nd. What we will do after reaching Sining will depend upon the conditions we find there. I hope to continue westward and examine the great basin occupied by Lake Kokonor, a large salt lake over 10,000 feet above sea level. From there I want to turn south across the first range of mountains to a large desert valley from where we will turn east and return to Lanchow via the Huang Ho valley. I do not expect to make an economically important discovery in this region, which is not one we are particularly interested in, but we would like to go this way for three important reasons: first, to thoroughly test out our transportation and camping arrangements before undertaking a much longer and more arduous trip into northwestern Kansu; second, to spend most of the mid-summer season in the high altitudes and drier climate of Tibet so that by the time we return to Lanchow the rainy season will be mostly over; and third, because much of this route will be near important streams where I think erosion will have produced better outcrops than can be expected in much of the northwest, enabling us to become more quickly familiar with the geological sections. This trip will take us beyond the outskirts of Chinese civilization into regions inhabited by Tibetans and Mongols. I saw the first of these kinds of people on the streets here the other day. They are certainly wild-looking individuals, dressed in sheepskin clothing, very dirty, with unbelievably matted hair. I shall undoubtedly have more to say about them later.

Last night we were invited to dinner by Mr. Wang, a nephew of T.C. Wang, the new Chinese ambassador to the U.S. He is in the Salt Revenue Services here. We ate at the principal hotel which was at one time a rather pretentious private residence with a number of courtyards surrounded by rooms. The doorways have very high sills to be stepped over carefully, a sure sign of importance and splendor. For the first time our room was perfumed with burning incense, but as usual the dinner of at least twelve courses was far too elaborate and filling for comfort.

Just east of our officers' club is a walled garden, a part of the government's buildings, which is opened to the public on Sundays and, although not worth very much, is crowded with people. At that time the wall is patrolled by policemen with drawn pistols bent, I suppose, on protecting the Governor. As usual there is no grass, and the plants that are there seem to suffer greatly from the dry climate. The principal attraction is the zoo, which contains a monkey, two bears, and several deer, all very pathetic looking, improperly cared for, and abused by the visitors. In the far corner of the garden is an open-air basketball court, and when I visited it a game was in progress. A considerable crowd was gathered around watching, as basketball seems very popular here in China, but it was played at a most leisurely pace. I wonder what these people would think if they could see a really good and fast pair of American teams at it.

On the other side of us across a narrow alley is a school. The building is apparently a remodeled temple and looks quite nice. Every morning at 6:00 sharp I am awakened by children chanting their lessons in the peculiar intonations used by the Chinese when reading aloud. Their reading and delivery techniques are quite different from their speaking voices. Also early every morning there are the tuneless bugle calls from close-by barracks and the distant shouts from the men going through their sitting-up exercises.

Lanchow
June 30, 1937

Here it is the fifth month away from home, and we are still not at work. Everything requires three times as much time as it should. Frequently I seriously think that our Chinese companions are keeping us back, but then again I realize that they succeed in making arrangements that we could not possibly manage for ourselves, so perhaps it all evens out. Also, it is pleasant to be with them; they teach us much and prevent us from getting into some complicated situations which we might well do without their assistance.

Today has been a peculiar day; the sky has been dull with no evidence of blue anywhere and the atmosphere so hazy that only the nearer hills are visible. Altogether the effect is that of a dust storm, but there is no wind and no noticeable dust in the air. It may be a kind of a fog, but if so, a very strange one with no humidity,

I am concerned that Suez seems to be packing up a lot of stuff for the first trip that he will not need. I realize it's easy to do if you don't ruthlessly discard everything that is not absolutely essential. I also know that he is not accustomed to this kind of travel, but I feel that I cannot make suggestions to him or insist upon procedures. If I don't humor him along he is likely to pack up his bags and return to Shanghai. Although we could get along without him it would be difficult, as none of the other Chinese have more than a very rudimentary command of English.

General Ma Pa-tsing, the military commander of northwest Kansu, is now in Lanchow. He arrived yesterday afternoon and is being entertained with the usual round of dinner parties. There will be a large one here at the club tomorrow, so we shall probably have to eat out. His visit may have political significance, but its meaning will probably not become obvious and we may never know what is in the air. Ma (which means "horse") belongs to a large and prominent Mohammedan family; his near relatives are powerful people in northwest China, eastern Tibet, Turkistan, and western Mongolia in both politics and military affairs. Three half-brothers are important generals with active commands, although I have heard talk that one of them was recently exiled to Russia.

Many of the women in these parts have bound feet; some of them are not yet twenty years old. Since I have not seen any women going through the process of binding I think this barbaric practice has been stopped, if only recently. Binding renders the feet absolutely useless, and these poor women must go through life as though perched on the tops of wooden sticks. Most of them can only walk a short distance and many of them require the aid of canes.

The last few evenings we have been treated (?) to concerts of fiddle music and singing by someone staying on the first floor here. It is not quite as bad as the radio programs and the phonograph records of Chinese music I have heard, which are Punch-and-Judy sounds with falsetto voices and much banging of gongs. This fiddle sounds a little like a bagpipe to me, high-pitched and quavery. It is very tuneless, and our performer continues until he gets tired. Unfortunately, I get tired first.

Peddlers are abundant here. They all carry noise-making implements whose natures vary with the trade. The commonest advertising instrument is a small drum with a long handle which looks something like a bed-warmer. A small stone is fastened to the side of the drum by a string, and by twisting the drum's handle one way and then the other the peddler can beat out a regular tattoo. Small gongs are used the same way. Hollow pieces of variously formed woods are sometimes carried and beaten with a drum stick or split pieces of bamboo to give a rattling sound. Tinkers have a number of pieces of tin suspended from their baskets which clink together with each step. It's noisy business.

Lanchow
July 3, 1937

It rained the night before last, so yesterday the streets were two to three inches deep in oozy mud. It was such hard going that some rickshaws had one man pulling and another pushing. I chose to walk and had quite a time trying to avoid as much mud as possible on the narrow sidewalk areas which are sometimes less than one foot wide. In places it was possible to avoid the street mud by ducking from one shop to the next through connecting archways.

The man with whom we have a contract for mules and riding animals has at last rounded up the required number of pack animals—about twenty-five. They were to be brought in yesterday for our inspection and approval. Along with the mules, which cost $1.70 (Chinese) per working day or $1.00 idle, fifteen men are included gratis. I don't know why we need so many men, but it is felt that number is essential. When we went around to the mule place for inspection, no one was there. If it hadn't been for all the mud I wouldn't have minded so much, but as it was I was totally disgusted. We went back today to find some of the mules but must return again tomorrow to see the whole show. The mule men who will be our traveling companions are a particularly filthy lot, however they seem bigger and stronger than the general run of Chinese. I wonder if they are a special breed who have followed this occupation for generations.

The mules were gathered in a shed at the back of a coal yard. Coal is mined a few miles south of the city and hauled in carts or on the backs of animals. It is very friable and arrives in a nearly pulverized condition. The coal powder is then mixed with clay in a proportion of 100 parts coal to 65 parts clay and made into large bricks which are sun-dried and sell for ten cents each. Chinese stoves have neither grates nor chimneys, and the clay holds the powdered coal together in lumps that will stay in the stove and burn. Smoke comes right out into the room and finally escapes through a hole in the roof. As there is no chimney attached to the stove, there is no draft to keep the fire burning well, so air must be pumped onto the coals by hand-worked bellows. The bellows used here are in the form of a square box with a sort of piston with appropriate valves which is worked back and forth in a sawing motion.

Of course everything is done by hand. Today I passed a carpenter shop where a man was turning wooden spindles on a very simple lathe. The stick to be turned was held by a pin at either end so it would turn easily and was rotated rapidly by a bow with a string wrapped around it and worked by the carpenter's left hand while his right hand held the cutting tool. I have seen men grinding metal in long narrow iron mortars with heavy iron wheels to fit. The wheel is mounted on a shaft which projects about four inches on either side. The operator sits on a bench with his feet on a shaft extending from each side of the wheel and rolls it endlessly back and forth all day long. Blacksmiths and brass workers pound and file laboriously to make the various metal objects that we turn out so effortlessly by machinery. Iron, incidentally, is worth more here than brass because all iron must be shipped in and brass is available in the form of old coins, worth more as metal than as money.

Suitcases would never stand the hard usage of being packed about on mules, so we have had Dr. Han's carpenter make us some sturdy wooden boxes in which to cart belongings not packed in bags. Of course the boxes weren't ready when promised but we finally got them yesterday, and I have unpacked my trunk and gathered together the things I will need for the trip. At least I am ready to start at a moment's notice, whenever that moment might arrive.

Today I learned from Sun that we can obtain here a series of military topographical maps of the eastern part of Tsinghai Province that I was unaware had been published. He got a governmental note of permission to use the maps, and we set out to see what we could get. We found the General Staff Office and, while our cards and governor's chit were taken off for approval, we waited in the guard room, carefully overseen by a very young soldier. Shortly, the messenger came for us and we were escorted to the officer in charge of the Survey Department. He received us most cordially and as soon as our wants were made known sent an orderly out for the maps we wanted. He said that he was not authorized to sell maps but he could give them to the "proper persons". I guess we are proper persons.

The calling card business in China must be a thriving one because wherever a person goes he hands out his cards and receives those of others. The reason for this is that a man's name means little without knowledge of what the characters look like since there are so many unrelated families with same-sounding names but with vastly different written characters. It is not in the least uncommon to see people conversing and writing out characters wildly in the air with their fingers just to convey their thoughts. The Chinese language seems to be an inadequate one.

Mr. Wang dropped in this afternoon for tea and a little visit during which he told me some interesting things about the Chinese Army. Soldiers are neither conscripted nor enlisted for a particular period of time, but are hired more or less like servants and, theoretically, they can give up their jobs and leave whenever they wish. Actually, the army seems mostly made up of homeless men without other work or a place to go, who probably expect to stay as long as they can. Many of them are paid $3.00 (Chinese) per month, out of which they must furnish their own food. It doesn't sound very attractive, but apparently the army offers better prospects for keeping body and soul together than two or three thousand men could find elsewhere. Some soldiers are only boys, fourteen or fifteen, but I guess one can be homeless at any age.

We received our first newspapers from Shanghai. They are dated up to June 22nd so you can see that we are far behind the times, news-wise. Suez has been translating the single local Chinese newspaper for us, but it's not very satisfactory. An old *Time* magazine has also come in with the mails.

Lanchow
July 4, 1937

I can say without reservation that this has been the quietest Fourth of July I have ever spent. In the morning we went around to the hospital to give our supplies a once-over and then off to see the mules that have been brought in. They are the sorriest lot of animals one could hope to find and don't really look as though they can stand the trip. Sun, however, seems satisfied, and he has been back through this country with mules twice before. It looks like we will be off tomorrow morning.

In late afternoon, Fred and I walked over to the Seventh Day Adventist Mission outside the city's south wall to call on Mr. Davies. We had waited until the last minute so that there would be no embarrassment between the missionaries and ourselves about invitations back and forth. Mrs. Davies stayed in the kitchen while we had a chat with Mr. D. and other missionaries from the Sian station who are visiting here. There was a flock of children around ranging in age from babies to a nearly full-grown girl. We heard mostly about people who have been through here recently, including an American councilman from Hong Kong who had traveled up to Sining and back. In spite of his high credentials and prominent position, he was unable to see Ma Pu-fang, the Sining general and acting governor of Tsinghai, and I wonder if we will fare any better. Actually there is little reason why we should wish to visit with Ma so long as he sees that we are looked after and no troubles befall us. We also got an earful about an American who was part of the Gardner Expedition a year or so ago. Among other things, they made movies of the devil dancers at the Kumbum Monastery south of Sining. It seems that this fellow was an unpleasant chap who got himself kicked out of the expedition and later returned to the U.S., was a technical director for the movie *Lost Horizons,* went on a lecture tour, and wrote a big book about Tibet. This was all certainly most ambitious of him since the missionaries say he never got to most of the places he talked about and apparently used other people's photographs to enhance his lurid stories. One of the missionary wives heard him lecture in Philadelphia and was appalled. He has just been up this way again, but his reputation so marked him that he was not allowed to go anywhere and was forced to leave.

Although we are due to leave with our mules tomorrow morning at 8:00, I will believe it when we actually get off. Our first day's journey is about twenty miles or so, during which we will follow along the south side of the Huang Ho, stopping for the night at a village where the river changes from a northerly to a westerly direction. The following morning we will ferry across the river, travel up a tributary variously known as the Sining Ho or the Huang Shui, and that night reach a tributary of the stream, the Tatung Ho. This is the boundary between Kansu and Tsinghai, and we will stay there to make a day's side trip upstream to a coal field. From there it is four days to Sining, where we will stop for four or five days and from where my next letter will be mailed. It will certainly feel good to get to work after so many protracted delays. I hope we can camp out and not be forced to spend our nights in villages along the way. We can be very comfortable in camp, and if only half of what I hear about native inns is true, they must be pretty awful. In spite of everything, I'll wager that Lanchow will look very good to us upon our return.

Well, here's to the success of our expedition with hope that everything will run smoothly and according to plan.

On the road
July 5-7, 1937

As I suspected, we did not get off at 8:00 in the morning. After a more than substantial breakfast at the Club, we packed into a whole fleet of rickshaws and arrived at the hospital at about 8:30 to find no mule men, although most of the loads had been roped onto the wooden yokes which fit on the pack saddles. When the men finally arrived we were much disgusted at the appearance of our riding animals which were no more than pack animals with the pack saddles removed. In search of the best beasts we looked over the lot, and such a pitiful group of animals they were; most of them had bad backs, some with open sores as big as my hand that made me sick to look at. At last we got things arranged, not to our satisfaction but at least so that we could start out. I chose a small horse with no shoes on his hind feet, and the others had mules. Fred's mule was in the best shape but turned out to go unaccountably crazy whenever he got near a horse, so he had to change to another mule, which he found later had to be constantly led by one of the men.

Our caravan finally set out with twenty pack animals, a litter carried by two mules containing Suez and the servants' bedding, and five riding animals. Fred, Sun, and I rode all the time, and our four servants took turns on the other two saddle mules. One servant pushed a front bicycle wheel with a cyclometer attached with which to measure the distance traveled, much to the amusement of the mule men and everyone we met along the trail. The main outfit started out just as Fred's mule wandered off somewhere out of sight. It looked for a while as though he would be left behind, but of course it reappeared at last, and we actually all got underway at 12:45 P.M.

Our road meandered west of Lanchow through a succession of suburbs and small villages so we were walled in between buildings and mud walls for some distance. When we came out into the "open" the road was the kind you read about existing in some places, worn down so far below the surface of the plain that we could barely see over its edges. At last, however, it became level with the surrounding land and there lay the upper Huang Ho valley ahead of us, some two miles wide, bounded by barren hills on either side. The plain lies in several well-marked alluvial terraces cut up into fields, all more or less contoured. Where irrigation is possible good crops are raised, but elsewhere crops are sparse, and many of the fields are covered with a layer of pebbles to conserve the moisture. Irrigation is accomplished at some places by wells fitted with a type of Persian wheel much like that used in India. Elsewhere there are great water wheels; one we passed raised the water some sixty feet into the air. River water is led into a channel where the lower part of the wheel dips. It is fitted with paddles against which the current flows, causing the wheel to rotate slowly, lifting the water up in long angled boxes.

I found the first day of riding a little painful. It has been at least fourteen years since I have been on a horse; my saddle is hard, my derriere is soft, and my horse's gait is not too good. The stirrups were fitted with toe cups which prevented me from getting my big feet in far enough to take the weight off my toes. My new boots are stiff and tight, and this all resulted in my toes going quite numb. Later that day I had

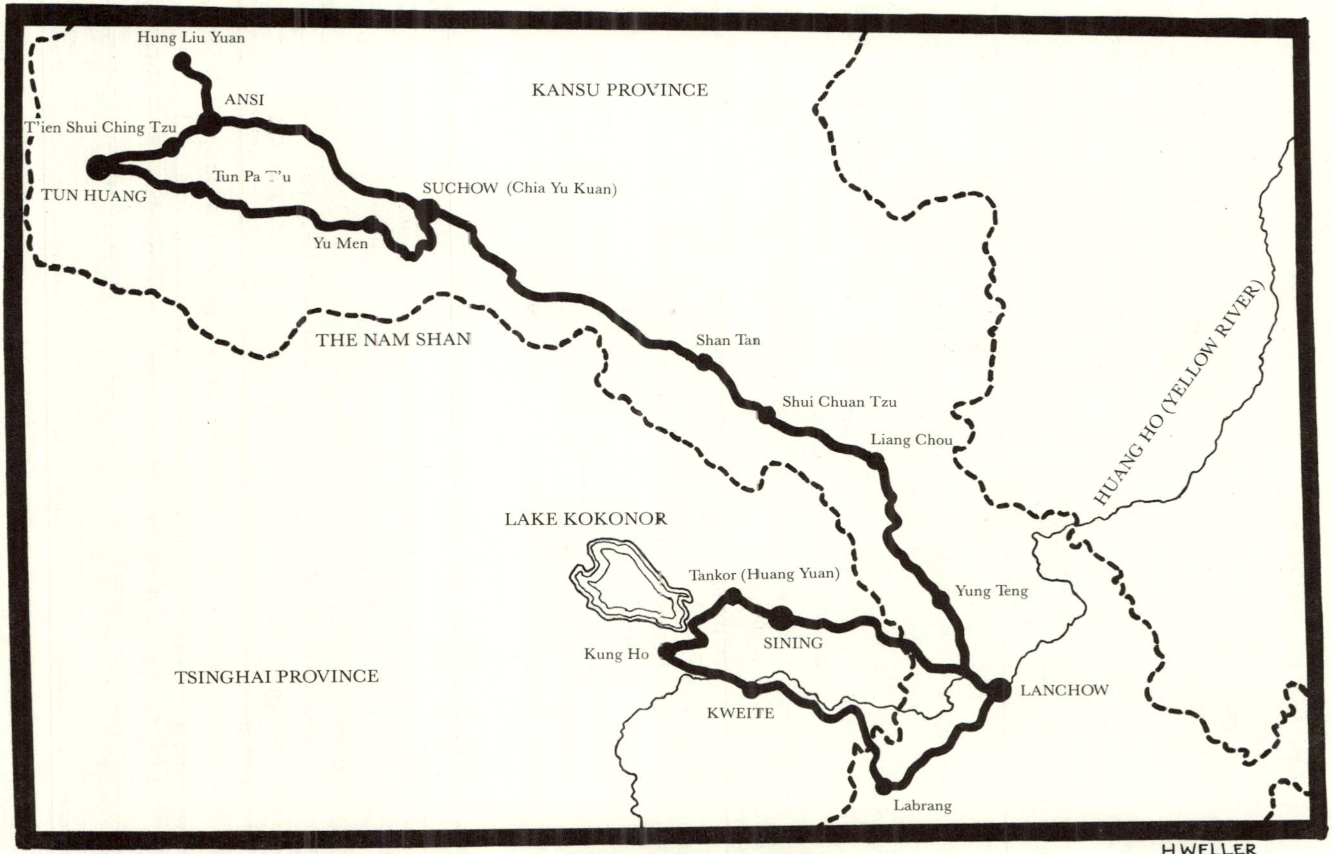

MAP II

Kansu/Psinghai

the sense to cut off the stirrup toe cups, which opened up space and relieved the pressure, and thereafter things were much more comfortable.

We passed through numerous small mud villages much like those in northwestern India. The children are particularly filthy and often naked, which perhaps saves their clothes, if they have any. Melons are grown here in pebble-strewn fields with neatly arranged vines, but the largest melons I saw were little bigger than oranges. We passed quite a few people on foot with loads on their backs, others riding or pushing carts, a few on muleback, and several men carrying small skin rafts walking back up-river, presumably to float another load of produce down to town.

The day was hot, the road dusty, and shortly after 6:00 we were happy to stop at Si Liu Ko, a small village nearly twenty-five kilometers from where we started our journey. The first inn at which we stopped proved unsatisfactory even to the mule men, who are not overly particular. So we and the animals progressed to another inn where we spent the night. It consisted of a courtyard about fifty by twenty feet, surrounded by tiny rooms fronted by a raised mud floor "verandah" about six feet wide. Our packs were unloaded all over the place and the mules stabled at one end. As soon as our sketchy supper was over, about 9:30, I was glad to go to bed. I put up my camp bed at one end of the verandah, spread a sheet inside my sleeping bag, crawled in, and was very comfortable.

We have complete camping equipment including tents, and I had hoped we would mostly camp out, but apparently Suez prefers the inns. They are not so bad in this dry climate, although the proximity of animals provides a distinct stable atmosphere. The sleeping rooms are very unappealing (small, dark, and dirty) so I shall certainly sleep outside whenever possible. Each sleeping room has a raised platform, or "kang", built so that it can be heated from underneath in winter. But although the nights are cool and covers necessary, we certainly need no heat now.

We also traveled about twenty-five kilometers during our second day. (One kilometer equals about 2/3 of a mile.) Our route on July 6th started out through a narrows in the river valley, caused by a thick hard sandstone that is tougher to erode than the soft red clays that lie above it. The valley widened and then constricted back to narrows again. About 2:00 P.M. we came to the mouth of the Huang Shui or Sining Ho where we had to ferry over. The boats are flat-bottomed scows about forty feet long and ten to twelve feet wide, pointed at both ends which are somewhat raised. Each is equipped with a great clumsy oar on one side and a large steering sweep. The river current is quite swift and a gang of men must pull the boat half a mile upstream with a big rope. There they get in and row madly across the river while the current carries them the half-mile back downstream again. The return journey is a repetition. We have five riding animals, two carring Suez in his matting-covered litter, and twenty-two pack mules. There are four of us, four servants, and fifteen mule men. It is quite a group and it took two boats to get us across. The whole ferrying operation took two hours, and by the time we reached the other side the first boat load of pack mules had gone on. They stopped at the first village beyond, but we missed them there and rode on to the next one. When we discovered our mistake, of course we had to turn around and go back.

Our second inn, at Ho Wan, was almost an exact duplication of the first. Before, however, our companions were not only the mules and men, but several goats, some pigs, chickens, and ducks. This time the livestock was augmented by a flock of sheep which was driven in just as we were eating dinner. Quarters were terribly crowded, so I set up my bed on the roof in spite of dark clouds that looked like rain. I was glad to retire early, having been up since 4:30 A.M.

Today, July 7th, we started out as usual at about 7:30 and traveled right through until 1:30, when we reached Hai Tsui Tzu, a distance of twenty-two kilometers. These have been short stages, but they have seemed long. The days are very warm, and in this thin air (over 6,000 feet) the sun burns badly. I started out with my sleeves rolled up, but after only a very few hours they came down, and my face, neck, and arms are sunburned and quite sore. My left hand, with which I hold the reins, is badly burned so tomorrow I must tie a handkerchief over it for protection. Also, I am extremely sore from riding. This first week will be the worst; after a coat of tan develops and I get toughened to the saddle I am sure it will get easier.

Actually, the worst part of this kind of traveling is the lack of a satisfying drink when one is needed. All liquids are warm, and whenever we stop we have to wait for water to be boiled for our tea, which does not really quench the thirst in any way. What I wouldn't give for a gallon of nice pure cold water! Also, our riding animals are far from satisfactory. I guess we will have to buy some good horses.

The inn where we stopped this afternoon was so filled with our own animals and loads that there was barely room for us, so I persuaded the others to move into another nearby inn where we are quite comfortable. I hope that no other travellers take it into their heads to patronize our spot tonight. We have just finished a belated lunch of sardines, corned beef, rice with milk and sugar, bread and butter, and tea. We have also just given ourselves the second typhus innoculation.

The country we passed through today became increasingly barren. We are in the midst of the opium region now and almost half of the cultivated fields are planted in poppies. Either they get better care than other crops or they grow better here than anything else does. They are not very pretty plants, and although there are some scattered white flowers and a few pink ones, they are mostly past blooming and the fields are a mass of pods. Each pod has been cut with two parallel incisions around the central part from which the crude opium has oozed and been gathered. It is worth $10 (Chinese) per catty (one and a third pounds). The villages here are most miserable and many houses, and in some cases whole towns, are in ruins. Also, many of the fields are uncultivated. Whether or not this is due to the opium addiction of the people I cannot say. Even after the opium has been produced the poppy plants are important, as the stalks and leaves are used for animal fodder and the people eat the insides of the pods. Furthermore, poppy pods are the principal playthings of the local children.

From the mouth of the river we are following there is a "motor road". This means that the road has been graded, but there are no bridges; it is badly washed out in places, and no motor vehicles could follow it very far. Here and there it is crossed by irrigation ditches full of mud and water that would stop almost anything. Still, it is a busy road and we passed quite a few people, mostly on foot, but some were riding donkeys and there were a few on bicycles. Among them were peddlers with their wares in boxes dangling from the ends of their carrying poles. They stop in villages and display bright-colored thread, buttons, socks, mirrors, combs, scissors, and cigarettes.

Some of the villages are walled and fortressed and at intervals along the way there are deserted blockhouses with holes for machine guns and rifles. Watchtowers crown many of the surrounding hills.

On the road
July 8-9 1937

Yesterday I rode out ahead of the procession and sat by the roadside across from a field of poppies to wait for the others to catch up. People passing obviously found me to be a curious sight and many halted to stare. One man stopped to sell me some apricots and to look at my saddle, which is western style and leather. Chinese saddles are made of wood and covered with quilted pads. Most of these people carry their belongings stuffed into bags made by skinning an animal whole and then tying up the legs. There are the inevitable donkeys loaded with the folded skins that only a short time ago were floating produce down the river. The country people's dress is not predominantly blue as I had expected. Many garments are black and most of the others are a very dirty white. Some of the men wear the large spectacles I first saw in Sian and others carry them in cases dangling from their belts. Some wear straw hats radiating out from conical peaks, others wear hats made of very coarse felt, turned down into a sort of visor in front and turned up along the sides and in the back, very much like Robin Hood.

Last night before dinner Fred and I wandered about the streets, but principally we watched a man pulling a gob of opium on two sticks much like taffy. It was certainly a black and sticky mess.

Last night I made up my bed in the inn yard where my immediate companions were the proprietor's farm donkeys, a dog, three pigs, and a flock of chickens, minus the three we had eaten for dinner. Sometime during the night I was awakened by a great disturbance that seemed to be caused by an agitated woman walking around with a lamp and talking loudly. I fell back into sleep without knowing what the trouble was but learned in the morning that a thief had entered and made off with a substantial amount of flour and oil. Tonight the family will load up their guns and set watch.

Today has been our longest stage thus far—thirty-seven and a half kilometers. The scenery is much the same as before, fields of poppies and small, partly ruined mud villages. The rocks around here are mostly red in color, and our trail wound precariously through deep gullies where at one place a pack fell off one of the mules and rolled down a steep slope. I don't know how Suez's litter makes it, but it does. I tired myself out yesterday by whipping my horse into a faster pace. Today I got out my spurs and made better time with less work on my part but with, I'm afraid, more damage to the horse. Most of the time I was well out in front of the procession.

Our route briefly joined the motor road between Lanchow and Sining. A tributary river flows in from the north here, cutting a steep, narrow gorge out of hard metamorphic rock. It is spanned by a picturesque bridge from which the road winds dangerously down in a series of treacherous hairpin turns. I would certainly want a very talented driver handling a good car in top condition before attempting to navigate it.

Tonight we are at a Mohammedan inn with a somewhat larger courtyard than usual. The only drawback is that we cannot cook ham or bacon in their kitchen.

On the road
July 10-12, 1937

I have just rejoined the main party after a side trip of two days. The night before last we were in Hsiang Tan Chen, which is just over the border in Tsinghai. During the night a fine drizzling rain began that continued until noon. Fred, Sun, and I, with one servant and a pack mule, set off in the rain up along the Tatuang Ho. We recrossed the bridge from Tsinghai into Kansu to find the guard soldiers who had challenged us previously fast asleep in their small hut at the end of the bridge.

and tomorrow before going south for a three-day trip to a town where there is a large Tibetan monastery. There are big doings just now because it has recently been determined that the reincarnation of the Dalai Lama of Lhassa (who died several years ago) is somewhere here in Tsinghai Province, and a delegation of 100 big lamas has come here to find him. But, to continue where I left off.

On the morning of the 10th, Sun and I left Yao Chiai in a persistent drizzle and ferried over the Tatung Ho by a boat that this time was sensibly attached to a cable stretched across the river, necessitating the labor of only one man. There was very little wait, and we got across quickly. We then rode on along the west side of the river, passing through several very small villages where grain mills were run by water in irrigation ditches. The current runs down a wooden chute to gain velocity and is directed against a water wheel operating in a horizontal position. A shaft from the wheel passes up into the mill-house above, where it turns the lower of the two millstones, grinding the grain. At one place we saw a mill boat tied to the bank of the Huang Ho. The passing of river water was strong enough to turn the paddle wheels which extended on either side of the boat, activating the millstones.

When we reached the old motor road to Sining, which was really little more than a track, we turned away from the river and proceeded a short distance up a valley eroded in red beds. The motor road snaked in a roundabout way, but the telegraph line was laid in a relatively direct route across the Ha Ka Lu mountains, so Sun and I set off with our mules along the trail that follows it fairly closely, leaving the others to take the road. We climbed steadily and often steeply up a mountain spur. The rain had made it muddy and very slippery, and our animals often had a difficult time keeping their footing. The total rise was something like 2,500 feet to an elevation of about 9,000 feet. Since I am not used to climbing in this rather rarified air, I rode practically all the way. Although the mountain is composed of rock, it is pretty well covered by loess, and many of the more gentle slopes had been terraced. While not exactly level, the natural slope had been reduced to something easier to work. The fields on the lower slopes were almost totally abandoned; in fact, much of this country shows signs of having supported a considerably larger population than is presently here. My guess is that the change is a result of drought as well as the civil disturbances. The upper slopes were more open and gentle, and it was obvious that they received more rain than the lower areas and, consequently, were much better suited for agriculture. As we rode along we were partly among clouds that rolled up from the northeast, completely filling up some of the valleys below us. The upper slopes were also terraced and all under cultivation with crops of mostly barley and peas. Barley is a source of a common dish, *tsamba,* utilizing unripened grain which is roasted, ground to a meal, and mixed with tea and butter to form a sort of thin paste.

The upper portions of the mountain were quite attractive, with the green fields and many scattered wild flowers. The prettiest flower was something like verbena, with small compact blossoms, pink on the outside and white within. There were delphinium, some of which were a distinctly coppery orange color, and a plant with a very pretty clover-like purple flower but with quite a different kind of leaf. Another plant with clover leaves had single flowers, yellow on the inside with reddish-brown outside borders.

We passed several mountain villages with mud-brick houses and no trees at all. I saw goats, sheep, and a few cattle, but not nearly as many as I would expect to be grazing here on this rather lush grass.

The trail down the southwest side of the mountain was extremely torturous, winding back and forth into a narrow gravel-filled valley. I am glad we were in descent, because the slope was so steep that I seriously doubt the mules could have carried us up. The drier condition of this side of the mountain was obvious—the rain comes in on the northeast winds and dumps on the top and other side. We followed the valley several miles and eventually met up again with the motor road near the entrance to the Huang Shui valley and the village of Lao Ya Cheng. We reached Kai Miau Tzu only a few minutes after Fred, Suez, and the rest of the outfit had arrived.

Between Sining and its junction with the Huang Ho, the Huang Shui flows through three steep and narrow gorges. The valley between the first and second is well irrigated and prosperous. In this area lies Le

Tu, the only real city between Lanchow and Sining. It is, of course, walled. Soldiers have been very much in evidence ever since we entered Tsinghai, and Le Tu was well guarded. I was, as usual, far ahead of the rest of our party when I came to Le Tu and, unaware that the road skirted the south wall, I boldly entered the gate. Like most Chinese gates, it was double, with soldiers stationed at each entrance. They were dressed in fairly presentable blue uniforms, armed with broad Chinese swords and rifles, and each man wore a belt filled with hand grenades of the potato masher or wooden-handled type. They peered at me dubiously, but as I didn't wish to provoke questioning in an unknown language, I just looked very sternly back at them and rode on past. The city was much like Lanchow, only smaller, with the usual narrow streets lined with small shops. Of course everyone stared at me, and some laughed. I guess I did look funny riding such a small horse that my feet barely cleared the ground. Also, my sunburned face was peeling and my whiskers were nearly a week old, so I must have been an unseemly sight. After successfully bridging the barrier of soldiers at the double west gate, I was again in the country. On a later occasion I was actually stopped by a soldier. He asked me questions I could not understand, so I finally handed him one of my cards. Apparently he could not read, but either it looked important or he considered the case hopeless, so he motioned me to proceed. Several times I have ridden right past a guard who later stopped Sun and demanded his passport. I can only assume that either foreigners are still somewhat privileged persons out here, or folks don't know how to deal with them so ignore the challenge.

Agricultural products of this part of the valley are the most varied I have yet seen. Principally the crops are wheat, barley, and potatoes, but there are also fields of rape, oats, and peas. Near some of the dwellings there are small patches of various vegetables. Incidentally, it seems that all green vegetables in China are called cabbages, whether they are cabbages or not. I haven't seen a real cabbage since leaving Shanghai, but every time I ask Suez what a particular vegetable is he says "cabbage", and that's that. There are some fruit trees, pears and apricots, but the most common are crab apples. No poppies are permitted in Tsinghai. Further back in Kansu I saw jujubes, whose dried fruit looks something like dates but the tree is not a palm. Along the irrigation ditches are poplars and willows which furnish the poles used in the local buildings. Along this particular stretch of the valley I saw new construction, a very rare sight.

At the last gorge before reaching Sining the road crosses a bridge to the south side of the river. Behind us the traffic had been slight, mostly small herds of scrawny sheep and goats, but on this side of the bridge congestion became comparatively heavy; soldiers and peasants afoot or on mules, travelers in carts, and a few bicycle riders, all raising a good deal of dust. Traveling carts here, with the bodies neatly enclosed in canopies of blue cloth, are in great contrast to the skeletal rural carts which look as though they will fall into splinters before your eyes. I imagine they are all rough-riding, however, with their two wheels and no springs. The wheels are seldom round, nor do the rims lie in a plane. Those that are iron shod do not have continuous hoops or tires, but have several curved plates held in place by enormous rough-headed hobnails which do terrible things to the road.

Just east of Sining we passed a huge military encampment enclosed by a high mud wall. As even this was not big enough to contain all the soldiers, there was also a considerable tent city spread out. The soldiers here are almost entirely Mohammedan and appear to be better equipped and better dressed than the general run of Chinese troops. They look quite presentable in their dark blue uniforms, which are even fitted out with zippers. It is obvious that Ma Pu-fang considers his army very important. It is, I think, one of the few semi-private armies remaining in China. Ma is said to have a return of about $40,000 from the salt revenue of the central government, but as that is not nearly enough to meet his requirements, he has relegated to himself a monopoly on wool, hides, and the sausage casing business, which is probably the most extensive export and money-maker of the province. I hear that he buys at arbitrary and nominal prices and sells at a huge profit.

We were met a Sining's east gate yesterday afternoon by a representative of Ma Pu-fang and escorted through the city to the Salt Revenue Office where we met Suez's brother-in-law, Mr. Ti. General Ma had made arrangements for us to stay at the "best hotel", but as it was

Mohammedan and we could not cook there, we reestablished ourselves at a Chinese one. Admission from the street is gained through a gate opening onto a long narrow court flanked on both sides by small one-story rooms, several of which are completely occupied by our luggage. We are housed in a two-story building at the end of the court, facing east towards the gate. Each floor has three rooms; a sitting room in the center and bedrooms on each side. Suez has a bedroom below, Fred and I have the two bedrooms above, and Sun is in the room between us. I sit now writing this on the small porch which gives access to our rooms.

Sining is in several parts, each walled and battlemented; its buildings are mostly one-storied and made of mud. The walls are constructed of piled up sun-dried mud bricks plastered over with mud mixed with straw, although a few of the more pretentious places use lime plaster on the outside.

As we have progressed westward the Mohammedan population has steadily increased. The men, usually bearded, wear black or white caps quite different from the common Chinese black skull cap. Some of the women wear headdresses very much like the European wimple of the Middle Ages. There are some Tibetans here and probably some Mongols, but I have not yet seen enough of them to recognize them easily. I have seen typical Tibetan dress, however; heavy sheepskin clothing worn even on the hotter days and high felt boots dyed in bright colors. There are probably also a few Turki in these parts for I have seen some white turbans, first in Yao Chiai, and here I have noticed a veiled woman for the first time. The Turki are a tribe of Central Asia who principally inhabit Chinese Turkistan and are a non-Mongoloid race.

Sining
July 14, 1937

On the night of our arrival here Mr. Ti had invited us for a courtesy dinner, so after cleaning up, changing clothes, and shaving for the first time in over a week, we ventured out from the hotel. Ti is employed in the Salt Revenue Office and stationed at Tankor, about thirty miles to the west of here. It is such a lonely place that he frequently travels in to Sining for a bath and a little companionship. There was a Mah Jong game in progress at the restaurant when we arrived, with lots of money on the table. We watched one man win $50.00 before we sat down to dinner. There were the four of us, Mr. Ti, who speaks English, and two of his friends, who do not. The food was much the same as we have had before except more highly seasoned with pepper. Also, the principal dish was sea slugs (somewhat crunchy things) cooked with pigs' feet and served in a greasy gravy. I much preferred the chicken, which was cooked whole, head and all. It was the first tender chicken we have had since leaving Shanghai. The most amusing part of the dinner was caused by their not having enough teacups to go around, so one of the Chinese drank his tea out of a rice bowl while our host drank his out of the spout of the communal teapot.

When we returned to the hotel we were promptly called upon by the Chief Magistrate of Tsinghai, who acts as official greeter for General Ma. We were informed that he had arranged for us to meet the general the next morning at 9:00.

We then went out to the public bath house which, like the telephone system, is one of the modern touches of the city. Mr. Ti had seen that the best section had been reserved for us. It was dark by this time, and we were guided through the streets by a servant with a Chinese paper lantern containing a candle. Apparently the importance of a person is reflected by the size of his lantern, and ours was a large one indeed. We went in through a gate, up some stairs to the second floor, and into a room, lit by candles, containing six towel-covered reclining benches which were arranged in pairs. Between each two was a small table bearing a candle, an ash tray, and teacups. Nearby was the inevitable spittoon. The attendants were half-grown boys who served tea, brought dishes of watermelon seeds and small hard candies, and helped us to undress. While our baths were being prepared we slipped on robes made of Turkish toweling and straw slippers and waited in our room which was steamy and hot. When my bath was ready I was ushered through a curtained doorway into a small room containing an honest-to-God enamelled bath tub half filled with steaming water.

Investigation showed the temperature of the water to be extremely hot but not enough to take the skin off, so I put my feet in and sat on a towel on the edge until the water cooled down a little and I became acclimated to it enough to immerse myself. I had brought my own soap, which was fortunate as none was furnished. I also had brought my own towel for drying because the Chinese habitually dip their towels into the water, scrub with them, and then after wringing them out attempt to dry themselves off with the same damp object. The bath certainly felt good, and I rid myself of literally tons of dirt, but I know that I won't stay very clean here for long. Back in the other room we sat around in our underwear until everyone finished bathing and then returned to the hotel. I finally got into bed at about 10:30, the latest I have been up for a long time.

Yesterday morning, accompanied by Mr. Ti, we made our social calls. First we stopped at the Post Office where we were received by Mr. Kuo, the Postmaster. He was a pleasant young man, English-speaking, dressed in European style, through whom we made the necessary arrangements to have our mail forwarded to us after we leave Sining. Next we went to the residence of the Chief Magistrate, whose name was Ma although he is not Mohammedan. He does not show it in his personal appearance, but he is apparently a wealthy man as his home is the model of local elegance. Spacious with numerous small rooms opening onto the central court, it is both attractive and very crude. Distinctly Chinese in style, it could be comparable to a rustic summer cottage in an American resort. The enclosure walls are of common Chinese grey brick, carved here and there with tasteful ornamentation. The tiled roofs are supported on poles and overhang narrow verandahs. The house walls are formed almost entirely of intricate wooden latticework, the inside covered with a layer of thin white paper. A couple of large openings are paned in glass, hinged at the top .to be opened outward. The inside walls are wood-paneled, and nearly every room contains a raised kang covered by a rug. The uncomfortable chairs and tables are all of soft white pine ornamented by elaborate carving, although the structural fittings and general workmanship is very mediocre. The wood is unfinished and already shows marks of contact with many dirty hands and bodies. At one side of the house is a walled garden where vegetables and flowers are indiscriminately mixed. The latter includes orange lilies, canterbury bells, dianthus, calendula, and peonies. In one of the rooms, whose walls were ornamented with scrolls of Chinese characters and an old finger painting on paper, we were served with tea, cigarettes, watermelon seeds, and candies. Mr. Ma appears to live here alone as the place seemed deserted except for a couple of servants.

After the proper length of time we left to be escorted to the General. There we went in through a Chinese roofed gateway guarded by armed soldiers who saluted, passed through a court, then through a gate into another court, and finally were left in a waiting room while a soldier took in our cards. The color scheme of the buildings was blue and white, the national colors. On the outer walls were a few very simplistic and amateurish paintings of war-like scenes with tanks and battleships, but most of the decorations were large inscriptions in Chinese and Tibetan. Our waiting room was furnished with chairs and small tables, and the walls were hung with bright red silk banners bearing Chinese characters in gold leaf. Presently our summons came and we were ushered through another court or two to be greeted by a gentleman bowing to us in front of still another building. This was the great Ma Pu-fang, one of the most powerful autocrats in China. He appears to be in his late thirties, is larger than the average person in these parts (as a matter of fact, he is almost as tall as I am) and, as nearly as I could tell, on account of his flowing blue Chinese gown, well-built and strong. His hair was cropped close, and he wore only the vestige of a mustache and beard. His face was one of "Oriental inscrutability", and one could easily imagine that he was a man capable of anything. Our reception with him was quite an honor as he is in the habit of refusing to see people, even important emissaries. He bowed us into his reception room which was carpeted with rugs of bright and clashing colors. Besides the usual chairs and tables there was a raised divan, much like the old thrones in the Peiping palaces, and a glassed-in bookcase full of boxes and bottles of medicine. Received at the same time was a German, an advisor in the mounted infantry of the National Military Academy.

(I had seen him several days before in a shop in Le Tu as I rode by, and again on the same day as I sat by the roadside eating my lunch, he passed by, walking down the road followed by his litter.) He is apparently here on vacation. With him is a Catholic father. They both spoke Chinese. Ma Pu-fang talked with Suez about our plans and seems to approve of our expedition. His approval is important to us because military forces in northwestern Kansu are part of his division and are personally commanded by two of his brothers. I would think that this insures our being able to travel about there freely a little later, as we are doing here now. When our interview ended, Ma escorted us out across the first court as a mark of courtesy and then returned to the German and his companion.

On occasions of this kind it is proper and customary to give presents, generally four in number. In Lanchow we gave Governor Ho a large box of Shanghai rice, a great delicacy in this region, several boxes of cigars, material for a suit, and some bricks of tea. General Ma does not smoke, so he received a bag of rice, suiting material, the bricks of tea, and Suez substituted the cigars with something else, I don't know what.

Our next call was on Mr. Wai, the Commissioner of Reconstruction, where our reception was much less formal. He was a pleasant man in his forties who looks very western in spite of his Chinese dress. Our last call was on the Commissioner of Civil Affairs, but he was not in so we left our cards and were spared another long conversation in Chinese.

In the afternoon I wrote up a short report of our work to date and mailed it off to Yen in Shanghai.

Upon our arrival here we learned of the trouble that has broken out with the Japanese near Peiping. We thought that things had quieted down, but the news broadcast we heard last night said that fighting had recommenced. Suez and his brother-in-law are much concerned because their families are in Peiping, however, Suez does not think the Japanese will bomb the city because of the presence of the foreign legations. We have been so busy since leaving Lanchow that we had not realized how out of touch we are with the world's news. The latest foreign reports we have are three weeks old, and it appears that it had done us little good to subscribe to a Shanghai paper as we don't seem to be receiving it.

We are well and as comfortable as can be expected. Today we took the last of our typhus shots, so now let them bite away. As a matter of fact, something has been biting me for the last few days; it's not fleas so I strongly suspect that it is lice. I have not cared to investigate too closely for fear of what I might find.

July 14, 1937

Section from a letter to Dr. Yen:

These Tertiary red beds are not the type of sediments which might be expected to give rise to petroleum, but the sands in the lower part would be ideal reservoir rocks for oil that might rise from underlying beds. The side trip that Mr. Sun and I made to Yao Chiai was for the purpose of examining some of the older rocks that might be present beneath the red beds. We saw there representatives of both the Permian and Cretaceous coal series as well as considerable thicknesses of associated, mainly sandy, sediments. Both coal series contain much dark grey to black carbonaceous shale that I think is of marine origin and which might be a source of petroleum under favorable circumstances. In this vicinity, however, the beds are much deformed by both folding and faulting, so it is probable that the carbon ratio of the coal is too high for the dark shales to be source beds.

At the present time it is my impression that the Tertiary basins which we have seen are too small in extent, too dominantly synclinal, or too greatly disturbed to be of economic interest. It is also very doubtful if the dark shales underlie the Tertiary beds in these basins. If they do, and if they have given rise to oil in any quantity, the general structural conditions are such that seepages should occur along some of the mountain fronts, but no seepages are known anywhere in this region.

Lo Sar
July 15, 1937

I am writing this in a Mohammedan inn near the great lama temple of Ta Erh Ssu, or Kumbum as it is known in Tibetan. It is 4:00 in the afternoon and raining. The elevation here is 9,500 feet, and it is cold.

Yesterday we were in Sining. Mr. Ma, the magistrate, and Mr. Yao, the Commissioner of Civil Affairs, both called upon us, and we received an invitation from Mr. Ti and three of his friends for dinner tonight. Because we were to be out of town we had to decline with thanks, but later in the day a coolie appeared at our quarters carrying a huge tray with an eight course dinner, each course carefully noted on a large piece of red paper. Since we were unable to accept the invitation and since our hosts were unable to change its date, they took this means to meet their social obligations. It was a very special dinner of delicacies not locally obtainable: sea slugs, fish maw, and abalone, none of which I care for very much. Other courses were imitation bird's nest soup made of some kind of seaweed, a meat dish, stewed preserved melon, a meat and melon stew, and "eight precious" rice. The "eight precious" rice was supposed to be a sort of dessert, a sweet rice pudding affair with eight surprising ingredients in it like maraschino cherries, almonds, etc. We saved it and ate it for breakfast this morning.

Dishes other than the local rough earthenware are much prized because of the difficulty of long-distance transportation to import them. As a result, broken dishes are not thrown away but are carefully fitted together and mended. The method involves drilling small holes into which small brass bands are fitted to hold the pieces together. This is quite an industry in Sining and there are many shops that do nothing but this kind of business.

We had hoped to inspect some new riding mules, but they never showed up. As I have mentioned, our animals are not very satisfactory. My horse, for example, is small and one of the laziest beasts on earth. He seems to fall asleep on the road and then suddenly wakes up and is frightened by the first thing he sees. On our last day into Sining he was especially bad. The list of objects that set him off that day were: every donkey along the way, a cart, a mud puddle in the middle of the road, two women sitting by the side of the road, a yak, a bicycle, and a pile of logs. In a spirited animal one might expect and forgive such actions, but with this particular horse I am just annoyed.

Our western saddles are a constant source of curiosity and amusement. So is our bicycle wheel. This is simply a front wheel with handle bars to which an odometer is attached; it is pushed along by one of the servants to measure our mileage. The people cannot understand part of a bicycle that cannot be ridden, and they all giggle and ask questions about it.

This morning we left Sining about 8:00 with five pack mules and Suez in his litter. The rest of our equipment remained behind with one servant to look after it. We passed through the south gate and turned away from the river and up a large side valley that merges from the southwest. For a very short distance sandstone outcropped the steep hillsides, the same rocks that make the bluffs along the north side of the Huang Shui at Sining. Interbedded with the sandstone were reddish clays and layers of white gypsum. The rocks dipped gently to the south and the road rose steadily so that these harder beds soon passed below the surface. As a result the topography changed and lower, gentler hills were formed by the soft overlying clays. The valley was quite wide in places and completely cut up into irrigated fields of barley and broad beans, which are something like limas but thicker and very good to eat. We passed many donkeys dragging pine poles from the mountains in the south to build Ma Pu-fang's new barracks in Sining.

As we progressed higher it became evident that this country receives more rain than the Huang Shui valley. Everything was green, and there were large patches of colorful wild flowers. At last we left the valley and turned west into a region of large rounded rolling hills that looked like central Kansas, except greener. Some of the farms were surrounded by high mud walls, but the loopholed block houses that had been so common were getting farther and farther apart. There are no trees here, although the valley below us had many poplars, something like our cotton-woods, which were all shedding their wool.

We reached Lo Sar in the rain a little before 2:00 P.M., having traveled twenty-eight kilometers in slightly less than six hours. It took the cook nearly two hours to prepare our lunch, which was filling but not very warming for a cool day.

Our inn is quite good as inns go. In fact, it might even be called a "hotel". It has three courts; our animals are stabled in the second court and we are in the third, so for the first time, except for Sining, we are free of them. Our court was apparently at one time an elegant residence but is now in considerable disrepair and used mainly for storage. The yard is about thirty feet square, its surrounding woodwork elaborately carved, with poles and panels painted in red and black on a natural wood background. Inside the principal room the woodwork is lacquered and painted with scenes. Our Chinese apparently had some difficulties acquiring accomodations for us here, but a Mr. Ma, the local tax collector, was interested in our presence, which gave us so much face that now everything is sweetness and roses. He also has sent us half a sheep, part of which we shall eat tonight.

Lo Sar
July 16, 1937

Today has been a beautiful sunshiny day, although cool. We first returned Mr. Ma's call and then headed for the temple and monastery of Kumbum which is a short distance over a small steep rise and down in another small valley. A large group of flat-roofed mud and brick buildings, it houses the 3,300 monks attached to the numerous temples. Most of the structures are in the Chinese style, facing a large enclosed court whose walls are covered with pictures. Some of the buildings, however, are very different and are built with glazed tile walls. The roofs of two of the temples, as well as the ornaments on some of the other roofs, are covered with gold leaf which glistens brightly in the sun.

The monks wear full-skirted gowns of dark purplish-brown material and wrap red scarves around their shoulders. Although these are not "red" lamas, the general color scheme is not the yellow that one sees on the monks of Ceylon and Burma. As a whole they are the filthiest group of people I have ever seen, and I am sure that many of them have never washed since the day they were born, if even then. They come in all ages and sizes, from small boys on up. At least one boy from each Tibetan family is obligated to become a monk, and I understand that about one third of the males in Tibet are thus "employed". We arrived this morning just in time to see them all seated in long rows in one of the large buildings having breakfast. Small boys were rushing around pouring a mixture of hot tea and rancid butter from large brass-bound casks into each wooden bowl. Back in the shadows somewhere a monk was chanting while another one was shouting and hurrying up the serving boys. The kitchen contained three huge covered cauldrons, ten to twelve feet in diameter, which were all steaming away while one monk poked at the fire under them and another knelt and chanted. The only other activity we observed was lamas spinning the prayer wheels and knocking their heads against the walls in places easily identifiable because these spots had become very dirty. Several places around the temples were sites for obeisance where over the years so many monks had prostrated themselves that foot and hand holes two or three inches deep had been worn into the heavy wooden planking of the floor. Some of the planks had been worn so deeply that patches had been inserted.

Unfortunately we got here just too late for one of the big Tibetan festivals which comes on the sixth day of the sixth month of the lunar calendar. This year the date was July 13th, and had we known we might have managed to come earlier and could have seen their devil dances. Things are still hopping around here, however, since it has been determined that the reincarnation of the Dalai Lama is somewhere in Tsinghai Province, and the hunt is on. It is believed that the Dalai Lama's soul is reinvested in a boy born at the same instant as the Lama's death. The old one died several years ago, and presumably the powerful Tibetan families and the big monasteries have been playing politics; the group here has won out. Currently there is a bevy of dignitaries from Lhasa here, searching the area for the boy who will become the new Dalai Lama, and a feeling of great anticipation is in the air. Suez says that during the Dalai Lama's boyhood the Tashi or Panchen Lama acts as Regent. He tells us that during the Manchu Dynasty it was almost always arranged for the young Dalai Lama to die of smallpox before coming of age. If that is the case, I guess that the selection for such a high position has not always been entirely a blessing.

There were many visitors here for the recent festivities, and the path between Lo Sar and the monastery is still lined with the tents of Chinese merchants who took advantage of the opportunity to show and sell their wares. After passing through this long line of tents we came to the first group of monastery buildings and, after entering through the monumental gateway built into a sort of chortan or stupa, came out into an open space marked by a row of eight small chortans which commemorated some high lamas who had been executed by a Manchu general 250 years ago. It is said that even after all these years the general is still burned in effigy annually. Behind the chortans are a pair of tablets engraved in both Chinese and Tibetan, probably honoring the donations of wealthy men. This particular monastery is reputed to be richly endowed, and it owns much of the surrounding farmland, although the monks do not work it. Near the chortans is the smaller of the gold-roofed temples, and beyond is a little ravine along the west side of which most of the other temple buildings are arranged. One of the most attractive is very small, its courtyard filled with flowering bushy trees with a heady scent like lilac. This was the only place in the whole establishment where plants seemed to have any importance. In the center of this court was an upright dark stone whose surface was covered with many copper coins plastered with butter. Unfortunately, since our Chinese do not speak Tibetan and very few of the lamas speak Chinese, we were unable to learn the significance of many of the things we saw.

The sound of thumping drums beckoned us to another building and into a series of courtyards. There, in a small court, a line of monks sat beneath large thin drums mounted on poles, beating them with long sticks shaped like question marks, making a quick and persistent rhythm. We were chased out by a young monk before we could make a guess at the purpose of this ritual, but we did have opportunity to wander about the temple and examine the walls which were covered with murals showing Buddha and various demons with brightly colored faces engaging in scenes of torment. Without particular artistic merit, they seemed to show a strong Indian influence. Inside the temple it was very dark, but with the aid of a few matches we looked about as best we could. Grouped around some of the pillars were old Tibetan flintlocks, which are ancient and cumbersome weapons, each equipped with a forked stick that could be unfolded and stuck into the ground as an aid in aiming. Hung from the rafters were many banners painted with images of Buddha, so dark with age and grime that it was not possible to make them out in the dim light. On the floor, supposedly in life-like poses, were a number of stuffed animals including tigers and bears, much moth-eaten and black with dirt, their heads liberally slathered with butter. You can imagine what the place smelled like! On the balcony along each side of the court was a large stuffed yak bull with a stuffed monkey sitting between its horns. The whole assemblage looked ghostly and unnatural. In the other buildings there were gilded images with butter lamps burning in front of them.

Prayer wheels were numerous, each bearing the Tibetan characters reading *Om Mani Padme Hum*, meaning "the jewel is in the lotus blossom". But there are other ingenious and easy ways for the monks to say their prayers. For example, there were a number of tall wooden poles topped by several flounces of cloth to which were fastened narrow pieces of material inscribed in Tibetan or covered with small representations of the wheel of life. Everytime the wind flutters the cloth, these many prayers are said automatically.

Tibetan people are very interesting in appearance. Better class women wear voluminous gowns, usually black but sometimes brightly colored, falling almost to the ground, gathered about the waist with bright cloth belts. Their hair is either combed straight down their backs or braided and confined below their shoulders in two long, narrow, flat cloth sheaths about three inches wide. These sheaths are usually red, heavily embroidered or ornamented with disks of mother of pearl and Chinese brass coins, and are looped into their belts before they continue on down to the ground. They wear much jewelry; large hanging earrings and many finger rings of silver set with turquoise and other stones. They are either bareheaded or wear men's felt hats with undented crowns. The men are often skirted, although their skirts are not ground length, and they generally wear heavy outer garments of dark plum color which are very full, with sleeves so long that they nearly reach their feet. Shirt or jacket collars, which are sometimes embroidered with gold, stand up around their necks. Most of them wear modern felt hats, although some men wear the native felt hat with a high pointed crown covered with bright ornaments. I saw one man wearing a straw hat on top of which he had placed his winter fur cap. Most of the men wear their hair in queues tied around their heads. Some of them wear earrings. If a man owns a rifle, he carries it with him wherever he goes.

Both the men and the women wear clumsy looking boots with stub toes and thick soles, usually of black leather, with very ornate and colorful upper portions of woven material reaching almost to the knee. Suez says they are Chinese style, but it seems to me that it is the Tibetans and not the Chinese who wear them.

Physically, Tibetans look so much like American Indians it is easy to believe that they are related. Their facial features are not Mongolian, and many of the women have quite fair skins. The ordinary Tibetan, however, is a rather sorry specimen; his clothing is sheepskin, old and ragged, and his matted hair is tied up with a loosely twisted rope of dark yak wool.

I have stayed up long after the others have gone to bed, and it is now the almost unheard-of hour of 9:30 P.M.. Darkness now causes me to stop writing because I can no longer see the letters. Our No. 1 boy has been watching me and marveling at my ability to write in the dark.

Sining
July 17, 1937

Yesterday, after investigating the Kumbum temples, Suez returned to town and Fred, Sun, and I rode out to the edge of the La Chi San mountains which bound the Sining basin along the south border. It was a lovely day, cool but sunshiny, and the surrounding countryside looked quite pretty. It is high enough to receive rain at this time of year, so rather fair crops can be grown without irrigation. The area was rampant with wild flowers colorful enough to grace anybody's garden, but they apparently are unappreciated by the local people. We followed a trail from Kumbum, and after crossing a couple of rather high hills we could look back down into the valley we had come up from Sining the day before. Rising up on the opposite side were sharply peaked mountains about 15,000 feet high. Their sides were green, although bare of trees, and clouds rolled over their peaks. As we rode south to the edge of the mountains we began to find outcrops of the old rocks which formed the range, clear evidence that we were beyond the limits of the basin we had been studying. We ate a lunch of canned beans and a loaf of native bread at an elevation of well over 10,000 feet and returned to Lo Sar for the night, arriving back in time to have supper at a decent hour. Our gift of Mohammedan mutton tasted very good for a change.

The journey back to Sining this morning was uneventful. We made it in half the time it took us to get there, perhaps because it was downhill all the way and the mules thought they were going home. We arrived here in time to have lunch with Suez.

The road was busy with considerable traffic going in both directions. Although there were some men traveling with packs on their backs or with carrying poles, there were no wheelbarrows—mostly animals carrying or dragging loads. Horses, mules, donkeys, cattle, and yaks are all used as pack animals and for pulling the clumsy and wobbly carts. One beast is harnessed between the shafts and, if the load is a heavy one, a couple of others may pull out in front attached by long ropes. Many animals wear long cylindrical bells with wooden clappers hung beneath them which make mournful notes as they jolt down the road. Both oxen and yaks have pierced noses inserted with wooden sticks bent into circles. The yaks are shaggy and short-legged and mostly of a dark color, with horns which extend upward, curled like two half moons facing each other. The noise they make is not like the lowing of cattle, but more like a fog horn. Some of the yak bulls are formidable creatures. Just outside of Lo Sar a large herd was being gathered and loaded with packs for a trip across the mountains.

Many of the horses and mules are so bedecked with tassles of red wool and bells that they are hard to recognize. They are commonly equipped with wooden sticks under their tails for cruppers, and they look as though they had just pulled away from their carts. The Chinese riding saddle is made of wood and sits high up on the animal's back, and often there are so many bundles and bags attached around and under the saddle that one wonders how such a small animal can handle such a big load.

We have seen a number of camels grazing, and today we passed a procession of them along the road, mostly young animals without humps. They did not look like Mongolian camels, but if they are the Indian variety I wonder how they got way up here.

Women work in the fields weeding. They wear dirty patches of Turkish toweling over their heads to shield themselves from the sun, over which sit hats made from white cotton stitched over eighteen-inch hoops. The children are filthy, covered piecemeal in last year's tattered quilted coats. They wear no pants. They seem to have as good a time as children elsewhere, and I suppose their mothers love them just as much, although they certainly are an unattractive lot.

We have seen a few pretty little birds in this region, but the variety is surprisingly small. Black and white magpies are the most conspicuous kind. There are also many blue pigeons which are wild but are not easily frightened, so one can approach them closely. We thought they might be good eating, so on our way up from Lanchow Fred got out the shot gun and in three shots killed six of them. His feat of getting three with one shot made quite an impression on our Chinese who have told everyone about it, which has made Fred quite cocky about acquiring so much face. When the birds were cooked they were so tough that I think there will be no further slaughter of them.

Sining
July 18, 1937

Today I received a letter from you, written just one month ago—not bad for Central Asia, I should say. The newspapers and magazine we subscribed to in Shanghai have not been arriving, however, and I think that effort was all a waste of money.

We had expected to leave this morning on our side trip to the north, but a hard rain last night continued all morning and into the afternoon, so we did not go but sat around feeling cold. After 5:00 P.M., when the rain stopped, Fred and I braved the mud and waded up and down the main street looking in the shops. I bought a small rug (about two by four feet) and a Mohammedan knife.

Many rugs are made in this district. I had not bought any previously because on our trip south we were to pass through the village where they are made. I expected to find some kind of local bazaar but there was none. Inquiry advised us that the price of wool has recently tripled, so no one is able to weave. The little rug I bought here today is not particularly good, but it has pleasant colors and cost only $1.25 (U.S.).

I have little to report. Of chief interest to me is that the boy who washed my clothes says he found lice in them. My companions are likewise lousy. However, if the lice don't bother me any more than they have to date, I shan't complain. The other morning I caught a big fat bedbug in my hat, just after it had bitten me on the forehead. That is one bug that won't attack again.

Sin Chung
July 19, 1937

Today has been a beautifully clear sunshiny day, and when we got outside Sining this morning we could see new snow on the mountains far to the north and west, although by noon it was all gone. In spite of the nice weather the going has been miserable due to the mud we have had to flounder through most of the way to the village of Sin Chun, which is about twenty miles north of Sining along one of the principal tributaries of the Huang Shui. I have been trying out a new horse which I am considering buying, and to make him show me his paces I caused myself to become splattered with mud from head to toe.

We left Sining's west gate and turned down the river past the site where Ma Pu-fang's soldiers were building a bridge. We are here a year too early, however, and had to ford the river which was swift, deep and muddy. I kept thinking of what would happen should my horse stumble, but he got me across safely. This is a side trip, so we have brought along only three mules and two servants, while Suez and the rest of the outfit remain in Sining.

The day's trip was uneventful, up through a valley filled with fields and an occasional patch of flax with pretty blue flowers. Flax here is raised for oil and not fiber. We stopped at a village called Hou Tzu Ho for lunch in a Mohammedan eating house. Sun ate a plateful of noodles which we saw being prepared in a particularly unsanitary fashion, but I had brought along a pancake of native bread which, with some boiled water, made my meal. While we were sitting there an auto came into the village, frightening all the animals. It was an open Ford containing three foreigners, probably Russians, and a back seat piled high with bedding, topped conspicuously by a gun. The proprietor of the Mohammedan inn where we are staying tonight is quite proud of the fact that the auto's occupants stayed here last night and that now he has two more foreigners as paying guests. This just may put Sin Chung on the map.

Gumosa
July 20, 1937

We are now at a lama monastery, after a pleasant fifteen-mile trip northeast from where we stayed last night. This was a short stage so we sent our servants and baggage straight through to here while Fred, Sun, and I ambled several miles up the main branch of the river to a small coal field. We passed through a narrows in the valley which at one time was utilized as a means of defense in conjunction with a man-made wall, labeled on some of our maps as part of the Great Wall of China. Now in ruins it consists only of a high irregular ridge of brownish earth with lumps marking the positions of the old towers.

The coal field is located up a small side valley and, like coal communities the world over, is a dismal place. Carts and beasts of burden throng the road, going up empty and coming back down loaded with baskets of pulverized coal. There are said to be fifteen mines here but, as they connect underground, this number probably refers to the quantity of shafts, which are about fifteen or twenty feet apart and located inside separate small huts. Each is equipped with a crude wooden windlass worked by three men who haul up the coal in bags at the end of a long rope. The coal is then carried outside in baskets and spread out to dry. In a separate large shed there is an enormous windlass with two great handles which is worked by seven men to drain out the water that is hauled up in large canvas bags. The mines are said to be 200 or more feet deep with three closely-spaced seams of coal dipping 30-40 degrees to the north. The men work seventeen hours a day for fifty Chinese cents. (What would John L. Lewis think of this?) Each mine produces about four tons of coal a day. There are no visible outcrops, and the age of the coal is in doubt.

We turned back to the narrows, crossed a picturesque bridge over the river, and passed through a gorge cut into limestone by a large tributary flowing in from the east. This valley opened out onto a most pleasant scene: a rushing stream, fields of grass, and blue and white iris-like flowers. As we continued we began to see trees on the mountainsides—small broad-leafed varieties on the lower slopes and evergreens at the higher elevations—a refreshing sight.

The Gumosa monastery is over 100 years old and quite large, in spite of housing only 300 monks. On a hillside facing eastward across the valley, it is better laid out than Kumbum. It has seen more affluent days, however, and its large court surrounded by buildings with tiled Chinese roofs seems almost deserted and uncared for. The building on the west side of each court is two-storied, while the rest are only one. We are living in the first court; the farther courts are reached by steep steps of granite blocks. The painted carved woodwork which has escaped the effects of weather is quite fine with brilliant reds, blues, greens, and a generous amount of gilding. The wall paintings, however, are neither as numerous nor as well-preserved as those at Kumbum. A sudden shower blew up shortly after we started our sightseeing, and almost at once long drawn-out trumpet blasts could be heard from one of the buildings. It sounded like mad bulls bellowing. We were told that it was part of a ceremony to ward off hail, which is common in these parts and often quite destructive.

The monks here look just as dirty as those at Kumbum, but they don't seem to be so caught up in their devotions. During our initial wanderings we saw only one attending to ceremonial ritual. He was seated inside a dark room before a drum rimmed with painted skulls, chanting monotonously while alternately banging the drum and clanging a pair of cymbals. The main part of this building probably houses the principal shrine because its planking was worn into grooves by praying monks. The doorway was covered by a piece of canvas, but when it was drawn aside we could peer into a darkened room at long painted banners and butter lamps burning in front of small images.

The tallest building was where the monks took their buttered tea and kept their Tibetan books. We entered with some lamas who were returning books made of many leaves of paper, about two feet by six inches, held between thick, heavy wooden covers. The room was very dark and cold with a damp musty odor. The floor space was covered with slightly raised sitting platforms topped with rugs and sections of felt; festooned from the rafters were hanging banners painted with holy pictures. The walls were in darkness, lit only by small butter lamps, but almost life-sized statuary figures could be made out in the flickering light, and I saw many small glass cases containing, I think, individual Buddhas.

The monastery is preparing for a festival, judging by the tents of Chinese merchants lining the road leading to it. These merchants are both ordinary Chinese and Mohammedan Chinese, known as *huei-huei*. The *huei huei* are invariably the proprietors of eating establishments. I did not see many Tibetans, although those I did recognize seemed to be of a somewhat different tribe from those around Kumbum. Here the women wear their hair in many little braids brought down in front of their shoulders and encased in long pouches.

The further west we travel, the less the Mohammedans look like usual Chinese and the more queues are worn by ordinary Chinese men. Women's hairstyles seem to become increasingly complicated.

Trouble seems to be developing with Suez. He and I get along fine, but Fred has been having run-ins with him, and Sun confesses he hates him. I feel that his sense of importance is pretty strong. Sun says that

Suez tells everybody that he is head of the expedition, when he is really only our travel agent and interpreter.

Hou Tzu Ho
July 21, 1937

We are back in the village where we had lunch the other day. We got a late start this morning and arrived here in the middle of the afternoon; our mules arrived somewhat later.

After breakfast this morning Fred and I returned to the temples for more picture-taking, during which we saw a small group of lamas emerge from a second floor balcony from where they blew a series of mournful sounds through great long horns. (As a matter of fact, they went on and off with this horn-blowing all night long—I awakened several times to the noise.) Next, along came a procession of lamas in bright robes and coxcomb hats, followed by the chief lama, or Living Buddha, who was ensconced on a throne covered by a rich-looking rug and backdropped by a large tapestry hung from a frame. The processional lamas formed a square about him and prostrated themselves while he chanted and read from a book.

The fair started today, and when we left the monastery we passed through a continuous parade of Tibetans and Chinese, garbed in their best clothes, going in. The Tibetan women wore small hats with the brims turned up all around, which were faced with velvet or a kind of gold cloth. A few of the men wore conical hats with straight brims made of dark material with red tassels fastened to the tops. These had elaborate bead work and mother-of-pearl ornaments.

Sining
July 24, 1937

We encountered some very hot and intensely sunny days on the way back to Sining, and I am still struggling somewhat with sunburn. My hands and face are scaly from burn upon burn, but at last I think I am beginning to acquire a protective coat of tan. The nights, at these altitudes, have been very cool, and I am glad for my eiderdown sleeping bag. Some recent mornings have been so cold at 6:00 A.M. that it is very difficult to climb out and get started.

The country we traveled through was really quite beautiful in contrast to the squalid villages. There is a great prevalence of goiter in this region; it seems to most often attack women, although there are also many men with swollen necks.

The first night out of Gumosa we stayed at a comparatively new Mohammedan inn where we thought we would be quite comfortable, but it proved to be inordinately noisy with people running around and talking loudly, and in the background there was a village dog that barked every second throughout the whole night. I was awake for hours and, instead of counting sheep, I counted his barks. I don't understand why he did not lose his voice in the effort.

With the exception of firearms, often old and in bad condition, and a few cheap bicycles (the other day I saw a man driving a loaded mule on top of whose burden reposed a small tricycle), the only product of western civilization that has penetrated into this country is the common felt hat. They are everywhere, on both men and women, with crowns dented or smooth, with brims turned up or pulled down. Upon coming to China one is at once struck by the incongruity of the European felt hat worn with the long Chinese gowns. Originally I had thought this combination was a result of East meeting West in the big cities, but I have found that this is apparently not the case as the felt hat is an important part of every wardrobe even in the most inaccessible parts of Central Asia.

We arrived back at our Sining hotel at mid-morning on July 22nd. The river we had to ford previously had gone down a bit since we set out so our return crossing was safer, although Fred took a dunking when his mule stumbled and went under. His first act upon reaching his room was to empty his boots of water.

Suez had quite a social adventure in our absence. At 10:00 one evening, just as he was ready to retire, a messenger arrived from Ma Pu-fang granting him the honor of naming the plays that Ma's favorite actresses would present that same evening before a group of high

Tibetan dignitaries who were in town from Lhasa. The excuse for the late request and invitation was that Ma had only just learned that Suez had not left Sining with us and was still in town. The messenger had also brought a horse on which Suez rode to the performance. Apparently he had a wonderful time at the affair and renewed acquaintance with the brother of the Panchen Lama whom he had known years ago when he was a diplomatic official in Tibet. The aftermath of the event was, as custom demands, that he had to send the actresses a present of $100 for having performed the plays he selected.

Last evening Suez gave a big Chinese dinner for his brother-in-law and several other members of the Salt Revenue Service. It was an expensive dinner and I am sure carefully planned to make a big impression. It was to have started at 6:00 but the last of the guests did not arrive until 8:00. This seems to be a Chinese custom—to come two or three hours late to dinner or not to arrive at all, sending regrets afterwards.

Yesterday I wrote up the geological section of our north-south traverse as well as another short letter to Yen telling him something about the area. I also started packing up my belongings which have been strewn about my room ever since we first arrived in Sining, selecting the things I shall take on our journey west to Kokonor. Items we don't want will go directly south to Kueite where we will be in about two weeks time. We had planned to leave today for Tankor, the last Chinese city on this route and the end of the telegraph line and mail service, but a hitch developed. Both Suez and Sun think we should take a small military escort with us into Kokonor country, not as much for protection as for show, as well as interpreters for the Tibetans. Also, since such an escort has been offered to us it would be impolite to turn it down. So yesterday we sent a formal request for a couple of soldiers to be released to us by Ma. This morning we received word that Ma had been sick yesterday and was unable to comply immediately with the request. Being sick is a good old Chinese face-saving excuse for not doing something. It can be a polite way of refusing a request, or an excuse for having forgotten it, or because one was too busy to attend to the matter, but almost never is it because of sickness. I do not know which of these reasons was the cause of Ma's "sickness". This evening, however, two army officers came for instructions, and it appears that they and two ordinary soldiers have been selected to accompany us tomorrow. One of the officers is a young Mohammedan with a downy beard; the other is a hard-bitten fellow with a pointed mustache.

Also yesterday, there was a threat that our mule men would go on strike. Our bargain with them was that the mules would be paid $1.70 a day while working and $1.00 idle. Of course, with this kind of arrangement the men would rather work, but since arriving here most of them have been idle because we have not had much to carry on our side trips, and now that we propose to send things directly to Kueite, which takes only two or three days, there are more idle days coming up. Our round-about way to Kokonor will take two or three weeks, and they all want to come with us to earn more money. But this is a problem for Suez to struggle with.

We have been enjoying dining on the broad bean which is grown widely in China. They grow in fields on stiff stems which make a thrifty-looking crop. The numerous flowers bloom close to the stalk; the petals are white with large brown spots. When the beans are young they are truly delicious boiled or fried, but for some unknown reason the farmers here will not bring them to market until they are old and tough. The other day Suez sent his boy out to get some young ones from a farmer. When the farmer balked at selling them, the boy told him that his master had been there the day before and saw that the beans were nice and young and that if the farmer would not sell them his master would come back with soldiers. This threat got him the beans, but the farmer was very angry and said loudly that he hoped the master would have an unpleasant death.

Suez's boy was his rickshaw coolie in Shanghai and, rather than be let off and have to look for other work, he begged to be brought along on the trip in any capacity. I think he is enjoying himself, and as Suez's personal servant he feels important. He loves to boss the mule men around; he probably never before has had anyone he could speak down to. The cook, the No. 1 and the No. 2 boys have all served on ships and been to Europe, and in that way they have acquired a little English.

They are not very respectful, but they are cheerful and do their work as expected. In any case, in China servants are really considered part of the family and a certain loyalty develops.

I have noticed that a number of young boys wear padlocks and chains around their necks, as does the hotel owner's son. Suez explains that these items are believed to protect the boys, rather like keeping them under lock and key. This is probably a result of horoscopes, cast at the time of birth, predicting that they most likely will not live to manhood. Boys from wealthier families wear elegant silver chains and elaborate elongated padlocks with intricate designs engraved on them. Some boys also have their heads shaved except for patches at the very top in the shape of the "fairy peach", a symbol of longevity.

Tonight we had dinner in one of the local restaurants with Mr. Ma, the magistrate, and eight other Chinese gentlemen. One of the guests was the newly appointed manager of the Farmer's Bank. He looked like a matinee idol and Fred felt compelled to ask Suez if he was an actor. He is probably thirty, extremely handsome with thick black hair over a low forehead and prominent dimples when he smiles. He was dressed in a light grey silk gown with a short black silk jacket. Dinner was good, except for the sea slugs and liquor, which was strong and peculiarly flavored. The walls were ornamented with the usual scrolls of Chinese characters and a series of interesting lithographs showing scenes of the fighting with the Japanese in Shanghai in 1932.

Tomorrow we leave on our Kokonor journey. Despite the fact that we will be out of touch with civilization for at least two weeks, you must not fear for my safety. As a matter of fact, unless we run into something quite unexpected, I am probably safer here than I would be in Chicago.

Tankor
July 26, 1937

When we got up yesterday the sky was overcast and it felt like rain. After much arguing among the mule men over the adjustment of the loads, we finally got started a little after 8:00 just as a fine drizzle began to fall. I was afraid the day would be a bad one from the very beginning, and I was not disappointed. As usual, I traveled out ahead of the procession and, at noon, stopped by the roadside in my poncho and ate my solitary lunch of native bread and Tasmanian plum jam while I waited for the rest to catch up. They didn't, so I plodded on slowly, thinking they would be along soon. I suspected that the animals were finding the going difficult, so I was not particularly concerned, only impatient. By mid-afternoon Fred and Sun came along and we waited together for awhile. We were beginning to think that we would have to stay the night only twenty miles out and ten miles short of our destination when the rest of the caravan eventually arrived to join us. We pushed on. That last ten miles was the longest distance I have ever encountered; the map seemed to have measured the distance in a straight line while the road itself twisted and turned, and the mileage was at least 25 percent further than our expectations.

Our Chinese maps had not prepared us for this stretch of the way. They look nice, but are so inaccurate that they are of little use. We knew that there was a gorge ahead of us, but expected it to be like the others we had experienced; narrow, straight, and comparatively short. What we actually found was a long narrow valley which wound its way for ten miles through small mountain ranges with steep rocky slopes rising sharply above us and with a river in almost continuous rapids spilling over boulders strewn in its bed. The mountains had a core of fine-grained grey granite which we had seen before, but there was much distorted metamorphosed sediment rock. The drizzle continued, and wisps of white clouds hung about the upper parts of the steep slopes.

The road along here is known as a motor road, but that name is misleading; it is only an exceedingly rocky cart track, and I would certainly never attempt to drive any car of mine over it. There were two or three small villages in the valley where there were spots level enough to be converted into fields, and at some places irrigation ditches wound precariously around the rocky hillsides. Some slopes bore stands of small broad-leafed trees, and here and there herds of sheep, goats, horses, and donkeys made clumps of lighter color on some of the distant greenish slopes. At several places Tibetan prayer characters were engraved on rocks, and at one place there was a wooden shrine with a carved painted figure and several small Buddhas. These were all much defaced by the smoke of small fires that had burned in front of them. The cliffs along one side of the valley were nesting places for the wild pigeons which are everywhere.

In the lower part of the gorge was a deep and turbulent river, but above the valley things opened up and the river became more placid as we continued westward. Eventually the mountains drew back from both sides of us and we entered the valley of Huang Ho (or Tankor, which is the Tibetan name.) The mountains are still formed of metamorphic rock, and each valley ends in a great alluvial fan of dark-colored gravel. We climbed up on one of the crests crowned by ruins of the great mud wall which formerly guarded the valley and looked down on the city of Tankor about a mile below. This is the last Chinese city in this direction. As usual, it is surrounded by an earth wall with brick battlements, and suburbs have sprung up outside the walls. To the east of the city we could see a large walled fort, now apparently deserted.

It was after 7:00 P.M. and dusk as I approached the east gate and dismounted to wait for the others. After fifteen minutes I knew something was wrong and thought they had probably entered through one of the other gates, but I also knew that if I was patient someone would come to find me. Half a dozen small boys gathered around me and with much curiosity examined my boots and spurs, my saddle, and me. Eventually one of our soldiers came along in his great white felt raincoat and escorted me through the dark muddy streets to the Salt Office, where the others were established. I was very tired and the Salt Office, with its several courts, was a welcome haven. The few Chinese officials there made us feel at home and, while we waited for our dinner, they served us with tea, hard candies, watermelon seeds, cherries preserved in sugar, and raisins from Turfan in Sinkiang Province. Much to my disappointment we were served a Chinese meal with sea slugs; I would much rather have had half a can of corned beef. However, we also had edible bacon, broad beans, cucumbers, and rice, so I made do. When I finally got to bed the tune of hard rain on the tile roof lulled me into instant sleep.

This morning dawned bright and clear, as is usual in this country after a rain. We investigated the Salt Offices to find two courts, the first quite large and paved with stones, occupied by some chickens and a duck, all actively engaged in tracking through the mud puddles. The second court was much smaller, with some discouraged-looking flowers and peony bushes. To one bush was fastened a stuffed pheasant, most bedraggled after the rain. Compared to our standards before reaching the interior, it is quite primitive, but it is elegant compared to some of our recent lodgings.

We are staying over a day here, largely, I think, because Suez was tired after yesterday's trip, but the reason given is that another soldier who is to act as our guide is arriving here tonight.

Sun and I spent the day investigating the city and river. It is quite an interesting place with narrow, twisting, steep streets between mud walls. The few shops display flashy cheap-looking articles. We visited several temples, the first of which was dedicated to the city god. Each Chinese city has its own city god who appears to be nameless and who is supposed to be changed every three years, just as the Imperial officers were supposed to change every so often in the old days. Here the city god has apparently done his job well and is considered quite important, as this place never fell before the Mohammedans like many other cities in northwestern China. His temple is unusually well kept and attractive. The god-figure stands at the end of a long court and presents himself as a big fellow with a drooping mustache, mostly covered with gilt. The walls have unusually nice paintings, not in the Indian Buddhist style, but distinctly Chinese. There were several courts and rooms where strips of paper inscriptions were hung. There were a number of women worshipping in the area. I took some pictures, attracting a group of people who were most interested in the chrome-plating of my camera. Sun explained to them that I was from *Mei Kuo* (America), the Chinese characters of which literally mean "beautiful country". Quite a happy choice of words, I thought.

A group of noisy boys guided us to another of the city's temples which was dedicated to the god of war, in reality an old general deified by the Emperor. His spirit was supposed to represent the virtues of faithfulness and honesty, rather than bravery and martial vigor. Alas, the temple was closed and, although we were led through a series of back doorways and passages, we could see only a small part of the interior, which was deserted and not well cared for.

After this abortive adventure, we went out through the west gate to the temple of the fire god. An old priest was sitting in front of the idol intoning a prayer that he was reading from a book while beating time on a hollow piece of wood with a stick. Here, also, there were large numbers of women devotees.

We then went down to the river, a considerable part of which is drawn off into a canal that operates several mills. Along the road were small boys with baskets and long-handled forks who were collecting animal droppings to be used for fuel and fertilizer. The river area was crowded; women washing clothes, men filling casks with water to be carried into town on donkeys, boys washing vegetables for market, and children swimming and playing.

After lunch we visited a Mohammedan temple whose tower rises conspicuously above the surrounding buildings. It is circular in shape with several tiers of Chinese-type roofs. The whole thing is very graceful and quite elaborately carved of wood, and because it is new it was rather awe inspiring. But it is unpainted, and in a very few years it will take on the dilapidated appearance of the rest of the buildings here. Inside the court in a plain temple building white-turbaned men, who had left their shoes outside the doorway, were saying their prayers against the blank wall facing Mecca. I assume they were Turkis.

This city is in a comparatively rainy area, and we are told that there are showers every three days. Once, in April, it rained for eleven days straight, but I am guessing that, for the most part, the rain is the fine persistent drizzle we have been experiencing.

Hsai Wa Yuh
July 27, 1937

Today we traveled fifty kilometers up the Turgan Valley, which comes into the Huang Shui at Huang Yuan from the southwest. We left at 8:00 A.M. and arrived here in mid-afternoon after climbing steadily another 2,000 feet. We are now at an elevation of over 10,000 feet.

We followed the so-called motor road up a narrow valley with gorges cut through coarse grey Prophylitic granite, which caused the river to create almost continuous rapids. At places along the road we passed groups of stone-cutters quarrying granite into long narrow blocks for door sills and lintels and an occasional large millstone. Their job of attacking huge chunks of granite with hammers and chisels seemed quite a hopeless task, but the number of dressed stones lying about showed skilled accomplishment. Many pieces had to be rejected, however, as the stone had split imperfectly. The cutters live in crude tents on tiny level spots; at one place there was a small forge with a minute pile of coal, obviously imported from some distant location.

As the valley opened we passed from granite to highly contorted metamorphic sediments which eventually divided into two mountains with jagged crests which receded to the right and left, enclosing a series of lower, more rounded hills of brown sandstone. The hills are without trees, but have enough grass and low bushes for small herds of animals to graze here and there. These bushes are uprooted, dried, and used for fuel, and we saw donkeys loaded with them heading for the city. We also passed several large herds of dark, hairy, wild-looking yaks. The villages have become smaller and further apart and Hsai Wa Yuh, where we stopped, is the most insignificant of the lot. We have put up at the local tax station, which is indistinguishable from a small inn except that it is connected with the military telephone manned by a one-legged ex-soldier. Our mules and horses have been turned loose to graze along a small stream and seem to be enjoying themselves. Their usual diet is chopped straw and black beans, so this must be rich fare for them. The soldiers have pitched their tents outside the tax station, and most of our belongings are piled up around the inside of the structure. We had dinner about 4:00 P.M. which, although early, was welcome after our scant lunch and pleased the boys who probably wanted to get their work over with as soon as possible.

The officer who rode along with Fred and me today was very interested in my camera. He thought it was a viewfinder telescope at first and looked all around the landscape with it. Since that was his inclination, I got out my field glasses for him to use, and he held up a thumb in the significant gesture meaning they were "number one". I thought I would please him by letting him carry them for me, but he soon returned them because everybody pestered him for a look.

I have been told that the motor roads, telephones, and the innumerable block-houses and fortifications around here were all built in a great hurry at the time of the Communist invasion several years ago

Intermarriage between the Chinese men and Tibetan women in this district develops many racial mixtures as well as combinations of costumes. Mohammedan Chinese men here rather fancy the Tibetan boots, and one of our soldiers sports a dark red woolen Tibetan robe. Some of the local Tibetan women have adopted the Chinese women's trousers and jackets, but still cling to their boots and the long embroidered pouches in which the ends of their braids are fastened.

Kokonor
July 30, 1937

We left our night's resting place and followed the road as it angled away from the valley and up the mountainside, getting higher all the time. At about 9:30 we reached the pass through the "Sun and Moon" Mountains and could look both eastward down into the valley that drains into the Pacific and west into the valley of the Tao Tang Ho ("River that Flows Backwards") which drains into Lake Kokonor ("Blue Sea"). We felt that we were at last really entering Central Asia, the vast area with only internal drainage. It rained a fine drizzle onto our faces for the entire day.

In the valley behind us there were scattered patches of cultivated fields which made a quilted pattern against the green slopes. The fields were mostly of mustard and rape and formed brilliant yellow splotches. Outside the fields were abundant and colorful wildflowers; some of the slopes were almost a solid mixture of yellow and purple. We crossed the "Sun and Moon" Mountains at their southern border, where they are comparatively low. My aneroid barometer read 11,820 feet. North of here they are very rugged, although not particularly high for this region.

The Tao Tang Ho Valley, which we crossed into, was very different. It was the most absolutely deserted country I have ever seen. Mountains formed both of its sides and sloped gently down to a small stream that flowed through it. There were no trees by which to judge the size of the hills which were doubtless larger, and the distances longer, than they appeared. Everything was covered with a short growth of green grass and scattered small flowering plants. The trail crossed several spurs on the northern slope as we gradually worked our way lower, and in the late afternoon, when we spotted our caravan slowly marching to the south of us, we were the only living things to be seen.

The climate in this part of Asia has probably changed greatly. About noon we came to the ruined city of Cha Han Cheng which is now entirely deserted, with nothing remaining but the old wall enclosing a square about half a mile on each side. When his party was here two years ago, one of Sun's men found a brick bearing the seal of the early Han dynasty, which dates it in the year 2 A.D. Later in the day we saw a similar old city in the distance and crossed what I am sure had once been a large irrigation ditch. Obviously, this valley was once better watered and able to support a fairly large agricultural population. Most recently the area was occupied by Mongols (Kokonor is a Mongol name) whose domestic economy depended to a considerable extent upon the Bactrian camel. At present, however, the valley does not produce the kind of vegetation upon which camels thrive, and the Mongols have moved on west to the Tsaidam Basin. Oddly, the Mongol period marked a more arid period than exists at present, and the area is now in the hands of the Tibetans and offers excellent pasturage for their animals.

As we gradually descended in elevation, the fine short grass gave way to tall coarse grass, which grew in bunches due to less rain. In mid-afternoon we saw several small groups of tawny antelopes in the distance.

We made camp on damp ground just above a small river, using our tents for the first time. We have five of them on this trip: four small ones—one for Fred and me, another for Suez and Sun, and two for the kitchen and dining area where the servants sleep; then we have a large one for the mule men. Our five soldiers have their own. When they were all pitched it made quite a tent city, but because everything was too cold and wet to seem very interesting, I did not stand around admiring the scene. I had worn my leather jacket with a sweater underneath, but as soon as we unloaded and I could get to it, I got out my sheepskin coat. The soldiers wear big coats of white felt to keep off the rain, and after making camp several of them also donned their great skeepskin coats with sleeves so long they almost touched the ground.

Our soldiers are all Mohammedans. Their uniforms are so nondescript that it is hard to determine their respective ranks, but I know that three of them are officers, probably captains or majors. They are armed with Mauser pistols and 1917 Remington rifles made for the Russian army. The officer I like best is also some kind of a priest, between forty-five and fifty, with a scanty mustache and beard. He generally accompanies Fred, Sun, and me as we scout off ahead and shows much interest in everything we do. Another officer is about the same age, but with a very red and villainous face. He is the official Tibetan interpreter for the 100th Division and is working in the same capacity for us. A third officer is a younger man with wispy whiskers and a nice smile. He is evidently quite a dandy, and when in camp he sports a black silk jacket with orange buttons and a very dirty lining. All have shaven heads under their old felt hats, but once in camp they change to little caps made of triangular pieces of black and white or blue and white material, which are disgustingly filthy. They carry all of their equipment with them, each man sitting on top of the load his horse carries.

By evening the drizzle had stopped, but it remained so cold and wet I was comfortable only in my sleeping bag on my cot. When we arose in the morning the sun was shining and we hoped that, as usual, a bad day would be followed by a good one. Clouds hung heavily over the mountains all around us, looking at times as though they were going to close in, but they didn't and we had a most lovely day. Fred, Sun, and I started off with three of the soldiers ahead of the rest as we were moving only a short distance and I wanted the tents to dry before being packed up. The only incident on our ride was furnished by Fred who shot a rabbit which had popped out of one of the numerous rabbit holes in the banks along the hillsides. We followed an old caravan route that leads to Kokonor, skirting its south side northwest into the Tsaidam Basin. In places the hooves of passing animals had broken the sod and given the wind opportunity to blow out depressions now filled with water from the recent rain.

As we set off in the morning we saw some Tibetan encampments up in the valleys to the north and south of us, which had been obscured the evening before by mist and rain. They first appeared as little black dots on the green slopes, and when we reached the southeastern corner of the lake a little before noon we passed close to several of their dark wool tents, pitched low in the ground at intervals along small streams. Held up by poles inside and out, they cover a considerable area. We selected a campsite on the bank of a little stream which rippled into the lake, but not before we were set upon by a pack of great dark shaggy dogs which emerged from a tent close by. The soldiers went after them with sticks and stones, and a disheveled woman came out of the tent and helped to drive them off.

While the soldiers unloaded their horses, we went to inspect one of the big black tents. An old man stepped out into the sunshine, dressed in blue cotton trousers tucked into boots, his big sheepskin coat peeled off and hanging down from a belt tied around his waist which left his upper torso bare except for a large leather-covered amulet around his neck. He wore a conical hat with a brim trimmed with sheep's wool, and wound around one wrist was a rosary of dark beads. He was a wild enough figure to suit anybody's imagination. We learned that he was a very wealthy Tibetan, although certainly nobody could have guessed it from his appearance or that of the rest of his family or their abode. In fact, he was so well-off that he had two lamas who lived with him to do nothing but say prayers. Most of his front teeth were missing, and his face was incredibly dark and wrinkled. His wife was also toothless, with a projecting chin and nose which made her look exactly like a Halloween witch. Her hair was braided into many tails, gathered together at the ends to make sort of a veil around her face. She and her two daughters also wore their sheepskin robes hanging down from their waists, but they made some attempt to cover up as we approached. Down their backs were the two long pouches ornamented with red beads and with convex, embossed silver disks which looked like bowls set with red stones. The sons were off someplace with the animals, which were scattered all over the landscape. We were invited into the tent, which was divided in two by a cooking place made of clay from which a dung fire made a terrible smudge that was supposed to escape through a slit in the top of the tent. On one side an old woman was churning butter from yak milk in a vertical churn. The other side seemed to be the living quarters, but a couple of goat skins were all that covered the bare earth floor. At the back of the tent a small brass image of Buddha sat in a dish of water. The old man said that Buddha liked water. One of the lamas wore flowing yellow and red robes, the other was all in red and continued reading aloud from some loose pages of a Tibetan book the whole time we were there. All of them were most obliging in posing for photographs; the old man even put on his very best sheepskin robe and boots for us.

When we returned to our camp for lunch the sun was shining brightly, but a thunderstorm was raging over the mountains to the south when after lunch we explored the lake shore. Kokonor has been rightly named the "Blue Sea". It is a beautiful deep blue color, with the wind rippling its surface and turning up whitecaps far out. It is much too large to see even the mountain tops on the other side. To the south rise the South Kokonor Mountains, which slope gently down to the water in shades of green. To the east are the "Sun and Moon" Mountains and in front of them a long high belt of sand dunes. The lake's water is slightly salty, but I think it could probably be drunk if necessary. At its southeast corner, separated by a wave-built ridge of sand and pebbles, is another lake into which the Tao Tang Ho empties. Its Chinese name means "Ear Lake", and it is fresh water. Its shoreline is the home of many ducks, some of which Fred tried to get with his shot gun, but they proved to be too wild and too fast for him. I rode around to the other side of the lake with my rifle, hoping my shots might scare them into Fred's vicinity but, of course, my three or four inept shots neither bagged a duck nor caused them to fly as desired. As the gnats were dense and flitting into my face, I soon tired of the activity and returned, only to find that Fred had got a duck after all. It was a specimen of the famous Kokonor yellow duck. It attains a good size; the forward part of its body is a tawny yellow brown which shades backward through grey to a black tail. Its shoulders are white and the outer wings are a dark iridescent green with black tips; quite a combination of colors for one bird.

Our caravan arrived in the middle of the afternoon, as it had taken until after lunch to dry out the tents, and soon we had our tent city constructed again. After tea Suez and I wandered down to watch his boy, Anyee, and one of the soldiers trying to catch some fish they had located in a hole along the stream's edge. At first they tried to bail the water out of the hole with a shovel and wash basin, which didn't work as intended. Instead it stirred the water up to a muddy pitch, and the scared fish came to the surface where they could be caught by hand. This created some excitement, and most of the men (including Fred) gathered about to advise or participate in the sport. Soon they had fifteen fish some nearly a foot long. These were the "yellow fish of Kokonor" which we had seen dried and in baskets in towns along the way. Closer observation showed them to be a grey color, not yellow, and I cannot understand the name. Their skins were quite smooth and seemingly without scales, and for this reason the Mohammedans will not eat them. Suez had some for dinner and Fred ordered some fried for breakfast, but didn't like them.

Yesterday was such a lovely day here we couldn't help but think that this would be a perfect resort area if only it were more accessible. But today all has changed. Fine rain started falling this morning before it became light and has been coming down ever since, making our camp a cold, damp, and totally unpleasant place. I have on almost all of my clothes under my sheepskin coat, and I'm still wet and chilled to the bone. About 6:00 A.M. a wind started coming in off the lake, which got stronger and stronger until I thought our tent might be blown down, so I got up out of my warm sleeping bag and into my damp clothes, thinking that I would rather be dressed if it did collapse about me. The tent sprang a leak on Fred's side, so he got up early also. He had planned to hunt big-horned sheep in the southern mountains today, but that has been called off. Worse, we have just learned that six of our horses, including mine, are missing. Either they strayed during the night, or they have been stolen. Some of the men are out looking for them now. It is still raining. Sun has gone back to bed, Suez is writing letters, and Fred is sitting in his chair, seemingly asleep. The thermometer registers 54 degrees, which is not so terribly cold, but inactivity and the resulting lack of circulation makes it seem much worse.

Our soldiers must be having a miserable time. Their tent is made of very thin cloth, and they sleep on the ground. They cook over an open fire, which I would think would be impossible to manage in weather like this. Yesterday they carried in bundles of brush and collected yak droppings for their fire, as there is no wood in this area, but neither of these items burns very well. In order to keep the fire going one man must constantly work a bellows, which consists of an iron tube about a foot long with a goat skin bag attached to one end. It is open at the other end and, by holding it in a certain way and pushing down on the bag, a blast of air is forced out of the tube under the fire.

For lunch we had part of a goat that the soldiers were either given or bought from the Tibetans. Last night we saw them kill it by cutting its throat in the orthodox Mohammedan fashion, a gory sight. When Fred shot a rabbit one of our officers immediately rushed over and slit its throat, because any animal to be eaten must die in that way. We didn't want the rabbit, nor did the soldiers, so it finally went to the mule men.

Nine of the original mule men are with us now, and I'll wager they all wish they had never come. They are inadequately clothed and have no bedding to speak of. The head mule man, who is responsible for my horse, has just returned from searching for it, soaked to the skin and crying with the cold. We have sent him to the servants' tent to get something warm to drink. He is mean-looking, with a nasty oozing sore on his neck that looks dangerous to me, but aside from making him move his head with care, it does not seem to interfere with his activities. On the whole, however, our mule men are in better circumstances now than they were when we hired them. They had been previously engaged in hauling coal and were literally embedded with coal dust. This residue has largely been removed by sweat and rain, and they have emerged as a bunch of husky and not unpleasant-looking men. One of the older men quite amuses me, but he drives Suez into a frenzy. He has a wrinkled, effeminate face and a high-pitched voice and wears a short queue with the front of his head shaved. He owns two white mules which he is much concerned about, and whenever the loads are redistributed he seeks out the lightest burdens, which always gives rise to violent quarrels and, the last time, to actual blows.

Our horses have not yet been found. One of our officers, certain that they would not be difficult to locate, returned to camp early and reported that they had been found and were on their way back. When the others came back, wet to the bone and empty-handed, the search was started in earnest, and a message was sent to the local Tibetan chief for assistance in locating them.

Towards late afternoon the rain finally stopped and the clouds slowly began to break up, lifting from the mountains to the south of us to reveal their tops covered with new-fallen snow. For the first time we were able to see the mountains to the north of the lake, their bases well below the horizon, their snow-capped summits clearly visible. There are some very high peaks over there, some that are above the line of perpetual snow.

Our camp also came to life. The soldiers butchered a sheep, and the mule men prepared and consumed a feast of stewed entrails. Our old Tibetan neighbor came over for a visit and greatly enjoyed himself viewing the countryside through my field glasses.

After dinner I went on a little walk to encourage my circulation. It was so quiet and still that I could hear the tousled ripple of mountain streams several miles away. Our camp is by a small stream with the most amazing meanders; it does everything but tie itself into a bow knot in its efforts to move a few feet closer to the lake.

On the road
July 31, 1937

Last night was the coldest we have had, down to almost 40 degrees.

For the first time I felt the need of a mattress under my sleeping bag, and Fred has been nearly freezing to death under his two blankets.

The soldiers finally came in about 10:00 A.M., driving our lost horses before them. They had located the beasts some fifteen miles to the east of us at about 6:00.

We had an early lunch and struck camp in the afternoon. After a very short march we set up a new camp, again beside the Tao Tang Ho, a few miles east of the place we had camped before. Tomorrow we split; Fred, Sun, and I will go south across the mountains to Cha Pu Cha and Kung Ho and then east along the Huang Ho to Kueite, which we ought to reach in about a week's time. Our route will be too rough for Suez's litter, however, so he will continue east on a direct route to Kueite, which should take three or four days.

From the lake we followed the so-called motor road, which is nothing more than two shallow furrows plowed about fifteen feet apart, with small piles of sod thrown up every fifty feet or so to mark the way. It does not seem ever to have been used. We are now camped in the middle of a wide valley with mountains on three sides of us; the lake is on the other side, but it is out of sight. Our tents are set up in a large open space with low weeds, while all about us are the bunches of tall coarse grass which seem to be a paradise for rabbits. Across the valley, on a bluff ending with a remnant of terrace, are the crumbling mud walls of another deserted city.

Cha Pu Cha
August 1, 1937

Last night was so cold we went to bed about 8:30. In the morning, even before I was up, the local Tibetan chief who had helped to locate our horses came to visit. Our major brought him into our tent to exhibit the particular wonders there, such as the camp cots and my sleeping bag with me zipped up inside. Our arsenal of guns is also displayed at every opportunity; it seems to be the best technique for dissuading potential Tibetan robbers from their chosen activity. Tales tell of two Americans who, several years ago, shot and killed some robbers, and a healthy respect for foreigners with guns has evolved.

Fred, Sun, and I left camp this morning with five pack mules, four mule men, two servants, and two of the officers. We went due south, crossing over at a low place where the mountains extend along the southern side of Kokonor. On the way we passed a couple of Tibetan boys herding sheep, and a little on the south side of the pass we sighted an enormous tawny wolf. We finally came out onto gently rolling plains covered with coarse grass and a small, dried-up lake, eventually met up with the "motor road" indicated on our map, and turned west along the cart track through the grassland where there was not one living thing in sight. After two or three miles we came to the head of a deep gully cutting into heavy gravel deposits which led into the first of a succession of steep valleys that flow into the Huang Ho. We passed by a small mud-walled Chinese village with fields of sickly looking crops surrounding it, and about ten miles further through several of these valleys we arrived at our fort at Cha Pu Cha. This is the most remote Chinese military outpost on the western frontier. It is mud walled, about 100 yards square, with small rooms all around the inside of the wall. The twenty soldiers usually quartered here are off somewhere, so the place is deserted except for a caretaker and a Tibetan robber who is a prisoner with irons on his legs. This is the end of the military telephone line, with connections to Huang Yuan in one direction and to Kung Ho and probably Kueite in the other. The telegraph line does not extend this far, so it was by military telephone that our arrival was announced. We were welcomed and furnished with a sheep and feed for our horses.

Our day was cool and partly overcast, a splendid day for traveling. We were not bothered, as we have been recently, by myriad insects and flies buzzing in our faces; instead there were thousands of small blue butterflies fluttering in the air, stirred by our movement and the breezes.

Although I am not disturbed by Suez's actions, it is becoming more evident to me that the others are glad to have him out of the party. He does a lot of grouching, particularly about the food, which gets on Fred's nerves, he is very hard on the servants, and is overbearing towards Sun, who dislikes him intensely. I have not seen him at it, but I am now pretty certain that he is an opium addict, and the shortness of his temper is probably in inverse proportion to the length of time since his last pipe.

Kung Ho
August 2, 1937

We left Cha Pu Cha fort this morning shortly after 8:00, with many bows from Mr. Lo, the local paymaster, and his friends. Our road led down a valley with fields of sparse crops scattered along it. Most of the farmers in this area are Tibetans, but I have seen a few Chinese women working in the fields, and the merchants are mostly Mohammedans. We traveled about twenty-two kilometers, during which we descended 1,000 feet, and are now at Kung Ho.

In this Tibetan country we see many *obos,* or piles of stones with branches and brush with pieces of sheep's wool attached to the tops. They are sort of holy places or shrines and are usually located on high spots where the road crosses over a ridge. It is arid country, and the earth supports only sparse bunches of coarse grass and short thorny bushes. I saw just one tree all day, an old gnarled tamarisk.

During the morning ride we overtook a good-looking young Tibetan woman whom one of our officers persuaded to pose for some photographs while she smoked one of Fred's cigarettes. She accompanied us a while, and our chief officer fell behind to walk with her. He apparently greatly enjoyed himself, being quite publically affectionate with her, which she didn't seem to mind.

Kung Ho is a tiny village of about 150 people, mostly Tibetan, and is the center of a cultivated area on the north side of the Huang Ho. To the north are barren gravel-covered terraces; to the south, steep high bluffs rise above the river, and to the east, where the land rises, we can see the beginning of a dark narrow cleft, a long gorge through metamorphic rocks.

We were met about ten li (about 1/3 of a mile) from town by the local acting magistrate and some of his friends, who had been informed by telephone last night that we were coming. They grandly escorted us into town, which boasts a few trees and a single street where the homesteads are enclosed by high mud walls. We were taken to the official block of buildings, surrounded by battlemented walls, through several courts and a small garden with mixed vegetables and flowers, and ended up in a back building where we were served tea, watermelon seeds, and some very doubtful-looking crystallized sugar. We waited there, while we and our belongings were carefully scrutinized, until our servants had unloaded our gear in the school building nearby. This place is almost indistinguishable from many other buildings we have been in but, wonder of wonders, it has a rough wooden floor along two sides. This is a government primary school, and we are told that when school is in session the pupils number about fifty boys, mostly Mohammedan.

This part of the country has little use for money because the Tibetans do most of their business by barter. A sheep and a brick of tea are each worth about $4.00 (Chinese). Silver coins are acceptable, but paper money seems to be unchangeable and, therefore, not much use. We brought some tea bricks all the way from Shanghai for just such times as this, but they are all with Suez on the road to Kueite and consequently are no good to us. As custom demands the officials have presented us with a sheep which we don't need and can't use because we already have a sheep from yesterday which has not yet been touched. In return, as custom demands, I must make a present to the official's servants, or I can give them a $5 bill and let them worry about getting rid of it.

Upon inquiring, I learned that common soldiers of the 100th Division are paid $5 per month, out of which they must provide their own food. Our major's pay is $50 a month, the same pay as our No. 1 boy.

Incidentally, I believe I have been mistaken in thinking that the turbaned men I have seen are Turkis. More likely they are ordinary Mohammedans dressed for prayer. This occurred to me as I observed our chief major wind a dirty rag around his head in a turban before praying; suddenly he looked quite like a Turki.

Since we arrived in town early we had the afternoon to fritter away, so Sun and I went for a short walk and when we returned found that our soldiers had rounded up a group of Tibetan women to "dance" for us. We contributed $5 to pay for a large jug of wine (really very strong distilled liquor) and some red cloth which was then torn into strips. Practically the entire village crowded into our court to watch the fun. One of the dozen women performers was our acquaintance of the road in the morning. Their clothing was quite colorful, and each had only her left arm in her large outer gown, with the right sleeve hanging down empty. First, a man in sheepskin with a weird mask and a fur hood came into the center of the court and sang a song. He wouldn't stop until we paid him ten cents. Next, one of the younger men, who had become rather liquored up, sang a long song in a peculiar monotonous quavery high-pitched voice. He was joined by one of the women who did the same, only she mostly sang into her left sleeve. There were long hesitations between repetitions of her song which, for the most part, she sang with her back to us. This lasted for an hour, first one man and then another, alternating with the women who sometimes came out two at a time, holding hands and turning about so that sometimes they were back-to-back and sometimes facing one another. Some of the women were quite shy, and there was a great deal of giggling and many false starts. Each time a performer completed this procedure a Mohammedan official would rush out and very roughly tie one of the wide strips of red cloth over her shoulder and around her body. There was much clapping and laughing among the squatting spectators, a few of whom got rather drunk, I'm afraid, but everyone seemed to have a good time. Among those present were several lamas who were dressed differently from any we had seen before. Bearded, they were wearing long red robes and turbans and looked more like Mohammedan priests than Buddhist monks, but each carried his prayer wheel and spun it constantly. The doings were amusing for a while, but later became so monotonous we wished they would all stop and go home.

In honor of our presence in town the main street is decorated with pieces of red cloth strung across it on ropes. I am sure that very few foreigners have ever been here; there is certainly nothing here for anyone to come for.

It was rather late when we sat down for dinner with the young magistrate, who is named Ma like all three of our majors. I don't think he liked our western food much.

Sticking up the thumb means that something is "A-Number One", so I have taught our officers the sign of "thumbs down", which they think is very funny. In Tibetan sign language holding up a little finger and spitting on it means something is no good.

Lo Han Tang
August 4, 1937

We have had two fatiguing days on the rough, little-used trail between Kung Ho and Kueite. It is easy to understand why it is untraveled; so far as I know only one other exploring expedition has ever been over it. Last night we stopped at a tiny Tibetan village named Chi La Ha, and tonight we are at another, Lo Han Tang, which is slightly larger and a bit more prosperous. We should reach Kueite tomorrow. We are getting used to stopping at places that we wouldn't have been found dead in a few months ago. This one seems almost like the height of luxury.

After a late start out of Kung Ho we travelled east for about five miles over a very dry plain, crossing a number of steep narrow gullies, some of which had small tamarisk trees growing in them and reminded me of the valleys we used to ride down in the Punjab. We reached the edge of the mountain range called A Lai Kung Shan, through which the Huang Ho has cut so deep and narrow a gorge that no road can follow it. The west slope of A Lai Kung Shan does not look steep, but it is really a pretty hard climb over the granite surface of the mountain which rises above 2,500 feet. It was a little after noon when we reached the top. Along the way we were joined by an old Tibetan with a queue and a curious felt hat, who sat down with us at lunch time and smoked his copper pipe which he lit with flint and steel. From the top we could see mountains in every direction rising to much higher elevations. To the north were the mountains extending along the south side of Koko-nor, to the east was the La Chi Shan range whose north edge we had reached near Kumbum, and to the southeast were the mountains beyond Kueite. In the other directions were more distant ranges. We crossed the rounded crest and made a precipitous descent down the east side by a section of the trail so steep that we had to dismount and lead our horses. The pack mules had a very difficult time of it. We descended nearly 2,000 feet into the valley, turned up a dried gravel stream bed until it became too narrow to follow, and then climbed up the hillside again to the top. To our surprise we came out onto a flat grass-covered plain which sloped gently up towards the northern mountains. These high plains are winter grazing grounds for the nomadic Tibetans' herds; we saw the remains of some of last year's fireplaces.

We traversed this plateau and, just as suddenly as we had come upon it, we reached the other side and peered down 1,600 feet into an amazing area of badlands. In my day I have seen many badlands with a relief of several hundred feet, but here was an area with depths of well over 1,000 feet. Our slow and tortuous trail led us steeply down into a valley of thick gravel where there was water for irrigation and, as a result, some small settlements of Tibetan farmers were supported. Although they lived in several tiny villages scattered along the valley for two or three miles, there is only one name for the place: Chi La Ha. We passed on to the last house where, to all intents and purposes, we simply moved in and made ourselves at home. The house faced onto the inevitable mud walled court; its single room had a raised kang and three fireplaces in the middle for cooking and heating.

No man of the house was in evidence, so all work and authority centered around a woman who was probably not as old as her wrinkled face suggested. She wore a red jacket that did not quite cover her stomach and, over it, a long heavy robe which was let down and tied around her waist by the sleeves. She wore clumsy Tibetan boots; her hair was tied in 108 small braids fastened at the ends. Down her back hung three beaded strips of cloth bearing large embossed bowl-like silver ornaments. Despite a swarm of hovering neighborhood spectators, the only other visible members of the household were the resident lama, who was spinning his prayer wheel, a little girl of five or six who wore her short hair in twenty braids lengthened with string—and little else, and a very old woman in a pointed witch's hat. We kept the younger woman busy hauling water up from the spring, which she did by using a tall, slender bucket carried on her back, supporting the bottom of the bucket with a rope knotted around her waist and holding it upright with a length of sheep or yak wool held around her shoulders.

It was late when we arrived and we were tired. We had a light supper inside with the heat and smoke of the dung fire because the breeze outside blew out our candles. Almost immediately we set up our beds along the side of the court wall under an overhang and crawled in. It was not until morning that we saw that the court contained a flag pole with a string of prayer flags and a small chortan made of mud mixed with straw.

This morning we sent the mules off ahead of us and, accompanied by a couple of villagers, went down into the valley to see the very narrow gorge where the stream cuts through the granite mountain to join the Huang Ho. Along the fault from several fissures in the rock issued a number of small springs of hot sulphur water. One of them had some steam which blew the water out in a spray, and one of our majors and our No. 1 boy had shower baths. We returned to the village from where we rode back up the valley we had come down the night before and began a stiff 1,600 foot climb up the hill to the east to a small remnant of the flat upland surface we had crossed the day before. Almost immediately we had to descend the other side along a gentler slope and about noon reached the bottom, where we overtook our mules. After many miles of very rough going, up and down through the badlands, we finally emerged into another valley, an area of treed terraces, which certainly looked good to us after the desolation of the country we had been through. Watered by irrigation ditches filled by an eastern tributary, these terraces flourished with prosperous looking fields. This is the setting of Lo Han Tang.

We went to the chief's house where we were expected. New, with wooden floors, it is almost like a palace to us. The chief, a man in his forties, was quite respectably dressed, with a queue wrapped around his head and whiskers down the side of his face and under his chin like an old-fashioned New England sea captain. Immediately we were surrounded by the whole household, several lamas, and many friends, who all examined us and our belongings with great interest. We have had absolutely no privacy from these people's curiosity, and whatever modesty I once possessed has long since disappeared. They think nothing of sitting in a doorway, watching and waiting; every aspect of our getting dressed and undressed is full of wonderment. However, these agricultural Tibetans are simple, friendly, and good-natured people, and I don't really mind their curiosity. As a matter of fact, it has permitted me to take a number of photographs which I hope will turn out well.

The chief must be rather wealthy because one room in his house is a private shrine with a life-sized Buddha, several smaller images, some holy pictures, and a number of the peculiar long, narrow, wood-covered Tibetan books. I don't think he has a private lama, however, as I have not seen one standing around chanting. In the courtyard there is a flag pole with its strips of prayer flags as well as ropes running from the top of the pole to the corners of the wall, also hung with small prayer flags. The wall is punctured with window-like openings in which small prayer wheels are operated by the wind.

After dinner we went for a little walk through the village with one of the local lamas, who opened the temple for our inspection. It was small but rather nice and certainly better lighted than others we have seen. Near it was a small building containing a large wooden prayer wheel run by water power. The Buddhists have thought of every possible way to make praying easy.

The lamas in this region all seem to be "red" ones, while those in Kumbum and Gumosa were "yellow" ones. The "yellow" church is supposed to be a reformation of the old "red" church, but I don't understand much about the differences. In outward appearances, some "red" lamas wear queues and often are turbaned while most of the "yellow" lamas cut their hair or shave their heads. I understand that "red" lamas can marry while "yellow" ones cannot.

Just as we came out of the temple, Ma Chou-hsiang, our chief major, came rushing up with my rifle, much excited, to tell us there were some Tibetan robbers, called *tu-fi,* nearby and he wanted to borrow my rifle. Of course I gave my permission, and he and the younger officer hurriedly saddled their horses and were off.

Our soldiers are good fellows, and I have taken quite a liking to them. When they first came to us they knew not a word of English, but by now have acquired a few and enjoy using them. The day before we reached Kokonor we found the rain had spot-rusted our rifles. The chief major picked up the word "rust" at once, and it has become sort of a password between us. Whenever he wishes to call our attention to something he says "rust-rust", and we do the same to him. The young officer likes to stick his thumb up and say "OK".

Kueite
August 5, 1937

I can now continue the robber story. Later last evening we learned that two, three, or four (depending upon who told the story) Tibetans made a raid on local herds and had driven off some horses. At about 10:00 P.M. the soldiers returned from their hasty reconnaissance with a group of villagers, and there was much guttural talking and gesturing. It appears that the soldiers had located the robbers in a nearby village and had shot at them, but the robbers ran away, escaping in the dark. Shortly after we started off this morning, the soldiers and some Tibetan peasants spotted the tracks of horses on the trail, and the major borrowed my field glasses to survey the landscape, looking for the robbers. He questioned everyone we met along the road, and about noon a man reported a number of strange horses far out on the flat land near the river. The major soon found them with the glasses and he, three soldiers, and I started out to investigate. Riding was difficult because the ground had broken into large mud cracks, and the horses' feet often slipped down into them. As we got closer we drew our guns (since the robbers were reported to have two rifles) and spread out, but as we circled in we found that the robbers had run off into the hills, abandoning the horses; apparently they had been badly frightened last night. We rounded up the horses and drove them triumphantly into Kueite. The major phoned his report of the affair to Sining, doubtlessly embellished with imaginary details, and said that he has been highly commended by

Ma Pu-fang himself. Sun tells me that if the horse owner claims the horses he must pay the major a reward of $100, and if no one claims them they will be turned over to the army. And so ends my biggest adventure thus far.

The valley where we stayed last night joins the Huang Ho as it emerges from the long gorge that caused us to cross several mountainous ridges. Here the river looks small, as it flows in a rather confined channel and is dwarfed by the size of the hills rising above it. Most of our journey to Kueite was through very dry and desolate-looking country where only the mud flats along the river were green with a low growth of tamarisks and thorny shrubs. To the north were almost continuous bluffs of reddish Tertiary beds until about five miles outside of Kueite, where the valley constricts between a long terrace to the south and the low northern hills. Our road became narrow and winding and finally brought us within sight of the city on the south side of the river. We crossed on a pontoon bridge whose boats had once been gaily painted but now are weather-beaten and drab. It was surfaced with loose rough planks which jumped and clattered under the horses' feet, frightening them. Arriving in Kueite in mid-afternoon we found Suez established in our "hotel". I had some letters waiting for me as well as two Shanghai newspapers, both over a month old. After a late luncheon we all had baths (our first in over two weeks), shaved, and changed clothes, and I, for one, feel quite restored.

From here we return to Lanchow by way of Labrang where there is a large Buddhist monastery, but first we will lay over here a day or two, so I can write up my geologic notes and send a report to Yen.

Kueite
August 6, 1937

I spent the morning poring over maps and with the aid of Sun, the major, and the hotel proprietor have plotted our route for next week. The original plan was to go to Labrang, a large Tibetan monastery four days' journey across the mountains to the southeast via a direct route, but recent communication with Sining has forbidden us that pleasure because the area has robbers. We shall, therefore, go by way of Sunwha, which will take us across the Huang Ho, east to the foothills of the La Chi Shan, and thence southeast to Sunwha and on to Hochow. This will take another four days at the least, but the change is actually a satisfactory one because of geological areas along the way which could be important to our work.

After the matter of our continuation was settled, Major Ma and I set off to explore the city. As our hotel is in a southern suburb of Kueite we proceeded to the south gate and climbed to the top of the thick mud wall for a view of the place, which is quite small. Residences of the local well-to-do sat within their own walls, and there were a number of temples as well as many open places where we saw wheat being thrashed. Having gained our bearing, we then walked about. The temples were mostly disappointing with the exception of an empty Mohammedan mosque with a graceful and elaborately carved wooden tower. The grounds surrounding the Confucian temple were planted in potatoes which later we were able to substitute for our rice, a very pleasant change at dinner.

Local farms seem to be thriving. The new wheat harvests large hard grain; a farmer told us that his yield was 300 catties to the mow, which figures out to about forty bushels per acre.

The "hotel" is a two-story building facing a court, entered from the street through a long, dark tunnel. It is operated by brothers who buy wool and hides from Tibetans, and in season the place is a hostel for outside buyers. If they buy from the brothers their lodging is free; if not, their room charge amounts to 2 percent of their purchases from others.

Our elevation is down to 7,500 feet, almost the lowlands to us at this point, and it has been warm enough so that I can have my bed out on the roof. The city is overrun with dogs, the municipal scavengers, who sleep all day and bark all night, apparently under the leadership of one beast who is persistent and incessant with noise from dusk to dawn. "Annoying" does not describe the din. The human population, almost entirely Mohammedan and Tibetan, is quieter, at least at night.

In the afternoon I wrote to Yen and drew up some geologic sections of our route of the past two weeks.

Hsia Ka Tzang
August 7, 1937

Our march today was longer than usual. The young major and I rode ahead of the others and reached here two hours before the rest of the party. It has been a warm day with a breeze strong enough to necessitate my use of the chin strap on my sun helmet to keep from losing it. Fred, who does not tan, has been wearing a wide-brimmed straw hat which, in wind like this, he has had to tie around his face with string, like a sunbonnet. He knows he looks silly.

We left Kueite the same way we entered it, by crossing the pontoon bridge to the north side of the Huang Ho. We then turned eastward toward the village of A Shih Kung and followed the base of the bluffs which changed from drab brown to an area of faulting which brought up the lower red beds and quite a thickness of grey clays. The contrast in color was startling and conspicuous for many miles. South of the river and east of A Shih Kung a ridge runs south and forms a gorge of the Huang Ho, which we had to avoid by crossing some rough country to the north. The Tertiary beds in the angle between the mountains have been squeezed, deformed, and faulted, and in a few miles we saw more real geology than anywhere on our journey so far.

The major and I stopped for lunch at A Shih Kung where I was escorted into a native hut. While I ate my sandwich my companion told the numerous occupants all about me and exhibited some of my wonders; the aneroid barometer and my dark sunglasses which clip over my clear ones seemed to be of greatest interest.

At Hsia Ka Tzang we made ourselves at home in a Mohammedan inn where the major and I had tea and munched on raw peas with a group of women and children seated on a piece of felt spread out in the courtyard. In the interval one woman washed the major's shirt, and the children had a grand time playing in the soap suds, which they probably don't often see. We were joined by some Chinese peddlers traveling on foot to Sining, whom we had passed earlier on the road. More tea was served, to which they contributed some apricots. I very much enjoy getting away from the rest of our party this way, with someone who is acquainted with the people. Under these circumstances I feel I can see the country's inhabitants as they really are.

Sun Hsien
August 8, 1937

This morning we left the main road and turned east up a small valley which led us through red beds over a probable fault and up a high ridge of metamorphic rock. We climbed 1,300 feet to the top; the last part of the way was exceptionally pleasant as the northward-facing slopes were covered by a fir forest, very reminiscent of northern Michigan. The trees were mostly small but grew rather thickly on mossy ground that was abundant with small plants and wild strawberries. These were small and red but with so little flavor they would have been a disappointment at the dinner table. The most interesting wild flower was a peculiar pink variety with highly specialized petals and a corolla ending in such a long, thin tube that, if it had any honey, it surely was safe from all insects.

Eastward from this ridge we passed more red bed country which was rough and deeply eroded, but the streams from the mountains in the north furnished water for the terraced fields and gave evidence of rainfall sufficient to grow decent crops. We let our horses graze along the edge of a field of shoulder-high oats and eventually were confronted by a very irate woman who, I judge, objected to the destruction of her crop and called us every bad name in her vocabulary. The soldiers merely laughed at her, which is the only evidence of animosity between soldier and peasant that I have witnessed thus far.

At noon we reached the village of Chi Tsa where there is a Tibetan monastery with about 500 lamas. Built on the steep western side of the valley and rising one above the other, the mud walls and flat roofs reminded me of pictures of the Navajo dwellings in the southwestern U.S. We rode up to the principal temple, which was flat-roofed and not designed in Chinese style, and after a bit of discussion the major persuaded a lama to open it for us. The walls of its raised porch were decorated with the usual fantastic paintings of gods and demons, and at either side were a pair of large prayer wheels. The interior was better lit than usual so we could see quite well. The building was mostly empty, but the back wall was lined with glass-fronted cases containing five nearly life-sized images and a myriad of smaller ones, one or two feet high, all different, and all heavily gilded. The lama said they were made in Peiping. The roof was supported by pillars, some ornately painted, others wound with rugs bearing barbarically colored dragons. These were woven in pairs so the designs met to make the dragons appear to be coiled around the pillar. I was told that these rugs were made in the village near Ta Erh Ssu (the Chinese name for Kumbum) where only a couple of weeks ago I shopped for a rug without success.

The road has been very steep in many places today, and Suez has apparently had a rough time of it in his litter. In any case, he called a premature halt to our journey about 3:00 this afternoon at a small village some distance from the one we had planned to reach. He was quite disagreeable until he had opportunity to closet himself and doubtless revive himself with a pipeful of opium. There is no inn here, and we were directed to a farmer's house where we simply moved in, regardless of the owner's absence. The only inmates were a fierce barking dog chained to the porch, a little naked boy who cowered in the kitchen, and a sleeping baby who never woke up during the whole disturbance. A man and woman finally came to claim the children, and after a hurried entrance and exit they all disappeared, seemingly frightened by our presence. I admit that this is an autocratic and abrupt way to secure lodgings, but it seems to be the way of the land, and our accommodations are quite adequate even though the court is very small. The advantage is that we are free from the noise and smells of the mules with whom we must usually share our resting place.

In a way I am glad that our route plans have changed, because this part of the country is really very pretty, with steep green slopes and cultivated fields; it is a relief after the very dry and desolate country we have traveled through recently. To the north of us lie the La Chi Shan, great masses of granite and serrated ridges of metamorphic rock around which the clouds have been playing hide and seek.

Wu Tao Ling
August 9, 1937

Today we traveled along the south flank of the mountains at an elevation of about 10,000 feet and crossed one ridge after another separating the streams that flowed toward the Huang Ho to the south. It is attractive country with prosperous hillside farms and little villages of mixed Tibetan, Mohammedan, and Chinese populations. Streams and rainfall provide full irrigation as well as green slopes sprinkled with wild flowers in full bloom.

This morning we met a monk on the road who was traveling up from Szechuan to the Kumbum monastery, prostrating himself all the way. He would walk two steps forward, raise his hands high in the air, and then fall frontwards full length on the road, only to rise again and repeat the process. The journey he is making is several hundred miles, so I guess it will take him endless months to complete it.

The young major left us yesterday to make an early appearance at his home village, Tsa Pa Pu, which we reached about noon today. He came out to meet us and, taking my hand, escorted me to his home, with Fred, Sun, and the other soldiers close behind. He is from an aristocratic family, and his father was a brigadier general. His home was much like other dwellings we have seen except for a brick-paved courtyard and wooden floors indoors. We were taken to the best room, furnished with two kangs and a large raised seat covered with a rug decorated with large storks and flowers, where we were served a meal of black tea sweetened with sugar, steamed bread, two dishes of mutton, one cooked with very hot green peppers, the other with greens, bowls of coarse noodles in a meat soup, and the usual watermelon seeds. Having already had our lunch we couldn't eat very much, but the soldiers made up for us and gobbled it all with gusto.

I think we have just about come to a parting of the ways with Suez, and I shall have to get rid of him. More and more, the expedition is being run to suit his convenience and, of course, this cannot continue. Yesterday we stopped early because of his insistence. Today we arrived at this village where he selected a good lodging for himself and left us to flounder on our own. Fred, Sun, and I have had to put up at a small Mohammedan dwelling overrun with women and children and must trek over to his place for our meals. The whole story is too long to tell here but, in essence, he has been disagreeable, has misinformed me about local conditions in order to change plans to suit his wishes, and has actively obstructed our movements. From the start his presence has slowed us down, and I am convinced that we would be better off without him. I now feel that I must write a letter to Dr. Yen asking him to recall Suez, although at the moment he is on his very best behavior, sweet and agreeable, apparently recognizing that he has gone too far and that something is in the wind. However, I am sure this state of bliss will not last long.

Sia Shih Chia
August 12, 1937

Our journey on the 10th was uneventful. We crossed some ridges extending south from the mountains and entered a flat valley descending to the southeast; its cultivated hillsides looked relatively prosperous. We found that we had unknowingly joined the "motor road" from Sining to Sunwah, and small platoons of workers were filling up ruts in preparation for the civil governor, Ma Ling, who is returning to the region by automobile. Ma Ling is a man over seventy, the uncle of Ma Pu-fang. Last year he made a pilgrimage to Mecca, and in his absence Ma Pu-fang increased the strength of his army and so entrenched himself in power as the acting governor that the old man was afraid to come home. A nephew sent a delegation to Shanghai, where Ma Ling was waiting it out, to assure him that it would be safe for him to return. It may be possible to get a car over this steep, narrow, winding road, but I wouldn't want to risk it. Local politics would be less dangerous!

We passed through a small walled city where we were stared at by Mohammedans and progressed southward to a valley which gradually narrowed into a gorge of metamorphic rock. To avoid it we took a road over the hills to the east, rising to an elevation of about 10,000 feet before descending steeply about 1,500 feet to the tiny village of Sha Nung Wan where we spent the night. Not only were we very crowded there, the water was brackish and tasted so bad that even strong tea could not disguise it.

Yesterday we left the rough country and reentered the same valley we had followed before, which widened out again on this side of the gorge. It led us straight south to the Huang Ho, which we followed for about five miles before it constricted and we were able to cross it on a rickety suspension bridge. On the south side we found a spring near the trail and, for the first time since leaving Sian, I broke my rule and drank unboiled water. As I may have told you, one of our real hardships is the lack of pure water, and I am constantly dehydrated. At this point my thirst was uncontrollable because the brackish water at the last village had kept me from filling my canteen, and I was parched dry.

We spent last night in Cha Han Ta Ssu, which Suez says is inhabited principally by people of Turki derivation whose language is unintelligible to him. I doubt it, however, because they look and sound the same as other villagers. In any case, we were more comfortable there than at any place since Kueite.

Today we passed over a good sized mountain with the highest elevation yet and have arrived at a Tibetan village so tiny that it is not even on the map.

Suez left us this morning to go directly back to Lanchow where he should arrive in about a week's time. We turned south and followed the motor road back into the red bed hills away from the river. This is drier country; its abundant grasshoppers have red underwings that make sharp snapping noises as they fly, like the click-click of hundreds of scissors. We zig-zagged up to the top of a ridge about 2,000 feet above Sia Shih Chia before dipping back down into the valley. It once may have been possible for a car to pass over this road, but it is now so badly washed out and so steep that the mules had a difficult time. The trail grew even worse as it meandered up the valley until suddenly I noticed that we had left the motor road behind us, were out of the red beds, and into the metamorphics of the main mountain mass. A beautifully clear and cold stream flowed over a rocky bed, and we found a fine spring with the best drinking water since Shanghai. It seemed like heaven to gulp sweet water, surrounded by fox gloves, campanulas, forget-me-nots two feet high, and some wild flowers I had never seen before—a large purple daisy-like flower with an orange center. I would like to bring some seeds home, but they are not ripe now and I would not be able to recognize them without their flowers. Wild strawberries were ripe red among the grasses.

We reached the pass at 6,000 feet above our starting point about mid-afternoon and again came upon the road. From this height we could look down into the Huang Ho valley to the north and see the general features of its geology for miles. We came down along the steep southwest slope and are now 3,000 feet below the pass. Riding horseback down a steep rough grade is uncomfortable for both beast and rider, so I walked and again got far out ahead of the others. I met three Tibetans and we stopped for a visit, they speaking their language and I mine. They seemed quite impressed by my notebook full of funny writing, my fountain pen, and the hairs on the backs of my hands.

On the road
August 13, 1937

Last night we stayed at a Tibetan house, which we simply usurped. An old one, its woodwork was all blackened by age and cow dung smoke, and it smelled so bad that we could not enter. We set up our sleeping cots under an attached roofed-over area for our night's repose, and Fred, who generally sleeps inside, joined Sun and me for obvious reasons. When we arrived the court was empty except for a couple of small calves that had been confined under two wicker baskets where they set up a great bawling for their mothers. After dinner Fred and I took a walk and encountered a young hunter who had just shot a marmot with an old muzzle loader which had to be fired with a fuse. Fred gave him a cigarette, and his face erupted into a broad grin.

It was so cold during the night the bed bugs were numbed so they could not run, and in the morning we collected them from all of our mattresses. Fred has been badly bitten by bed bugs and, he thinks, lice, although I have not noticed either as much as I have the fleas. If I do have lice I haven't really been bothered by them, but with everyone and every house infested, it is inconceivable that I should escape their attention.

I don't think the people expected to be paid for our lodgings, and when in the morning I handed over a silver dollar (worth 35 U.S. cents), big smiles went all around the family, and I felt like a real philanthropist.

Lung Wu Ssu
August 14, 1937

Today we continued down the valley to its junction with the river flowing northward into the Huang Ho, descending nearly 2,000 feet to the village of Lung Wu Ssu, the last outpost of the government in this direction. It was a warm day and men, women, and children were in the fields harvesting and thrashing wheat, all stripped to their waists. Thrashing was done by a stone roller dragged around by any animal available or by the people flailing at the wheat with sticks. Farmers here seem to be Tibetan; the Chinese and Mohammedans are merchants and artisans. These Tibetan women have a different hair dress from elsewhere. They wear two or three braids gathered into a short red pocket in back, ornamented with either a silver bowl or a brass ring from which a long braid of dark yak hair hangs nearly touching the ground. Some of the men wear pieces of felt as eye shades, bound onto their heads with their queues.

The distance we covered today was short, and after fording the river we reached this place early in the afternoon. I was ahead of the others with two of the soldiers as we entered the village down a very narrow street full of evil-smelling mud where I was stared at by the neighborhood children while lodgings were found for our party. We were eventually set up in a very crowded inn where we had a couple of rooms on the second floor, decorated with some very brilliant lithographs that looked like pictures from packages of fire crackers.

After a hasty lunch of tea and canned beans, we visited the temples which occupy the terraces above the town and, as the home of over a thousand monks, far surpass it in size. There is nothing noteworthy about their buildings as Tibetan temples seem more or less alike. In one building an orchestra and choir was in session with thirty to forty lamas seated in two rows facing each other. Some were beating with long curved sticks on thin drums set on head-level standards; the rest had cymbals, except for one old lama on a high seat who appeared to be the leader. They chanted, beat the drums, and clanged the cymbals for some time before the monotony made us turn and leave. In the center, between two rows of lamas, were two horns twelve to fifteen feet long supported on wheels. At the moment of our retreat loud blasts were blown from these trumpets that were most startling. The message may have been that they were glad to be rid of us; the noise certainly made us jump.

I asked the major what became of dead lamas because I had seen no graves anywhere. He said that bodies were disposed of in one of three ways: taken to a high place and left to the eagles, thrown into the river, or burned. I suspect that most of them go to the eagles, as the streams are mostly too small to carry off corpses and fuel too scarce to waste on cremations. Eagles, on the other hand, are abundant everywhere and seem to be the only avian scavengers besides crows and magpies. There are no vultures. After death the Living Buddhas are mummified in a praying position, encased in clay, and stored in the temples.

We had dinner after returning from the temples, and while we were still at the table a Swedish missionary named Carlsson came to call. He invited us to his place to meet his wife and have some coffee, and of course we went. They have been in Lung Wu Ssu for two months and, as they expect to work among the Tibetans for the rest of their lives, are fixing up their quarters which they rent from the monastery for $10 silver a year. Their dwelling, finished except for the plaster on the mud walls, is very plain, but it is the first really clean place we have seen since leaving Shanghai. They are now building a chapel and some stables. They plan no educational or medical work; they are here only to save souls—I wonder if it is worth the effort. Tibetans are extremely superstitious, and any conversion would be very superficial at best. Carlsson says that the term "lama", properly used, is only for the Living Buddhas (who are reincarnated). There are eleven of these here now; the principal one is only twenty years old. Living Buddhas are worshipped by the people as gods; the others are merely priests or monks, although greatly admired and respected by the populace. The only educated members of the community, they are all taught to read phonetic Tibetan writing, but this must be very superficial learning because the literary and spoken language are different from one another, and few of these monks really know what they are reading. I imagine the Roman Catholic priesthood was like this 500 years ago. Although "lama" is apparently a Chinese word, it is widely used by Tibetans although their own language has a word for it, *alúng*. Ordinary priests are called *ahkáh*.

We had a pleasant visit with the Carlssons and thoroughly enjoyed the coffee, as ours ran out several weeks ago. They had only three chairs which Fred, Sun, and I occupied while Mr. Carlsson sat on the bed. Mrs. C. spent most of her time in the kitchen. We were their first guests and they pressed us to come back for breakfast, which we could not refuse, and as a result we had our first really good breakfast in months, cereal made with *tsamba* (which the Tibetans make into a thick paste with tea and butter), boiled like farina with fresh milk and sugar, fried eggs, sweetened bread, and coffee. I went through our supplies to see what we could offer them in return and took a meager gift of a can of asparagus, one of marmalade, and a glass jar of lemon candies.

On the road
August 15-16, 1937

We finally got away from town about 8:30 in the morning, crossed the small river on a little bridge near which we paused to fill our canteens from a nice spring, and climbed out of the valley to the east. The hills here are covered with common drab loess-like silt, and the trail, which was quite steep and zig-zagged, was worn down into the material ten or twenty feet. At a few places we could see over the top a bit, but we climbed about 2,000 feet before we came out to where we could get a good view of the town and monastery below us to the west. Beyond them rose a range of mountains with clouds drifting around their summits. To the south we were separated from another mountain range by a small steep valley with patches of forest on its slopes in between terraces planted with nearly ripe grain. Among the fields were scattered a few tiny Tibetan villages with their poles of prayer flags and small wind-driven prayer wheels. We passed through one village to the accompaniment of barking dogs and soon were beyond the last signs of civilization.

Again in the grasslands, we passed through fields of wild flowers and small fluttering brown and black butterflies, where streams flowed with beautifully clear water. Here and there along the ground and under the other plants showed the red of wild strawberries. Our trail continued westward, up and down, to 11,500 feet above sea level at the ridge's summit. We flushed out a covey of partridges, and Fred shot three before the rest were frightened away by the mule men running to retrieve the dead birds.

We descended on the east side of the ridge through a steep, rocky, V-shaped valley cut in flinty metamorphic rock and finally entered a larger valley where our trail led southeast up a tributary from the other side. This valley is one of the nicest we have seen thus far, with a scrubby growth of willows through which we could seldom see for more than a few yards. I was leading the procession when suddenly I came upon a bevy of pheasants, beautiful jet-black birds with red and yellow heads. I stopped so quickly that the men behind me thought there were robbers ahead and rushed up with their rifles, frightening the birds which took off with a startling whir of wings.

Up to this time we had not seen a single soul since leaving the village. As the valley widened, however, we came upon a group of monks struggling along the trail. By far the best-looking monks we have encountered, they seemed clean and their clothes were neat and in good repair, but they carried with them that overwhelming odor of rancid butter. They were of all ages, and at the tag end of the line there was a small boy carrying an animal skin filled with butter and a stack of repulsive-looking cakes.

We came out of the valley into extraordinarily different country. I don't think I have ever seen such a sharp break in scenery; it seemed quite unnatural. We passed from a deeply eroded valley into open country with wide flood plains along the streams and rounded slopes that led up hills high enough to be mountains, but without the appearance of mountains. Everywhere the surface was covered with grass and other low plants, but there was not a single tree or bush, and we could see in a broad sweep for many miles. The explanation was simple. We had come into a region which was characteristic of this part of China and Tibet before the great rivers cut down their valleys to the present depth. Erosion progressed backwards up the Huang Ho and its tributaries, and this open countryside has not yet been attacked. It was as if we were ahead of time. Of course the future will bring erosion which will result in rugged mountains and gorges, and some day this place will look like the country we have seen before it.

We continued eastward and presently came upon marks of cart wheels, which we followed for several miles to a monastery built in the shadow of granite hills. The name of the place in Chinese was Kua Shih Chih Ssu; the Tibetan name, as nearly as I could make out, was Gwarshgirsh. Here we put up for the night among a throng of filthy monks who pushed about to see the strange foreigners. Among them was a small boy about four years old, dressed in red robes like the others. He was made much of by the older men and seemed to be the pet of the place. A brook flowed along the foot of a slope near the monastery with part of its water diverted into a canal which turned two large prayer wheels. Each wheel was equipped with a bell that was struck with every revolution. We are rather weary of ordinary temples and did not investigate this one.

There has been much talk of robbers these past few days. Carlsson said that as long as soldiers are stationed throughout the country conditions are generally peaceful, but as soon as they are removed the nomads recommence their raids. We have been traveling with our guns prominently displayed, and today our major used my field glasses to scour the countryside. I think he just likes to use the glasses, as much of this region is so open that we could not possibly be surprised by the approach of anything, much less a band of marauders. In any case, I think we are a fair match for at least twenty robbers, as they are evidently not noted for their bravery.

We left the monastery rather late in the morning, headed up an open valley whose slopes were covered with blue larkspur, and finally crossed a ridge at an elevation of 12,000 feet. At the summit there was the usual Tibetan *obo* with tufts of wool attached to poles. Coming down the other side we met some Tibetans and stopped to talk. One was an old man whose two teeth showed prominently when he grinned. He pulled out a pipe made from the thigh bone of a sheep and happily sucked through it on a cigarette butt of mine while I took his picture. He said six robbers passed through the valley yesterday, but had been driven off after trying to rob two men who shot at them. Further on we met fifteen men with rifles on their backs whom our soldiers greeted with friendly shouts as we passed them by. How robbers are identified, I don't know. Although this troop of men looked suspicious to me, they easily passed inspection. We stopped for lunch near a camp fire where two Tibetans were skinning and cooking marmots. They had recently been robbed of their horses and saddles, whether by the robbers mentioned previously, I don't know. We pitched our camp beside a creek, across from some kind of fortified government building. We are now back in Kansu Province, where the grazing lands are used for pasturing army animals. I took advantage of the creek for bathing and, when I stripped off my clothes, was quite honestly amazed to find how badly bitten up I am. It is clear that my body has been furnishing feasts to sundry jumping and crawling creatures for a long time. I changed my underclothes and socks and feel clean for the first time in weeks.

Later in the afternoon when I joined the major at the cook tent for a cup of tea, the excitement started. The major, per usual, was peering through the field glasses, this time intently focused on the south slope of the valley where the trail disappeared over the hill. In a joking way I said "*tu-fi*?" to him and, as I took over the glasses to look for myself, a band of Tibetans crested the hill and started down the trail toward us. I turned in the direction of the fort to see a group of about fifteen soldiers with rifles advancing from the other side. It appeared that the soldiers were coming after a bunch of robbers who were coming after us and that we were about to be in the middle of a ruckus. Our soldiers grabbed their rifles and ran off to join the fun, and I got out my pistol in case of need. I could hardly believe that the Tibetans were robbers because of the calm way they came over the hill in the direction of the fort. They steadily headed toward our camp, shouting and gesticulating, and right in front of us the soldiers closed in on them and very roughly relieved them of their rifles and horses before herding them as prisoners into the fort. As best I can piece the story together, some soldiers were returning to the fort when they met a band of armed Tibetans whom they took to be robbers. Shots were exchanged, the soldiers beat it back to the fort to spread the alarm, and a small troop rushed out to capture the supposed bandits. Since the soldiers could not speak Tibetan the band ran toward us to have us intercede for them, to tell the soldiers that they were good men and not robbers. This didn't work as the soldiers were convinced of their evil purpose and marched them off to the fort as accused. I do not know whether or not they are guilty or what will happen to them, but at last we have been a part of the local robber scenario.

Labrang
August 17, 1937

After the excitement of last evening, our soldiers slept in the open to guard our mules and horses while the rest of us were as comfortable as possible in our tents during the chilly night. In the morning we resumed our journey southward through the same uninhabited country. During this time of year the nomad Tibetans keep their flocks and herds in the higher mountains and come down to these low pasturelands (about 10,000 feet) only for the winter. Much of the country we passed through was formerly cultivated, and signs of ancient terracing were distinct along the distant hillsides; however, now there is nothing but weeds, grass, wild flowers, and marmots rustling about the remains of last year's fireplaces. There are white dandelions with pale yellow centers and a peculiar kind of thistle whose spiney leaves form a rosette with a whole group of purple flowers on practically no stems springing from its center. Along the road which led us up and down a number of low ridges we passed several groups of Tibetans, all heavily armed; some carried two rifles and many also had swords. We crossed a broad valley and ascended a tributary valley until we reached the crest of a low mountain range at an elevation of 11,500 feet. At the pass we rode between two poles connected by a rope with many small prayer flags fluttering from it, looking from a distance like a miniature wash hung out to dry. From there we descended nearly 2,000 feet along a very steep valley which brought us to the city of La Pu Leng (Chinese) or Labrang (Tibetan).

This is undoubtedly the dirtiest town we have yet seen. Our road took us down a long gully through the center of town, which seems to be the community refuse heap. We clomped along in a cloud of dust rising from all kinds of filth, including half-burned dung, bones, fragments of hide, and innumerable tufts of dirty wool. The toilets of all the over-hanging dwellings likewise dumped their debris into the gully. Apparently an occasional stream of water from the mountains is relied upon to clean this street, but it does not seem to have rained here for a very long time.

We are now established on the second floor of an inn (which is not too bad as inns here go), overlooking the mud roofs of neighboring houses. A chattering Tibetan woman is in charge and in constant motion, coming and going in a bustle of activity. Here the hairstyle is again different, with one large braid in the back and many smaller ones on either side. The large one is enclosed in a flat red cloth tube at the back of the neck, and the others go into wider pouches on either side at the small of the back, ornamented with large disks of polished brass, a large clam shell in the middle, and a row of pearl buttons at the top. The whole thing ends in a fringe at the bottom which almost sweeps along the ground. Although it is quite warm here during the day, many people wear large pointed hats of sheepskin with the fur inside. These are turned up in the back, projecting in a sort of peak in the front.

Our first activity was to call on General Huang Cheng-ching, the local potentate, whose Tibetan name is Ahlóh. We left our inn in the eastern part of town and walked west through narrow dirty streets, past a small stretch of open plain between the mountains forming the valley, until we reached the monastery. Temple buildings cover an area about half a mile long and a quarter of a mile wide on the north side of the river. We walked past the south wall which was faced with a series of open sheds containing large prayer wheels made of skin stretched over wooden frames. Originally painted in gaudy red and gold, they are now so old and dirty that the characters which form the Tibetan prayer are almost illegible. There must be at least a thousand of these wheels, and the monks, as well as other people who pass this way, give each one a spin as they go by. South of the monastery was an open market where a great number of people were squatting about on the ground.

The general's quarters are just west of the monastery. At the gate eight soldiers in old grey-blue uniforms were jumping up and down, engaged in some game like hopscotch, but as they saw us approach they stiffened and became quite dignified. One was armed with a Chinese broad sword with its handle wrapped in blue cloth; the others had rifles which seemed fairly modern in design. We presented our cards and were conducted through the gate into an outer court and through another gateway to a large central courtyard on which a two-story building opened. We were taken upstairs and, after a short wait with the general's secretary, were told the general was ready to receive us. We were escorted around the balcony to the far side and into another room which contained a large table covered with oil cloth and two enormous vases of garden asters. The walls were hung with colored lithographs, the kind one might find in a primary school, and across the ceiling were stretched several cords with paper national flags hanging from them. Presently the general appeared. He was above average size, nearly six feet tall and powerfully built. He wore a coarse cotton shirt with a stand-up collar embroidered in gold, with a loose purple woolen robe over it which left his right arm free. He had on the traditional heavy dark Tibetan boots. We were accompanied by our two Tsinghai majors and two servants who carried our gifts—silk material with which to make a Chinese suit and three bricks of tea. Suez had implied that General Huang would be unpleasant and might create all kinds of difficulties for us. Apparently he is the community autocrat, with younger brothers in the monastery here as No. 1 and No. 2 Living

Buddhas. (They keep all the good jobs in the family!) However, we found the general to be most genial, and we learned from him of the very serious situation with the Japanese. We have been so cut off from the rest of the world, it is only recently that we began to hear rumors of fighting near Peiping. The country people here know little about the outside world and seem to care less. The general, however, has a military radio and has consequently received the latest news—that on August 15th Japanese planes from Formosa bombed Shanghai, causing great damage. The Cathay Hotel was practically demolished and, according to the general, 1,000 people were killed. Another bomb fell in the French Concession, doing much additional damage and killing many more. Since the Cathay Hotel is owned by Sir Victor Sasson, a British subject, and located at the junction of the two principal streets in Shanghai's International Concession, I cannot see the British taking this lightly. If the reports are true and the interests of all the other foreign nations are involved, almost anything can happen. It seems a strange and stupid action for the Japanese to have taken. Sixteen planes are also said to have flown over Nanking dropping bombs. Six were supposedly shot down. But enough of such news, as your information is undoubtedly more complete and current than ours. In any case, we are far away from the trouble here and safe from harm.

This afternoon we were accompanied by one of Huang's staff officers on a tour of the temples. This monastery is the largest and most important in this section of country, Kumbum being second. There are said to be nearly 4,000 monks here. From a distance the temple buildings are seen to rise above the mud-walled dwellings of the monks in true Tibetan style. Built mostly of stone and painted brick red, they are placed close together, many of them several stories high. They have flat roofs and regularly placed windows, many of them with little cloth canopies or awnings over them. Actually, they look like our apartment buildings, and the overall effect is that of an American city. The walls of the upper half story are made of tightly packed brush, trimmed off evenly and painted a reddish-brown. At the eastern entrance of the monastery are two poles with prayer flags and several large white-washed chortans, one of which is topped by brass with large figures worked into the surface. It is highly polished and shines brilliantly in the sunshine. The roofs of the temple bear big brass ornaments, some of them figures of deer. Although much of the ornamentation and furnishing is similar to the other temples we have seen, there are fewer mural paintings of gods and demons than at Kumbum, and none of the interior pillars are encased in rugs. The images are mostly gilded and range in size from small to giants up to twenty or thirty feet tall. We stopped to look in the kitchen where several enormous cauldrons were being heated over brush fires to the accompaniment of a chanting priest and, just as at Kumbum, the whole place reeked of smoke and rancid butter. Next door was the refectory where the monks partake of their buttered tea, and the pavement of stones between it and the kitchen were polished and slippery with spilled butter. The main temple was a dark and spacious room with the only light coming from one small door and a row of butter lamps across a back wall. The air was stale and rank with the odor of rancid butter. On the floor were rows of very dirty mats where the monks would sit; the wooden floor between them was caked with spilled butter and my hob-nailed boots slipped and slid about on it. The lamps across the back inadequately lit up the many images and figures, among which, we were told, were the mummified bodies of former Living Buddhas. If so, they must have shrunk a great deal in the process. There was also a pair of elephant tusks whose rounded ends glinted in the dim light, having been polished by the touch of innumerable hands.

We climbed upstairs on steps slippery with butter, out onto a flat roof. Beside a pair of brass deer an old priest in red robes pounded hollow sticks together at regular intervals, making sonorous sounds. At the back was another recessed story where a second monk was engaged in a series of obeisances. He looked as though he was going through sitting-up exercises. Through windows covered with wire netting we saw some silver pyramid shapes which, we were told, contained more bodies of ex-Living Buddhas. Hanging from the roofs were a number of bells, mostly brass, although the largest was cast iron with figures and characters in Chinese and Tibetan. They gave a very pleasant sound.

In one of the courtyards the boy monks were learning their lessons, without much seriousness, and our presence quite distracted them. Their books had wooden covers, and they practiced writing in damp sand spread out on the ground.

We returned to town through a bazaar where we bought some small watermelons which were not very good, although quite expensive as we also purchased a leg of mutton for about half their price. The watermelons were wet and refreshing nonetheless. They are not raised here but are brought in from Lanchow, a week's journey away.

Sun has received a letter from the man in charge of the fort where our robbers were incarcerated. Part of it was in Chinese and part was in very bad English, just to show, I suppose, that the man knew the language. It explained that the robbers had been let off with a slap on the wrist and a promise to be good. We also have received an invitation on large red paper from General Huang, inviting us to luncheon tomorrow. It would be impolite to refuse such an invitation, and we shall take great pleasure in informing Suez as he was so sure we would get a poor reception here.

Labrang
August 18, 1937

This morning we did little but sit around in our one-room apartment over an odoriferous stable. We asked our Tibetan hostess and one of her friends to put on their best clothes and come up to the roof to be photographed. They obliged with enthusiasm and giggles. Our hostess wore the same hairdress with polished brass disks, but appeared in a splendid robe with two large silver ornaments hanging from the girdle; to one of these was attached a case containing a knife and two chopsticks worked in gold and silver. The other woman's hair was covered with forty silver dollars as well as smaller coins, in place of the usual brass disks.

Our luncheon invitation was for 2:00 P.M., so at about 1:30 we started off on horse and mule-back so as to arrive with dignity. The three of us, plus our two majors, conversed with General Huang for a short time and then were joined by three American missionaries from local missions, a Pentecostal one and the Christian Alliance. They seemed like good fellows for missionaries, and we all had a very pleasant time. The meal was strictly Chinese but one of the best since Shanghai, and we thoroughly enjoyed it—all but the sea slugs, which I was disappointed to find on the menu. The wine was very strong, and it fell to Fred and me to drink most of it for the missionaries did not drink, one of our majors is a practicing Mohammedan, and Sun knows how to get out of it gracefully. Before we were finished my head was spinning. General Huang had a nice silver service in the Chinese style consisting of two small dishes apiece, a small cup and saucer for the wine, and a large spoon, all intricately engraved with Tibetan patterns. The chopsticks were made of ivory.

I have wanted to get one or two of the paintings Tibetans have in their temples, so Sun told Huang of my wish. It happens that such pictures are not usually sold as they are painted only on the order of someone who wishes to present them to a temple. However, the general will try to find one for me that some painter may have available, although I am dubious of the success of the search. Sun told him that I had previously acquired many Buddhist paintings from India and made obeisance to them in my home in America. The general was surprised and noted rather bruskly, "Protestants do not like Buddhist pictures."

In the evening we went by invitation to the Christian Alliance mission across the river to listen to radio broadcasts from Nanking, Manila, and Tokyo. There was too much static, but we did learn more about the Japanese situation. This time we heard that the bombs which fell on Shanghai were dropped by Chinese trying to hit Japanese gunboats in the river there. They flew high and made no allowance for the strong wind which was blowing, and although the Japanese flagship was hit and considerably damaged, more of the bombs went astray. The Cathay Hotel was hit and forty killed, and the English Hong Kong-Shanghai Bank and the National City Bank of New York were both set on fire. Street fighting was taking place on Nanking Road. Mr. Griebenow, the permanent Christian Alliance missionary here, says he believes the Japanese have created this disturbance to distract from their operations in the north where they are attempting to grab off another piece of territory and an important railroad which is the outlet for Inner Mongolia.

Mr. Carlson, the other missionary visiting from a station further south in very rugged country, is on his way to Hochow to a missionary conference. He and Griebenow appear to spend most of their time treating people for syphilis, which is prevalent here. It would seem that there are few real conversions being made; in fact, Griebenow tells of one of their converts who returned to his home village where he was set upon by his neighbors with knives and killed. He says that although General Huang and his No. 1 Living Buddha brother appear to be friendly with the mission, most of the monks are openly antagonistic and vehemently hate the missionaries. Griebenow has just returned from a trip among the nomads in country near a mountain that some believe to be higher than Mt. Everest. He is an excellent photographer and has a great collection of pictures taken during his fifteen years out here. I am sincerely sorry that I did not have the time to study them more carefully. The American who authored that infamous book on Tibet stayed with Griebenow for about a month. Fred has borrowed Griebenow's copy which we will read and return to him from Lanchow.

I almost forgot to mention that we were served apple pie!

On the road
August 19-20, 1937

We have been traveling with the Carlsons and the Griebenows, who are on their way to the conference in Hochow. They, their wives, children, and servants added to our own entourage have made a sizable caravan. They usually travel across the uplands, but we wanted to see the outcrops along the valley so they have come along with us for a few days' change of scene. We spent much of the first day going all the way down a lovely valley cut in metamorphic rock and granite. We passed through small Tibetan villages where the grain was being harvested, and the women worked in the fields with their robes hanging down from their waists on account of the heat, although they continued to wear their sheepskin or fur hats. In some places the bottom of the valley was full of large bushes and trees, among them a kind of sumac, a spiney gooseberry, and big rose bushes with a few flowers still hanging on them. This area is a great one for pheasants. The south side of the valley is covered with fir trees, and we saw more forest in one day than in all the rest of the trip so far. It is the abundance of trees here that enables farmers to build pole racks for hanging grain waiting to be thrashed. Also, many of the fields are separated from the road, not by mud walls as elsewhere, but by brush fences made of branches woven between slender stakes driven into the ground. In and about Labrang we saw mud walls in which sheep and yak bones were used in place of stone and brick. In comparison to Labrang this place looks pastoral and refreshing.

The river we have been following is swift with rapids, but it is generally narrow and we have crossed and recrossed it over numerous rickety bridges. Local forests supply the wood for the rafts going down river. The rafts, made of poles, are about 100 feet long by 6 feet wide and are bound together so that they are flexible and can bend around curves. Men at either end steer them with large sweeps.

We spent last night at a miserable inn in Wang Kan T'an where the innkeeper retired early with his lamp and pipe to enjoy the solace of opium.

Today we continued down the same pretty valley which shows some interesting geology. Except for a light drizzle that started about noon and stayed with us into the afternoon, it has been an enjoyable day. This region seems to get more rain than others we have traveled. The north-facing slopes of the hills are covered with fir forest and the south sides with bushes and grass. The trail has been rough and rocky, bordered by many small trees, among them wild apricots and crab-apple, a birch much like our yellow species, and an oak of the general white variety. The local elderberry produces orange-red berries instead of the blue-black fruit we are accustomed to.

At one point we passed through a gap in a very old stone wall that the missionaries say is the ancient boundary between Tibet and China. Just outside the village where we have stopped is a mud wall, supposedly part of the Great Wall of China, which was repaired here and there a couple of years ago when the Communists passed through this region. The Carlsons left their mission only three days ahead of the Red arrival. He has a specimen of their paper money with a portrait of Lenin and Chinese characters.

We had tea and cookies with the missionaries and later a wonderful dinner of roast duck and the first loaf of real bread we have seen in months. Tomorrow we should be in Hochow.

Hochow
August 21, 1937

We are now back in China, and I suppose that our adventures in "Forbidden Tibet" are a closed chapter. Late yesterday afternoon I noticed that the architecture had changed rather suddenly, from houses with flat mud roofs to gabled roofs covered with tiles or slate. I thought at first that this reflected the "Chinese Style", but then remembered that all roofs were flat on our way west from Lanchow—we slept on them—and those were all Chinese villages. Then, influenced by the falling rain, I decided these roofs were designed for a wetter region and the slanting was needed for drainage. It has been raining steadily most of the day, and our road along the Tao Hsai Ho has been one mud hole after another. We have been caked with the stuff from the knees on down. The cultivated valley we passed through was covered with fields of grass; the wheat has been cut and stacked against the farmers' houses, and broad beans and rape are being harvested. We are in melon country, and we see small piles of them along the wayside and in eating stands. We are again in the poppy district, but this crop is smaller than that of the valley west of Lanchow. The season is long since past, and only stalks and pods are in the fields.

In mid-afternoon we arrived in Hochow, the largest city we have seen for a long time, probably about the same size as Sining. We scouted for an appropriate inn and found one, where people had to be chased out of the principal apartments so we could move in. It is better than many places we have stopped recently except for the flies which, for the first time on our trip, are really bad. Sun, our two majors, and I went to the Post Office where I found a note from Suez and cashed a check for $100. Although I have had enough money for our traveling needs, I have not had much excess, and it feels better to have pockets bulging with paper cash. We presented our cards to the pleasant elderly postmaster who escorted us into his private office off a small courtyard planted with dahlias. We had tea and asked about the war. The local newspapers are quite inadequate, and we learned little new about conditions east of us.

Fred and I bought some not very flavorful "drunken melons", but they were wet which gave them purpose. At dinner we ate a local cantaloupe which I found as good as some I have eaten at home. I also tried some white peaches, which were small, specked, hard, and without much merit.

Ho Tzu Kuo Men
August 22, 1937

This morning we packed up, said goodby to our Tsinghai soldiers, and left Hochow—gladly, because all of us got fleas from the inn we thought so fancy. Outside the south gate we passed through a rather extensive suburb with its main street lined with shops and great piles of vegetables and melons, and as we approached the river we noticed the establishments of the timber merchants who raft the many stacks of poles downstream. We crossed a bridge built of poles and covered with brush and earth and eventually connected with the cart road we have been following all day. For about forty li it went south up a tributary valley to a ridge 1,500 feet above Hochow and turned generally eastward down another valley. A fine rain started falling, so after riding another twenty li we decided to stop here. Although our ponchos have kept us relatively dry, the road became very slick and the animals had a hard time keeping on their feet.

Except for places where the road followed along a stream bed or was intersected with bottomless mud holes, it was not too bad; I have driven over worse ones in Illinois. In fact, there were places where trees and bush obscured the terraced hillsides, and I could easily imagine I was in southern Illinois. As this is the main road between Hochow and Lanchow, we passed several groups of carts outward bound, loaded with blue-striped Chinese mail bags, each pulled by one or two small mules or horses which struggled desperately to keep the carts underway. A few of the carts were equipped with motor truck wheels and rubber tires, and the tire marks left in the mud looked ridiculously incongruous in this setting. At one place, parked by the roadside and partially covered with weeds, was an old and battered four-wheeled hack of faded green, much like the old-fashioned cabs we had in Chicago before taxis. Minus one wheel, the door secured with a cheap padlock, it obviously belonged to someone of substance who had met with grief in the middle of a journey.

Today, for the first time, I saw corn growing in the northwest countryside. It is grown elsewhere, because we have seen boiled ears being sold in the markets, but I have not seen the fields before. The stalks are short and runty, the ears little and irregular, and it would take no prizes in our country. Our return to civilization is evidenced by the number of bicycles on the road. I have also seen one cheap motorcyle, which was the wonder of all beholders. The peddlers are again our fellow travelers, trinkets swinging from the ends of their carrying poles.

Our inn here is small and doubtful, but we had no other choice because it's the only one there is and the rain was falling fast. We came in through the gate to a court full of mud and water and dismounted in a building whose roof leaks from at least a dozen places. We had tea in the family's quarters at the back of a second court and are to sleep upstairs in the building beside the gate. I have yet to survey the accommodations, but my expectations are not high. The cook has just reported that dried eggs are cheap here; seven for ten cents Chinese (less than half a cent U.S.). In Labrang the same price bought only four.

Liu Chia Tsan
August 24, 1937

I did not write yesterday because I was not in good humor. Though we had fleas in Hochow, our inn at Ho Tzu Kuo Men was alive with them. Before going to bed Sun got nearly twenty out of his stockings. They bedded down with me in regiments and, after trying to ignore them, at 1:30 A.M. I finally had to give up. They were not only crawling and biting, they were dropping from the ceiling like sand and jumping about my face. I got up and, after shaking out all my clothes, got dressed and spent the rest of the night sitting out on the balcony. It was cool and my clothing was not very warm, so I spent the time until morning shivering, although not violently enough to keep the fleas from their irritating business. Last night when I undressed, I went over my clothes carefully and caught dozens of the damned things that had been at work on me for nearly twenty-four hours. I am a mass of bites (too many to count), all itching like blazes. Sun was restless that night, but I think he mostly slept through it, and Fred was totally oblivious, snoring away in grand style. Anyway, I sat out on the balcony and surveyed the place. Although the night was cloudy, the moon was full and quite a bit of light filtered through. There were four watch dogs and one of them, seeing me, an unfamiliar object in the shadows, barked endlessly. For want of something better to do, I counted his barks at the rate of over 100 per minute. The family and the mule men were quiet and peaceful; they seemed used to and undisturbed by the fleas biting and the dog barking. The first sign of life in the morning was an opening door in the small building across the way from which a man in a short sheepskin coat emerged, followed by a dirty white horse. After an interval a young woman came out, sat down on the doorstep, and proceeded to search herself for fleas and other vermin, starting with the wrappings of her bound feet.

Last night we were more particular about our lodgings and selected a small inn in a very tiny village because it looked neat and clean. It cost the princely sum of $1.00 for the night. Its court, unlike the usual swill of trampled stable refuse, was nicely swept, and along one side were planted several bushes of tall dahlias and a squash vine. There was only one sleeping room, so even though it looked a bit like rain Sun, No. 1 boy, and I set up our cots in the courtyard, and Fred and the cook took over the room.

While our mules were being unloaded we sat in the room on the kang to write up our geological notes, since we continue with our reports even though we have not found the oil we have been looking for. It was much too hot for comfort. Apparently, at many places through here, kangs are heated even in summer. The space beneath is stuffed with straw and other more objectionable rubbish and set on fire. The opening is closed, and it smoulders on almost indefinitely.

A Kan Chen
August 25, 1937

A small shower did overtake us in the small hours of the morning while we slept in the courtyard, but ponchos spread over our beds prevented serious discomfort.

I am falling rather sadly behind in my accounts, but after riding some eight hours and then writing up my geological notes, I do not always feel like writing letters. Also, it is beginning to get dark earlier, and we go to bed as soon as the sun goes down as our only light is a candle, and there is usually too much breeze to use it.

It was cloudy when we set off in the morning. We were annoyed on and off by misty rain, although it was not as bad as the day before when a stiff, raw wind blew it straight into our faces. Our road led northwest away from the river, through heavily covered loess land where it was badly washed-out and, in some places, deeply sunken. Although the fields were terraced except on the steeper slopes, the area was totally deserted, and the mule men mumbled about robbers. Presently we came to a small city and, as we skirted its western wall, soldiers appeared and demanded Sun's passport. It was taken inside for inspection and not returned for some fifteen minutes, while we waited. They did not bother either Fred or me. We continued up the valley and, just beyond Chun Pu, came into some very rugged country with desolate barren hills of Tertiary sandstone like that which forms the first gorge of the Huang Ho west of Lanchow. The valley forked, and at the intersection was an extremely small village where the mule men paused for bowls of noodles. We rode on further and ate our sandwiches made with native bread by the side of a stream. From here the trail became a narrow and rocky defile that has a particularly bad reputation for robbers so, at the suggestion of the mule men, our guns were unslung. It is my belief that a few robberies along some sections of the road assures the whole area a bad name forevermore. In any case, weather and fears aside, we found the geology of the region interesting and gave the beds along the streams some careful study as we went along. We reached an elevation of nearly 8,000 feet along a ridge before descending again through the same kinds of rocks and dropped some 1,500 feet to A Kan Chen.

The word for this village, like most of the others we have been through, is "dismal". The principal differences are that it is the center of the coal trade, and the population is now less Mohammedan and more Chinese. The streets are endless holes of mud. We are only about forty li outside of Lanchow and ought to be there tomorrow.

The last few days we have seen some very interesting country. From Ho Tzu Kuo Men, we traveled through Chi Chin Chi to the valley of the Tao Tsai Ho, which was a wide and fertile place with many small corn fields and walled gardens full of pear and apple trees and another tree whose clusters of red berries are used like pepper. A good crop of pears seems likely this year as the trees are heavily laden with growing fruit. An ingenious device is used here to prevent branches from breaking from the weight of the crop. A tall pole is erected in the middle of each tree's growing area, and from the top hang many small ropes to which the drooping branches are tied. It seems a better scheme than propping them up from below as we do, but it makes an orchard look like a cluster of miniature radio towers. Flower gardens are common, mainly planted with dahlias, orange and Chinese lilies, and cosmos. Some of the squash and pumpkin vines have been trained onto poles so that the fruit hangs in mid-air about eight or ten feet above the ground. In one garden I saw a pretty yellow pumpkin (the Chinese name means "good-looking melon") on which someone had carved a lovely, intricate design of flowers which was preserved as a scar on its surface.

When we reached the Tao Tsai Ho, we ferried over on a rather small boat fastened to a cable stretched across the river. It could carry four or five mules at a time; with our eleven animals and their loads, several trips back and forth were required, which took about one and a half hours. On our side of the river we found a small eating place and bakery, and while we waited for the ferry we observed the baker who was making bread. He cut the dough and rolled, twisted, and flattened each piece in a peculiar way. It was smeared with yellow oil and finely chopped onion tops, and then the flattened disks, which were thin in the middle and thick around the edges, were slid into the oven four at a time. The oven was a round, cast iron, concave pan set over a fire and covered by a large sheet of iron full of live coals. The bread looked and smelled so good when it emerged that we could not resist, and we bought a round and ate it right on the spot while it still steamed.

Having crossed the river we went downstream along the other side, past two paddle-wheel mill boats. Here we were in an extensive tobacco raising district. At first I didn't recognize the plants as they didn't look at all like the Kentucky variety. In flower with yellow blossoms, they were small and sickly looking. The walled gardens produced crabapples, some of which were ripe. These were arranged at wayside stands in neat piles of five to tempt the passersby, but most of them were wormy and blotched and not very attractive.

We passed through one city whose well-kept wall was fronted by a very respectable suburb, but once inside we discovered only fields and a few houses along the main street. I wondered if this was the result of recent fighting in the area, if perhaps the city had been demolished and not yet rebuilt. Since crossing the river we have entered another military district and have been stopped several times by soldiers armed with both swords and rifles. They have all questioned Sun, closely inspected his card and, not infrequently, his passport. Chinese is certainly a peculiar language; a few simple questions and answers seem to provoke an endless period of conversation.

Lanchow
August 25, 1937

This morning Fred, who has developed a case of diarrhea, came directly into Lanchow, but Sun and I and one of the mule men climbed nearly 1,000 feet up the hill north of A Kan Chen to see the Jurassic coal fields there. We passed through the home village of the mule man, and he disappeared just long enough to exchange the tattered wide-brimmed straw hat he has worn all during the trip for a "new", somewhat soiled, stiff straw one of western style. He also exchanged his padded black jacket for three white cotton ones.

As I expected, the coal mines were primitive, with steeply inclined shafts up which naked men carried sacks of coal on their backs. The largest mine employed twenty men; each produced about 300 catties (400 lbs.) of coal per day, worth about $3, each miner earning 75 percent. If the miners did not have to pay all the mine's expenses out of their percentage of the take, they would be relatively rich men. I doubt if any of them were over thirty years of age; the work is so strenuous that an older man could probably not endure it. The coal is carried to Lanchow in wicker baskets or yak hair bags by mule-back and, as we continued towards the city, we passed an almost continuous procession of men and mules with empty loads returning for another trip.

This road led down the hill, a decline of almost 2,500 feet, the steepest part in loess worn down in places some forty feet. As the grade became gentler we passed through a succession of small villages which, due to the rains, were filled with vile smelling slimy mud. The children, however, seemed to love it, and many were deep in it making mud pies of the repulsive stuff and smiling from ear to ear.

It had rained in Lanchow during the day, and its streets were a mass of sticky black mud. At last, we are back in the city where we started from about two months ago. We are stopping at the Kun Lun Hotel, Chinese of course. We were not satisfied with the officers' club here before, but this place may turn out to be worse.

Lanchow
August 27, 1937

It seems quite natural to be back in Lanchow again, as the streets are familiar even if they are ankle-deep in mud. A pile of mail was waiting for us, mostly newspapers, too old to be of much interest, and magazines. Unfortunately, we have forgotten what was happening in the continued stories we were reading in the *Saturday Evening Post,* and one issue is missing. I have arranged the newspapers in order, from June 20 to August 9, and glancing over them I find no news of the outbreak of hostilities in the north. I understand that little mail has come from Shanghai since the martial situation developed there. I also received five anxiously anticipated letters from home and the first of my Leica photographs. They are small prints and hard to see, but I have some good pictures. I am wondering what has happened to my second batch, sent from Kueite; they must have reached Shanghai after the hostilities began. Also, what has become of my letter to Yen asking for Suez's recall?

Our hotel is the best place we have roosted in since leaving Lanchow in early July, but it is far from a palace. Fred, Sun, and I have a suite on the first floor at the end of the second court, consisting of a small bedroom where Fred is established and a large sitting room with our other two beds. Suez has a small room to himself (thank God) nearby. Our greatest objection to the place is the noise. Last night there was a spirited Mah-Jong party overhead that went on with much talking and tile-clicking until early morning. All afternoon there has been a dinner party across the way where the finger game was played, accompanied by loud shouts. At first we were plagued by pesky flies until, at last, our Flit was dug out and they were exterminated.

Last evening it rained again, and the mud in the streets has been reactivated. As I have probably mentioned before, there are no real sidewalks here, only narrow ledges of uneven width and height, and because each walkway is interrupted by stairs and pillars, etc., one must be an acrobat to navigate it. When you add the hordes of Chinese going and coming and dodging one another, progress is slow and uncertain.

In the morning Sun and I "walked" to the post office to mail letters and found it closed for Confucius's birthday. We then went to the hospital to pay our respects to Dr. Han who had returned yesterday from Nanking and Sian, but as he was not expected to report there today, we went to his house and found him still in bed. I went on alone to the Seventh Day Adventist mission outside the south gate of the city where I had a nice visit and got the latest news from their radio. The situation in Shanghai is indeed serious. It is estimated that $500,000,000 in damage has been done. The American flagship aboard which we had dinner last spring was struck, killing one sailor and injuring eighteen more. Yesterday the British ambassador, driving from Nanking to Shanghai, was attacked and wounded by a Jap airplane. I am sure you have probably heard all of this and more, and I am glad that you know I am not in Shanghai. Here, we are about as far away from the trouble as one can get and in no danger. It is rumored, however, that thirty Japanese spies have been rounded up in this part of the country and brought here today to be imprisoned. I certainly do not envy them.

Our plans for the future are a little bit uncertain. What I want to do is ship our provisions and equipment by motor truck to Suchow, which is the last city in northwestern Kansu inside the Great Wall. We would follow by plane, now that the Eurasia Company's weekly service has resumed in that direction. From Suchow we would set off with mules and make a circuit to the west around the Yu Men and Tun Huang areas, which would require a month or six weeks, and then work our way back to Lanchow, also with mules, which would take us up to early December. Just how all this would work out I do not yet know. I do know that no trucks can leave here at present because of the mud-clogged roads.

Section from a geologic report of this area:

The oil possibilities of southern Kansu and northeastern Tsinghai appear to be entirely negligible. Although structures favorable for the accumulation of oil may be present in some of the Tertiary basins and although the Tertiary sandstones and conglomerates are suitable for reservoir beds should oil be present, the Tertiary beds are not the type of sediments that might be expected to give rise to petroleum. Possible source beds do occur, however, in the Permian and Cretaceous systems, but strata of these ages wherever seen are much deformed, compressed into close folds, and broken by many faults, and there is no way of determining where these strata may underlie the Tertiary red beds. The general structure of this region is such that if oil were present, there would almost certainly be some seepages along the mountain flanks where the generally synclinal Tertiary strata are faulted against or overlap the older rocks. The total absence of known seepages, therefore, seems to be sufficient to condemn this region as being unworthy of further consideration.

Lanchow
August 29, 1937

Fred and I spent most of yesterday working on our sections and maps, and we now have more than 1,000 kilometers drawn up. I have practically finished my particular tasks, but Fred has been reducing the maps to a scale suitable for showing the geology seen along our routes, which takes more time, and he is still at it. Today is cloudy and cool, and I have polished off our stack of newspapers, probably the last we shall see for a long time.

The news, of course, is largely concentrated on the Japanese conflict. It is obvious from the sequence of events that this has been a deliberate aggression by the Japanese. Dr. Han was in Nanking at the time of the first air raid, and there have been others subsequently. The one he witnessed involved a small group of Jap planes which engaged the Chinese one night, and while they were thus occupied, fifty bombers flew in and did much damage. Among other buildings, the Communications Administration was destroyed, but this has been kept out of the newspapers.

The Japanese say they are determined to beat China to her knees. Chinese sentiments are unanimous for a prolonged resistance. One plan that is being given consideration is to retreat, fighting every inch of the way, moving the entire population inland and destroying everything that must be left behind so that the Japanese will claim only empty and desolate land, thus emulating tactics used by the Russians against Napoleon. Such a decision would be a desperate one, but the situation to be met is also desperate. Dr. Han, who probably reflects the thought prevailing in Nanking, says that if these tactics could be employed, Japan would probably crack from the strain within two years. To do this, however, he feels that one fifth of the entire Chinese population would have to be sacrificed, which would be several times the total casualty list of the Great European War.

The Japanese trouble will necessitate no particular change in our immediate plans. Suez and Sun have been received by Governor Ho, who will issue our passports for travel to the northwest and give us letters of introduction to the generals in command out there. Arrangements have been made for two motor trucks to transport us and our equipment in as far as Suchow. We are supposed to start next Thursday.

We are I think in one of the two safest areas in the country; the other is Yunnan in the south. In the extreme west, the intervening country between the east and here would have to be conquered before hostilities could reach our vicinity, and because of the slight economic importance of this region, it seems unlikely that Japanese air raids will be extended here. The question of getting out of the country is another matter; by the time we return here after our work is finished, it may be impossible to leave from any Chinese port. There are other exits, however, through French Indochina, India, or Russia. These routes would involve inconvenience and considerable time, but they will be open because, though other countries may be drawn into the conflict, it is inconceivable to me that France, England, or Russia could ever become allied with Japan. Therefore, you need have no fear for our safety. My only concern is that the outgoing mails may be greatly hampered or stopped and that you may hear from me most irregularly, tardily, or not at all.

Lanchow
August 30, 1937

After two fairly nice days the streets were just beginning to dry, and then it rained again. I braved the mire this morning and walked out to the Seventh Day Adventist mission to check on the news. I also saw a couple of Shanghai newspapers dated August 12 and 13 and noted with interest that the American who wrote that ludicrous book on Tibet is covering the conflict here for the *March of Time*. So you do not have to believe everything you see in the news reels.

It appears that today a government order went out commandeering all motor trucks so we may be out of luck as far as that type of transportation is concerned. It looks like preparations are being made to run munitions and guns down from Russia. It has been announced in the local papers that a treaty has been arranged between China and Russia agreeing not to encroach upon one another's territory, although one may suspect that its provisions and implications go much farther than that.

If we cannot get trucks our trip northwest must be made with mules. This would mean that it will take a good three weeks just to reach Suchow. However, we shall be in no great hurry to start because developments in the next week may be very important to our future plans. I would not be surprised if we should be recalled; on the other hand, with transportation pretty well disrupted near the coast, I don't know how we could get out that way even if we wanted to. One of the missionaries told me that their people in Sian had been advised to move inland, which means here. Obviously, if and when we move northwestward, we shall have in mind that it may be necessary to keep going in that direction rather than coming back this way. We shall certainly be prepared to do so if necessary and to that end plan to take all the essentials with us.

In a way all this uncertainty is quite intriguing, and could I be sure that you were not terribly worried about me I should rather enjoy my personal situation. We have enough money and provisions to get clear of China; the only thing that concerns me at all is that we may not be able to get at our money when we need it. The govenrment has issued stringent regulations regarding withdrawal of money from banks, intended, I presume, to prevent the flight of capital from the country. However, I believe an exception could be made in our case, which is all very well and fine, but there are no banks west of here so we must rely on the post office for funds. This is something to worry about when the time comes.

Lanchow
August 31, 1937

Another miserable day. It has rained steadily and is cold—almost down to 50 degrees. There is no place to go and nothing to do.

Today Governor Ho's representatives returned our passports for Suchow, so that formality is over and we are free to go when we can. The roads are impassable to trucks, so even if we had them they wouldn't be very useful to us now.

We have been doing a great deal of talking about plans and have almost made up our minds not to return here but to continue west and go out through Russia or India. If the war continues it will be impossible to get back to Shanghai, and our only other alternative is to stay here for the duration, an unpleasant thought at best.

Lanchow
September 2, 1937

Time passes so tediously there is little to write about. We went to Dr. Han's for dinner one evening and met a Mr. Taylor of the British Boxer Indemnity Board, who is here inspecting schools. A rather small man in his fifties who has spent the greater part of his life in China, he did not seem greatly perturbed by the present situation. After dinner we stayed and listened to the radio, but the Nanking broadcast was interrupted by static that Dr. Han said was of Japanese manufacture. Before hostilities these air waves were quite clear.

The mail plane came in today, but in spite of our hopes there was nothing for us. We did get a paper that came by truck, dated July 16.

This afternoon I wandered out to the mission to find out what they had heard of the war. The principal item of interest was received by the American Consul at Hankow and strongly advised all Americans in the interior to get out while the getting was good. The British have not been ordered out, but I understand they have been told that if they stay they take the same chances as the Chinese and will not be protected. The missionaries intend to stick around and see how things develop. Meanwhile, telegraph communication is slow and uncertain, and the last air mail took eight days. It is our guess that Yen has left Shanghai because we have not heard a word from him since the trouble began. So, for all practical purposes we are cut off from the rest of the world. I would hate to have to give up our work just as we are getting started; if we have to leave now all our time spent would be wasted. If we had assurances that we would be allowed to pass on through Chinese Turkistan, I could make up my mind what to do. We are going to try to see Governor Ho tomorrow to ask him to wire General Sheng in Urumchi for his support. If it is forthcoming, I think we shall just go ahead about our business as though earthshaking events were not in progress.

Lanchow begins to pall. The streets are awash in foul-smelling black mud, and we have not seen the sun for days. We are fairly comfortable in our large room, but that is all. One wall is decorated with a large portrait of Sun Yat-sen between two lithographs of stags in attack positions. They are super-realistic, even to the billowing breath issuing from their nostrils. On the other wall is a calendar advertising something or other and an official-looking document with Chiang Kai-shek's picture and flags across the top, which is most likely either a permit of some kind or appropriate and friendly instructions to the hotel guests. Next to these are two scrolls of Chinese characters on gold paper edged with red and between them a water color of a poorly proportioned horse with polished hooves and a wild eye. The other two walls are lattice covered with thin paper, one facing out onto the court, the other separating the big room from Fred's bedroom. In it he has another pair of gold paper scrolls and between them a lion, probably by the same artist who painted the horse. This King of Beasts has a great mane which dwarfs the rest of him as he stands on an overhanging rock that looks ready to fall on Fred's bed.

I have solved a mystery. Every morning I have heard a peculiar whistling noise that waxes and wanes but is rarely ever silenced. Now I know that it is made by pigeons who fly about with their feathers humming in the air.

Lanchow
September 3, 1937

One more day. It is still cloudy with slight sprinkles, but it is warmer.

We had another noisy night. A loud individual above us, a salesman for a tobacco company, seems to run his promotions with the aid of Mah-Jong games. There was disruptive yelling and clicking and clacking into the wee hours. Suez says that when this gentleman learned two American geologists were here, he wanted to interest us in some gold and jade mines he owns in the Kun Lun mountains. Suez squelched him.

One of the rooms opening onto our court is occupied by a woman who is the wife of an army officer stationed here and two or three small children. She is quite a shrew, and on occasions streams of the most violent sounding language issue from her apartment. Suez says she swears most horribly and profanely. Today there was a great commotion again, and Suez reports that it is a fuss over the husband's new concubine.

This morning we received word that the local governor cannot help us obtain permission to pass through Sinkiang Province should it be necessary for us to proceed out of China that way. On a more positive note, however, Suez has received a telegram from Mr. Chow in Shanghai, which has relieved my mind considerably. If Chow is still in Shanghai, then conditions there must not be so very bad. Since this telegram reached us in two days, it appears that we are not as cut off from the east as I had supposed. Also, his request that we continue with our work must mean that he believes we are in no particular danger from the war. Furthermore, Suez has been instructed to remain in Lanchow rather than accompany us into the northwest, which must be a result of my letter to Yen. This means that we will be relieved of the irritation of his company in the field, plus his presence here will provide us with a rear guard to keep us posted as to conditions and to pull any political strings that may be necessary. So, it is without misgivings that we prepare to follow our original plans.

Lanchow
September 7, 1937

We were scheduled to leave yesterday by motor truck for Suchow, but the contractor announced that our departure must be delayed a day or two. As it happens, it is just as well because today the sun was out, the first nice day since we have been here, so by tomorrow the road west out of here should be partially dried up and in fairly good shape.

We will leave town pretty well-healed, with over $1,000 in cash and a money order on the Suchow post office for $1,500 more, which ought to see us through a couple of months. We are feeling not only terribly rich but important. All trucks are being held for goverrment service, and gasoline to run them is almost impossible to find. We, however, have two trucks of our very own as well as money and a dry road! Morale has risen several notches, and we are anxious to be out and running again.

Most of the missionaries are staying. It is impossible to tell from the Chinese papers exactly what is happening, but propaganda is flying about thick and fast. This morning the paper carried a tale about the Japanese putting rings through the noses of their prisoners and tying them up like cattle. Can it be true?

On the road
September 9, 1937

Afternoon:

I am taking advantage of delay caused by a hot box on our truck to write.

We thought we would get away early yesterday morning because the trucks were loaded the day before, but Suez did not get the proper clearance papers from the tax office so the police made a detailed inspection of our baggage and wanted to tax our canned goods. This necessitated a special trip to the govenrment house by Suez and Sun to get the matter straightened out. We finally got away from the hotel about noon and crossed the Huang Ho bridge where we were stopped by soldiers on guard who spent an hour reviewing our passports.

We have two trucks, a new International and an older Chevrolet, and there is another one, also a Chevrolet, traveling along with us. We must carry all of the gasoline and oil for the trip up and back, which takes up about half the load. When our goods are piled on, we sit on the top. Riding is rough and we must hang on desperately. The third truck is not only fully loaded but is also carrying thirty people who cling anywhere they can. The theory that a live load doesn't weigh anything keeps trucks overloaded and abused. The third truck had a flat tire yesterday, which is no wonder; I expect we shall experience many more along the way.

The road was fairly good at first as we drove west along the north side of the river. A section of the Great Wall once extended along here and in some places is in ruined evidence, although in other spots it has been repaired and crowned with small block houses. The rocks that formed these hills are metamorphic and grey granite. We turned to the north up a gorge and began to rise in elevation, gradually working up into the beds that lie over the metamorphics. The valley widened out and a good rain could easily flood it, making the road impassable. We did get stuck several times in wet gravel; once we sank down to the running boards but, with time and the efforts of a dozen men, were freed.

After the gorge the road led through much eroded red beds covered by loess. The area was dry, and many of the small streams were salty. We went up and down several divides, the highest about 1,500 feet above Lanchow. At dusk, after covering about forty-five miles in seven hours, we emerged into a large valley coming down from the north and stopped at a small village called Hsu Chia Mo. There was no inn so we slept out in front of some shops right in the street.

Today we continued up the valley, passing through a number of small mud villages and individual farmsteads like tiny castles, their mud walls about twenty feet thick with watch towers in the corners. At one we were stopped by soldiers and our guns and licenses were carefully examined. This valley, irrigated by the Chuang-lang Ho, seemed prosperous, but the crops were nearly all harvested and it looked very bare. The dried bean and poppy stalks were bundled and piled high on the roofs for winter fuel.

A good straight motor road has been graded for a distance up the valley, but we could not use it because it has no bridges, so we wound in and out of the fields and through the willow trees planted by a Manchu general who campaigned here some 100 years ago. They have been topped so many times for fire wood that they are very misshapen and strange looking. We have seen many caves dug into the hillsides, but practically none of them are now inhabited.

Evening:

After two hours the truck was fixed and we bounced onward. After witnessing this demonstration of unskilled labor, I should hate to entrust my own car to the care of these fellows. We had further delays when the third truck got stuck in a mud hole and, later, had trouble fording a stream. Both times the thirty passengers pulled it out with a frayed rope. Later in the afternoon a small thunderstorm blew down the valley and we took shelter in a small village, but the rain didn't amount to much more than a dust settler. We soon got into country where it had hailed and rained hard, and the road was so flooded in several places that it had to be drained before we could proceed. Slipping, sliding, and plunging through muddy ruts gave us an excellent shaking-up, causing one woman passenger on the third truck to be very sick and spew up over everything. We made fifty-four miles today, which will give you an idea of the quality of the road.

Tonight we have put up in an opium joint—the best place in Cha Kon Yi we could find.

All day we have traveled up the same valley and are now about 3,500 feet above Lanchow. In opium country again, we've seen dried stalks being gathered and bundled and the seeds beaten out of the pods with sticks. This northwest opium is said to be of better quality and cheap, in some places about $1 per ounce. One of our drivers says that he intends to take $10,000 worth of it back to Lanchow. Taxed at seventeen cents per ounce, he will make a heady profit.

A little after noon we passed through Yung Teng where the motor road branches southwest to Sining. There were two walled cities about a mile apart, one the old Manchu city which is now only a mass of ruins, its population killed off by the revolution in 1911 or in the Mohammedan uprising about fifteen years ago. The other was the Chinese city with one whole side of its wall now totally demolished and the area almost all farmed. It is obvious that this area was once much more densely populated. These ruined villages are due either to intermittent fighting here or to the great earthquake that killed thousands of people here in the early 1920's. Long stretches of the Great Wall still stand in this valley, but it is not very remarkable as it is only made of mud and looks just like all the other walls.

Liang Chou
September 11, 1937

We reached Liang Chou safely last evening after a trip of seventy-five miles. We are now approximately 175 miles north-northwest of Lanchow and are staying here to pay a call on General Ma Pu-tsing, Ma Pu-fang's elder brother and commander of the Chinese Fifth Army.

We were quite comfortable in our opium den except for the reek of the smoke both evening and morning. Our start yesterday morning was delayed for fully an hour because our truck motor was so cold it would not start. The driver began working on it at 6:00, and after the battery was completely run down and all other means had failed, the other truck was put to use and pulled us to a start.

Our road continued up the same valley most of the morning. As we climbed, the areas under cultivation grew smaller and the hills greener with grass and wild flowers. Most of the blossoms are gone now except for some purple asters. There were two patches of fir forest, but for the most part the country was treeless. We have been following the Great Wall which has stood as a raggedy mud barrier first on one side of the river and then the other. At the small village of Chen Chong Yi a section of the wall extends clear across the valley from the mountains on one side to those on the other. Here we turned up a side valley to the north and climbed steeply up a very rough track to pass through the mountains at nearly 10,000 feet. The wall also extends up this smaller valley, but here it is in ruins; there are marks on the hillsides showing where still older walls once stood. Down from this pass we came into the great central Asian region of interior drainage where the river which flows down this valley finally loses itself in the wastes of the Gobi Desert. There are no Tertiary beds in this valley; it is cut first in soft metamorphic rocks, then in dipping Triasic red beds, and then back into metamorphic again. The valley is very narrow, like a gorge, and the road is exceedingly rough and rocky. At its narrowest part, the river cuts through a mass of limestone that looks reddish on the steep hillsides, but is beautifully white where worn and washed by the water.

At Ku Lang the valley opens out into the great alluvial plain that extends all the way to Liang Chou and then beyond to the Great Gobi. We stopped there for a belated lunch. So far we have been traveling at a rate of about eight miles an hour. Ku Lang was full of soldiers, and we were delayed after lunch by one of them who insisted on getting a free ride. He first got onto our truck, but Sun managed to get him off; he then added himself to the thirty passengers on the third truck where there arose a long, frantic verbal and gesticulating melee which I thought might result in real trouble, but he was finally pulled off.

Meanwhile, our second driver got out of town with his truck before the soldier could clamber aboard, and ours also lumbered off before the hitchhiker could attempt another assault.

The plain we crossed to Liang Chou seemed level, but slopes gently most of the way. It is composed of fine, light, drab silt much like loess and, as it is irrigated by water from a number of streams flowing out of the hills to the west, we forded one after another rather than trust the bridges, which didn't appear to be any too stable. Along the streams were wide sections of gravel and, at other places, gravel areas that seemed to have been formed by the soil having blown away. It was very dusty, and at places the road had sunk far below the surface, wide enough for only a single vehicle. When there was much traffic there were serious problems, and several times we were held up by carts. Buildings made from local soil blend into the landscape so well that they are not at all conspicuous. Almost everywhere there are ruins of uncertain age.

The people in this region are dirtier and duller looking than any we have encountered thus far. I presume that life has been so hard on them that only the sturdier ones who can live like animals survive. The children are mostly naked, never washed, and invariably each one has a gob of snot hanging from his nose. Most of the women look half-witted, but I suppose that also is a result of their lives as many of the younger girls certainly look bright enough. For the first time I saw a child undergoing the foot-binding process. She was only about eight.

The place where we are lodged is outside the city. It has a very large court, and our three big rooms surround half of it. They are unusually clean because the place is being renovated, but there is as yet no paper plastered over the lattice walls, and we have a constant audience peering in at us. Apparently all the trucks and buses stop here; a while ago one from Suchow came in. The trip took five days. I might add here that the Japs need not be concerned, at least for the present, about the Chinese running munitions down this road from Russia. It is in too poor a condition and the trip takes too long.

I have learned that these trucks cost about $5,000 in Sian. Our trip is costing us $900 for each truck, out of which $100 goes to the renting agents in commissions.

I spent most of the morning hours drawing up a geological cross-section of the road from Lanchow. It is sketchy in parts because a jolting truck is not a very good observation post, and much of the time I was not exactly sure where I was. Anyway, it is done to the best of my ability, and it looks good.

In the afternoon we received word that the General had finished inspecting his troops at the air field and would receive us. His office is nearly a mile from us, but it was a warm day in bright sun, and we enjoyed our walk through the east gate into town. We were followed by our No. 1 boy carrying our presents wrapped in a dirty table cloth. These were two nice pieces of cloth for a suit and ten bricks of tea wrapped in two packages of red paper. The boy soon tired of his load and hired a street boy to carry it for him. The soldiers at the gate were armed only with broad swords, whereas the soldiers we passed in smaller villages have carried not only swords but rifles and belts of hand grenades as well. One soldier stepped smartly up to Sun and brusquely demanded to know where we thought we were going. He seemed quite taken aback when informed that we were calling on the General.

Inside the city wall the main street was unexpectedly wide and smooth, which led me to believe that trucks and carts were not allowed to pass through on it. We turned off on a small side street and arrived at a gate near a parked automobile. Received by the secretary, we were ushered into a waiting room furnished with the usual chairs with soiled blue covers and a few small tables where we were served tea and cigarettes. When the General appeared, he did not look at all like his brother. He was short and chubby, his head was shaved, and he wore a sparse mustache. He shook hands with us and seemed most cordial. Sun told him of our plans, and he promised to wire his officers in towns we expect to pass through and asked us to telegraph him if anything was not done to our liking. The interview was short and to the point.

Many people in China keep crickets in little cages. Actually, they are not crickets but insects something like our cicadas. They keep up a nearly continuous chirping. Yesterday I saw a man carrying a small hawk fastened to his wrist, so apparently hawking is still practiced here to some extent.

Sun has told me about a strange thing in Manchuria. Until 1922 there were no mining laws in China. A code was drawn up giving the landowner the surface rights to his land extending only a foot or two into the ground and giving the underground rights to the government. In Manchuria, coal mining rights were acquired by individuals. The coal was shallow in some areas, however, and the roots of trees worked down to penetrate the coal seams. The miners claimed the trees belonged to them, but the farmers who had planted the trees also claimed them. The dispute was finally settled by dividing the trees equally between the miners and the farmers.

Liang Chou
September 12, 1937

Well, we are delayed here in Liang Chou. As I mentioned, we have three rooms undergoing renovation and there is no paper over the lattice work, so except for the roof over our heads, we are practically living out of doors. During the night a hard wind blew up and covered us with dust, and in the early morning a heavy rain began to pelt in over us. It rained on and off all day, and the court is a mass of mud. The temperature has dropped below 50 degrees, and we have had to get out our sheepskin coats to keep warm. Even if tomorrow is a nice day, I doubt we can leave.

Liang Chou
September 13, 1937

Another day of inactivity. This morning the sun was out, but it gradually clouded over again. I think, however, that the mud produced by yesterday's rain has largely dried up. The streams west of town are said to be high, but if there is no more rain tonight they should be down by tomorrow and we can get off westward.

Shui Chuan Tzu
September 14, 1937

We made fifty-six miles today and are now established for the night in a small Mohammedan restaurant in this village.

We started out about 8:30 this morning and to my surprise, drove right through the center of Liang Chou along the main street which I had supposed was in too good a condition to be used for ordinary transportation. Beyond the west gate, instead of a suburb similar to the one in which we stayed, there were some very extensive cemeteries. The graves were either small mounds covered with pebbles or little brick walls with miniature gateways facing east or southeast. We crossed many streams and irrigation channels and had not gone more than two miles before our second truck got stuck in the mud. It was pulled out in short order with a long rope and the help of some passersby. Farther on we came to great stretches of gravel-covered land quite unsuitable for cultivation. To the northwest the alluvial valley gradually closed in, and the northern hills that were at first barely within sight steadily drew closer to the road. South of us the mountains rose abruptly, the higher peaks covered with snow.

It is dismal countryside where farming is not possible without extensive irrigation. The people look miserable; they are dirty and clothed in rags and tatters, and their homes are walled and turreted. This is all poppy country and most of the people are addicted to opium, which probably explains their condition. But which comes first—the sorry state of the land or the sorry state of the people? We stopped for lunch at Yung Chang (which has a particularly bad reputation for opium) where I was told that most of the girl children are sold into slavery . We ate at a restaurant which advertised itself as the "best", but even our Chinese, who are not too particular, examined their food carefully to be sure it was clean enough to eat. We drank a little tea and ate some hot bread to the accompaniment of noises made by a slobbering idiot beggar who sat in the doorway. While we waited, the mechanic worked on the steering gear of our first truck, which had gone bad.

We have been climbing steadily but slowly all day and are now 2,500 feet above Liang Chou. The sun shown brightly during the morning, but in the afternoon it clouded up, and during the last part of the day we drove into a strong wind.

Shui Chuan Tzu and Yung Chang are the only walled cities I have seen that do not have soldier guards at their gates. Apparently there is nothing worth guarding.

Kanchow
September 15, 1937

Much to my surprise, we made eighty-one miles today in spite of being delayed two hours while a blowout was repaired. It was fixed in such a way that I expect it to blow again any minute.

Our route this morning was up the same valley we followed yesterday, with mountains closing in on both sides until we reached the divide at an elevation of over 8,000 feet. We have come down gently and are here in Kanchow at about 4,000 feet, the same elevation as Lanchow. We traversed through some grassland around the pass, but the country has become steadily drier again and is cultivated only where water is available for irrigation. The Great Wall paralleled the road for more than half the day and for considerable distances was fairly well preserved. I suppose this is due to the dry climate. Ruins and evidence of terracing along the hillsides indicate that this area was once more densely populated than it is today, but it has long since been abandoned by farmers. As we traveled westward we came into view of the snow-covered outermost range of the great Nan Shan system. The range of metamorphic mountains just north of our road is the Pei Shan, which is not nearly as high. We traversed along their foothills for about twenty-five miles where they are flanked by Permian beds with coal seams marking the hillsides with black lines.

We had a late lunch in Shan Tan. While the driver of the first truck had his smoke of opium we sat in a shop stocked with bolts of cloth, matches, cigarettes, candles, a few stockings, women's hats, and dishes. The proprietor kindly offered us tea, and our boy came in with some steamed bread which we ate without anything to go with it.

The land on both sides of town is mostly waste, with low granite mountains to the southwest. There was a group of temple buildings in better than usual repair and a number of others in all stages of ruin, with their plaster images exposed to the weather. Just outside Shan Tan was a large cemetery where almost all of the mounds were marked with upright sandstone tablets with characters chiseled on them—something we have not seen before.

The next thing of any consequence to the west was Tung Lo, with irrigated land around it and trees which looked better than anything we have seen for some time. However, we rapidly left that behind us and came into very desolate country—regular desert, badly eroded by the wind which had stripped all the soil away except for ragged remnants standing on the prevailing surface of sand and gravel. From here on the going was very heavy with many stretches of sand, and we got stuck repeatedly.

As we approached Kanchow we came to a marshy area with lots of stream channels; irrigated and cultivated, the canals were marked by stands of trees. Getting stuck in sand was replaced now by being mired in mud because the canals were raised and the roads sunken, so that overflow water runs down onto the road. We entered the city through its triple east gate, well guarded with soldiers, and turned south to an inn which serves as the bus station. Although small, it is certainly better accommodation than we had last night.

After supper Sun went to call on an old friend of his who is the assistant magistrate here and brought him back for a visit. Mr. Liu is about forty and has the first really long fingernails I have seen. He comes from Hopei, and he and Sun went to school together as small boys. He told us that General Ma Pu-Kan at Suchow has been ordered to Shensi Province with his soldiers and is soon to be replaced by General Han Ch'i-kung and his troops, who are in residence here at Kanchow. We had intended to go on tomorrow, but under the circumstances we shall stay over a day to see General Han. Otherwise we might return to Suchow in a few months to find an officer in command who knows nothing about us.

Kanchow
September 16, 1937

We were not even dressed yet when Mr. Liu called upon us to advise us that General Han leaves his office every morning at 9:00 to return home to bed. In order to see him, therefore, we had to rush to his office before breakfast, so we had to hustle. Since we had not intended to make this sudden social call we were not prepared with presents for him, but we dug around in our baggage and took the blue silk meant for General Ma Pu-kan and eight bricks of tea that were extra, and off we went to the General's office. On the way we met companies of soldiers, some marching, others rigidly drawn up for attention, and were impressed by their neatness and discipline. We went through the gates and courtyards to the office area and were shown into the waiting room. Presently the General's adjutant and several other officers came to us and, after learning what we wanted, went off in search of the

General. I was beginning to fear that he had left for home when an unmistakable figure entered and strode across the room. He was a well-built man of medium height, about forty, a Mohammedan with a better than ordinary black beard. His uniform and cap were of the cotton that is worn by common soldiers, but new and clean, and although he wore no insignia to show his rank, he wore a brass dagger on his Sam Brown belt and a magnificent pair of cordovan boots that came up above his knees. He chatted pleasantly with Sun and every once in a while Sun translated something he said, for instance, that he gets up each morning at 4:00 to drill his troops. A military air pervaded the room, aided by his presence and a series of large colored posters depicting details of various drills hung on the walls. Obviously a capable military officer, he is second in command of the 100th Division under Ma Pu-fang. I think we can continue in safety, protected by this local potentate.

We returned from the General's office to our inn for a late breakfast, which was light because we had been invited to a 10:00 luncheon by Chief Magistrate Ma and Mr. Liu.

The government office is on our street, not too far away. Passing through a number of courts, we were received in a newly decorated room with a large table and vases of flowers. Mr. Ma is a small man and had not shaved for several days. He has very bad teeth, and as a child he must have suffered from that common skin disease that causes hair to fall out in patches, which resulted in bald spots he tried to cover with his remaining whisps of stringy hair. He is Mohammedan, but not a good one because he smokes and drinks, and many jokes were made about the liberties he takes with his religion. Although we arrived at 10:00, the other guests did not come until noon, so I was glad we had eaten some breakfast. There were twelve people there, but I never found out who they all were. Because there was not room enough around the table, our hosts ate in another room. In spite of the excuses made for bad cooks and poor food, it was an excellent meal and, lacking strange things like sea slugs, we really enjoyed it. As usual, we had much too much food and too many courses and we were full well before the meal was over. A number of finger games ("bottoms up", "dry glass", or *kanpai*) were played, and the one other Mohammedan present played along with everyone else, but because he could not drink when he lost, someone else obliged when necessary. Hot scented towels were passed around after the meal. During the party our No. 1 boy brought word that General Han had sent us presents in return for ours, and I had to hand out $5.00 to pay his servants for bringing them. When we returned to our quarters we found that the presents included a live sheep, a package of dried Hami melon, one large package of hard candies wrapped in cellophane, four cans of Chinese fruit, four bottles of Chinese soda pop, and four tins of cigarettes. This is the first time we have had any return of presents made to us.

After lunch one of the men took us to the silk stores to buy a piece of material for Ma Pu-kan, to replace the one we had given to General Han. At a second shop we found some that met with Sun's approval and bought five yards of it at $3.60 (about $1.00 U.S.) per yard. This is twice what it would have cost in Nanking because transportation is expensive and new stock cannot now be obtained, so prices have risen.

Instead of returning directly to the inn, we walked north to the tall Drum Tower in the center of town, then east on the east-west street, which was quite wide and smooth for a Chinese city, with a row of trees planted along each side. Kanchow appears to be prosperous, in sharp contrast to the other places we have seen in this region with the exception of Liang Chou. There are many temples in and around the city, and we stopped at the most famous, that of the Lying Buddha. The temple is now deserted by its priests, and its buildings are used as barracks. We presented our cards at the gate and were permitted to enter. Inside we found a large court surrounded by small buildings, while at the back stood the large main structure, its center doors painted with two large dragons, and phoenixes adorned the doors on either side. The painting was old, faded, and dirty. Flanking the doors were two large carved brick panels painted with Buddhas and other holy figures, and along the front wall were colossal figures of gods and demons in black and white, their lower portions almost totally obliterated. As we entered, a dozen or more officers who had been eating lunch inside rose courteously, and we passed through to a side room containing a kang, a table, a number of chairs, and a supply of automatic pistols and cartridge belts hanging on the wall. A large key was produced to open another door where we were ushered into the main temple. There, lying on his side, was the figure of Buddha, about 120 feet long and mostly painted gold. Two other figures, nearly twenty feet tall, stood at his head and feet, with several dozen more figures, double life-sized, arranged around him. Although it was a large display it was covered with dust, and there was nothing very remarkable about any of it. The room is now used for storing saddles.

We returned to our inn and received a number of callers. Mr. Liu had supper with us. He, with some other men, had been captured by the Communists here last year; their lives were probably saved by the arrival of Mohammedan soldiers who drove out the Reds. I guess there have been some pretty rough times here, with each side trying to massacre the other. We opened one of Han's cans of Chinese fruit but were disappointed when it turned out to be twelve grapes floating in sugar water. The sheep, however, was much more satisfactory. The cook killed it and served us the liver for supper, which tasted very good for a change.

Nan Hua Tsun
September 17, 1937

We got a late start this morning from Kanchow and are here for the night, after traveling only forty-nine miles. Several of Sun's friends saw us off; one is the government treasurer, who gave us a box of really good apples and two wooden boxes of moon cakes. These are small sweetened pastries which look like little round moons and are the special treat of the "Festival of the Middle of Autumn" which will be celebrated in a few days when the moon becomes full.

Beyond Kanchow's south gates we found ourselves on the edge of a wide sand and gravel area which is the bed of the Hei Shui Ho or the "Black Water River". The gravel is about two miles across, and the river flows through it in a number of channels. It is said to be very dangerous when a hard rain falls in the mountains, for that causes a sudden flood to gush down, sweeping away everything in its path. I have to hand it to our drivers for getting us across; they repeatedly throttled the trucks through water much deeper than I would have dared drive into. All told, the crossing took about an hour. On the far side we passed a village surrounded by fields and then entered a sand dune area where the going was very bad. We got stuck countless times. Beyond the dunes was cultivated ground with many irrigation ditches and canals where we traded sand for mud, and one or the other truck was in dire difficulty most of the time. When we stopped for lunch we had gone only twenty-two miles. The drivers took over an hour to eat. (I never saw such eaters as the Chinese. They can hold unbelievable amounts of food. I suppose that in a country like this where food is scarce, people stuff themselves as much as they can whenever possible.)

We had only five miles of really good going in the middle of the afternoon when we crossed some level prairie land that apparently has never been farmed. It was dry with rufts of grass and weeds, and in many places its surface was encrusted with white salt. A few cattle and a herd of camels were grazing there. We soon came into low dunes again, and our troubles returned.

We brought two men with us from Kanchow who have some kind of government positions in the Kai Tai neighborhood. They directed us to a high-walled farmstead where we are spending the night. I don't know exactly how many people live here, but there are at least twelve full-grown men and a corresponding number of women and children of all ages. It is one of the paternalistic families, named Chong. We are established in the ancestral hall, which is the largest and only decent-looking building in the whole place. It has a sort of wide shelf along the back of the room on which the ancestral tablets stand. Over them hangs a picture of gods, and incense is kept burning before it. (This nicely drowns out the odor of opium in the air.) The rest of the room is vacant except for a medicine cabinet with many small drawers and some spare farm implements. Nothing like us has ever happened to this family and, of course, they are all shoving about showing excited curiosity.

It has been a fine day, but summer is definitely over. The air has not been clear and the lower part of the jagged, snow-covered Nan Shan mountains have been lost in haze although the white upper slopes show vividly against the blue sky.

Photographs

Photo 1. Skins of rapeseed in Lanchow

Photo 2. Waterwheels near Lanchow

Photo 3. Rafts of inflated skins ready to be floated down the Huang Ho

Photo 4. Sutton and Sun amidst baggage in the inn courtyard at Ho Wan

Photo 5. Bridge over the Tatuang Ho into Tibet

Photo 6. Sining street scene with a blind beggar

Photo 7. Kumbum Monastery

Photo 8. Gurmosa Monastery

Photo 9. Mulemen preparing to feed the animals at Hsai Wa Yuh

Photo 10. Attending soldiers cooking dinner at Hsai Wa Yuh

Photo 11. Preparing to break camp

Photo 12. Tibetan family in front of yak wool tent by Lake Kokonor

Photo 13. Tibetan women performers at Kung Ho

Photo 14. Badlands forming the Chi La Ha Valley

Photo 15. Woman dressing her daughter's hair into 108 braids at Lo Han Tang

Photo 16. Kweite street scene with Tibetan women

Photo 17. Tibetan lamas along the road near Gwarshgirsh

Photo 18. Prayer wheels at the Labrang Monastery

Photo 19. Ferry across the Tao Tsai Ho

Photo 20. Attending soldier and Mongols in front of felt yurt near Hsiao Ma Lien

Photo 21. Thousand Buddha Caves near Tun Huang

Photo 22. Interior of one of the Thousand Buddha Caves

Photo 23. The author's caravan in dust storm near Pei K'an Kou

Photo 24. The author's truck stuck in mud on the way to Liang Chow

Photo 25. Human-drawn road roller near Feng Hsien

Photo 26. Sun in carrying chair on the way up Omei Shan

Photo 27. Salt wells at Ta-feng pao

Photo 28. Chungking

Photo 29. Junk on Yangtze River

Photo 30. Entrance to "Wind Box Gorge" on the Yangtze

Suchow
September 19, 1937

Yesterday was the last day of our truck trip, thank the Lord. We had a terribly rough ride for about eighty-five miles, and by the time we reached here I felt that my teeth had shaken loose, and my rear end was actually rubbed raw. The Chinese, however, seem never to have gotten past the stage of thinking the trip was all fun, and whenever we hit a particularly hard bump and were all but pitched out of the truck on our heads, they would laugh uproariously. Unfortunately, my humor left me after the second day and I replaced it with swear words.

We journeyed along the southern border of the alluvial valley within a few miles of the mountains with their snow-capped summits. The land was waste. We passed within 200 yards of two antelope; one did not even rise from its lying position as our truck rattled past. Shortly before we reached this city we saw cultivated fields, but their crops have already been harvested. As we bounced across innumerable irrigation ditches and gullies, we were not troubled by mud or water.

Suchow's brick wall is in pretty good shape, with many stones piled on top of it to be hurled down upon attacking forces. We were detained at the south gate by soldiers who took half an hour to examine Sun's passport before carrying it off to the Chief of Police. It seems odd that the authorities seem overly concerned with the movements of respectable looking persons (that's us, of course) while the tattered and disheveled walk in and out of towns without the slightest notice.

Suchow
September 20, 1937

The main north-south and east-west streets of Suchow are surprisingly wide and smooth. At their intersection is the usual Drum Tower, where we turned east to the best hotel in town where we engaged one of two first class rooms at the back of the second court for the enormous sum of forty-eight cents (Chinese) a day. It is a huge room and quite big enough for the three of us. The other first class room is occupied by soldiers from Sining who have a small boy with them as a servant. Last night they beat him so that he cried for a very long time.

Before we were settled, we had callers. One was Mr. Wong, the magistrate of a city we passed through on the way up; another was Dr. She, a chemistry student who has returned from Belgium. Although he holds a licentiate degree, he insists on using the title "Dr.". He was an assistant to Dr. Wellington Koo at the Peace Conference, which is how he happened to hear of us, but what he is doing out here I cannot imagine. I think he is one of those second or third class students who continue to wear European clothes and ape European mannerisms but in the essentials relapses to Chinese ways. Later in the evening the police came around to finish checking us over.

Yesterday morning I drew up the geological section of our route and only went out with Sun on a brief shopping expedition to look for long sheepskin coats, without success. In the afternoon we took our letters and presents to call on General Ma Pu-kan. We were kept waiting at the gate a long time during which we were examined by a group of curious soldiers, and eventually we were ushered through a series of courts to a large room with a kang on which two soldiers were asleep. Sometime later the General appeared. Mohammedan, of usual height, with a scanty mustache and beard, he is probably about fifty, and is the least impressive of any of the high dignitaries we have met, although I understand that he is quite well liked. I do not think he reads Chinese for, although he carefully studied our letters of introduction, he had his aide read them aloud. He seemed friendly and invited us to dinner, but as a formal written invitation did not follow the verbal one, either he forgot about it or didn't mean it.

Today I cashed a check on the Lanchow bank at the local Provincial Currency Bureau and then went to the post office to meet the postmaster and draw some money from him. There were letters from home awaiting me, as well as a letter from Suez and one from Dr. Yen, dated last August 31st, which said that he was fleeing the Japanese and leaving Shanghai for Hong Kong or perhaps Singapore. Then Sun and I walked around the eastern part of town for a look-see. We also ordered long sheepskin coats to be made, which we will need for cold weather before too long. When I was in Peiping I bought two books written by three missionary women who had traveled through this part of China some ten years ago. We have gotten more useful, worthwhile information from these books than from any other source. The missionary establishment where they lived is in the western part of Suchow, so later in the day I wandered over there where I met a Mr. Wong of the Tibetan Mongolian Council.

This city is as nice as any native city I have seen, or maybe I am just getting used to them. It is longer east to west than north to south, with only three gates. There is no gate to the west because of a local superstition, although there is one at the end of the Great Wall where the main road passes through, about twenty miles west of here, which is sometimes referred to as the "West Gate of Suchow". Our hotel is located on the main business street, which is lined with the usual succession of small shops stocked to a considerable extent with goods from Russia, mostly printed cotton cloth.

Here, for the first time, we are seeing Turkis. They look less Chinese than the *huei-huei*, and many of them have prominent hooked noses. Their clothing is different from anything we have seen—enormous baggy sheepskin pants and high leather boots. I saw one pair of boots with green heels that looked very much like our cowboy boots. Mohammedans are not nearly as numerous in the northwest as in the southwest part of Kansu, where their principal center is Hochow.

Suchow
September 21, 1937

Nothing much has happened today. Sun told us that Suchow is famous for small stone wine cups, so he and I set out to find some. We were directed to a small court behind shops near the south gate where a woman showed us some cups made out of limestone that had converted to marble and colored black or greenish by contact metamorphism. They are very small and delicate, graceful in shape, ground quite thin and polished. I thought they would be nice for liqueur and bought two sets of ten each $6.00, although her original price was $11.00. Of course they are all made by hand, cut and ground with fine sand. First, round cylindrical blanks that look like pieces of core are cut from the rock. These are trimmed to proper length, bored out, roughly shaped, and finally finished. Three workmen were at work in the shop at the time, so we watched them a while. Their cutting and grinding apparatus was turned by foot pedals while the workman held the stone in one hand and fed sand to the wheel with the other. It is certainly a long laborious process, and many pieces break before a set is completed. When we returned to our quarters I showed my cups to Fred who, for the first time, seemed interested and anxious to buy something. Sun and I took him back to the shop where I bought another set of twelve for $5.00, and Fred ordered four dozen, half of them larger than mine to use as cocktail glasses. They are to be finished in six weeks when we return through here and can pick them up. I figured that my thirty-two cups cost about twelve cents each in American money. (I don't think I could guarantee making a good cup via this process, but if I could I wouldn't charge a penny less than $12.00 U.S. for it!)

I paid off the truck men, and negotiations are now underway for horses and camels for the next stage of the journey.

This northwestern region is one of the most backward in all of China. We see more long hair on the men here, and younger women have bound feet. This is also the land of the ox cart; it seems that the further inland we go, the larger the wheels and the smaller (although it may be comparative only) the oxen. I am impressed, however, with the youth of men in important government positions. I don't think we have seen any who are past their forties and, as most of them have come here from the eastern provinces, they have undoubtedly brought relatively progressive ideas with them.

Sun says that the crops have not been good this season, that wheat is five times as expensive as it was two years ago when he was through here. Cotton is currently $1.50 per cattie, which is three times as expensive as in the U.S., yet it grows well here and we have seen many cartloads of it going down-country.

This is melon season. Watermelons are small but good; some have orange-colored pulp instead of red. The famous Hami melons are something like honeydews. We passed fields where melons too small to be sold were being broken open and the seeds removed; they are practically a staple delicacy with the Chinese. On our last day on the road we lunched on a watermelon and some apples in a very poverty-stricken village where several naked children scrambled for our apple peelings and cores and ate the melon rind and seeds off the road where we tossed them.

There are no newspapers either here or in Kanchow, nor do the government offices seem to have radios, so we are without news of the war. A new air field is being built, however, and during the last couple of days on the road we passed nine or ten empty trucks going back east that had probably brought up gas and oil for it. They were all American makes—Ford, Chevrolet, Dodge, Studebaker, International—and mostly rather new.

Suchow
September 23, 1937

We are again in a period of patient waiting, and I have little to report.

Yesterday the Sining officers in the adjoining room left and were replaced by Mr. Yu and family. He is returning to China after having served three years as director of the postal service in Sinkiang, headquartered in Urumchi. A good-natured man who speaks fair English, we have had several interesting visits with him.

From all we have observed, it is fairly easy to go from here to Sinkiang but difficult to reverse the direction. This is probably because the authorities there do not want information concerning the conditions to leak out. Mr. Yu received orders in December to return to Nanking, but was not allowed to leave until last month. His journey here from Urumchi was made by Ford truck in a roundabout way that took thirty days.

About three years ago the governor of Sinkiang, a very corrupt official, aroused such ill will among the local people that they revolted and called to their aid Ma Chung-yin, a young Mohammedan commander stationed in northwest Kansu. The governor fled, but about the same time the Russians introduced General Sheng, who had been driven into Siberia by the Japanese during their takeover of Manchuria. The forces of Ma and Sheng met and fought, each claiming to represent the national government. Sheng, with his Russian assistance, succeeded in running Ma out and has remained in power, but subservient to Russia. His influence, however, does not extend into southwestern Sinkiang, and in recent months there has been some fighting there.

Much of Sinkiang Province is very nice, but entirely undeveloped. Financial and business conditions are, apparently, very bad, the local currency having depreciated to the point where the official rate of exchange is 1,700 taels for one Chinese paper dollar. There are few private merchants; they have been replaced by government shops. And the soldiers, constantly stopping and searching people, have made travel both difficult and disagreeable.

Yu originally went to Urumchi via Siberia, having left his wife in Shanghai. He is now returning with another wife and some new children. This wife is a Sinkiang product; her father was a Mongol and her mother a Turki. She is quite young and seems pleasant, but I fear there may be complications when she meets wife No. 1.

We have just discovered that we are occupying two rooms instead of one, as we had supposed. It seems that in these parts rooms are not defined by walls but by beams in the roof. Because a beam in the ceiling divides our apartment down the middle it is, therefore, two rooms.

The walls and ceiling of our quarters are covered by thin white paper, mostly quite dingy, with many holes in it where it covers lattice work. Some of these holes have been mended with paper of different colors or parts of old letters, but many gaps remain, and one or another of them usually frames a curious Chinese eye. Our only decorations are a number of small colored posters, about four by twelve inches, which advertise the New Life Movement, exhorting the observer to Cleanliness, Thrift, Diligence, Study, Truthfulness, and all the other virtues. The poster on Truth is particularly interesting because it tells the wolf-wolf story straight out of Aesop.

Sun received two letters from Nanking today. Apparently some of the stories we have been hearing about bombings by the Japanese have been greatly exaggerated and little actual damage has been done. Fred has bet Sun that in three months the fighting near Shanghai will have stopped. I hope he is right.

Suchow
September 26, 1937

Our current delay is caused by transport animals. Horses used to be cheap here, but last year many of them disappeared with the Communists, and I suppose the Mohammedan soldiers have also helped themselves freely. The result is that we have only seen one horse that would serve our purpose and there are no camels anywhere near the city. We found one camel man and had practically reached an agreement when we learned that his beasts were 100 miles away and it would require ten days to bring them here. I think people are afraid that if their camels are commandeered by the government they won't be paid, so they keep them as far away from the soldiers and police as possible.

The day before yesterday, when we realized that we would probably be here some days longer, Fred and I started to draw an outline map of the country we are covering. The area is so large that curvature of the earth must be taken into consideration. Our first project was not a success, but the second turned out all right, and Fred has been locating the principal towns on it by latitude and longitude. It will look nice when finished.

A recent trip to the post office netted two copies of *Time* and several June issues of *The Saturday Evening Post*. There was also a Shanghai newspaper for us, dated July 15. While I was there, telegrams were being sent out. There is no electric plant in this city, so the necessary juice was made by two men turning the cranks of a big magneto.

Yesterday noon one of General Ma's aides came by to advise us that we had been invited to a 4:00 dinner party; of course we accepted. He had hardly left when another invitation came from the magistrate, also inviting us to dinner at 4:00. Sun sent word back to the magistrate asking that the time be postponed to 7:00, but instead it was advanced to 2:00 so, although we had just finished lunch and were not at all hungry, we dutifully put on ties and clean pants and sallied forth to our 2:00 engagement. As usual, we were the first to arrive, the remainder of the party of twelve did not show up until well after 3:00, and we finally sat down to eat at 4:00. At 4:15 we excused ourselves (as is permitted in Chinese etiquette) and went to our other dinner party. We arrived at the General's doorway just as he rode up on his bicycle, and he ushered us in himself. While waiting for dinner to be prepared, we were served dried apricots with the stones removed, Turfan raisins, watermelon seeds soaked in soy, large chunks of brownish crystallized sugar, Russian lump sugar, thin cookies from Shanghai, and hard candies wrapped in cellophane. The accompanying tea smelled and tasted so strongly of mold that I could barely drink it, but nobody else seemed to notice. Although our first dinner of the day had been regular Chinese style, this second one was quite different. First, steamed rice was brought in, then dumplings containing meat and onion tips chopped fine and twisted up in the dough. This was followed by a whole roast chicken which we had to tear apart and eat with our fingers, and then another chicken, ditto. Next came a platter of great chunks of boiled mutton with a side dish of stuffed intestines. And last was a plateful of very pasty noodles in a broth strangely flavored with vinegar. The table was aswill with grease, and our fingers and hands, of course, got very slimy. Instead of the usual hot wet towels, we were furnished with very coarse swatches of brown paper with which to clean up. There were only two other people there and the General, pleading indigestion, didn't join us to eat. On the whole, it seemed to me that the dinner was neither very good nor very successful.

This morning Sun and I went out to see how our sheepskin coats were progressing and shortly after our return became aware that we had been part of a small spy hunt. It seems that yesterday afternoon a foreigner, thought to be German, appeared at the air field and took photographs. Today the General ordered that he be found and arrested, but first the General's aide and the police chief came around to make sure the spy was not one of us. This was a curious supposition, since we spent a good portion of yesterday afternoon attending the General's dinner party.

Suchow
September 30, 1937

We have succeeded in buying two horses that seem fairly good, although small, and arrangements for our camel caravan have been made. The animals should arrive in town today. We still need one more horse.

Suchow has quite a military atmosphere because Ma Pu-kan has about 6,000 soldiers encamped here, practically all of them Mohammedans. They belong to the 100th Division under Ma Pu-fang of Sining and are part of one of the few private armies remaining in China. Many of the officers are very youthful and have probably obtained their positions through influence rather than experience. For example, the General's chief aide is only about thirty years old, but already a Lieutenant Colonel. Nonetheless, the troops seem to be well disciplined and are, at present, undergoing very intensive training. We hear them every morning while it is still dark, blowing their reveille bugles. I have never been very alert at 5:00 A.M., and in my dozing state it almost sounds like an orchestra tuning up. A little later we begin to hear drumming, which I assume means that the men are marching. But the big demonstrations come late in the day when, just before sunset, a number of buglers ascend the east gate tower, which is quite near us, and start tooting with all their might. When we first arrived the discords were awful, but either they are improving their technique or we are getting accustomed to the sounds. They keep up this noise for at least half an hour; I would think that they would be staggering from the effects of all that blowing. When the men are in their barracks after dark we hear them singing in unison, not the quavery Chinese kind of song, but tunes rather Western in style. Sometimes there is yelling reminiscent of our football games and I can only guess that they are shouting answers to questions put to them in a sort of catechism. Later, first from one part of the city and then from another, taps sounds and all becomes quiet. Some of their bugle calls start like ours, and then the notes run off in an unfamiliar pattern which gives me a slight feeling of disappointment. Somehow the sound does not have the spine-tingling quality of our own military tattoos.

The soldiers all have two dirty white labels stitched to their uniforms. One, on the upper part of the left sleeve, bears the number of the army or division, and the other, on the breast, bears calligraphy and a red chop mark indicating rank. There are three grades of officers and three ranks in each grade. The label for the lowest grade has a blue border and one, two, or three black triangles indicating ranks equivalent to our second and first lieutenants and captain. The second grade has a yellow border and also one to three triangles indicating major, lieutenant colonel, and colonel. Generals supposedly have red borders around their patches, but those I have met wore unlabeled uniforms.

Our news of the war continues to be scanty. What we do know comes from Sun's translations of the ten-day-old Lanchow newspaper or from conversation with others. We have been told that Japan has sixteen divisions at Shanghai, which is about 160,000 men, and that their progress in the north has been greater than in the south, but still the gains do not seem to be alarming. If Chinese reports can be believed, the much vaunted Japanese military machine has made a rather miserable showing. Their tactics in bombing cities and trains back of the fighting line has done little damage, but instead has greatly aroused the anger of the people. There is no doubt in my mind that the Chinese are almost solidly united to oppose the invaders—probably more unified in their purpose than ever before in the history of the country. The Japanese do not seem to recognize the opposition. They expected a quick victory and apparently do not realize that they have bitten off more than they can chew. The longer the fighting lasts, the more advantage the Chinese can expect to gain, and if they can hold up their resistance the Japs are sure to lose. I certainly hope the Chinese can succeed in driving them out of the country and then confiscate their property here. If she can do this, she will have securely established herself as an equal to other nations, and no one can look down on her again. She would then be in a position to demand that extraterritorial rights by foreigners be abandoned, which I think would be right and just.

I have no idea whether or not my letters are censored. If censors are at work I do not know to what they might object. At any rate, things are happening in this part of the country which, if not reported outside, certainly must be suspected. It is obvious that Russia cannot afford to have the Japanese win. Her actions have shown that she is unwilling to fight Japan openly because such an action would probably start another world war. The only possible conclusion, then, is that Russia must give major help to China without actually entering the conflict. It now appears elementary to me that the road along which we are travelling is the obvious one to use for transporting material. Viewed from another angle, China has manpower but lacks equipment; therefore, anyone might guess that it would be brought in from Russia over this route. In actuality, large air fields have been or are being laid out at all the main towns along this route. Gasoline and oil are being transported to them, and there are said to be fifty truckloads here right now, enroute to Ansi. Rumor has it that 500 planes are expected to pass through here shortly. Every day we see Chinese government planes coming and going; a few days ago one of them was said to be the Generalissimo's personal machine. I have also heard that the authorities here are rounding up camels to transport guns from Urumchi. (I hope we can hold on to our caravan.)

Suchow
October 1, 1937

Autumn is certainly here. Although the days are sunny and comfortably warm, the nights are quite cool, and when it clouds over and rains a little it is downright cold. Our room faces north and never gets any sunshine; I think it is the coldest place in town. When I am in it I almost always wear my sheepskin coat. Enormous flocks of black birds and magpies are ready to fly south, making a terrible racket with their preparations. The people are also preparing for winter by getting out their padded clothes, and it is amusing to note how bowlegged the men look in their padded pants.

Tomorrow we leave. We have not yet seen our camels but have been told that they are here and ready. We still need a third horse for Sun, who will ride a camel until we can buy one someplace beyond the threat of confiscation by the military. It will be good to be out and working again. This waiting around is boring.

PART IV

Beyond the Wall

Hsi Tsang Ssu
October 4, 1937

At last we are out of Suchow and back at our field work again. Three cheers!

We didn't leave Suchow on October 2 until almost 4:00 in the afternoon because the camels, which were supposed to be ready to embark first thing that morning, were late. We were up early and packed, but the camel men didn't show up until noon, at which time there were no camels in evidence. They set to work, however, making up the loads, and during the afternoon the animals began to appear. As I said, it was late in the day when we finally set off with eight lightly loaded camels, two camel men, and an army officer on a mule. The No. 1 boy and the cook each ride a camel, as does Sun until we find a horse for him. Fred and I are on horseback, and our groom, or *ma-fu,* pushes the bicycle wheel in front of him to measure distance.

We headed toward the mountains southeast of Suchow where an oil seepage has been reported and spent what was left of the day retracing the motor road, stopping for the night at a high-walled farmstead where our officer directed us. Some of these country people are scared out of their pants at the sight of soldiers, so when we arrived at this farmstead, most of the inhabitants ran away as fast as they could. We dislike frightening them, but without an official escort we would have difficulty obtaining shelter away from the towns. The ancestral hall in this place had no space for us because there were two nice new coffins lined up waiting for their future occupants to die, so we took over the next best room.

Yesterday we traveled over twenty miles along the alluvial valley that is the main part of northwestern Kansu, rising about 1,000 feet towards the southern mountains. It has been boring country except for the wildlife. We have seen hundreds of birds soaring in rough V-formation, their necks and legs extended, honking loudly. I thought they were wild geese until Fred winged a couple with his shot gun, and we discovered that they were a kind of crane, light in color with dark wing tips. They do not have webbed feet, and their bills are rather sharp. Millet grown in this area is now ripe and being cut, so the birds have converged here. When asked if they were good to eat, we were told that they were "good but not too good", whatever that means. Later we passed through sand and gravel desert country with low tufts of spiny weeds where I saw nine antelope. I took a couple of shots at them with my rifle, but of course missed. As dusk began to settle, our soldier investigated several farmsteads, finally picking a place to sleep at the home of a young man of twenty whose father had died about three years ago, leaving him 100 mow (six mow equals approximately one acre). Each mow produces crops worth about $20, which is then taxed $1, making his annual income around $2,000. In these parts he is a rich fellow. He does none of the farming himself, but has a number of coolies who do the work for him. He said that this year was not a good one because water from the melting mountain snow used for irrigation has been scant.

We are back among the Tibetans. Here they all speak Chinese and are known as "ripe" Tibetans, as distinguished from the "unripe" ones who do not.

This morning we continued south toward the Nan Shan along a steep and rocky valley of grey granite. There was a question whether or not our camels could make this kind of trek, and as we were unable to obtain any other kind of pack animals, we were stuck with having to use them. They are certainly out of their element and, although lightly loaded, they have lurched along very slowly and grumbled their complaints every inch of the way. Actually, they have come over rougher ground than I thought they could manage. A swiftly tumbling stream of clear cold water came down from snow in the mountains, but the valley itself did not hold my interest. We left the main valley after eight miles and started up a small one coming in from the west. Two miles further brought us to this small Tibetan settlement. There is one temple building and several smaller houses where the people live who farm the small mountainside fields. Even tiny patches of level land are scarce. Irrigation water has to be carried long distances along the slopes through a network of ditches which show considerable skill in engineering and construction.

The soldier, cook, and I got here about 3:00; Fred and Sun arrived a half hour later. It is now 4:00, and the camels have not yet been sighted. We are putting up at the most pretentious house in the village, which belongs to the head man, now in Suchow. In his absence the honors are being done by a young and intelligent lama in a red gown, cut Chinese style. We have been entertained in a room with a very large kang and a small cast-iron stove for additional warmth. I suspect it is needed, for the elevation is about 8,000 feet and it is quite cool even in the sun. Our sleeping room is the "best" room. It has a shelf full of knickknacks, including a broken alarm clock in a glass case and two burnt out electric light bulbs sitting on little red cloth-covered stands. (Heaven knows where they came from or why they are on altars.) There is also a mechanical doll that once flipped around on a horizontal bar, but now the spring is broken.

I have seen only two women. They are not as picturesque as the Tibetan ladies we have seen elsewhere and wear small hemispherical black caps like those worn by Chinese men. One of them has her hair sewn into two red cloth narrow strips ornamented with large mother of pearl disks; the other has a wide red cloth back-piece covered with pearl disks of various sizes which hangs down from her cap.

Later:

The camels finally got in about 5:30 after a good portion of their loads had been carried up by villagers. As soon as our provisions arrived, we warmed up on hot tea and, after dinner, felt quite contented.

Hsi Tsang Ssu
October 5, 1937

We are back at our farmstead after a wild goose chase to an oil seepage, which turned out to be nothing more than a damp spot on a cliff of metamorphic rock.

We started out this morning about 8:00 with our soldier and the No. 2 lama from the temple. Sun rode a horse borrowed from the farm. There are two ways to the seepage, so we went via the short route (seven miles) and returned the long way (ten miles). Setting off through the valley, which was steep and rocky, we climbed for about an hour over nearly 2,000 feet of frozen ground along an ice-covered stream before the sun finally reached us. Eventually we approached the divide above 10,500 feet, where there were patches of snow and the usual Tibetan *obo* crowning the pass. The lama told us not to stand too close to it or the mountain god who lived there would give us headaches. The small valley on the other side was more open, with its slopes covered with grass. Descending about 1,500 feet, we came to the main valley with a granite gorge containing a small area of Permian coal series. We got to the seepage about noon and, after determining that it was nothing but water, sat down to lunch. Also lunching by a small camp fire were three Chinese gold miners from the placer mines which are five mountain ranges distant along this road. Gold has been mined up there for a long time; the gravel is now being washed for the fourth or fifth time. The take is about $10 per man per month, of which 10 percent must be paid in taxes to Ma Pu-kan.

We started back down the main valley to the mouth of the tributary we climbed yesterday and retraced our steps. I have never seen so much granite in my life. Geologically it is most interesting, but it makes rough going. Our trail was up, over, and in and around boulders, and we sloshed through many streams. It could not possibly have been managed by the camels. Yaks can handle this terrain, but they seem to be unmaneuverable creatures. We followed ten of them, loaded with sheaves of barley, being driven along the trail by two men. They wandered all over, into streams and up steep hillsides where they rubbed against rocks and thorn trees and got all tangled up, losing much of the grain along the way. They were more trouble than the two men could adequately manage.

People in these hills are very poor and must work terribly hard for a meager living. Those who work the farms are paid fifteen cents Chinese a day with food, and the food must be pretty terrible. Although we saw a few black tents on the hillsides, herds and flocks are very small in this rough country.

On the road
October 6-10, 1937

We picked up our camels and baggage at Ju Fe Ssu and started westward again, along the edge of the Nan Shan. During much of the first day I walked while Sun rode my horse. He is so infernally polite that it is difficult to share with him; he said he didn't want to use my horse, but when I walked out ahead and quite literally left him holding the reins he had no choice but to bring him along. On the second night out we stayed at the farmstead owned by the head man of the district and bought a horse from him for Sun. It is not a very good one, but it's better than nothing and will probably be OK.

While there, we were joined by one of our gold miners, a man about sixty with a deeply wrinkled face and hair that had neither been cut nor combed since he set off for the gold fields last spring. His donkey, carrying all of his possessions, had lain down in a stream so he had to unpack everything and spread them all over the courtyard to dry. Mostly they were medicinal substances—rhubarb-like roots and a kind of fungus that when dried looked like crumpled black paper.

The day before yesterday we came to the Hung Shui Pa Ho, which provides water for irrigation in this area. Its valley is a gravel trench about half a mile wide, cut thirty to forty feet below the plain. Not much water runs through it because it is mostly carried off in ditches. The banks are high and the ditches are actually tunnels dug out through the gravel deposit. We noticed one that was marked on the surface by a row of pits connected underground. Some of them run along for many miles underground and represent a tremendous amount of work. West of the river were a few farms, but beyond them only bare stony desert. At the last farm we filled two five-gallon gasoline cans with water and kept going. We later made dry camp, pitching one of our four tents for the boys to cook in. Although autumn is definitely here and it is cold, the weather is fine, and we have been sleeping out. The mountains are quite impressive along here, with peaks over 15,000 and some nearly 20,000 feet, all of them very rugged and snow covered. We can see a number of small glaciers in the range just to the south of us. The other night a full moon rose over the Nan Shan and illuminated her snow-covered peaks just as if it were daylight.

Yesterday we continued westward parallel to the mountains, through desolate country with nary a tree in sight. At times I rode far ahead of the others and could barely recognize the specks in the distance as our camels strung out against the plain. I was able to get close to a dozen antelope and would have tried a shot or two if I had had my rifle with me. A little after noon we came to a small valley with a trickle of water where there was a ruined clay wall of an ancient city, inhabited now by a single Tibetan family. It was not on our map, nor do our maps show any water in the whole area. I suggested that we fill our canteens at this place, but the camel men said there was no need, so we continued to plod on our way. It soon was evident that we could not possibly reach the river to the west of us by nightfall, and I became quite concerned about the water situation. However the camel men, who graze their herds in this country during the summer months, led us directly to a small valley where there was a spring. Again we pitched our cook tent and slept out. The elevation was 7,000 feet, and it was cold. At 2:00 A.M. a strong northwest wind blew up and it became colder, and by morning the sky was overcast with low clouds obscuring all the hills around us. There was ice on the water, and I got out my woolen underwear for the first time since Kokonor. As we broke camp a fine hard snow began to fall. We set out in the teeth of a cold wind that made the going most uncomfortable. As we descended a little in elevation, the snow changed to a fine rain that froze when it struck us. During early afternoon we arrived at this small coal mining village, Ta Hung Kou.

The miners are all Kao Tai men and, like other coal miners we have seen, they never wash. The mines are little gopher holes back in the valley, and the miners live in tiny two-room huts partly dug into the hillsides. None have windows, only small holes in the roof which furnish exits for smoke from their fires. The men live in one room, their mules in the other. Nonetheless, we were so cold and damp that we were glad to venture inside one of the dwellings for tea, which warmed us enough that we could face the world again.

We spent the afternoon prowling up and down the valley figuring out the geology, which was complicated enough to be quite interesting. Here we found the first thrust faults we have seen.

The boys pitched a tent on level ground for Fred, Sun, and me while they have moved in with some of the miners for the night.

Erh Hung Kou
October 11, 1937

Early last evening the clouds blew away and the sky became beautifully clear. It was a cold night, however, and this morning the water in my canteen was frozen solid. It was with great joy that we welcomed the morning sun and its warmth.

Emerging from the valley onto the plain, we found that the north wind was still blowing, but because sunshine had replaced the snow and rain we rode along in good spirits. Still, sitting on a walking horse is not an ideal way to keep warm.

All day we moved northeastward and after traveling almost thirty-two kilometers are nearly back to Suchow, staying at the same house where Sun stayed two years ago. We are pleasantly established in a room with a coffin in readiness for future need and a lamp of burning incense at the altar.

We had to travel in this direction because directly to the west is the Pei Ta Ho, which is impassable at this point. It flows in a deep trench cut into the alluvial gravel with sheer bluffs on either side, sometimes as much as 100 feet high. The Nan Shan has a new coat of snow which extends much further down its flanks than before. To the north, nearly twenty miles distant, we could see Chia Yu Kuan, which is the town with the gate where the main road passes through the Great Wall. There was considerable mirage, so from time to time the town seemed to be floating in the sky, its walls magnified until they sometimes seemed hundreds of feet high. There also seemed to be immense fields of water where of course there were none. Early in the afternoon we passed the end of the Great Wall on the other side of the river, marked by a blockhouse on the edge of the bluff. We sighted more antelope.

On the road
October 14, 1937

On the 12th we were able to cross the Pei Ta Ho. Fred rode his horse into some quicksand, and we had a devil of a time getting her out. It was finally accomplished after about an hour and with the assistance of some passersby. On the other side of the river we reversed our direction and now, after two days of travel, are not far from where we started.

At 1:00 we crossed the Great Wall where we had sighted it from the opposite bank and at last were outside this rampart of Chinese civilization. The wall ends at the vertical cliff bordering the Pei Ta Ho, and we edged along the river rather than journeying up to the gate at Chia Yu Kuan. We literally stepped over the wall here as it is little more than a mound of earth and drifted sand. We had filled our canteens at the river and pushed on until late afternoon, to make dry camp on the desert. The wind, strong all day, had swung around to the west, so we were still facing it. We pitched two tents, one for ourselves and one for the servants. The other men didn't want to go to the trouble of putting up tents for themselves, so made a windbreak instead from the baggage and camel saddles. At dusk the wind died down.

The 13th was a nice day, almost warm. We continued to the southwest, slowly but steadily climbing the alluvial slope to the foot of the mountains, reaching them about noon. Along the way we passed two strings of camels, ridden and driven by Turkis who were wild-looking individuals wearing low conical sheepskin hats with flaps that tied down over their ears and necks. Some of the hats were covered with colored or figured cloth sewn on the outside, and one had a bunch of feathers attached to the peak. They wore sheepskin trousers, huge and baggy, and felt boots. In this bulky attire they certainly looked ready for cold weather. Their faces were ruddier than the Chinese, and I noticed that some of them had grey eyes. One of the caravans included a small flock of sheep, their traveling food supply. Many of these sheep were brown which meant that they had come from the Tarim Basin, since the local sheep are either black or white.

Sun says that there are two kinds of Turki in Chinese Turkistan. The Sa La Hui, the ones we have been seeing, mostly inhabit the Tarim Basin. To the north, in Szungaria, the Turkis are Chien Tou Shui, and they are distinguished by their turbans. Recently some 2,000 of the Sa La Hui have resettled near Tun Huang as a result of persecution by General Sheng of Urumchi. They have given up their arms to General Ma Pu-fang here in Kansu and have been alloted land on which to live. Probably these caravans were enroute to Suchow for provisions.

Most of this region is very desolate and barren, with neither soil nor water. The surface is gravel with streaks of sand which we can see over for miles. Whether there is wind or not, there are almost always dust devils or little whirlwinds in the air; sometimes we can see a dozen or more at different places at the same time.

Our Chinese followers have been picking the leaves of a small onion or garlic-like plant to flavor their monotonous diet of stale, coarse bread. It gives them a terrible breath. Their camels have also been eating the wild onion and, as they snort and bellow all the time, the smell around us is overpowering.

We spent last night at a single farmstead on an isolated bit of cultivated land. Although I was told it was a wealthy household, the buildings were all falling to ruin. They had over a thousand sheep grazing, and most of the rooms were stuffed with bales of wool. When we were in Sining the price of wool had risen to $70 per 100 catties. Now, with the war, wool cannot be sent out to market and the price has fallen drastically. Sun says that people with ready money are buying great quantities of it for speculation and will hold it until the price rises again.

This morning we sent the camels on ahead and rode up into a valley which presented a long section of the Cretaceous with the Tertiary overlying it unconformably. We easily caught up with the camels after lunch and continued west along the mountain front. In one valley we saw our first yurt—the felt Mongol tent in circular form.

There has been a slight northwest wind and the air has been sharply clear, making the snow and ice on the Nan Shan to the south glisten in the sunshine. To the north of us are some much lower mountains, and between them we can see far into Mongolia.

Antelope are now so commonplace that it is hardly worth mentioning them.

Yu Men
October 23, 1937

My letter writing seems to have suffered recently. The country we have been traveling through is much less interesting than Tsinghai, and I have been wondering if the effort is worth it. Are my letters getting out? We expected to find mail from home when we got here, but there was none. The last letter I received from the States was dated July 17. Oh well, on with it.

We were first approaching Mongol country when I last put pen to paper—so to continue. We headed south to the mountains guided by a Mongol head man whose services we had purchased with a brick of tea. He turned up the first morning with a riding camel, but as the badlands we were going into were too rough for pack camels we sent our caravan around the longer way while we took off for the oil seepage known as Kan Yu Chuan, or "Dry Well Spring". His camel got over the ground surprisingly fast, and our horses had to hurry along to keep up with him.

This seepage was in a small deep valley of pale colored red beds where there was a small anticline, probably with a thrust fault on the north. A thick sandstone was much oil stained, and a few pits had been dug where the oil collected on the surface of the water. We continued west down the valley and up a side ravine through a range of conglom erate hills that extended along the mountain front until they dipped off to the north, evidence of very recent uplift. In one of these valleys we came across half a dozen wild sheep. They stood closely bunched together for just a few minutes on the top of a small hill and looked us over before suddenly turning to disappear from sight. We have seen the skins of these sheep at various places; they are covered with a thick blue-grey fur rather than wool, which leads me to think they must be the blue sheep we have read about and not the Ovis poli that the Roosevelts hunted some years ago.

At last we came upon a gravel plain stretching out to a basin north of the mountains, which proved to be a terrace about 350 feet above the Hsiao Shih Yu Ho, or "Stone Oil River". At its edge we could look down to the river snarling and roaring over the boulders in its bed. On a lower terrace about 100 feet above the river level stood a small, red, dilapidated temple. Still lower we could see black oil-soaked spots, said to be the smallest of three seepages in this vicinity, but which turned out to be one of the biggest I have seen. Our camels arrived from the north shortly afterwards. The camel men thought the trail down the bluff to the river would be too rough for the animals, so we set up our tents on the high terrace. The only difficulty was that water had to be carried up the long steep path, but because we did not have to do the fetching and carrying ourselves, we had no objections whatsoever.

Fred, Sun, and I walked down the hill to a small stone hut on the river bank where the men live who collect the oil. There were three of them and a boy about ten. One of the men had the worst case of trachoma I have ever seen, with red eyes rimmed by swollen lids filled with pus. The boy was dressed only in a very tattered sheepskin coat that came halfway down to his knees. He was black with oil. I don't think he had ever washed and was in such a condition that only sandpaper could have gotten down to his skin. Perhaps this protective covering helped to keep him warm.

The oil drains out at the contact between the alluvial gravels and underlying red clay. It is collected in a number of shallow pits just above the river bed, bailed out with a dipper, loaded into buckets, and carried up the hill on donkeyback to be dumped into other pits. Oxcarts come in from the town to the north and carry it off in small barrels. It has been collected this way for over sixty years, ever since its discovery by gold miners in about 1870. The seepage belongs to seven households who hire men to collect the oil. On a good day 100 catties (one barrel) are recovered, but since the oil does not flow in the winter when the water freezes, one year's production is only about 20,000 catties, or between one and two hundred barrels. It is sold for ten cents a catty and taxed at 10 percent.

The next day we explored the gorge as far back as we could go. It was tough going and geologically disappointing, so we turned around and came back as there was no other way out of the canyon. Along the gravel cliffs there were hundreds of small caves that the gold miners had dug for living spaces. We saw a few primitive sluice boxes where men had recently worked, but I understand that the military has levied such a tax on the miners that most of them have abandoned the occupation. The amount of gold obtained would be very small to us, but here it gives the men a living wage, and there is every reason to feel that a fortune of gold could lie in this gravel to be retrieved.

It was quite cold at our elevation of 7,000 feet, and a bitter headwind was blowing, so we were glad to head northwest to lower country. We traveled all day through foothills, which made the going hard for the camels, and they were unusually slow. By noon we had progressed only six miles before reaching a spring called Hsiao Ma Lien. There was a small encampment of Mongols there, except for our guide the first we had met. Established in four yurts, they were grazing camels and sheep. We were invited into one of the yurts for tea served in greasy bowls with rounds of thin bread fried in rancid butter. A yurt is far from elegant in appearance; round, about fifteen feet in diameter, with a straight wall about four feet high and covered with a low conical roof, it is made of thick felt on a framework of sticks, with a hole in the top to allow smoke to escape from a small fire always burning in the center of the floor. It was surprisingly comfortable, however, more so than our tents. Our hosts were four men, one a lama in a yellow robe, a woman, two small children, and a large, vicious, shaggy dog. The Mongols are much like the Tibetans and, of course, are Buddhists. At the back of the yurt was a small shrine with brass dishes and an offering of bread. The men shave the front of their heads and gather the remaining hair back into scraggly queues. Their clothing is mostly quilted, at least at this time of year, and their heavy leather boots have upturned toes.

We continued traveling down the eastern side of the river and then out over stoney desert, crossing one river terrace after another until we reached Chih Chin Pao in the evening. It looked impressive from a distance, with its clay wall enclosing a group of temple buildings and a slender white chortan contrasting sharply with the deep red of the rocks. Within, it was a poor place indeed. The main motor road and telegraph line pass to the northwest, so it is off the main track. We stopped at a small inn, the first since leaving Suchow. Fred and I occupied one tiny room and Sun took over another in which we set up our table. The room partitions did not reach the roof, so we got the benefit of the smudge fires built under kangs in all adjoining rooms, as well as fumes of opium enjoyed by their occupants. We stayed there a couple of days, investigating several of the surrounding hills which had originally fooled us as to structure. We found that they were not actually upfaulted, but were old buried hills of pre-Tertiary rocks, reexposed by erosion. We are now satisfied that we have the explanation for the local geology. So we headed north for Chih Chin Ssu, a miserable place in a gorge where the Chih Chin Ho cuts through a range of red granite.

Yesterday we traveled from Chih Chin Ssu to Yu Men. The distance was said to be ninety li, or about thirty miles, and since we have found that sixty li is a good long march for the camels and there was no stopping place in between, we decided to get an early start. Our servants awakened us at 2:00 A.M., which was a little earlier than we had bargained for, but we had breakfast and saw that the camels were packed off at 3:30 by moonlight. We decided to wait until daylight so we could see the country along the way and moved into the smaller room vacated by our servants, where the remains of their tiny fire still glowed on the clay altar-like hearth. Here we awaited the dawn. Sun promptly lay down on the kang and fell into a deep and snoring sleep, but I was too cold to do the same so stayed awake and smoked while Fred busied himself keeping the fire going. While we waited, two carts came in off the road and the drivers established themselves in the next room, noisily drinking tea before finally quieting down and going to sleep. It is the custom here to travel by night because the sun is so bright and hot at this time of year. At about 6:00 I noticed the first light in the east, and by 6:30 it was bright enough for us to start. The sun had not yet risen, but presently we saw its first rays strike the peaks of the high mountains to the south and soon it rose behind us, casting our shadows far ahead of us on the roadway.

This was the most barren countryside we have yet seen —the clumps of vegetation growing out of the bedrock got smaller and smaller and further apart as we traveled along. Here and there the monotony of the landscape was relieved by a small hillock and ridge of rock with sand drifting around it, but after a time this also became dull. We followed a motor road which was only a couple of uneven tracks in the sand, and some distance to one side was the long, lonely telegraph line. We passed a few horsemen, mostly soldiers wrapped in long sheepskin coats, and a couple of oxcarts that had traveled through the night. At first it was very cold, and my fingers holding the reins became so numb that I had to alternate hands. I was glad to be wearing my long sheepskin coat, made to order in Suchow. As the sun rose it felt good on my back, and by midmorning I had to peel off the coat. Before we reached Yu Men I was perspiring freely underneath my felt hat.

We passed several deteriorating watchtowers by the roadside. Eventually trees marking the edge of the Yu Men oasis came into view, and as we approached the city, patches of yellowish clay soil began to bear bunches of coarse grass. We came to an irrigation stream which is one of the diverging branches of the Shu Lo Ho, an important river heading back towards Kokonor. On the west side of this stream farm land begins. We expected to catch up with our camels before they reached Yu Men, but arrived after them. Sun still lagged behind, so Fred and I entered the city alone to search for the rest of our party. It soon was evident that it would be more difficult to find our camels than we had anticipated, and we rode down the main street amidst many staring people without locating either them or our inn. We had just about decided to ride back to the gate and wait for Sun when I caught sight of the track of our bicycle wheel in the dust and, even though it was almost obliterated by footprints, we managed to follow it to the inn.

The missionaries' book mentions Yu Men, which means "Jade Gate", in somewhat glowing terms, so we had expected more than it offered. It seems that as we travel westward the cities get poorer. This inn where our caravan has stopped is undergoing reconstruction. A carpenter is at work, his wife is peeling bark from poplar logs for new timbers, and two plasterers are mixing mud and chopped straw. The rooms are very small. We were standing about with our hands on our hips when one of our soldiers entered to announce that he had found a more suitable spot and led us through some dark rooms and devious passages to a back court used as a stable for a small flock of sheep. The rooms were definitely larger, so we ordered them cleaned out and had the proprietor move the sheep. Across the court is a mill where a blindfolded donkey goes around and around, turning the millstone, so the redeeming feature of this place is that we can get fresh baked bread. It is coarse and dark and contains considerable grit, but is a relief from our cook's fried bread-like pancakes which are all right when hot, but become soggy and doughy when cold.

Our knowledge of the outside world is nil. There are no newspapers or radios, and for three weeks we have not been in a place that even boasts a post office. Although the telegraph line goes through Yu Men, there is no telegraph office. But everywhere there are rumors about the war. We heard that Lanchow was bombed on the 11th, but I find that hard to believe. My doubts were confirmed today when some gasoline trucks came in from Sian, bound for Ansi. They had been in Lanchow on the 15th and not only had it not been bombed but Sian which is 500 miles closer to the Japanese army, has not been touched. Yesterday we saw four large, white, two- and three-engine airplanes flying east, and today six more flew over. They are probably Russian and carrying supplies. Also today we have learned that Russian trucks have been bringing engineers to work on the road, and we know that considerable road work is being done by villagers east of here.

This evening we were invited out to dinner by the city magistrate. The red paper invitation named the hour of 4:00, but the servant did not pick us up until 6:00. When we arrived there were seven others, including two of General Sheng's soldiers from Urumchi who were traveling through on Russian trucks with the road engineers. They reported on the numbers of planes and tanks in Urumchi ready to come in to China. After the usual tea in shallow bowls and watermelon seeds, we all sat down at a circular table and, by the light of one candle, ate a meal composed chiefly of chicken cooked several different ways. When we left I forgot my cigarette case and sent one of the boys back for it. It was returned minus most of its contents.

Section from a later official geologic report of this area:

West of the Shih Yu Ho is an extensive area of very roughly eroded country. Seepages were seen both here and at Kan Yu Chuan. Oil is collected from both places and sold for lubricating cart axles. One or more seepages occur in the intervening area, as fragments of asphalt were observed in the gravel of a stream draining it, but possibly because they are not "live" they have not attracted the attention of the local people. The principle seepage occurs on the crest of the anticline where this is exposed in the east bank of the Shih Yu Ho. It was discovered by gold miners about 65 years ago and has been exploited on a small scale for the last 60 years. The oil drains out at the contact between the Tertiary red clays and the overlying gravel and is collected in a number of small shallow pits from which about one barrel is recovered on good days. The source of the oil here is not visible, and no oil-stained Tertiary sands were observed. At Kan Yu Chuan, an oil sand showing a maximum thickness of about fifteen meters outcrops on the south flank of the anticline. It is oil stained to a height of thirty to forty meters on the hillsides, and oil is now seeping from it where it is exposed in the bed of the valley. A few pits have been dug from which small quantities of oil are recovered.

As to accessibility, the ancient caravan route extending from China into Turkistan and more distant countries passes through the entire length of northwestern Kansu. Since time immemorial the native two-wheeled carts have traversed this road. Two or three years ago, however, motor vehicles were introduced into this region, and their use is constantly expanding. At the time this expedition proceeded to the northwest, practically no improvements had been made along the old cart track, and six and one half day's driving time was required to travel by motor truck from Lanchow to Suchow, a distance of about 750 km. The military importance of this road during the present Sino-Japanese struggle will necessitate its rapid improvement for future use. Another possible route extends from Pao Tu at the end of the railroad west of Peiping, across Sui Yuan and Ning Sia Provinces, to connect with the road described above at Liang Chow. This way is some 200 km. shorter than by way of Sian and Lanchow, but the condition of the road is not known and no improvements are currently being made along it. Northwest Kansu also may be reached from Siberia and Russian Turkistan.

If the Shih Yu Ho anticline is to be drilled, the fuel problem may prove to be a serious one. There is no fire wood available in sufficient quantity anywhere in the district, so reliance must be placed upon coal derived from one or more of the small coal fields that exist within a sixty to seventy km. radius. These coal fields, however, are worked in an extremely primitive manner and on a very small scale, and because of their complicated structure and the thinness of their coal seams, it may be difficult to secure any material increase in their production.

The Shih Yu Ho is the only permanent stream in the immediate neighborhood of the anticline which will furnish as much good water as desired. There is a spring at Ma Lian Chuan whose waters are apparently derived from the red beds. Water could also be obtained by driving shallow wells in the gravel beds of dry streams, but the amount that could be obtained from the spring or wells in this region is invariably highly mineralized, principally with sodium sulphur, which might cause difficulty in a boiler.

It can be said that oil is present in northwestern Kansu, and the Shih Yu Ho anticline is a structure that, under favorable conditions, might prove to be productive. There is of course no way of determining how much oil is present in the anticline except by drilling, and if this structure were more accessible it would undoubtedly be a worthy site. In this district, however, development costs will be very high, and if oil prospecting here is to be considered as strictly a business proposition, most careful consideration must be given to all of the factors involved in development, production, refining, and marketing aspects before a decision is made to proceed farther. If, on the other hand, the development of an oil field in the northwest part of China is required for national defense, to be accomplished at any cost, the Shih Yu Ho anticline should certainly be drilled. It cannot be expected, however, that oil from this source will be of much importance in the present Sino-Japanese crisis, for even with the utmost dispatch and the best of luck, it is likely that at least two years would be required to drill the first wells and install a small refinery.

San Tao Kou
October 24, 1938

Today we traveled just over twenty-two kilometers and reached this place at about 2:30 P.M. One hasn't much choice about distance covered each day; one simply takes off across the desert to the next inhabited spot. All day we passed over the alluvial fan of the Shu Lo Ho, and there has been no geology to see, only ruined land with the soil blown away. There has been a steady wind at our backs to speed us along. The largest item of interest was a three-engine bomber passing overhead, painted white and bearing no distinguishing marks.

As we were eating dinner tonight, three carts bound for Tun Huang drew up to the inn. Two were loaded with cigarettes and one with coarse paper. Each was drawn by four mules, one between the shafts and the other three pulling on ropes out in front. The cart men drive them without reins, using only a long whip and loud shouts. We passed one oxcart on the road today whose ox had apparently given up and lain down. The driver was trying in vain to get him up. It must be a desperate job for the poor animals to pull heavy, clumsy carts over these roads that are either very rocky or deep in sand.

Today we saw a farm house burning. The owners had stacked their cut grain on the roof to await thrashing, and somehow it caught fire. They were desperately trying to save what they could, and we were sorry for them because, not only were they losing their home and all their possessions, but the results of a whole year's worth of backbreaking work as well.

Our horses live on a diet of chopped straw and peas. Every inn and farm has a straw chopper, which is something like a big paper knife mounted on a piece of log. One man wields the knife while the other feeds in the straw, and I wonder how many fingers have been lost in the process. The peas are small and black and coarsely ground. We have just purchased a fresh supply, and a man is outside in the darkness now, grinding them up in a hand mill. Local veterinary medicine is most peculiar. Our *ma-fu* has reported that one of the horse's urine has been yellow, for which the remedy is tea. In Sining my horse was supposedly ailing, although I had noticed nothing wrong with him. The cure consisted of taking some of his tail and mane hairs and burning them to make a poultice which was then applied to his belly. Recently the soldier's mule was supposed to be sick and was cured by boring holes in his nostrils and ears with a very dull knife. I suppose that human doctoring is practiced in these parts on much the same scale.

Pu Lung Chi
October 25, 1937

We got here today at about 5:00 P.M. after a journey across a grass-covered prairie which sloped gently north to the Shu Lo Ho. Probably the region's dead soil was once used as farmland, but now it is without water and has been abandoned to wild grass. After nightly frosts this time of year, the grass stretches away in a waving brown expanse in every direction. Today has been a little colder than yesterday, but the inevitable wind has been at our backs and is not particularly objectionable. There was a dust storm to the south of us, and we could see the mountains in that area only through a dense haze.

One more tri-engine plane came over today (local people call them "three-headed" planes), and another is grounded here with a broken oil line.

The village inside the old wall dates back to a time when this was an important place with a large garrison, but about 100 years ago the water supply began to fail and the population has dropped steadily ever since. Inside the current wall are the remains of a much older wall, marking the boundaries of a quite ancient city. They say it belongs to the Han period, in existence some 2,000 years ago. Its construction suggests that this may be true. More recent walls are built of sun-dried bricks, but the Han walls were made of pounded earth held together with loosely-twisted strands of the local tall grass. In the ruins of this wall the grass is so perfectly preserved no one would suspect its antiquity.

Tu Hu Lu
October 26, 1937

All day we traveled over the same grassy prairie. In many places the soil was white with salt brought up to the surface by evaporating water which forms a hard crust over soft earth, and the horses' feet sink through it at every step. The grass is dry and dead. We have seen several little prairie fires sending up columns of smoke that are visible for miles. At one place we passed twenty or thirty mounted soldiers going east in such a thick cloud of dust that at first I thought it was a column of trucks approaching.

We continued west for sixteen kilometers along the motor road, drawing ever closer to the Su Lo Ho where, in the distance along its north bank, we could see the remains of the old Han wall. We passed the village of Shuang T'a Pao which is almost deserted; most of the people live in huts outside its east gate. Blocks of sod are used extensively for building in this prairieland, I suspect because cutting them involves less work than making bricks. Here we turned off the main road and have stopped at a farmstead where we are established in the principal room with ancestral tablets at one end. Sun and I have set up our cots on the kang while Fred has chosen the uneven floor next to the ever-ready coffin.

T'a Shih
October 28, 1937

We have continued steadily south across the prairie. Yesterday we spotted nine planes passing over us, probably on their way to Suchow. We are now some distance from the main road they follow, and although we could not make out what kind of planes they were, it is reassuring to know they are there. I hope they will be of good service to China in her fight against the Japanese.

Today has been something of a fizzle. We sent the camels straight off to this city while the three of us set out with a villager to make a circuit to the south to examine a low range of mountains that I believed were not shown on our map. We went through some terraced fields, over ditches, and across marshes of icy water to the edge of a belt of dunes. In the distance, back in the sand, lay the ruined wall of another old city, now entirely deserted, which was investigated years ago by Sir Aurel Stein. The going was very bad for the horses whose feet sank inches deep into the soft earth through the thin salt crust. Also, the grass had given way to low, thickly growing thorn bushes that the horses tried rather unsuccessfully to avoid. It became apparent that the mountains we saw were the ones shown on the map, but so different in topography that I had not recognized them. Since they did not need to be discovered after all we turned away, leaving the dunes behind us, and continued west in the direction of a clump of trees which we took to be T'a Shih. As the thorn bushes became more scattered and the ground firmer, we picked up a faint cart track to follow which was joined by other tracks, leading us to the trees and a small group of farmsteads. Sun engaged some of the local citizenry in an interminable conversation to learn that our camels had not been seen and that T'a Shih was still to the west of us. So we continued to wind about through the fields westward into a stiff and annoying wind for at least an hour before walls of the city appeared on a slight rise ahead of us. With a graceful pagoda at one corner, it looked imposing and seemed too good to be true. And it wasn't true, for when we drew closer I saw that the pagoda was falling to pieces and the wall much decayed. The east gate was closed so we circled around to the south. Inside, the houses were mostly deserted, and even the licensed opium shop was empty. I spotted our soldier's mule down a side street and knew we were "home for the night".

I have had a nice cup of tea and feel somewhat better to be inside a court and out of the wind and dust. We are established as before, but happily minus the coffin.

Mo Ku T'ai Tzu
October 30, 1937

We came southwest yesterday up the eastern side of the small T'a Shih Ho to this place in the foothills where we are staying over a day to enjoy the sights. All morning we traveled over a fine gravel surface that is part of the alluvial fan of the river. At first there were bunches of grass and considerable tamarisk scrub which gradually dwindled into bareness. We saw several small groups of antelope which seemed unconcerned by our presence, watching us from a broadside position or nonchalantly trotting back and forth. A little after noon we approached the hills that formed the eastern edge of the low range rising farther off to the west and crossed them through drifted sand and over sedimentary rocks and conglomerate. This led us down into the river valley to a second range of low hills that presented a jagged edge to the sky. We passed through a gorge of complex crystalline rocks and entered this valley area containing a small Taoist temple and the farm belonging to it. There is a priest and several laborers, but no women are in evidence nor are any dogs, which are usually numerous around Chinese farms. I think there has been one here recently, though, as I saw a large black dog skin staked out on the ground in front of the temple. This must be an attractive place in the summer when it is green with grass and slender poplar trees, but everything is brown now and the trees have lost their leaves. A bevy of pheasants flew up from the grasses and, after some tea, Fred went out with his shotgun, but they proved to be too shy and he returned empty-handed.

I have heard of an ancient library of Buddhist manuscripts and paintings which was discovered by Stein in the early 1900s in some very old cave temples near Tun Huang. We are headed there now, but have stopped here on our way to see a smaller cluster of similar caves known as the "Mushroom Terrace". We set off to see them this morning with Ma Fu Kuan, our Mohammedan soldier escort, and a local guide. We traveled about ten li up river across the gently rising gravel terrace that flanks the valley. The gravel was so smooth and hard it appeared to have been packed down with a steam roller. As we approached the cave temples, the river valley narrowed and deepened until it was about 100 yards wide and 100 feet deep, with perpendicular sides of consolidated gravel. At the temples we were met by a priest in coarse blue padded clothing, his long hair knotted on the top of his head. He served us tea before we started our sight-seeing tour. The cliff side is honeycombed with passages and chambers. The main caves open off a gallery that parallels the face of the cliff about halfway up. In all, there are fifty-three caves, all very much alike. An opening in the face of the cliff admits light into an antechamber, which again opens into a larger main chamber. These main chambers, about fifteen to twenty feet square with roofs about ten feet high, are connected by passageways just large enough to walk through. The walls and ceilings have been plastered smooth and painted. Most of the chambers contain a single larger-than-life-sized Buddha seated on a low pedestal, and a few also contain groups of figures on central platforms. Some have more figures on low shelves bordering the walls. These figures are the usual Chinese type, many of them grotesquely proportioned and fierce-looking, obviously not very old. The older caves supposedly date back to the Tang Dynasty, some 1,500 years ago, when Buddhism was first introduced into China from India, and a number of the wall paintings are very interesting. Those in the passageways and outside chambers have been badly marred and faded by exposure, but those inside the rooms have been fairly well preserved. Mostly the pictures represent people and demons, with brown as the predominant color. Some of the walls and ceilings have been repainted in common Buddhist and Chinese motifs. The most impressive temple, although probably relatively new, has a forty-foot high seated Buddha, with gilded face and hands and brightly colored robes, that is covered with dust. One enters the lower level at his feet, while the gallery above is level with his face. The chamber is very dark and, unfortunately, the view from below is obscured by a larger-than-life-sized figure seated in front of the Buddha. The priest told us that thieves had stolen a valuable ball that had once hung from the big statue's roof which gave off a mysterious light at night. In another chamber there is a statue of a life-like deer; he said that sometimes he finds hoof prints in the dust on the floor and is convinced the deer wakes up at night and walks around.

While we were investigating the caves, our guide's horse, which had been left untied, started off for home. I set off after him, chasing him all the way back before I finally caught him. I kept at a full gallop most of the way and had the best ride of the trip, far better than plodding along behind a string of camels. When I dismounted back at camp my horse was in quite an unaccustomed lather.

We arrived for a late lunch and tea. Our cook made Mongolian bread which is fashioned in thin round disks of dough and then fried in boiling mutton fat. It is quite good when hot, tasting something like Ritz crackers. When it is cold, however, it is terribly tough and taxes the masticating muscles. Fred went off with his shotgun to hunt pheasants and got five of them. They look almost as large as chickens until they are plucked of their feathers; then they are half the size one would expect.

It has been a nice day, bright, clear, and with not much wind.

Tun Pa T'u
October 31, 1937

Tonight we are in a miserable mud farmhouse in a tiny settlement made possible by a little bit of soil and some springs of brackish water. We only made eighteen kilometers today, but this is the last place with water; tomorrow night we shall have to make dry camp.

This morning one of the farm coolies from Mo Ku T'ai Tzu took us across the river and pointed us to the right track over the desert. From that point to here we did not see another soul. Our trail led over a barren pebbly surface that was flat out of the river valley, but as we slowly descended to a lower terrace the ground became covered with fragments of disintegrated granite. We then traversed an area of buff-colored soil that appeared in patches supporting bunches of coarse grass, covered in places by a white salty crust. The first sign of habitation here was a ruined watchtower within its enclosing wall. We stopped at the first farm we encountered, the poorest place we have graced with our presence yet, and that is saying something.

Water here comes from springs flowing out of marshy places where the grass, better than elsewhere is grazed short. Near one of the marshes I saw two pairs of large crane-like birds that I think were storks. They had white bodies with black heads, tails, and wing tips. I rode quite close to them; they side-stepped a little, but did not take flight. There was a flock of wild ducks at a nearby irrigation ditch, and Fred shot two of them.

Dinner tonight was some of yesterday's pheasant. They were excellent, truly one of the better meals that the Northwest Mineral Expedition has yet enjoyed.

Ma Fu Kuan seems to have a liking for babies. Often, shortly after we arrive at some house, he will appear with a baby wrapped up in the front of his voluminous coat with only its head showing. It suprises me a little, and I wonder if it is merely a gesture of good will to help quiet farmers' fears of the Mohammedan soldier.

Today we have had some light clouds and a strong west wind, but with my long sheepskin coat I hardly minded it at all. This coat is one of my better investments, even if it does smell rather strongly. I also approve of the Chinese invention of the long sleeve.

The days are getting shorter, and the chill that descends with the setting sun puts us in bed at an early hour to await the warmth of morning. One could say that the primary thing we get plenty of around here is sleep. We manage at least ten hours every night, and sometimes more.

Thousand Buddha Caves
November 4, 1937

I have had no opportunity to write for the last three evenings. The first we spent in camp on an open plain, the second we did not reach our destination until well after dark, and last night it was again quite late when we reached here.

We were delayed in leaving Tun Pa T'u because our camels wandered off, and it was some time before they were rounded up and driven in. It is the custom in this region for caravans to travel by night, which allows the camels to graze by day when they can be watched. Traveling by day as we do, time must be allowed for the camels to pick up their food in the evening and early morning. When we stop they are turned out to graze until dark, when they are brought in and fastened for the night. At daybreak they are again turned loose and allowed to roam until the packs are made up. It is surprising how far they can stray in that two hours or so.

Our guide across this part of the desert was a stooped old man in a dirty sheepskin coat and cotton trousers. His head had once been shaved around the edge, but time had mixed new growth with his longer hairs in the middle, creating a matted mess that I'm sure could never be combed. He led us along a path parallel to a range of hills into the next valley and across some springs where the road forded at a large muddy puddle. The camels were driven through, stirring up the black slime on the bottom before the men squatted down to fill our canteens. At least I managed to have them wait a little until the mud had started to settle. We then marched westward into the next valley through an area of moist sand that soon formed a tiny stream where a few gnarled poplar trees grew. We stopped here long enough to gather a bundle of firewood to add to one of the camel's packs. Late in the afternoon we made camp. The wind had died down, and we enjoyed a fairly good, not too cold night. The horses and mules probably did not feel as satisfied. They had their usual peas to eat, but we had not brought any straw and there was not a blade of grass anywhere for them to nibble on. By morning they were evidently quite hungry. The mule ate his own dung, and the horses were chewing on dead sticks until they begain to go after the pack pads on the camels' backs and had to be driven off. The camels, on the other hand, enjoyed themselves for there were some nice thorny bushes and tiny xerophytic plants (look that one up in your dictionary!) for them to munch. They chewed this fare thoughtfully, staring off into space as camels seem to do. Unfortunately, horses and mules do not like the taste of these juicy plants nor do they go for the local horsetail, which even the camels disdain.

We continued westward on the second day. The hills dropped away to the south as we slowly approached those to the north. A man on foot with a quilt over his shoulders joined us for awhile, and we passed a small string of camels heading east, driven by two Mohammedans. When we first noticed them, the mirage so distorted their appearance that we could not make out what they were. Many times during the day large pools of water seemed to spread out before us with rising, swirling dust devils looking like water spouts.

At about 4:00 we reached the edge of the hills to the north and found them to be almost replicas of the ones we had passed, upfaulted portions of an old crystalline peneplain. I think this is the same Mongolian Peneplain that was named by the Roy Chapman Andrews Expedition. We came into a valley and started down through a gorge along a stream bed which was sandy, dry, and without vegetation, which gave way to small clumps of tamarisks and then bunches of coarse grass, a sure indication of water. In favorable situations this grass grows to a height of six feet, with large feathery heads and seeds plumed like dandelions so the wind can carry them long distances. People cut it for animal fodder. The gorge finally provided a trickling stream from which the horses and even the camels were glad to drink. Rocks here were an intricate mass of igneous and metamorphic types which showed intense squeezing and many periods of intrusion. As we progressed they became more eroded and the gorge more rugged until at one place the trail led up a side of grey granite, and we had great difficulty getting the camels over it. The pads of their feet are admirably adapted for loose sand and gravel, but they slip around helplessly in mud and can get little traction on bare rock.

It was beginning to get dark, but we had passed the fault and were again in disintegrated rock where the going was easier. We left the valley and turned up a ravine that came in from the west, cutting across the bad country; it began to seem as if we would never get out into open country again. It was rapidly getting darker so we could see very little, but at last we heard dogs barking and headed toward the sound, finally finding ourselves in some small fields with a single farm house which proved to be a miserable place with no possible sleeping quarters for us. By groping our way, we pitched a tent and got a candle lit. It was after 10:00 before we had our dinner and went to bed. The dogs barked constantly.

Morning showed us to be at the foot of some hills that rose steeply 600-800 feet in bare eroded rock. A spring flowed out of the fault providing the water for a pathetic family: a man and his wife, three daughters, a coolie, and six ill-mannered dogs.

We pushed off before 9:00 and angled away from the hills down a descending gravel slope at their foot to the edge of a large area of tall feathery grass. There was silty soil here with a crust of salt and to one side a pond of salt water with banks as white as newly fallen snow. Here we joined the cart road leading to Tun Huang, but left it shortly afterwards for a faint trail leading off to the south. We passed a hovel of sod blocks where the old man living there offered to show us the way to the Buddha caves.

Under his guidance we cut across country back towards the foot of the hills and were soon out of grass on firm sand and gravel. The larger pieces of rock on this surface were mainly limestone so etched by solution that they looked as though they had been in an acid bath. Many had assumed fantastic and grotesque shapes; a landscape architect would have loved a collection for his models. Although the rocks making up these hills were not mainly limestone, there was such a preponderance of limestone fragments on the ground that, in this case, I felt it proved limestone to be more resistant to the elements than granite. These pieces must have been lying here an exceedingly long time to be so etched by the scanty rains.

Fred's horse has gone lame and is being led by one of the camel men; consequently we have been switching off walking and riding one another's horses. I found walking in my heavy sheepskin coat most arduous, so I was glad to ride Ma Fu Kuan's mule yesterday afternoon. He had his bedding in its rug casing tied across the saddle, which added about four inches of girth to the width. This plus the short stirrups made mounting difficult, and when I was finally astride my head was almost as high in the air as the boys riding the camels. At first this high perch felt soft and comfortable, but after a short time of stretching my legs around the thick pad I was more than happy to clamber down. At one point during the afternoon, Ma Fu Kuan and I got far ahead of our slow moving camels and sat down to wait for them in some low dunes. The sand was fine and clean and packed very hard; we had a wonderful time playing in it like children in a sand box.

At last we approached the edge of a valley with cliffs of gravel and much drifted sand, and as we ventured along this difficult stretch we saw in the cliffs before and across from us the openings of many caves. Since it was late in the day we did not investigate, but continued toward a line of trees in the distance where we found some buildings. One, with a pair of doors painted with vivid but unreal tigers, was open, and we passed through into a court where we have established ourselves in a sleeping room off to one side of a Taoist temple. There are two priests in residence; one does the cooking and the other attends to the religious rites of burning incense and ringing bells. Nearby there is a little settlement of four Buddhist priests and a small farm. Fred and Sun went to call on them and found them to be a miserable opium-smoking lot. As we ate dinner, however, we heard the drums going, so at least they attend to that part of their business.

Today we have explored the "Thousand Buddha Caves", made famous by Sir Aurel Stein who, in 1907, discovered a large number of very old manuscripts and paintings bricked up in one of the chambers. Tun Huang is a crossroads of the old Silk Road and caravan routes, and it was along this pathway of the ancient world that Buddhism was brought into China from India to the south. Since their prominent days in the distant past these caves have been visited by few foreigners: Stein, a French archeologist, two professors from Harvard, a few missionaries and, of course, the Russians.

The caves extend along the gravel bluffs on the west side of the valley for over a mile. The ones we viewed first from the edge of the valley yesterday are so ruined that there is little left but holes in the wall. Here the stream cuts against the bluff, causing the outer part to slough off. Unfortunately, the whole cliff-side has suffered this way to some extent, and the caves are not nearly as much in their original condition as those we saw a few days ago. The best preserved caves are behind a line of poplar trees, so it is difficult to get pictures of them.

There used to be 1,000 of these cave temples, hence, of course, the name of the place; there are only 360 of them left. Each year, beginning on February 8 of the lunar calendar, there is a three-day festival here with visitors journeying long distances to participate.

Much of the way along the bluff the caves have been dug on three levels as closely spaced as possible. The original passageways which connected them have been largely destroyed by the erosion of the rock face, so wooden balconies were built along the cliff front. By now, however, these too have decayed, and narrow openings just big enough to get through by stooping have been cut through the walls to connect main chambers. Still, many of the caves are totally inaccessible while others are completely exposed, with figures and painted walls flush with the sides of the cliff.

The most conspicuous structure is a recent idol house measuring the height of the cliff, between sixty and seventy feet high, with a series of tiered balconies surmounted by a pagoda-like roof. Inside is an enormous seated Buddha. Another much older cave, reaching to the top of the cliff, was carved out of gravel, then plastered over with a mixture of mud and straw and painted. A third large chamber contains a huge sleeping Buddha, surrounded by a hundred or more life-sized figures, each of them different. Many of the caves seem to follow a set plan: a square room containing a raised alcove or a broad nitch to the rear with a seated Buddha in the center, flanked by four to six upright figures. Some of these latter are ferocious in appearance. A few of the larger rooms have figures against the side walls; although other rooms are too small to enter, the plan seems similar. A few of the chambers open from anterooms; perhaps more of them had these anterooms which have been destroyed by crumbling of the rock face. Some of the larger chambers have four-sided pillars supporting the roofs from the center, with figures in niches decorating the sides of the pillars.

Many of the figures are obviously relatively recent, some with elaborate folded draperies and some very ill-proportioned. However, I found the wall paintings the most interesting. Their common design is an all-over pattern of small Buddhas in succeeding or alternating colors. Some of the walls have been replastered and painted over two or more times, and in places where the outer layers have peeled off, something of what was underneath is clearly revealed. The older paintings are not well preserved and are badly faded or mutilated. Darkish red is the prevailing color in the oldest paintings, while the newer ones run to black and green. The patterns of the roofs are conventionalized geometric designs, although there are some borders with small human figures in flowing robes floating in the sky that look like versions of Michelangelo's angels. At one time much gold leaf was visible, but this is now almost all gone; the present monks say it was scraped off and sold by the head priest some seventy years ago. We were told that the Living Buddha at Kumbum has arranged to give $7,000 to regild some of the figures although, to my mind, he might better give the money to help fight Japan. An enormous amount of work apparently has been put into digging the caves out from drifting sand and in restoration work, yet much is still in ruins. At the same time, it is easy to see that in its heyday the cave temples must have been dazzling to the eye and mind; an impressive place, indeed.

We were joined in our exploration by Ma Fu Kuan and several of our camel men. One of the latter took advantage of a holiday away from his beasts to knit on a sock he is making from hand-twisted camel's hair yarn. He knits to the left, starting at the toe, and uses four short needles. He has been working on this sock ever since we left Suchow, and it is now about half finished. When done it will certainly be very warm and strong. Ma Fu Kuan, a Mohammedan, has no respect for idols, and I couldn't see that our other companions showed much reverence for the area either. It is obvious that many previous visitors had but little regard for these holy precincts because many of the walls were scratched with inscriptions in Chinese and Russian. I even saw a *pater noster* in Latin that probably records the passing of a Catholic father.

It was late in the afternoon when we returned to our Taoist temple for a dinner of pheasant and wild duck and a sample of the bottled beverage given to us by General Han in Kanchow. This was a grave mistake as it was very sweet and heavily flavored with something not carbonated which caused all of us to run to the open air W.C.

Tun Huang
November 6, 1937

We arrived here yesterday after traveling twenty kilometers from the caves to what is called "the Paris of Central Asia", but it doesn't look much like Paris in any of its aspects.

Most of the trip was along a plain skirting an enormous line of sand dunes, which is really a small mountain range smothered in drifting sand. Just outside the city we passed through a narrow, barren belt of land where the soil has been almost all blown away, remaining only in little steep-sided hummocks separated by sand and gravel. The farmers are now flooding their fields to soften the ground for farming so, as usual, the roads, most of which are sunken, are a mess of mud and water. First Fred's horse slipped and fell in a ditch of ice water (she is the lame one, and fortunately Fred was not aboard her), and then, 100 yards further on, one of the camels went in. She did not seem to mind, but lay there chewing her cud until she was unloaded and helped out of the trench. The camels made such slow progress that the cook and I went on ahead and reached Tun Huang shortly after Ma Fu Kuan, who always precedes us to make arrangements for our accommodations. We were stopped at the east gate by a policeman clad in black, but when we mentioned Ma's name he was aware of our pending arrival and destination, and we were escorted to empty military barracks where we are now ensconced in a room once occupied by the colonel. Over the door is painted the white-rayed sun of China on a blue background.

There are no soldiers here now. They left a year ago to fight the Communists and never returned. Our colonel's office is the cleanest and probably the best place we have stayed since leaving Sian, even though it has a dirt floor and the paper is off the windows so it is almost as open as the outdoors. I have changed my clothes and washed my feet and feel clean and virtuous. It's the first time I have been out of my clothes since leaving Yu Men.

Tun Huan is a city of considerable size; it almost looks larger than

Suchow, but commercially seems insignificant. The shops I have seen are awfully small, displaying such common articles as printed Russian cloth, buttons, pins, matches, cigarettes, etc. Sun bought an imitation wool scarf to protect his face from the wind for $2.50, which I thought expensive. Oh yes, we have bought another horse for Fred—a grey. By the end of this, we will have quite a collection of bum steeds. The most interesting sight are the Turkis, who are more in evidence here than anywhere we have yet been. They wear high boots and round hats trimmed with black fleece, and we have seen our first turbans. Some of the faces look quite Semitic.

Our cook has been busy locating supplies, since we are beginning to run low on provisions. Our progress has been slower than anticipated; although we had planned to be back in Suchow within six weeks, it has taken us fully five weeks to get this far. The cook has found some coarse dark bread with an incredibly thick crust, but reports that eggs are scarce because the military authorities were taking them without payment so the country people simply stopped bringing them to town. However, we will never starve because we can always purchase mutton and potatoes.

We went to the post office where the postmaster, a young man with a cropped head of hair and pominent ears, casually cashed a check of $150 for me. Apparently my beard does not completely obscure an honest face. We have been told that surface mail gets from here to Lanchow in twenty days and that air mail is still functioning, so I hope that you are receiving my letters.

Young officers sent by General Ho to organize a local militia gave us some news about the war. Hopei Province, Sun's home, has been lost to the Japs, and much damage has been done by bombs in Nanking. The central hospital there is said to have been destroyed; because it is close to the Geological Survey, Sun fears for the safety of their new buildings. Italy is reported to be aiding Japan, just as Russia is helping China. We are told that Russian tanks are now passing through Ansi on their way to the front. But you probably know much more about these conditions from the home papers than I do out here.

In his book, Peter Fleming tells about the paper money used

further west, and I had hoped I could get a sample of it. Ma Fu Kuan went on an unsuccessful search, but did return with some ragged, dirty pieces of cloth, two by three inches, which are used here for small currency. They are issued by merchants and bear numbers and Chinese characters. The samples he brought me were in such shabby conditon that they could not be read. I think I wrote earlier that the number of copper coins equivalent to one cent varies from one place to another. Our No. 1 boy has been saving the coppers he gets in change with the idea of taking them back to Shanghai and making a profit. Today I chanced to see his hoard in a large tin can about half full. Looking it over I found forty different kinds of coins from all parts of China. What a story some of these coins could tell about their travels if they could talk.

Tomorrow we shall turn northeast to Ansi.

T'ien Shui Ching Tzu
November 8, 1937

We have completed the second stage to Ansi through fifty-eight kilometers of desert and are now at T'ien Shui Ching Tzu, which is even worse than the place we stopped last night. Here there is no temple, and the inn is smaller and dirtier. It is run by an old man whose cough proclaims he has TB.

Yesterday morning we were held up briefly at Tun Huang's gate by a policeman who had to announce our departure to his chief, but we finally struck off northwestward along the outer edge of a cultivated area. This is the main motorized road north to Ansi, so one would expect it to be in fairly good shape. The first part of it was not flooded by irrigation water, and we saw recent prints of truck tires in the dust, so took heart. In fact, the road was being improved—we passed gangs of men leveling a new stretch marked by tiny triangular red or white flags on long thin sticks. Later in the afternoon, however, the road worsened, and we got badly tangled up in extensive salt marshes where there were pools of water and low hummocks of clay covered with white salt that looked like snow and ice. In some places the salt had formed long slender crystals that were thin, empty shells—nice specimens for a museum, but so fragile they shattered as soon as they were touched. I think they had formed over crystals of ice. After a while we found that somehow we had wandered off the main road into a marsh where the camels could not navigate, so we were forced to turn back and find a better way. This unexpected detour delayed us so we didn't reach Ko T'a Ch'uan Tzu until sunset.

Shortly before daybreak this morning a strong wind came up out of the west and blew clouds of dust onto us in our doorless room. A little later, when the first light filtered in, sparrows in a nest above began to stir, showering me with bits of straw but fortunately with nothing worse. As we were leaving, three carts pulled in and, as soon as we vacated our room the cart men took possession of it. (I suspect someone was well settled in the room before we arrived, but was chased out by Ma Fu Kuan to make way for us, because there were embers in the raised clay hearth when we moved in and enough smoke lingered in the air to make my eyes smart until well into the night.)

One of the arrivals this morning was a Turki whose features were so sharp and hawk-like that he appeared very alien and somewhat fierce. He wore a small round hat trimmed around the bottom with black fleece, an old long sheepskin coat, and much scuffed high boots all wrinkled round his ankles.

The wind has kept at us all day and raised so much dust that we could hardly see the range of low mountains on our right—only their profile against the sky was discernible. Fortunately the wind was at our backs. I turned the collar of my coat up to keep it from blowing down the back of my neck, which helped keep me "snug-as-a-bug in my rug"! The wind was not very cold, but such a steady blow is penetrating. The people we passed who had to face into it looked frozen, and their faces were stiff masks of dust.

This place is the next well along the road, which crosses nothing. It's hard to believe that it is one of the main roads in Central Asia. Today's traffic: a string of camels, several carts, a few persons riding or on foot, and the postal courier with mail bags slung over the back of a small donkey. When we reached this inn we found it occupied by an officer and several soldiers from Ansi bound for Tun Huang, who kindly vacated for us. General Ho had telegraphed orders for them to investigate the rumor that troops at Kotan, south of the Tarim Basin, had turned bandit and were headed east for Kansu Province. I wonder how this word reached the General back in Suchow, because there is no communication with Kotan. We certainly had no indication of such activity when we were in Tun Huang.

In addition to wind and dust, the day has been cloudy. After crawling along behind a string of camels over nothing but cold, drab desert and ending up in a foul place like this, I find it all very depressing. Maybe there is lots of local color, but one gets very tired of it.

Liu Kung
November 9, 1937

Tonight we have reached the southern edge of the Ansi cultivated area after a march of thirty-four kilometers and are again established at a farmhouse, which seems like the height of luxury after the miserable inns of the last two nights. There are fresh paper decorations inscribed with calligraphy above and around the doors, and on the pillars of the courtyard are announcements of the dismissal of one old family god and a welcome to the new one. I assume the old god did not bring the degree of prosperity to which the people felt entitled, so they decided to make a change.

Our way this morning was over the same desolate, fine gravel desert we have seen so much of lately, to the east the same line of hills which we could see clearly today as the wind had died down and settled the obscuring haze of dust. This morning, for the first time, my ears got really cold, but by noon the sun was warm enough for me to take off my coat for a while. Although the sun may feel hot, the air is still so cool now that the ice on the streams and pools does not melt until afternoon. We passed a watchtower and some ruined houses at a place where there was soil and a fair-sized stream of water, strangely, the first place we have seen where suitable farmland was not being cultivated. From here we rode on over silty land with dust rising in puffs around our animals' feet until late in the afternoon when we came upon a ruined clay wall of a small deserted city. Part of the wall was unusually thick and high and bore upon its uneven summit two small temples of recent vintage. Just north of here the farms begin; we are housed at one of them now.

We were accompanied today by a man from the Tun Huang magistrate's office who is going to Ansi to telegraph a report about the bandits from Kotan. Ten of them were captured by the police west of Tun Huang three days ago, so the rumors of trouble are true.

Ansi
November 10, 1937

Today we traveled only twenty-one and a half kilometers, much of it through farmland over an unusually bad road—full of mud and water with half an inch of ice on top. The old Manchu city of Ansi is abandoned, but the airfield is there and as we passed it a couple of planes warming up threw great clouds of dust into the air. The new city, a short distance away from the old one, looked relatively large, but once inside the walls we found considerable vacant ground. As we approached the Drum Tower we saw several Russians in heavy, high felt boots and visored caps.

We are spending the night in a private home where Ma Fu Kuan and General Liu stayed a year ago. Tomorrow we go on to Hami along the main road to the west and will return here within several days.

If all goes well, this series of letters might reach you about Christmas. If so, Yuletide Greetings to the family from Central Asia. On the 25th we should be somewhere in northwest Kansu, not yet back to Lanchow, if we return there at all.

On the road
November 11, 1937

We left Ansi this morning about 9:30 and crossed the Shu Lo Ho over a make-shift bridge where we filled our canteens from the muddy river full of floating ice. The day has been bright and cloudless, but the persistent west wind was so cold that it instantly froze the water that slopped from one of the canteens carried by a camel so that the fur on her left front leg was a mass of tiny icicles. Another camel is loaded with straw for the horses because there will be no other feed for them where we are going. She has discovered what she is carrying and frequently turns her head to snatch a mouthful of it. I think she will get more of the straw than the horses.

We have come only twenty kilometers along the main road toward Hami in Sinkiang and are now camped under a telegraph line that, except for some tire tracks in the sand, is the only sign that anyone has ever been here before us. The ground is flat, with mountains rising to the north and south of us, and is covered with fine hard gravel that makes a natural motor road. Since Roy Chapman Andrews showed that trucks could be used advantageously in Mongolia, they have found their way out here. The gravel in some areas has a dark surface and appears black from a distance; I presume this is what has been called the Black Gobi.

There has been much mirage today. Although the country is flat, many small depressions, some quite close to us, have seemed to contain water. A different kind of mirage appears in the distance where the mountains have been duplicated, with one chain floating in the sky just above the peaks of the other.

Pi Tung Tzu
November 12, 1937

We have come another twenty-one kilometers north across the desert today. To my surprise we found here a tiny mud village existing by a spring and a few salty marshes. Our quarters tonight are elegant. We have three rooms, each about ten feet square. The center one has a door and no windows, while the others contain a kang and a window exactly ten inches high and three inches across. We drew lots for them, and Fred got the middle room. The window in mine was stopped up with clods of earth, but you may be sure that I opened it to its fullest extent. In a small way I will miss my telegraph line of last night. It seemed to lull me to sleep with its hum.

The first part of our journey today was over country exactly like yesterday's. We passed a small caravan; as it first came into sight, two startled antelopes skittered across the path. After a while the country assumed a broken aspect with small gullies and ridges, and soon we came out onto the old peneplain surfaces that we first recognized on our way to Tun Huang.

The wind we had all day yesterday died down at sunset, but the night was cold and I hated to crawl out of my warm sleeping bag this morning, even though I had on all my clothes except my boots.

Ansi
November 16, 1937

I have let several days slip by without writing, but conditions have not been favorable for the muse.

On the 13th we continued to Hung Liu Yuan, which means "Tamarisk (literally "red willow") Garden". Not at all what its name would suggest, it was a god-forsaken spot with ruined buildings on a surface of sand surrounded by barren black hills. If there were ever any tamarisks here, they were long ago cut down and their roots dug up for fuel. This used to be an important station on the caravan route to Turkistan and Russia, but since the Russian Revolution that nation has had little to export to China and trade has withered away. Also, since General Sheng established himself in Urumchi, travel between the two provinces has been discouraged. However, it is still a station for the postal system, operated by a Mr. Soong who has been here only two weeks and lives in the only building boasting a roof. The others have all been demolished, their timbers used for firewood. We selected the best spot to pitch our tent on a site which used to be an inn. Many camels had been there before us and, by using a shovel, we cleared a sufficient space free from their droppings. Mr. Soong called on us and presented us with a package of Russian lump sugar; cards were exchanged, and in the morning we returned his call and were rewarded with some very sweet tea and a small piece of Russian chocolate.

That night the wind died, but with the setting of the sun this country cools rapidly, and tents are little protection against the cold. The temperature dropped to 10 degrees above zero, and in the morning our eggs were frozen. Fred and I were snug enough in our sleeping bags, but Sun has neither sufficient bedding nor warm clothing, and he must have been miserable. He never complains, however, so one never knows.

Our map, charted by the famous Sir Aurel Stein, is not very good. The distance between Ansi and Pi Tung Tzu was not as great as shown, while it was much farther to Hung Liu Yuan than we expected, so we did not arrive until sunset, making it a longer march than anticipated. It was too cold that evening to jot down my daily mutterings.

Most of that day we passed over the old peneplain, sometimes perfectly flat and covered with black gravel and at other times bearing low rounded hills about twenty feet high, formed by old sandstone and cut by quartz veins. About mid-afternoon we came to the base of the low mountains we had seen to the north of us for several days. I had expected them to be faulted like those south of Ansi, but they were entirely different, composed of diabase intruded into the other rocks of the region which had never been eroded down to the peneplain surface. Although from the distance they looked jet black, they were actually a mixture of dark greens and reds. Our road led up a valley between these hills which became lower and more rounded, and as they were completely barren, it was with pleasure that we sighted Hung Liu Yuan on the horizon. Needless to say, arrival at the watch-tower and ruined buildings was another bleak disappointment.

I had expected to write of this day that we had not seen a single living creature, but I once caught sight of two antelopes in the distance, and in the afternoon a Chevrolet truck carrying several passengers came bouncing down the road. At the time, Fred was under the telegraph line taking a bearing with his compass and our camels were out of sight behind a hill. The truck stopped quickly, and the Chinese rushed over to Fred thinking that he was a Japanese spy cutting the line.

We had intended to continue past Hung Liu Yuan to Hami, but it seemed useless, so we turned back to Pi Tung Tzu. Yesterday, by getting up at 3:00 A.M. and starting a little after 4:00, we made the two stages back to Ansi in a single push. We are now staying over for a day of rest.

On our way up to Hung Liu Yuan we found an unexploded airplane bomb by the roadside. It was rusty and looked as though it had been there for a long time. We wondered about it, recognizing that it would have been dangerous to tamper with it. We told Mr. Soong about it so that he could arrange to have it picked up and disposed of, and on the way back we marked its spot with a small flag. Also, coming back, we noticed fragments of another bomb and a hole in the ground where it had exploded. It made us curious enough to investigate the small mounds with protruding rags that we had barely noticed on the way up. At the first one I found a pair of legs sticking out with the skin mummified around the bones and the feet missing. Later I saw another from which the body had been dug up by animals and the skeleton and tattered clothes scattered around the gravel. Later inquiry brought out information that last year provincial soldiers and a bunch of Chinese Communists had a set-to on this road, and the little mounds were the graves of Communists who had been killed. Only enough earth to barely cover them had been scraped over the bodies where they lay.

Yesterday was one of the most unpleasant days we have had. We started out as the moon was setting. It was very dark, and there was a wind out of the east, although it was not very cold. Two hours later the first faint light in the eastern sky announced the coming of the sun, which finally showed itself above the horizon one and a half hours later. The wind switched to the west, and it became bitter cold. This frigid wind continued steadily all day, whipping up dust that obscured even the sun. When we reached the Shu Lo Ho, its floating ice looked colder than ever, and the soldiers guarding the bridge wore not only their black sheepskin hats but also their big sheepskin coats and were crouched miserably around small fires.

We have returned to the same house here in Ansi and are in the same big room. The wind still blows today and, although the windows are completely covered with paper and the place is about as weatherproof as any place here can be, it is cold sitting around. There is no provision for heat, so our boy built a small bonfire in the middle of the floor which we huddled around until the smoke became unbearable, so we have now dispensed with the fire. I think when I get back to Suchow I will invest in some felt boots.

We lay in bed until a late hour this morning, and for the first time since Suchow were entertained by the blowing of bugles. It seems that several hundred soldiers moved into town while we were away. There are other ovservations I could write about, but prudence forbids.

We shall start our return journey to Suchow by a different route from the way we came up and should reach there in about two weeks.

Pei K'an Kou
November 17, 1937

This has been a bad day. We started from Ansi rather late and were met by an east wind that we had to face all day, which was both strong and very cold. It whipped up so much sand and dust that the sun looked like the moon on a misty night and sometimes, riding at the end of the procession, I could not even see the lead camel. On horseback, my head is mostly above the worst of the road dust, and my coat kept all but my nose and my toes warm, but the camel men were walking and must have had a horrible time of it in their short coats without buttons which they had to hold closed with unmittened hands. After about an hour of this I put on goggles to protect my eyes from the dust, and in the very short time it took to do this my fingers grew so numb that I could not tie the string that fastens my earflaps under my chin. After three hours and twelve kilometers we were only too glad to crawl to rest at a farmhouse where the fire in the main room seemed like heaven after the outside. I was almost blinded by the dust and did not discover for some time that the smoke from the fire caused the smarting of my eyes and not the dust as I had originally supposed. Anyway, we have settled down and, after some hot tea and toasted native bread, are feeling much better.

Pei K'an Kou
November 18, 1937

Last night the wind howled continuously, and this morning it was still blowing violently so we decided to stay until the storm was over. We have done nothing all day but sit by our fire. It burns on a brass tray about two feet in diameter which rests on a small table. Since the table periodically catches fire, we have a bowl of water handy to douse it. The chimney does not seem to have been discovered yet in China, so the smoke just goes out into the room. In some places there is a "heaven window" and the smoke filters out through a hole in the roof, but here there is no heaven window and we have to leave the door open to let it out. Of course, the cold air comes in through the same open door, so the total effect of the fire is more optical than thermal. The rafters and beams of most ceilings have been so blackened by smoke that they seem to have been painted black first and then varnished. A persistent smokey smell is also characteristic of all houses, and I think that we will carry the smell with us for quite some time, maybe the rest of our lives.

Hsiao Wan
November 19, 1937

The farm where we stayed the last two nights belongs to a widow with five small daughters. This is very bad in China, where girls are of no account. But these girls should have no difficulty in getting good husbands when they grow up because part of a good farm will go with them.

Last night it snowed just enough to make the ground white between the bunches of grass. The day was very dull, with the sun just a light spot in the sky, and only in the afternoon could we begin to see the hills a little to the south of us. With their covering of snow, they looked bleak and more like mountains than before. We came twenty kilometers to this farm where we are in a tiny room with a small fire burning under the kang. The smoke doesn't seem so bad, however, because all the paper is off the windows and it easily escapes outside. This is the coldest day we have had, down to 20 degrees, and tonight the temperature has dropped even lower. There has been a moderate wind at our backs from the west. Going the other way we would have been much worse off, and the cart men we passed were all bundled up in their coats and facing backwards.

San Tao Kou
November 22, 1937

Our dust storm, which started in Ansi, is winter's harbinger. The last few days have been uneventful except for weather. The snow has taken most of the dust from the air, but the sun gives little warmth and my feet have been quite cold. We passed through the end of a line of hills that our road paralleled all the way from Tun Huang, the Wang Shan Tsu, which Sun says means "Mr. Wang's Hills". We came out at Shuan T'a Pau where, on our way west, we left the road and turned to the south. It was still early in the afternoon so we decided to push on to Pu Lung Chi, which we reached an hour after sunset. We stopped there at the same house where we stayed on October 25.

From there we planned to turn northeast and follow the south side of the Shu Lo Ho, north of our previous traverse. Accordingly, we set out in that direction. After two hours, however, we came to a small marshy valley, all frozen over, and could find no way where the camels could cross it. Looking for a feasible route we turned southeast and eventually found ourselves all the way back on the main road, so the sum total of our morning's effort was many lost hours in vain wandering. Much work has been done on the road along here since we came this way and, except for heavy dust, it would not be so bad in dry weather. Having lost so much time that we could not make San Tao Kou our next stop, we turned north off the road to a cultivated tract called Wu Tao Kou, where we found shelter. It had been another cold day, and my breath froze in my mustache and on the collar of my coat.

Today started as a dull day with no clouds in the sky but with a thick haze. There was considerable wind from the west, and at one place where we had to ford a stream, the water froze instantly on the legs of the animals as they clambered to the other side. Later the sun began to shine more brightly, but the wind also increased in force and, although we had not planned to stop here, we did. We are out of bread so, with the combination of bad weather and lack of food, we decided not to push on.

I must admit that the last few days have caused my enthusiasm for field work in the northwestern provinces of China to evaporate almost to the vanishing point. We could stand the cold if it were not for the wind. So, after consultation tonight, we have decided to cut things short and go back to Suchow by the most direct route. Perhaps it would not be so bad if we had more comfortable places to stay at night. The people here could certainly live better than they do, if only they would, but things have not changed in 2,000 years or more, and apparently what was good enough for sixty past generations is good enough for people now.

PART V

The Eastward Journey

Suchow
December 3, 1937

We returned to this city December 1 and were very glad to get here, indeed. We were disappointed to find that our old hotel was filled, and we have had to go to a Mohammedan inn in the eastern suburb, where our room is large but impossible to heat and so dark when the door is closed that we cannot see or do anything. (And I had been looking forward to a weather-tight room with a stove and a stove pipe.)

We arranged for the postmaster to have our mail sent around to us, and within two hours a postman on a bicycle appeared with a satchel full of letters and a great pile of newspapers tied on behind. You may be sure that we seized them eagerly as for two whole months we have been without any communication from the outside world. Since my last letter from home was dated August 1, anything might have happened. We were afraid that the war might have caused mail to be held up, but it has filtered through in surprisingly good shape. There were fourteen letters from home, dated up to October 2, four issues of *Time* to August 16, and Shanghai newspapers from August 13 to November 6. Our first evening was devoted to reading letters by candlelight, with the result that neither Fred nor I got any sleep; at least I know that I didn't close my eyes until after 4:00. The excitement so stimulated our minds that we simply could not quiet down. Our existence of late has been anything but intellectual; most of our time has been spent plodding behind our caravan like a couple of dumb oxen. I am sure that you cannot possibly realize how uninspiring it is to go along all day looking at the rear end of a camel. And that summarizes it.

November 23 was a cold day, with sunshine and not much wind.

We turned away from the main road and went north and then east to have a look at the rocks on the north side of the large alluvial basin we had been traversing. We were headed for a small cultivated area known as Shih Esh Tun, but sallied too far north and wandered around on flat silted land covered with loose sand and clumps of coarse grass for about an hour, finally arriving at our farm as the sun set. North of the farm low hills rose from the silt, continuing northward to the horizon. While our camels were being packed up on the morning of the 24th, Sun and I rode over to these hills and determined that the rocks were igneous and metamorphic and therefore of no interest to us in this expedition.

From there we turned south and headed for the eastern end of the Yu Men oasis. All day we passed over silt and grassland, following no road or pathway. Although some of this land was marshy, it was frozen solid so we were able to traverse it with ease. We stopped at another prosperous farm where we made ourselves at home in the principal room. The master had just returned from Yu Men where he had subscribed $40 to the Chinese "Liberty Loan" that is being used to raise money to fight the Japanese. The people in this distant area seem aware of the situation, and anti-Japanese sentiment runs strong. The national feeling is such that I am sure the Japs are in for a very bad time; their initial superiority cannot last in the face of continued Chinese resistance.

The 25th was Thanksgiving Day, but not for us. We had a long stage ahead of us and arose at 5:00 A.M., getting off just as the sun appeared on the horizon. It was very cold, and my breath froze thickly all over the collar of my coat. We left the cultivated area almost at once and all day passed across the desert's surface of gravel toward a region of low hills, which are part of the slightly eroded peneplain we have seen previously. The rocks of these hills are all igneous and metamorphic and showed up as a patchwork of different colors—red, black, and green with white smears formed by weathered quartz veins. Although it started out as a bright day with almost no wind, by 3:00 P.M. the chill of approaching evening began to be felt; my big coat was a great comfort to me, per usual. We finally reached Chih Chin Ssu, where we stayed at the same inn we patronized on our way west. I recalled that it had seemed a pretty poor hovel at that time, but now it did not look at all bad to us—we have seen so many worse places. Our canned goods have been frozen for some days, and when the boy was thawing out a can of beans by the fire it exploded unexpectedly with a dull pop, which set him back on his haunches. He had neglected to open it first. Our provisions have run very low, so our Thanksgiving dinner consisted of plain boiled potatoes, dried beef, which our cook has never learned to prepare properly, beans, native bread, and tea. I felt as though I was coming down with a cold and went to bed with aching eyes and a runny nose, but as I awoke with few symptoms I guess it was just the effect of the smoke. By this time Fred, too, was beginning to feel the effects of smoke from the fires, so I have had more cooperation from him in keeping the doors open so the smoke can escape. Sun is immune, but I guess this is an inheritance from countless generations living under similar conditions. As far as comforts are concerned, these people have nothing on the cave men. Most of them are inadequately clothed and miserably cold. I have seen travelers in the grass country simply stop and set fire to a bunch of grass in order to warm themselves.

On the 26th we followed the main road to Yao Chuan Tzu. A stiff and cold west wind made me recall that when we passed this way before it was warm enough to remove my coat. How I wished that day would repeat itself. We stopped at a farmhouse where our quarters were the most cramped yet and were glad to be up and off again in the morning. We continued along the main road through desert that had been uplifted and considerably cut by erosion. Our inn at Huei Huei Pu was a poor one, but we could not help but feel cheered that it was another step eastward towards civilization.

The stage from Huei Huei Pu to Chia Yu Kuan was a long one, so we again started out early on the 28th. We had not been on the road long before the innkeeper came running after us claiming that one of our servants had stolen an iron pot stand. They denied it vehemently, but he was obviously in earnest so I finally gave him a dollar and he departed satisfied. It was a dull day but exceptionally clear, so we could see the great snow-covered mountains to the south very distinctly. This is all desert country, part of it uplifted and eroded with some exposures of red beds. Before we reached Chia Yu Kuan we passed through some terraced country which recorded clearly the recent uplift of the northern mountains. Part of them were formed by a valley that now passes through the eastern end via a gorge that could not possibly have been formed under present climactic conditions.

As you may remember, when we passed over the Great Wall south of Chia Yu Kuan on our way westward, it was little more than a mound of sand and gravel. However, in this direction and to the north the Wall is better preserved and predominant as it slashes its way across the landscape. It is, of course, only clay and not brick like the section near Peiping which we usually see in pictures. It is here at Chia Yu Kuan that the main road to Turkistan and Russia passes through the Great Wall. The city itself sits upon a barren gravel terrace surrounded by its high brick wall, and as we first glimpsed it from the west it looked desolate, indeed. Two gate houses with carved Chinese roofs rose conspicuously above the wall, but a third had been demolished, with only a few of its timbers standing. The west gate remained hidden from view by a gravel ridge until we came close to it. Outside stands a black stone tablet with four enormous Chinese characters proclaiming this to be "The World's Number One Big Gate". On either side of the arched opening there is a large hole in the brickwork exposing the clay core of the wall, below which is a big pile of rubble and stones. It is the superstition that bells are concealed within the wall here, and to throw a stone against the wall and ring them would bring good luck. Millions of heaved stones have caused the holes, and I couldn't but wonder how many of those who had thrown them had heard their bells. Of course each of our camel men threw his stone as he passed by. The inside walls of the passageway were covered with Chinese inscriptions proclaiming the sorrow felt at leaving China and the joy of returning.

The small city is deserted now and, except for its wall, in ruins. Most of the damage was done ten years ago when Ma Ching-yin's soldiers pulled down the roof beams for firewood. Between the walls and the west gate are some small ruined temples, although there is one outside the east gate in fairly good condition with a roof of green glazed tiles—the only ones we have seen in all of this northwest country. We stayed at an inn in the small eastern suburb where our tiny room was so open to the elements that we had to hang sacks and matting over the windows. Firewood was expensive here (twenty coppers for a small bundle of twenty or thirty sticks), but it was good and dry and burned well, maybe because it was also old roof beams seasoned for hundreds of years.

On the 29th we left Chia Yu Kuan's suburb and turned north off the main road, following a cart track along the inside of the Great Wall. It is about fifteen feet high and ten feet thick at the base, narrowing at the top. On the outside at the top is another much narrower wall, maybe two feet thick and four feet tall. As you know, the Wall was intended as a protection against the central Asian tribesmen who always fought on horseback, and against horsemen it was probably an effective barrier. This section of the Wall ends at the mouth of a gorge through the eastern end of the mountain, where there is a small fort. From here it branches off up rocky slopes as far as it might be possible for horses to go. On the east side of Chia Yu Kuan cultivation extended about half this far, and at that point another branch of the Wall runs off to the east. This part seems to be much older and is in very poor condition.

The day started nicely, but a sudden strong wind sent swirls of dust into the air around us. It blew so hard that once or twice it nearly pushed the camels off the road. We faced straight into it until we came to the mouth of the gorge, where we turned east and took it on our flank for the rest of the day. This is all flat gravel desert. To the north we could see through the dust a range of low hills with watch-towers. Our route and the raggedy line of the Great Wall gradually converged again, and here and there watchtowers stood out conspicuously. At last we passed through a breech in the wall and found ourselves again on the edge of a cultivated area. We put up for the night at Yeh Mao Wan.

Since leaving Ansi it has been so cold that I have had to get off my horse and walk occasionally, just to warm up my feet. Some days I end up walking much of the way. This has proved effective in warming the lower digits but has also caused them to perspire, and at night my boots don't dry out with the result that every morning my boots are frozen stiff and it is a struggle to get them on. It also means that my nice warm feet, right out of the sleeping bag, immediately become frigid in frozen boots and stay so until the boots thaw out.

We continued eastward on the 30th to see some hills shown on the map north of Suchow. For a couple of hours we followed the margin of grassland and a line of drifting sand encroaching upon it from the north. It was marshy, and in spots there were frozen ponds. The air was so filled with dust and flying sand that we plodded blindly along our way and were surprised when the hills suddenly loomed up in front of us, proving to be gravel covered terraces fifty to sixty feet high. Our way wound through them for some distance, and eventually we came to the other side into more open country where we sighted a small line of bullock carts. Following these a short way we came to another farming community, called Pa Ho Lang, where we stayed at a prosperous homestead. The high wall was newly repaired and brush had been built into the upper part of it, projecting outward, to prevent prowlers from climbing over.

The day before, our cook fell off his camel again; he went over backwards onto the frozen ground while trying to rearrange his seat. Apparently he bruised his hip rather badly because he still limps. The night before, we bought a sheep and had it butchered, and in the morning Ma Fu Kuan bought another sheep for himself that was carried into town alive, tied on top of one of our loaded camels. We kidded the cook and told him that he should have been tied on in the same manner. I guess the sheep had a rough ride on top of a couple of boxes and did quite a lot of struggling along the way, finally getting its feet loose. After that, every time it thrashed it kicked the camel's hump which protruded from the packs, and the camel would jump, bellow, and switch her head around to try to bite the sheep.

Our road headed almost due south towards Suchow. Leaving the farms behind us we ventured through remnants of terraces into grass country again where men were gathering the tall stalks to twist into rope used to weave mats and baskets. We saw more pheasants, and Fred shot one hen. These were slightly larger than the pheasants we had seen before; the hen had long tail feathers, and the cock was more brightly colored. They are truly beautiful creatures.

Soon we observed the first farms of the large Suchow cultivated area, all irrigated by ditches and tributaries of the river. Here we saw wild ducks, which again brought out Fred's shotgun, but although he fired several times, none fell. He said he was sure he hit a couple, but ducks are harder to shoot than pheasants; their feathers are a regular coat of mail and will often turn light shot.

The rest of the journey was uneventful. We came to the river bank bounded on the north by a bluff thirty to forty feet high, formed of silt and sand, from which we could see the battlemented wall of Suchow among trees to the south. As we approached we met more and more people. Many were out searching for fuel to heat their kangs. Some were gathering dung along the road, others were sweeping the ground with stiff brooms to get the last of the grass whose stalks had long since been picked. We came to the north gate but turned east along the side of the wall past the city dump. I was surprised to see a number of dog skeletons. Most of them were picked clean, but a crow was sitting on one carcass which still possessed a little meat. It was not at all disturbed by our close passage but continued to stick its head between the bare ribs and pull out dainty morsels. We turned in through the east gate, and our long, thousand-mile journey was over.

Section from geologic report of this area:.

Some White Russian acquaintances of Mr. Harry Hussey have informed him of the existence of a great oil lake in northwest Kansu. This is described in a letter to him as follows:

> The big pertroleum lake of which I have mentioned to you before is situated in a hollowish valley intersected with the ramifications of the Nan Shan Ridge. It is a desert without a blade of grass. Nobody is living near that place. The area of the petroleum deposits is about 250 square miles. It is a big oil lake. About 10 percent of its surface is asphalt, 50 percent is petroleum (in places more than one foot thick), and 40 percent is earth soaked with petroleum. When our friends came for the first time to this place,

> the smell of oil was so suffocating that they did not dare to penetrate too far into the place for fear of fainting. The two sources which they have discovered are just at the foot of the mountain range running along the frontier between Kansu and K'uk'unor. It shows that the main belt of oil must be situated under that ridge and oil, being pressed from inside, flows from under the mountain into the valley. That place is well known in the region.

Although Mr. Hussey's correspondent offered, for certain considerations, to furnish one of his friends to lead an expedition to the oil lake, he repeatedly refused to inform him of the approximate location of the place. In another letter, however, he stated that "It would be sufficient to ask the local people at Tankor or Suchow. Everybody in those localities knows that place." Accordingly, when the expedition passed through Huang-yuan (Tibetan name is Tankor) and Suchow (modern name: Chiu-ch'uan), inquiries were made, but no information about an oil lake was obtainable.

It is entirely possible that an oil lake actually exists, although no account of such a place has been given by any exploratory expeditions that have passed through this region, and it is entirely unknown to the Chinese who have penetrated every part of the Nan Shan in search of gold. The only possible conclusion, therefore, is that either this report is a hoax perpetrated with the hope of getting something out of Hussey and his friends, or else it is a gross exaggeration of the Shih Yu Ho seepages.

It was reported in Suchow that an oil seepage occurred near Hsi-Tsang-ssu, but a visit to that place revealed the supposed oil to be merely moisture seeping out upon the face of a cliff of metamorphic rock.

The only area in northwest Kansu that appears to offer any definite promise of possible oil production is the Shih Yu Ho anticline. If this structure should be drilled and prove to be productive, additional studies of the geology of the immediate foothill belt should be made along the front of the Nan Shan from the Su-lei Ho eastward.

Suchow
December 4, 1937

Suchow seems more lively than it was before. There are more people out on the streets, and the price of everything has increased. For example, bread costs double what it did two months ago. I suppose this is a result of the war and the fact that shipments inland are less frequent. Formerly things were brought in by camel caravan, but that source of supply has been practically cut off, so articles of trade will probably begin coming through from Russia.

Winter clothes are in style here now and big sheepskin coats much in evidence. Most men have fur hats—some much worse for many seasons' wear. The common type has a fur border that can be turned up or down over the ears at will. Ours are like that, and my ear flaps have been down most of the time since we left Ansi. Sun, however, persists in wearing his up; I suspect he thinks it looks undignified or bumpkinish to turn them down. Sun is a good fellow in every way and I like him immensely, but dignity in appearance seems to mean much to him. He wears his shirts until they are filthy, but will never go without a necktie. He is dusting himself constantly, as well as everything in sight, but real dirt does not seem important to him. He often wipes off his shoes with his towel and then uses it on his face. But back to my subject of winter fashion. Some of the dandier hats are astrakhan (made of black lambskin) and look quite jaunty. People of lesser means wear similarly shaped hats made of black felt. Thick felt shoes are popular among those who can afford them, and I have been looking for a pair myself. Unfortunately, I can't find any large enough for my big American feet. Ordinary peasants look much the same in padded clothing as they did before winter set in, as they are still in patches and still very dirty. It seems that no rag is ever in so bad a state that it is thrown away. We still see children with no pants sitting and playing on the frozen ground, thinking nothing of it. One must be really tough to survive under such conditions. Older children play a game with feathered shuttle cocks like those used in badminton, which they kick back and forth with the sides of their heels, and some of the girls as well as the boys are quite expert at it.

The eastern suburb where we are lodged is mainly Mohammedan, while the city proper is mostly Chinese. There are a number of *huei-huei* at our inn; these are the Chinese Mohammedans. Morning and evening we see them washing hands, faces, and feet in preparation for praying. This is one good commandment of the Koran, and the Chinese could do well to have a similar rule. Many shop proprietors are Turkis, with sharp foreign-looking features. They like high leather boots, which are usually black, but I saw one proud peacock of an old man wearing a pair that came above his knees in bright orange-brown leather.

The gateway between the suburb and the city always has a line of beggars who keep up a perpetual sing-song appeal to passersby, holding out hands caked with dirt. The most annoying ones, however, are ragged little boys who run whining along beside you and cannot be driven away. Fortunately there are not many of them.

Suez wrote that he feared money would be scarce here, so he has sent us a formal money order for $500, which cost him $25—a pretty steep rate, I would say. I had left $600 in the post office, and his worries made me fear that I might have trouble getting it out. However, when Sun and I called on the postmaster, he handed it over without a fuss, in fact he had it already tied in a piece of string waiting for us.

In the evening Fred, Sun, and I had a council of war and jointly decided that the season for field work is over in this region, and the best thing for us to do is to get back to Lanchow as soon as possible. So yesterday we went to the truck depot to dicker about our return journey and met with the disturbing news that there was no gasoline and that trucks are stranded along the road for lack of fuel. The Director of Comniunications confirmed the report, and we began to have terrible visions of a 500-mile trek by mule cart. However, in the afternoon our truck man returned with the good news that he knew where he could get gasoline for $3.75 a gallon, and it didn't take us long to reach a verbal agreement concerning the price. In order to get away we must have a travel pass, so this afternoon we returned to the Director of Communications. He told us that if we could find the gas, he could issue the proper papers, so that seems to be all fixed up. Tomorrow we go for the gas, which I understand is hidden in a small village near here by a profiteer who fears it might be confiscated by the authorities before he can sell it.

The first day here Fred and I almost ate ourselves into permanent horizontal positions. Provisions had run quite low on the trip and we had resorted to only very scanty lunches, supplemented with unexciting suppers. Anyway, when we returned to the food we had left here we were overzealous in our enthusiasm and quickly and painfully learned that three big meals a day were too much for us. I am on the road to recovery, but Fred, who says his system has never been the same since the army is still on the queasy side. Sun seems immune to everything and eats with enormous gusto.

Suchow
December 5, 1937

Our arrangements for departure are almost complete, and we expect to leave tomorrow by truck. We have eight cans of gasoline, which will get us to Liang Chow where the truck man is confident that he can get some more.

We have just been visited by our camel men bearing presents from their master. Our contract with him was for six weeks; when we did not return by that time he was sure that we had run off with his camels. Previously he had lost 500 of his herd of 800 to the army and was more than apprehensive. When we returned and paid him in full, he was most happy. The presents he sent were several large bunches of onions, a basket of millet, a number of small packages of noodles, and a large tray of sliced dry bread. Pretty swell, I should say.

Our disturbing news of the day is that a telegram has been received by authorities here informing them that Lanchow has had an air raid. Eleven Japanese planes dropped three bombs on the air field there, killing three workmen. It was a complete surprise. A watch is to be set up so that they will not be surprised again. It was suggested that similar precautions be taken here. Actually, I feel that Lanchow is too far away for the Japs to venture there often, and they probably made that one trip primarily for reconnaisance. When they saw so many planes on the ground they scampered off in a hurry. In any case, large dugouts were being constructed there before we left, so I feel that the city is well prepared for what may come. This news and the onslaught of winter all point to our getting out of here, as well as out of the country, as fast as possible. I don't know how we will do it, but feel that when we return to Lanchow we will get the best advice and aid possible. I have the suspicion that we may go to Szechuan Province. Mr. Chow, our big man in Shanghai, now holds an important government position and should be able to pull the necessary strings for us.

We have been told that General Ma Pu-kan has gone to Tun Huang to incorporate Ma Ching-yin's soldiers into his army. These are the men who were driven out of Kotan by General Sheng about whom we heard bandit rumors in Ansi.

The days have continued bright with little wind, but it is very chilly, and I am afraid that our truck ride will be a cold one. I am going to wear all of the clothes I have.

Lanchow
December 12, 1937

We reached Lanchow fairly early today and came at once to the hotel where Suez has been staying. He had a room engaged for us and, wonder of wonders, there is a small cast-iron stove with a fire burning in it, and the room was warm for our arrival. My very first action was to get out of my clothes and bathe. It required several basins of water, and I feel clean again. The last overall bath I had was more than three months ago, and most of this time I have been sleeping in my clothes; going to bed merely means taking off my coat and boots and crawling in.

We did not leave Suchow until December 7 because of delays in selling the horses. We had made a bargain with a Mr. Yang to buy our horses for $125, which is about half of what we paid for them and was certainly an advantageous deal for him. He didn't have the money and had to borrow it, supposedly to bring it to us on the evening of the 5th, but he didn't show up. We waited around all the next day for him while the truck was readied for us. On the evening of the 6th we sent our servants out to look for him because by then one of our camel men had informed us that his master was interested in the horses, but because Yang had already taken them from the *ma-fu* we could not close that deal. At 2:00 P.M. on the 7th word came to Fred and me that Yang and the money had been located, so we clambered onto our loaded truck and the money was handed up to me just before we drove out through the south gate.

We were joined by two other trucks rented from the same owner. One was filled to overflowing with passengers, but the other was empty. Ours, a Chevrolet formerly chartered by the post office, still bore the Chinese postal characters painted yellow against the green of the truck body. We departed Suchow by way of the same road we had taken with camels two months before and in a surprisingly short time passed the farm where we had spent our first night. We continued until about 5:00 when we stopped at an inn at Ching Shui, a distance of only about forty miles. We carried a bag of charcoal with us and enjoyed a relatively smokeless fire. The quarters we occupied belonged to the innkeeper and his family who were routed to heaven knows where, but in the morning as we packed up, the children all filtered in and squatted on their little bare bottoms around the dying embers of our fire.

On December 8 we rose before daylight and were off before the sun peeped over the eastern mountains. In the early morning hours the air is usually very clear, so I rode outside on top of the load and watched the sunlight appear on the highest mountain peak to the west and gradually work its way downward. Sun and I were settled facing backwards with our backs against our bags of bedding leaning against the top of the cab. The servants were on the back end, and Fred sat in the cab. In the afternoon Fred and I changed places, and I rode up front with the driver and his helper. Quarters were terribly cramped there. For some unknown reason the Chinese rebuild their truck cabs and substitute the nice upholstered seat with a sparingly padded plank. But at least the jolting is not as bad as it is up on top, and certainly one is out of the wind. Our driver, a young man in Russian felt boots who needed a shave, haircut, and general cleaning up, was a good driver and seemed genuinely interested in getting somewhere. On this return trip there were no stops at every village to eat and no hour off at noon for opium smoking as there had been going up. The helper seemed to be a boy in his teens, but may have been in his twenties with a very childish face. He wore a sort of aviator's helmet of cheap leather which didn't fit properly and rested on the top of his ears in such a way that by the end of winter I am sure both ears will be misshapen permanently.

We reached Kanchow that night, a distance of about ninety miles, where we put up at the same inn where we had stayed before. We got another room, however, somewhat larger than the first and newly papered, so that it seemed unusually nice. We thought Suez might have sent mail up here for us, so I sent my calling card around to the postmaster. There was no mail, but in the evening he called on us and alarmed us with his report that the Japanese had bombed Lanchow several more times and that the Chinese monetary exchange had dropped drastically.

Meanwhile we had noticed that considerable work has been done along this stretch of the road and that many bridges had been built to make the way easier.

We started early again on the 9th because Kanchow was scheduled for anti-aircraft practice at 8:00 A.M., and we felt it was necessary to get out of town before that time. I rode on top of the load all day and, although it was somewhat colder, I devised a system for keeping my feet warm. I took off my boots and wrapped my feet in the short sheepskin coat, pulling a blanket up over it all. Sun, the two servants, and I were packed in so tightly that we simply could not rattle around despite the bumps. In the afternoon a west wind arose that blew our dust back over us, and by the time we stopped for the night we were plastered solid with it. The truck could seldom do more than fifteen miles an hour, and at times the wind carried our dust ahead of us in such clouds that the driver could not see the road, and we were forced to stop early at Yung Ch'ang, patronizing an inn where our quarters were far from weather-tight. Part of the window was covered with straw matting, and the double doors failed to meet by a good four inches. There was a large smoke vent opening above the door, but because our room faced west against the wind, the wind came in without the smoke going out. Although we had brought coal with us the innkeeper did not have the proper fire dish, and our boy was unsuccessful in getting the coal to burn in a cut-down gasoline tin. Finally we procured a fire from the innkeeper, which was made from a mixture of our coal and clay and contained in a deep earthenware vessel. It was covered over with broken pieces of brick which made it resemble a gas grate. It didn't last long, but while it did it was a nice fire without irritating smoke. In addition to the dogs, which are always awake and bark all night, this inn had a large black pig that several times tried to force an entrance into our room. Fred and Sun shared the kang while I put up my bed on the floor in the midst of a pile of chopped straw that appeared to be the reserve fodder supply.

I sat in the cab with the driver the next day. It was only about forty miles into Liang Chow, and we would have been there by noon had our truck not gotten stuck with its back wheels in a deep narrow ditch full of icy water. The driver's efforts to get it out only served to sink the wheels deeper. Then the helper crawled under the truck on his belly in the water and managed to put on one chain, but that helped not at all. Next, one of the other trucks backed up in front and a heavy rope was made ready to pull us out. At the first tug the rope snapped in two places, and we were still quite firmly stuck. Finally a series of jacking-up excercises began during which the back end was eventually raised sufficiently to push rocks under the wheels. A small boy with no pants and a straw basket half filled with dung gathered from the road had been attentively watching the procedure. His basket was commandeered and its precious contents dumped so it could be used to haul stones from some distance down the road. After an hour and a half the pieces of rope were tied together, the front truck hitched up again, and by the united efforts of both motors at last we were freed. A countryman who had helped received the small pieces of broken rope for his efforts; the boy with the basket got ten cents.

Although we had no difficulty entering Kanchow, we were held up at Liang Chow's gate while unintelligible things were shouted back and forth between the officer on guard duty at the gate and his apparent superior on top of the wall. Finally we were allowed to proceed, passed through the city, and out the east gate to an inn near the one where we stayed before. Here we had a room with a kang large enough for all three of our cots. The floor space was largely occupied by bales of cotton, while piled around the sides of the courtyard were bundles of ginger wrapped in burlap. That evening a call from the local Communications Director brought more war news. He said that Japanese planes had flown to Lanchow twice. In the first raid eleven planes dropped a number of bombs at the airport; in the second raid there were seventeen planes but no bombs. Sun bought a newspaper which announced that the Japs had penetrated to Nanking and were attacking that city.

Trucks leaving Liang Chow must have permits from General Ma Pu-ching. We were advised by the Communications Director the evening before that our pass would be issued first thing in the morning. It was rumored that General Ma, fearing that the Japanese may drive westward through Mongolia to this city, was commandeering trucks to transport his personal property to Sining. We wondered if our truck would be endangered, but it was still there in the morning and, after loading up, we waited patiently for our pass which was finally issued at 11:00. We took off immediately with a man in the Communications Service as an added passenger and five other trucks which had joined our caravan to the east. We rolled merrily along about 100 miles and stopped last night by moonlight at Ping Fan, where we engaged a fairly large room with what appeared to be three kangs. This morning, however, we found only one real kang and two platforms constructed of boards on top of gasoline cases. Nonetheless, we were charged for three kangs and a space for ten men. I paid the price, but Sun was very angry at the deceit and overcharging. War profiteering has already started in this region, and inn charges are much higher than they were.

While our driver was warming up the truck by building a fire under the motor, we unexpectedly met the red-faced major who accompanied us on our Tsinghai trip. He is now engaged in supervising shipments of timber by mule cart from Tsinghai to northwest Kansu for bridge construction. He looked more Tibetan than *heui-heui*, and I did not recognize him at first. He wore Tibetan boots, a big sheepskin coat of Tibetan style, and a hat with a wide band of fox fur around it.

Our driver obtained another case of gasoline in Liang Chow which he said would get us to Lanchow, but before we had driven far from town one of the other trucks ran out of gas and we siphoned some of our supply for it. I was afraid that this would not leave us enough to get to Lanchow, but we made it OK. Another truck ran out closer to Lanchow, but we just left it and its passengers marooned by the roadside and motored on into town. We encountered no delay driving across a bridge over the Huang Ho, which was now quite low with gravel bars showing where before there was high water we had to ford. We were not stopped at the city gate for inspection as we expected to be.

Since our trip west, much road work has been done. Before, it was only a cart track whereas now much of it is graded and forty to sixty feet wide. Some of the grades are steep, some of the curves are sharp, and it is unsurfaced, but otherwise it works well; in fact, certain stretches compare favorably with U.S. highways. We were particularly impressed with the manner in which this was accomplished, not, of course, with sophisticated road building machinery, but by bare backs and hands with primitive picks and shovels. Some of these implements seem to have been handed down through generations; the metal blades are so worn that little remains to work with. Some of the men were pecking away at solid rock with their inadequate picks, but the rock was giving way under the sheer weight of their numbers. Other men were carrying large stones on their backs to build up the embankments. At one place a large group under the direction of a single officer was building a bridge. While a hundred or more were placing logs in position, six- or seven-year-old pantless boys were carting heavy baskets of stones for the approaches. Even the main street in Lanchow is being paved with hard packed, broken stones; its endless stretch of mud will soon be a thing of the past. It seems a shame that a war is required to bring much needed improvements to this region, but perhaps it will be better off in the end.

In the same vein, each of the principal cities we have revisited on our way back has become more prosperous. In Lanchow the streets are thronged and the shops seem attractive, at least in comparison with those poorer ones of the extreme northwest. More soldiers are in evidence than they were three months ago, stationed in many of the smaller villages along the way. They are garrisoned somewhere near our inn here, and their bugle calls ring out loud, long, and discordant, night and morning. There is also much military shouting and singing, although I would think that target practice might do them more good.

Our quarters are comfortable and even luxurious after our recent standards. Our rooms on the second floor open from a balcony facing south. Instead of glass windows there is lattice work at both ends of each room, covered with thin white paper which lets in a good amount of light in the daytime. Fred and I share a room about fifteen feet wide and twice as long; Suez is in a similar room, while Sun's quarters are smaller. We have another tiny space we shall use as an office. Each room has a little coal stove with pipes made from gasoline tins which keeps it nicely warm. We have run an electric wire through from Suez's room so we can have light at night, but the current is so weak that it is really little more serviceable than a candle. Partitions are very thin, and the wood has shrunk in places so that there are many cracks pasted over with bits of paper, so both sound and opium fumes penetrate almost as though there was nothing there. It does feel good, however, to get settled and to spread things out, and it is a particular relief not to be packing and unpacking our beds every day. We are also enjoying a change of diet, made possible by the cook having time to prepare a proper meal or two.

Upon our return we learned that conditions are not so bad as we had been led to believe. Chinese exchange has not gone to the dogs, and although the Japanese took Nanking yesterday, it is an empty victory because the government had moved inland to Hankow some time ago, and the Chinese are determined to continue fighting. Warning was recently received here of another Jap raid, but fighting planes stationed on the ground were in the air to meet them and drove them off before they had an opportunity to bomb. In any event, there is a bomb-proof shelter in the back yard of our hotel so we feel fairly secure. The fact that we have had no orders to get out seems good evidence that our Chinese sponsors believe we are safe. Also, it is apparently not too difficult to get out of the country either from Hong Kong, Indochina, or Burma.

Airlines fly regularly to Hong Kong despite the fighting, and Mr.

Chow has recently traveled from Hankow to Shanghai. We have received a telegram from him requesting that we stay here for the moment, so as soon as we are caught up on our mail we plan to work on our geological report. I have reminded him that my year's contract will soon be up and announced that I am unable to remain in China much longer. The most disturbing news, which reached us today, is the sinking of the American gunboat, *Panay*, in the Yangtze River. My feelings about this are very mixed. On one hand I fervently hope that the U.S. does not become involved, but on the other, it is unthinkable to me that the Japanese should be allowed to win. Surely it would lead to another world war in which Japan, Italy, and Germany would ally forces, a combination that would be much harder to defeat than Germany and Austria were last time.

Lanchow
December 20, 1937

We have not been very active since returning here; I have taken care of some business correspondence, and Fred and I have started work on our report. Our kerosene lamps with incandescent mantles are working now and, with the combination of good light and a fairly warm room, we find it unnecessary to go to bed with the chickens, so can achieve a decent day's work. I am doing the writing and Fred is working on the maps. Much as I despise writing, I have been pretty steady and stalwart about it and by this time have a respectable start. Sucz received a wire from Mr. Chow asking for the correct English spelling of our names, so I suspect that fresh passports are being obtained preparatory to our proceeding to Szechuan. Our mail and the telegram have come by way of Hong Kong. Letters go by boat from Shanghai to Hong Kong and thence are flown to Sian where they are picked up by truck for the remainder of the distance here.

The other night we had roast suckling pig for dinner. A man brought the pig, built a charcoal fire on the brick floor of our dining room, and barbequed it there on the spot. It was eaten, skin and all—the skin was wonderfully brown and crisp. As it was all done Chinese style there were no potatoes, only small, thin pancakes in which we wrapped the pieces of meat. It was very good, but somehow meat with little else does not make an entirely satisfying meal. We invited Dr. Han to share it with us. I was glad to see him again; he is a very nice person. He has stopped by several times for short chats since we have been back and has informed us of recent unpleasantries he has been experiencing on account of professional jealousies with some of the local doctors who are attempting to have him removed. People here seem to be antagonistic toward outsiders and join together in guilds of common bonds. Han is originally from Shantung and, although he belongs to a small guild of people from there and four other neighboring provinces, his guild is not influential or powerful enough to help him. He is very discouraged and depressed over the situation, and I am entirely sympathetic because I like him and think he has done a superlative job with his hospital.

On the same note, Governor Ho has left the province under somewhat mysterious circumstances. There was a question about his Mohammedanism, and he had brought in too many outsiders for government positions to be popular with the local people. There is now a new acting governor, but I don't know his name yet.

The recent reverses of the Chinese army in the Shanghai and Nanking areas do not seem to be discouraging to people here. I think they expected to lose ground at first and were actually surprised that successful resistance in Shanghai lasted as long as it did. They believe that if they stick it out doggedly, sooner or later the Japs will collapse. I tend to agree.

Lanchow
December 26, 1937

'Tis the day after Christmas and not a creature is stirring, not even The Great Central Asia Explorers. I wish I were home, but it won't be long now, and we are actually making plans for the trek out. There are two possiblities: first, to go out at once by plane to Hong Kong; second to go to Szechuan Province for a couple of weeks' work and then leave by way of Yunnan Province and French Indochina. I think Mr. Chow would like us to do some oil snooping in Szechuan, and while we are there it would be an excellent opportunity to explore the famous gorges of the Yangtze River. This area is far enough from the coast and the fighting that the extension would be a safe activity for us. Meanwhile, we have been living quietly and working on our report and maps. We are about half finished.

I have been wanting to go to the Chinese theater but have not had the chance before to go with someone who could tell me what was happening. Last night Dr. Han got tickets for himself, Sun, and me. There are no reserved seats and, because the show begins at an unearthly early hour, he sent a servant to squat in some seats and hold them for our arrival. Han came by for us about 7:30, and we set out on streets lit by sickly electric lights and occasional pressure kerosene lamps in the few shops still open. The theater was full when we got there and the play in progress. The hall held nearly 1,000 people squashed on benches so close together that we had to squeeze down the aisle. Each bench was long enough to hold four people. They had backs and were not quite as uncomfortable as you might imagine. Attached to the back of each bench was a six-inch shelf which held teapots, handleless cups, and dishes of watermelon and pumpkin seeds for the benefit of those seated on the bench behind. All the lights were on and the spectators were talking and laughing with each other, slurping tea, cracking seeds, squirming about, and apparently paying very little attention to the play. Our seats were excellent—third row center. After we routed the servant, struggled into position, and sat down, Han removed his shoes and wrapped his legs and feet in a blanket he had brought along as, of course, there was no heat. I wore my big coat and fur hat and found that all the surrounding humanity created enough warmth to make things relatively comfortable.

The stage was raised about four feet with a low railing across the front, which was lined with a row of dim unshaded electric lights. Four pressure kerosene lamps which hung from the roof had to be lowered and pumped up every now and then. On either side of the stage were two curtained doorways from which the actors made their entrances and exits. On one side a section of the audience was seated behind two musicians, one who played the flute and the other who alternated between sawing away at a fiddle with a small head and blowing on a wooden horn. On the other side of the stage were four men, a drum, and a sizeable collection of brass gongs and wooden and bamboo clackers. There were also a number of other people who seemingly had nothing to do with the play but wandered around talking with each other and the actors, and a prop boy with two coolies who moved tables and chairs on and off stage.

The play was not a continuous one but a series of separate acts which were the favorite scenes of several different plays. The stories were chiefly concerned with emperors, plots, and love affairs. For instance, the first play was a court intrigue in which an ignoble official was deceiving the emperor until he was found out. The second was a story about a young man pursued by enemies, who took refuge on a barge with a young woman who hid him in a coffin. After he was saved, she appealed to him to avenge her father's death, which of course he did; they fell in love, and he presented her with a magic token. The third was a complete story (as near as I could tell) about an eastern king who hoped to capture and kill a western king. However, the plot was so involved and complicated with double entendres involving princesses, deceits, disguises, misunderstood messages, etc., it would be impossible to describe. Han informed me that most plays are based on actual historical events in Chinese lore. Like opera, a lot of the dialogue is sung rather than spoken. Chinese singing is different from western singing in that it sounds very monotonous and is done in a quavery voice, often in falsetto with occasional lapses into normal range. Most of the women's parts were played by men, so it was a little disconcerting when their falsettos broke. Actually, the music was not unmelodious, but the racket of clackers, gongs, and drums, combined with the noises from the audience, made it difficult to hear the tunes. I am sure that people sitting halfway back could hear nothing.

The acting was stylized and unnatural, with much strutting and posturing and use of arms, hands, and fingers, and there were little dances from time to time that appeared to have a questionable relationship to the music. The costumes were gorgeous—brilliantly colored mandarin robes and great ornate headdresses with wild clusters of artificial flowers and Christmas tree ornaments. Most of the men wore false whiskers made from red or white horsehair which they continually stroked and combed with their fingers. Their faces, painted like masks, were startling. Although some of the actors used no make-up, others had their whole faces grotesquely painted in vivid colors. The eastern king, for instance, had a white face with heavy black lines accentuating his eyes, wrinkles down his cheeks, red eyebrows, dark frown lines across his forehead, and a red upper lip that blended with his whiskers. His bride also had a white face with rouged cheeks that started low and increased in brilliance to the upper parts of her eye sockets. Many faces looked like the demons we have seen in Chinese temples. Props were few and the coolies were constantly in motion, putting down cushions to be knelt upon, moving chairs and tables around, holding up pieces of blue cloth with painted bricks representing walls, etc. To show he is on horseback an actor carries a whip; a paddle is held up to show he is on a boat; messengers carry white flags with red borders; generals are indicated by having the sticks of four triangular dragon flags stuck down the backs of their necks. Unimportant parts were filled by the same seven men whose tattered trousers showed beneath their costumes. They carried swords, banners, or anything else required for the moment, and represented soldiers, a crowd, or whatever was called for. They were a dirty-looking lot and stood around with their mouths hanging open, looking a bit dull. Two things were particularly amusing to me. One, a teapot was circulated among the actors; a man would take it, pull up his false whiskers, take a slug, and pass it on. Second, the prop boy was always running around lifting up the backs of costumes when any of the actors sat down, arranging and rearranging all the drapes and folds. The evening was lots of fun.

It is said that the Formosa air squadron that raided Nanking has been based on the island for two years in preparation for the attacks—and that the Japanese pilots had spent at least two months in Nanking and environs, also on reconnaissance. We have been told that a German radio station in Hong Kong furnishes Japan with information which has been intercepted by the Chinese. For instance, one message reported that a fleet of Japanese bombers bound for Canton was caught in a storm and lost at sea, a fortunate twist of fate if true. The paper here had a story that Chinese bombs have sunk twenty-five Jap war vessels, including one battleship, just in the last two weeks.

From what the local papers say, I judge that feeling in the U.S. is running high against the Japanese and that Americans are clamoring for war. As I am sure I have said before, I certainly hope we don't get mixed up in this affair, but on the other hand Japan must be whipped. Neither England, Russia, America, France, nor Holland can afford to see her win, and it appears that everybody is just setting around waiting for someome else to come to China's aid. Of course, if England comes in Italy will attack Egypt, and there is no telling what Germany might do.

I wonder if England could make a deal with Germany to give back her colonies. Then England and Russia could clean up on Japan and Italy without much German interference. I would like to think they could do this without U.S. aid, but I suppose it is more realistic to be a fatalist.

Lanchow
January 2, 1938

Here it is, another year, and we are still in Lanchow. We have already been here longer than necessary because Suez makes all arrangements in the most circuitous fashion possible. It only took us a week to get out of Suchow, and motor transportation is much easier to obtain here, so I can't help but feel that Suez is trying to drag things out for some personal reason. However, I don't really care all that much just now because we have our work to do and there are few distractions to interfere. Also, we are comfortably situated, and I am momentarily content to let him do as he likes. Suez is a real problem in many ways, and I shall be glad when we finally part company. He does practically nothing, but acts and talks as though he were the busiest, most overworked man in the whole world. And nothing happens without him meddling in it.

Last week we had a lovely roast duck dinner. Sun bought the bird with the $5 he won on Fred's bet that the war would be over by Christmas, which was made three months ago when we returned to Lanchow from Tsinghai. We have also gone to the theater again, this time taking the servants with us. There was a series of sword dances and a modern four-act play about a peasant who mistakenly joined a band of robbers. The servants enjoyed it all greatly and sat there entranced. Actually, they seem to know more about theater than Sun does, and this morning at breakfast they explained some of the things that went on. They say that acting here is as good if not better than in Shanghai, and I must agree that there was some very good pantomime.

Suez gave a dinner party on New Year's Eve. He invited six men; one declined and two never showed up. We waited around for about an hour and finally sat down without them. Those present were the telegraph master, the superintendent of the electric plant, and the local General Motors agent. Suez acted as though he did not like the telegraph master and quarreled with him at the table because, apparently, the man would not drink with him as much as he wished. I liked the electric man; he spoke English well and had spent some time in the U.S. at Western Electric, Westinghouse, and AT&T. The other man was exceptionally quiet and hardly spoke to anybody at all. They left soon after dinner was over, and we went right to bed. It must have been about 11:00. As far as I know there were no New Year's Eve bells or whistles, although I guess if there had been it would have been interpreted as an air raid.

The newspaper reports that the incident of the sinking of the *Panay* has been closed, remarking that the U.S. had "come in like a tiger's head and gone out like a snake's tail". There seems to be a lull in the fighting, and we all wonder what Japan is cooking up—perhaps an attack on Canton. Their air raids within 500 miles of here have not been severe and mostly confined to bombing air fields and railways. Urban areas are pretty much left alone, probably because the cities of north China are not worth the price of the bombs to blow them up. In spite of what the Japanese press says, the Central Chinese Government is intact and firmly in control. I rather think that China is conserving her strength at the moment and building up for more important action in the spring.

We have had a call from a representative of the governor and one from the police because of a telegram from T.V. Soong in Hong Kong asking about our whereabouts. I suspect that the possibility of a U.S.-Japanese war has the New York office worried and inquiry was initiated by Dr. Koo. Meanwhile, Suez is working to obtain military passes from the governor for us.

Lanchow
January 9, 1938

Another week has rolled past during which we have been hard at work. The first draft of my report is finished except for a stretch in northwest Kansu for which Sun must furnish the data. Also, I have typed a copy of my field notes for reference which amounts to fifty-two single-spaced pages, a more monumental effort than I had expected.

We have been out to dinner only once, to Dr. Han's. It was an interesting meal that perhaps we could duplicate at home because there was not a succession of courses with exotic ingredients. We started with a samovar of boiling chicken soup with dishes of various kinds of pickles and sauces arranged around it. The servant brought plates of raw mutton, chicken, and liver, all sliced very thin, which we picked up with our chopsticks and held in the boiling soup until cooked, which took almost no time at all. Each of us had a bowl in which we mixed the sauces, principally soy and sesame paste that tastes like peanut butter. After everybody had enough meat, chopped cabbage and other leafy vegetables, noodles, and bean curd were cooked in what remained of the soup. We each broke a raw egg into our bowls and filled them with the broth. With this we had *shao-ping*, small round pieces of toasted bread covered with sesame seed. For a finale we had tea and fresh pears. It was awfully good, but neither Fred nor I can possibly consume the quantities of food the Chinese can, and we again left the table much too full. I don't see how they can eat so much.

I have begun to push Suez into making the necessary arrangements for our departure. We now have two passes from the governor, which are large and very important looking documents with enormous red seals. Last night when an officer came around to check our passports, Suez flashed them to make an impression. I think we will be leaving within a few days, by truck or bus or by air, I don't know yet. In any case, I shall be glad to be gone from here; the coal smoke in our rooms gets into everything, and we simply can't keep clean. The towels, pillows, and all our clothes are filthy with it, and I am sure we are much dirtier than when we were working in the field. This is also a noisy place, which can be expected when so many people live so close together. Every afternoon and every evening there is a dinner party downstairs, with much shouting and guessing of finger counts. There are several children; the young ones cry and the older ones play loudly in the courtyard. Everybody screams at the servants, and boisterous Mah-Jong games sometimes last all night.

I have been whiling away the hours talking with Sun about the world and the war. I am constantly amazed at his ignorance of life outside China. Although he once went to Sweden for a few months, he knows practically nothing about world geography and is totally blank about foreign countries. A partial explanation might be that the schools here have to devote so much effort to plain reading and writing that little time remains for other subjects. The Chinese language must be a terrible handicap to the whole country.

Back in Shanghai Hussey once told me that the Chinese do everything backwards. Of course this is not true, but they do enough things the opposite from us to be interesting. Some of these customs are: 1) a guest sits opposite his host, not beside him; 2) one shakes hands with himself, not the person he is meeting; 3) soup comes at the end of the meal, not the beginning; 4) men wear skirts and women wear pants; 5) they write from top to bottom, but from right to left and begin at the back of the book; 6) a person's last name comes before his first name; 7) letters are addressed with the city's name first and the person's name last; 8) one never signs anything, but uses a stamp; 9) here one uses the sound to stop a horse that we use to make him go.

I have begun to sort through my things and pack up for the trip east. Fred, Suez, and I have also made arrangements to have our money transferred to Chungking.

I would like to buy some old Chinese paintings, so Sun and I went out to see what we could find. The most interesting item we saw consisted of twelve long, narrow panels apparently intended for a screen. It was painted on silk; fantastic mountains with temples, trees, clouds, people, and animals were all perfect down to the last detail. I was told that it had been painted by a court artist and given by the emperor to one of the great northwestern Ma's. I was not interested in purchasing it, however, because it would have covered the whole north wall of our Urbana living room, windows and all.

We visited the temple of the city god, north of the main street not far from our hotel. The buildings were closed; the courts and passageways that separated them were being used as shops. There was one poorly arranged museum exhibiting all kinds of products made in Kansu Province. The area, full of people, seemed to be a favorite meeting and lingering place. Groups were sitting around little tables drinking tea and eating, while several wandering musicians and singers circulated about performing for coppers. A blind man played a large two-stringed fiddle and a pair of wooden clappers on a stand that he operated with one foot. The result might be considered something like Chinese jazz.

Lanchow
January 11, 1938

We have just received a batch of Shanghai newspapers dated November 25 and 26, and December 23 and 24. They all came via air mail! Both of the later papers had accounts of Japanese air raids on Lanchow; one stated that the city is being subjected to repeated and severe raids, and the other said that the Japs had shot down and destroyed fourteen Chinese planes here on December 21. These Japanese accounts of the action are untrue. Actually, there were two air raids; one we heard about while in Suchow and the other, on December 21, we witnessed ourselves. When it was announced by sirens, whistles, and bells at about 11:30 A.M., Fred and I were both working. Although the warning signals were very faint we were disturbed, but when nothing happened we went back to work. There was more tooting and ringing just before noon, but still nothing happened and again we returned to our tasks. The planes finally came about 12:30, and when I heard the first bomb I thought it was the noon gun that is fired daily. Not until it was followed by a number of other explosions did we figure out what was happening. The bombing was a considerable distance outside the city to the east at the airfield, but it was strong enough to shake our paper-covered windows. We rushed out to see what we could and at last discovered the Japanese planes so high that they were hardly visible and too far away to count. Since the first alarm Chinese planes had been circling the city; we saw them chase after the Japs, their machine guns stuttering away faintly in the distance. Another alarm was sounded in the afternoon, which turned out to be a false one, but it kept us in suspense for over an hour. Reports that evening informed us that nine Jap planes had dropped twelve bombs. One man, one woman, and a horse were injured, some pigs were killed, and thirty mud huts were damaged. That was the extent of it all. Japanese statements in newspapers cannot be believed.

Sian
January 18, 1938

By the time you receive this letter you might just as well stop writing to me. We have definitely started on our way out, and unless something very unexpected happens we shall leave here in a week to go overland into Szechuan Province where we will do a little field work. From there, and after our reports are finished, we will be ready to start for home. I suspect that this will be about April 1. I have written an airmail letter to Dr. Koo in Paris telling him what we have done and what we propose to do. His reply will determine how we shall return to the States—whether by way of Europe or the Pacific. Meanwhile, I am glad our work is nearly finished and shall have no regrets when we can finally shake off the dust of Asia and climb aboard a boat for home.

Sian was not very impressive when we came through here from Shanghai last June, but the frame of mind we are in coming from the reverse direction is, oh, so very different. I had a real bath in a bathtub, the first one in six months, and I was in heaven. I lay soaking in the water until it was cold. I slept in a real bed, the first one in seven months, but it took me several nights to fully appreciate it. At first the pillow was too hard, the covers too heavy, and it did not fit just right. I guess I had become so accustomed to my camp cot and sleeping bag that I hated to give them up. But the greatest delight has been the toilet. After having to go out in near zero weather to find a place to squat where there was some protection from the wind, it has been a luxury and a joy to be able to sit leisurely and in comfort for as long as I want. Actually, the appointments of a modern hotel which we usually take for granted at home are so foreign to our recent experiences that I find it difficult to adapt myself. It did not occur to me when I checked in on the 16th that I could wash up before my bags had been unpacked; I was sitting around talking with Sun when Fred came in and announced that hot water really ran out of the taps. That brought me to my feet with a start, and I had to rush off and splash in the water myself. It was like instantly passing from the Middle Ages into the present day.

Also, I have shaved for the first time in four months. When I looked at myself in the mirror I was shocked at my whiskers, which were over two inches long. I thought I looked like pictures of Robinson Crusoe, Sun said I looked Mohammedan, Suez said I looked handsome, and Fred said I looked like hell.

The last couple of days we were in Lanchow, Sun had some interesting callers. One was a geologist working for the National Economic Council who is investigating the coal fields thereabouts, and another was a hydraulic engineer. The engineer went to Cornell, Michigan and had lived in the U.S. about seven years, probably seeing more of the country than I have. (But then, I have probably seen more of China than most Chinese.) They both spoke English, and it is always nice to meet people with whom one can communicate. Language difficulties greatly hamper the personal contacts a foreigner can have here, although I am amazed at the number of people who know a little English, even in the most out of the way places.

The night before we left, Dr. Han had a farewell dinner party for us. The main dish, which is apparently customary for departures, was steamed dumplings with chopped meat and other things inside. A later course was the same thing, only fried. It was all quite good. At his request, Dr. Han is being relieved of his post and will be replaced by one of his own doctors. Since this man is not a local either, the agitators are not getting what they wanted. Most of Han's staff want to leave with him, but he has persuaded them to stay with the exception of his secretary, Mr. Wu, and his servant, both of whom traveled out with us. Han will follow in a few days when he gets things wound up. He doesn't know yet what he is going to do, but several different posts have been offered to him; it seems that in some way he is not entirely free to choose for himself.

Arrangements were made for us to leave on the 12th, and much of our baggage had been loaded on the truck the afternoon before. However, past experience has taught me not to expect morning departures so we did not get out of bed early. As final bits were being loaded that morning, it became apparent that we had too much baggage for one truck and our bus. Suez was so busy writing last minute letters and telegrams that he was not available to assist with the problem until I forced the issue and finally got him out of his room to convince the drivers that they were putting too much on our bus. It was too late to get another truck, so by redistribution and division the two vehicles shared the burden and, at 1:00, without any lunch, we at last pulled out, overloaded and cross. We had one Russian-built 1935 Dodge truck, which was nearly new and seemingly in good shape, and a 1935 Ford V8 with a bus body which had been used on a bus line from Inner Mongolia to Turkistan. The motor sounded good, but otherwise the thing was a wreck. There were seats along each side facing inward which were all broken down, with ragged cushions and sprung springs. It was said to accommodate sixteen, but inside, in addition to the eight in our own party, were Dr. Han's secretary and servant, the driver, his helper, the owner of the truck, our more than ample baggage, and our supply of gasoline for the entire trip. We were very crowded and uncomfortable.

We drove out through the east gate, past the eastern suburb and the airfield, which was larger than I had remembered and guarded by soldiers stationed at intervals. A number of military planes were on the ground, standing with wide spaces between them so that one lucky bomb hit would damage no more than a single machine at a time. We drove down the Huang Ho valley a short distance before we turned south and started to climb a curving road cut in gravel and silt deposits of the great river terraces. After climbing some 750 feet, we came out upon the top of the first important terrace and at this level started up a tributary of the river that comes in from the southeast. This part of the country is built from a succession of river terraces too numerous to keep track of. Each time we would reach the top of one, another flat-topped line of hills appeared before us. This country is all under cultivation, even though it is a dry region and at these high levels there is no water for irrigation. Most of the fields were covered with gravel to conserve the moisture in the ground, so the area appeared more desolate than it actually is because at this time of year there is no green anywhere—it is all drab brown. There were a few trees and small mud villages along the way. The road was in fairly good condition in comparison to some we have been subjected to, so we rolled along, sometimes as fast as twenty miles per hour. It was very dusty, however, and continued to be so all the way to Sian. At first we were protected by being enclosed in our bus, but gradually the dust filtered in, and during the later part of the trip the constant bouncing kept the dust in the air agitated so that it ended up being worse than if we had been riding outside. We got such a late start the first day that we did not complete that stage until 8:30, so it was long after dark when we arrived at the truck depot of a small village named Ting Shi. We were also held up by the bus's motor which had a dirty feed pipe, requiring a stop to clean it out every half hour or so. Then, when daylight faded, the head lamps did not work and the driver and helper puttered around with them for a while until they got one of them to work, which satisfied them, and we went on. It went out several times, fortunately never at any dangerous places. We were all crowded into two small rooms at Ting Shi where we had nothing but a kang and one tiny paper-covered window. It was freezing cold. We got a charcoal fire started, but were quite disconcerted when one of our servants told us that there was no place to cook our supper. Suez and Sun went to a local restaurant, but this did not appeal to Fred or me, in spite of our having had nothing to eat since breakfast. We finally made out with a can of Campbell's soup and fried eggs that the cook fixed over the charcoal fire in our room. It was 10:30 by the time we crawled into bed.

On the 13th we went on to Ching Ning, a distance of over 100 miles, reaching there in mid-afternoon. We began with breakfast of tea and round cakes slightly sweetened inside and stamped on the outside with the red chop marks of the shop where they had been made. We ate no lunch except for a small piece of native bread and some peanuts we bought in a village along the way. They were cold and not fresh, but tasted good for a change, anyway. Our road went up the valley for a way and then climbed to the top of a loess ridge that we followed for most of the remainder of the day. The natural terracing of the country so noticeable on our first day out of Lanchow was replaced by great ridges and steep valleys. The relief was everywhere more than 1,000 feet, and in some places well over 2,000 feet, from hilltop to valley floor. I imagine that eastern Kentucky, stripped of its trees and rock outcrops and covered with loess, would look like this. Much of the region is farmed, and all but the steeper slopes are terraced in patches a little less steep than the natural incline. Most of the people live in the valleys where they can get water more easily. We also saw some of the cave dwellings which are so typical of the north China loess areas. These are dug back into the hillsides with only small outbuildings around the entrances. Our ridge rose to a maximum elevation of 7,500 feet and was most irregular, causing the road to twist continually. It was high enough to have been recently among the clouds, so there was heavy white frost on the telegraph lines and poles, and the scanty dry grass and the few trees near houses sparkled beautifully in the sunshine, enlivening an otherwise dreary landscape.

The road was built a few years ago by the International Famine Relief Commission to give employment to these destitute people, who suffer serious droughts every few years. It is well laid out, in fairly good condition, but is only a dirt road built upon loess, and after a rain it must become a sloppy mess. They are now in the process of surfacing it with broken rock. Stones are carried from gravel beds of nearby streams and outcrops and must be transported sometimes very long distances and up steep hills. There is a continuous line of these stones along the roadside, miles in length. Every means of transportation is used for hauling: mule carts, oxcarts, pack animals, even the backs of men and boys. It is this kind of project that shows China's unlimited manpower to its fullest extent. Further toward Sian, the process of breaking up the stones is being done entirely by hand. The only piece of modern equipment I saw was a heavy iron roller pulled by a hundred or so men and boys. This is really an important road, and once the surfacing is completed it will be very serviceable.

Eastward, traffic increased with motor trucks loaded with mail, freight, and passengers, two-wheeled carts of every description, wheelbarrows in ever-increasing numbers, and the inevitable walkers carrying shoulder poles and packs on their backs. Carts and wheelbarrows are loaded so heavily that the animals and men can barely stagger along a level stretch. When a hill is reached (and there are many steep ones), cooperative effort becomes essential. Animals from one cart are unhitched and added to those of another, and once that cart is up the hill they all return for the second. In the same way, a wheelbarrow is left at the bottom of a hill so its owner can help another wheelbarrow get to the top by pulling on a rope. The wheelbarrow is an important piece of property and to many workers probably makes all the difference between eating and not eating. They are made of wood, with large lopsided wheels which turn to a tune of unceasing squeaks from the wooden axles. The handles are wide apart, connected by a heavy strap which passes over the pusher's shoulders on which he bears the weight. He uses his hands on the handles principally for balancing.

Suez left the bus to ride in the front of the truck with its driver and helper, which released his space in the crowded bus. Because of this we were all more comfortable the second day out. On this day we were stopped several times by soldiers, one of whom gave us a particularly careful looking over and asked repeatedly if Fred were German. Apparently Germans are under great suspicion because of their treaty with Japan.

We got into Ching Ning early enough to get as good accommodations at the inn as possible and to allow for a complete dinner of corned beef, potatoes, and canned peaches—the first substantial meal we had had in several days. Fred, Sun, and I occupied one large room while Suez had a smaller one to himself where he could smoke his opium pipe in peace. Half of this inn was occupied by a detachment of soldiers who were bugled in and out several times. The driver worked on the bus for a long time and, by the light of Fred's flashlight, succeeded in cleaning out the gas feed line so that it gave no more trouble. The engine had been using a terrific amount of gasoline, one gallon every three miles or so, a condition which we could not afford to let continue. Also, on long climbs the engine got overly hot and boiled water in the radiator fiercely. After this engine overhaul our gas consumption was much reduced, but in spite of cool days the motor still overheated on the long hills.

On the 14th we crossed the Liu Pan Shan ("Six Turn Mountains") to Ping Liang, a fair-sized city. A short distance out of Ching Ning the valley is restricted to a gorge which cut through metamorphic rocks, but aside from this all the country between Lanchow and the mountains seems to be a red bed region. The thick deposits of loess and alluvial material near the Huang Ho conceals almost all of the bedrock, but as we got farther away from the river the loess became thinner, and the red beds showed through here and there up to the hilltops. Our road rose steadily until we were again in a frosty world, but because the day was grey and overcast the grass and trees did not sparkle to light our way as they did the day before. The Liu Pan Shan is a low ridge formed of cretaceous sandstone dipping steeply to the west. The road made a series of hairpin turns, necessitated by the steepness of the slopes, and we climbed up through the clouds to the top at an elevation of about 8,500 feet, where the sun was shining but a cold, penetrating wind blustered about us. The slopes here were barren, covered by short brown grass. Elsewhere are the forests we had noticed from the plane going west, which provide cheap fuel to nearby towns. We started down the east side and, after rounding a turn, came to a vista where the sweep of country spread out before us for miles and miles. The road then zigzagged down the steep slope of thick, dark red clay. We got to Ping Liang reasonably early and pulled into the principal motor inn. The rooms were small and not very good, and someone soon discovered better accommodations about a block down the main road, so we moved there. This was unfortunate because our truck pulled into town some time later, and the driver was advised by the first innkeeper that we had gone on ahead, so he continued further along the road, thinking he was following us. On the truck was my bed, Sun's bed, and the beds of two of the boys. Suez asked the truck station master to telephone the next station, thirty or forty miles down the road, to order the truck to return. However, the station master did not want to take the responsibility, for the intervening country was bandit-ridden and it would be unsafe for a solitary truck to return after dark. So, I spread a piece of canvas on my kang and borrowed two of Fred's blankets, and Suez bought a new quilt and a couple of sheets. Sun was somewhat less well provided for, so he rented some dirty quilts and used both his fur coat and mine. I do not know what the boys did. While we were waiting for dinner a peddler came along with hollow sticks of barley sugar rolled in sesame seeds, and we bought some. They were really good, sort of like molasses candy.

The next day's journey took us along a valley for quite a way and eventually up a thousand feet or so to the top of a loess plateau. The view was amazing; all the slopes, except those that were almost vertical, were terraced into almost level fields, rendering the steep hillsides into a series of narrow steps from bottom to top. The amount of work required to construct those terraces must have been enormous. With the exception of the skyscrapers of New York City, no landscape I have ever seen has shown more evidence of the working of man. Unfortunately I could not photograph the spectacular scene as it was a very grey day; later in the afternoon there was a small snowfall. The top of the plateau itself was absolutely flat and, except for being treeless, it could have been somewhere in central Illinois. We dropped back down into another valley through similar tightly terraced slopes and eventually passed our truck in one of the villages. It was having tire trouble, doubtless from being so badly overloaded. When we reached the outskirts of Pin Chow we were stopped by soldiers who told us to get out and line up. An officer began the search with Fred and then all the servants. He must have become tired before he got to me for I was not bothered, despite my belt with its leather attachments for compass and aneroid containers which look enough like cartridge cases to make people think me fully armed. We got to our inn about 4:00 to find it dark and somewhat smelly. Later we learned that the truck had broken down again, so Sun and I were once more without our beds. I made up a makeshift bed on the kang and Sun again rented some foul-looking quilts.

The next day, the 16th, we reached Sian. It had snowed during the night, just enough that the ground was white as we started out from Pin Chow in the morning. We climbed up out of the valley to another flat-topped loess plateau and down into another valley with terraced slopes. We began our climb over a range of low mountains rising about 1,000 feet. At the top the air was so brisk and misty that it caused ice to form on the windshields, and the driver had to hold his head out of the window to see his way. This stretch of the road was so difficult for carts and wheelbarrows that the country folk who lived along the way did a brisk business renting themselves and their livestock for hauling. Mules, horses, donkeys, cattle, men, boys, and women were all pushing and pulling carts, while many a wheelbarrow had a cow or a calf hitched in front of it. From the point where we reached the loess plateau on the south side of the mountain, the surface gradually sloped downward, interrupted only by low terraces near the river. One of these terraces was covered with a number of big burial mounds that probably dated back to ancient times when Sian was the capital of China. We easily kept track of distance by milestone markers every two kilometers. The last sixty kilometers of the road were troubleless, and when we bumped over the railroad tracks that extend westward from Sian we knew we were approaching civilization. We crossed the Wei Ho by means of a railroad bridge and soon came to the edge of the city, drove through the first gate, then the west suburb, and entered the city proper via the west gate without being stopped by soldiers. That seemed strange, but when we came to their station just inside the gate we passed muster with ease. We came at once to our guest house. It had taken us five days to travel the same distance we flew in five hours last June. However, since the air service between Sian and Lanchow has been discontinued, we had no other choice.

Before our arrival we had heard reports of air raids in Sian; now that we are in town we have learned what is really happening. The Japanese are in the habit of raiding here about every two weeks with their attention confined to the airfield west of the city. Little or no damage has been done so far. It would seem to me that such tactics do the Japanese no particular good since the results are not commensurate with the cost of the operation, and they serve to stir up patriotism in the Chinese people who might otherwise have felt lukewarm about the war.

It is now midnight and the mail plane leaves for Hankow and Hong Kong tomorrow so I shall close this long epistle.

Sian
January 23, 1938

Time flies, and we have not been here a week. We have more American and English acquaintances here than at any time since coming to China, and it certainly is an interesting change of scene for us. Smith, an Englishman who is in charge of the post office here, was born in Patagonia but has lived thirty or more years in China and recently has been transferred up here from Chungking in Szechuan. He is very un-British, friendly, and has such an endless stock of stories and jokes that one never knows when to take him seriously. He has told us about the exceptionally crowded conditions in Szechuan cities, so we have changed our plans and are staying here to finish the report and maps and will pass straight through Szechuan rather than stop over there. Another more typical Englishman is on the Boxer Indemnity Board and is an agricultural advisor to the Chinese. Besides ourselves, there are three young Americans staying at our hotel. One, a University of Missouri boy, was a member of the Olympic team that went to Germany a couple of years ago. He became acquainted with the Chinese delegation and was offered a job teaching physical education at the

Chinese University at Peiping. The university moved here when the Japs took north China and sooner or later will journey on to Szechuan. Most of the students are in a very bad way, without resources and unable to return to their homes. Everything they have comes from the university. Their food consists of cabbage soup for breakfast, cabbage for lunch, and both cabbage and cabbage soup for dinner. Once every ten days or so they get a little meat. They sleep on boards in unheated rooms, and each student has been issued a cheap overcoat to wear. In physical education classes they will not engage in any competitive sport or anything rough which might hurt them in any way. The two other Americans are from Carlton College, which uses a fund of $1,000 a year to send a junior here to teach English in a middle school. One has been out a year, the other arrived just before the trouble started. Their school is north near the Jap lines, so they came south and have just succeeded in getting jobs as English teachers here at the university. Big athletic fellows, they are typical college boys having a whale of a good time and are always up to things that must make others think Americans are crazy. A third boy, from Oberlin College, is here on a similar plan. He does not live in the hotel but drops by occasionally. They are a good bunch and lots of fun.

On our first day in town we were invited to lunch by banker Liu for a good Chinese meal. Afterwards, quite openly, Suez lay down on a bed for his smoke of opium. When I expressed curiosity, he demonstrated the process, showing me how to prepare a pill. I had no wish to smoke it, so he did. He carefully explained that he smokes very little and can take it or leave it, and I, of course, pretended to believe him. On our way back to the hotel we stopped by a shoe store and, surprisingly, I found a pair of padded Chinese shoes that I could get on my feet. At first they felt a little short and cramped the ends of my toes, but now that I have worn them constantly they have stretched and are quite comfortable. They are wonderfully warm and only cost one gold dollar.

Sun and I have found paper suitable for typing the report and have called at the Office of the Reconstruction Commissioner from whom we learned that they can make prints of our map tracings. So again, as in Lanchow, Fred and Sun are working on maps and I on the report.

This time, however, it is the finished product we are turning out.

Mr. Han of the Forestry Service has dropped in on us and is as funny as ever. He has heard from Maxwell Dorsey, but the war, of course, has interfered with their planned exchange of seeds and pods.

One night I went to the movies with the young Americans. We saw Eddie Cantor in *Roman Scandals*, but although we enjoyed ourselves neither the picture nor the theater was much good, and I have been bothered by fleas ever since. Most evenings we sit around the dining room with other foreigners and one or two Chinese, talking and listening to the radio until midnight. (These are late hours for us!)

This noon we found the dining room prepared for a big wedding party. The proceedings transpired as we had lunch, so we watched with interest. The people were all connected with the university; there were over 100 of them, mostly men. One of the men, a young Hong Kong Chinese, had just come out with a Ph.D. from the University of Chicago. He was very well dressed in American clothes and seemed rather out of place among all the gowns. Tables were arranged around the room on three sides like a big "C". In the center was another table where the bride and bridegroom and a number of the groom's friends were gathered, all wearing red ribbons. I think the actual ceremony took place there, with a simple declaration to friends by the principals that they were married. The bride and groom then returned to their places, which were located as far apart as possible, two men made funny speeches we could not understand, they all drank to the bride's health from wine glasses filled with beer, the bride and groom bowed to all, and then total attention was given to the dinner.

Sian
January 30, 1938

We've been busily occupied the past week with maps and reports. In the evenings we generally talk with the other foreigners, listen to the news broadcasts, and even have some "new" borrowed books to read. I have just finished *The People of Tibet* by Sir Charles Bell, who lived for twelve years in Lhasa. He is a miserable writer, but in spite of this handicap he tells many interesting things. After reading it, however, I realized for the first time that we really saw Tibet, in some ways, better than Bell. Although he refers to the Lhasa area as "central Tibet" it is really on the southern border, and the people there are a mixture of many races, much too civilized and influenced by Chinese and Indians to be typical. I have also seen several movies; Joan Crawford in *I Live My Life,* for which the Chinese title was *The East Wind Blows the Flower,* and Zane Grey's *Thunder Mountains,* which was called *Brave Wash Gold.* The theaters are well patronized, but for the life of me I don't understand what the Chinese can possibly make out of such pictures.

Even if we had wanted to leave here within a week we would have been unable to do so, particularly with Suez's assistance and management. We wanted to send unneeded baggage ahead of us on a truck that was scheduled to leave January 20, but snow in the mountains has blocked the road, and now it is Chinese New Year's and everything must wait out the five-day holiday. It is unwise to travel at this time because bandits make a good business from robbing people returning to their homes with presents for the holidays.

Our hotel is overflowing. We have had several generals here, which fills the lobby with soldiers staging sit-down strikes and demanding back pay. These Central Army soldiers are better off than those in Kansu, but I guess they still have their problems. Because they must buy food out of their pay, if they are neglected or underpaid they have no choice but to become bandits. There have been some serious riots involving wounded soldiers, minus limbs, from the large military hospital here. Many of them have left the city to prey upon the surrounding countryside.

This is the worst place for beggars I have seen, with terribly diseased and crippled specimens lingering about; one man with one arm and one leg rolls along the sidewalk pushing a can with a few coppers in it. Some beggars block doors to shops so the only way you can go inside is to pay a coin or two. Then there are small boys who come running out of nowhere, whining whenever they see us. When that has no effect they run ahead, fall on their hands and knees, and bang their heads on the ground. They keep it up for blocks and never seem to give up the hope of receiving something. Late at night there are always small boys lying almost naked on the freezing sidewalks, sobbing loudly. I am told that they are forced into this practice by their parents or masters.

I saw my first Chinese typewriter at the bank the other day. It is very different from ours in that the characters are too numerous to put on individual keys. The roller is large and the paper is fastened tightly upon it. The characters are separate pieces of type like those used in printing; about 2,000 of them are held in a tray that moves on ball bearings in all directions. At the front of the tray is a handle and a pointer. Printed characters corresponding to those in the tray are displayed on a glass-covered platform at the front of the machine. The handle of the tray is grasped and moved until the pointer is on the desired character, which is picked up by an arm from below, inked on the roller, and struck against the paper. It is possible to use this machine faster than a brush, and carbon copies can be made, which is impossible with hand-done calligraphy. Still, it is a cumbersome procedure.

Suez is not enjoying himself here. He has been cock of the walk so long that he finds our independence disturbing. We really see very little of him because Fred and I eat most of our meals in the dining room. He seems quite glum most of the time, although I try to make him feel useful by asking numerous questions which he never fails to answer in an authoritative manner.

I was asked to give a talk to the Rotary Club the other evening, and it came off very well. In an audience of about forty, half were Chinese and the other half mostly English missionaries. Suez had a frightful time because he was not the center of attention. Sun told me that the "old man" (as we refer to him among ourselves) was much elated when he was asked to speak before a university group; however, when Suez spoke of the invitation to me, he pretended to be doing it under great pressure, against his wishes.

We have heard that Lanchow has been bombed again. And again, I say to you, don't be alarmed about my safety because I honestly believe that I am safer here than I would be driving on an American highway or crossing the street in Chicago's Loop. These air raids (called *chin pao* in Chinese) are more terrifying than dangerous. To be effective, a bomb must make a direct hit, and the chances against this are enormous. Also, the Japanese don't seem interested in cities in this part of China, but go for the airfields which are always some distance outside the city limits. Smith says foreign mail is not being bothered by censors so I guess it has been unnecessary to hold back my observations. There are rumors that Jap planes have been sneaking over Sian unobserved, that everyone at the airfield is full of jitters, but I doubt these stories. There is quite a tale involving a German pilot of a Eurasia plane. Because of Chinese military planes, Germans are forbidden to circle the airfield and must make direct landings. The other day this German Eurasia pilot was about to land as a Chinese plane was taking off from the runway; the Eurasia plane, being diverted, was forced to circle and wait for a safe moment to land. He had no sooner made his landing and rolled to a stop than a Chinese officer came rushing onto the field, lit into him, and accused him of spying. The German talked back so as to make the officer lose face, and a great fuss ensued. As a result, the departure of the plane was delayed and Eurasia has discontinued flights here until the situation is adjusted to their satisfaction. Consequently, we are now without airmail service. The pilot in question is staying at our hotel. He also tells us that a Eurasia plane was fired upon by Chinese planes in Canton and that a Chinese pursuit plane shot down a Chinese bomber over Hankow in error. Apparently foreign pilots flying with the Chinese military have not been treated well, have been deserted in the middle of attacks and have not been paid their bounty money. They are getting disgusted.

We are enjoying our young American friends, and sometimes in the late afternoon we desert our project and go behind the hotel where there is a basketball court and throw a football around.

Tonight is New Year's Eve, and we are invited out to dinner by Liu again. And that's it for now.

Sian
February 6, 1938

This last week has not provided me with much to write about because of work on maps and my report. As I think I mentioned, we have decided to stay here to do our office work because we are comfortable here and probably could not find another place comparable to it until we leave the country.

The New Year's dinner given by banker Liu was one of the most elaborate we have had, with innumerable courses, most of them good. In addition to the four of us, there was Liu, his wife, and his sister-in-law. It was the first time that women have been included in any of the dinner affairs we have attended; I guess socializing is not part of the woman's role here. Liu does not drink, which is unusual for a Chinese, but Mrs. Liu more than made up for his abstinence and proposed *kan-peis* fast and furiously. After dinner she quietly lay down on the bed for her smoke of opium. There is nothing modern about Liu. He dresses in the Chinese manner and is quite a sight. On the outside he wears a long gown that buttons down the side and is lined with some kind of fur. When he goes out he covers it with a long overcoat and a fur hat like mine, but made out of much nicer material. At home he removes his gown, uncovering a suit of pajamas made of beautiful dark blue silk lined with a woolen material which shows when he turns back the long sleeves to free his hands. The trousers are large around the waist, with the extra fullness doubled over in front and held by a white sash which hangs below the bottom of the jacket. The trousers are tied around the ankles. Hanging from short strings attached to various parts of his clothing are jade and ivory charms, all in peculiar shapes. Layers of padded clothing make him look like a bigger man than he is, and he should certainly never suffer from the cold. The most incongruous part of his get-up is the footwear—ordinary woolen bedroom slippers. When we visited Liu's home last summer I was not impressed and thought that this was a hell of a way for a big banker to live. Since that time, however, we have seen China and have come back here with a very different viewpoint. Now his place seems to us to be opulent and the ultimate in comfort.

New Year's is followed by a five-day holiday, and almost all of the shops have been closed and boarded up. We were able to get one truck load of our things sent ahead to Szechuan with our No. 1 boy in charge. Richardson, a young New Zealand agricultural advisor, went with them.

We have a group of League of Nations doctors here now: three Swiss, one German, and one Austrian. The German came up by plane a couple of days ago; the others made the trip from Hong Kong by train last week. Dr. Mooser, the Swiss chief, told me that they had been very foolish to take the train because Japs are bombing the railroad almost every day, and their car was the only one of the whole train whose windows had not been broken by explosions. The railroad is a single track system, now bordered on each side by massive holes in the ground from bombs. The train moved slowly, spending long hours waiting in stations so other trains could pass. Whenever possible, it took shelter from the bombings in tunnels. Although the Japanese did little actual damage, it was still a frightening trip. Smith, the post office man, told us that eighty trains, each carrying about a thousand first-class troops, had gone through to the end of the line at Pao Chi, which is almost at the Kansu border. They are headed for Lanchow, so it looks as though the Chinese expect the Japanese to push through Inner Mongolia next in an attempt to cut the supply road to Russia. The postmaster in Lanchow has asked Smith to send provisions from Sian because prices there have risen sky high as a result of the army buying everything in sight.

Mooser is an interesting fellow—very outspoken against fascists and missionaries. He has been all over the world and worked a long time in Mexico. His speciality I think, is in diseases carried by blood-sucking insects and other creatures. Just what he and his men plan to do here I do not yet know, but I have a feeling it is mainly preventive medicine, delousing stations, etc. This part of the country is in the typhus zone, and we have recently heard that the disease has broken out in Lanchow.

We have been to two dinners here at the hotel. Suez had a small one on New Year's Day for Mr. and Mrs. Ling, who have returned from the University of Michigan where they knew Suez's son, Robert. Mr. Ling did not speak English easily, but his wife sounded just like an American girl. The other dinner was given by Mr. Wang, who is president of the university, so almost all of the guests were faculty members. Mr. Wang and two guests were University of Chicago students, and with me as a fourth, the University's representation was quite strong. I have been asked to speak to the advanced geography class in the near future.

We had another *chin pao* alarm yesterday, about 3:00 in the afternoon while I was typing. I continued working, intending to finish a page before running to the dugout, but word came a few minutes later that it was a false alarm so I was saved the effort. The Japanese appear to be so busy elsewhere that they have forgotten Sian, which is all right with me.

Almost every evening we gather in the hotel dining room to listen to news broadcasts from Shanghai. Our group consists of Smith, Shaberg, the student from the University of Missouri, Caton and Domke from Carlton College, an Alsatian named Bernard, Fred, and myself. For the past several evenings the static has been so bad that we suspect the Japanese are sending interference. In between and around the broadcasts, when we have our heads bent towards the radio, a hilarious crap game has been going on. The boys have taught Smith how to play, and he is now the most enthusiastic of the whole wild bunch.

Sian
February 12, 1938

Another uneventful week has slipped past. My report is almost finished, and the first ten sheets of our map (which will be twenty-one sheets in all) will be sent out tomorrow for blueprinting. Both Sun and Suez have given talks at the University, Suez on the habits and customs of the people in the northwest and Sun on the geology of the region. I am due for my speech on physiography some time this week.

Caton set off yesterday to return to the mission school in Fen Yang, where he and Domke had been teaching, in order to take some necessary cash to the missionaries there. This place is up in central Shansi Province, only twenty or thirty miles from the Jap lines. He figured it would take him anywhere from four days to a week to get there. He spent his last night here making secret pockets in his clothes in which to hide the $5,000 he is taking. I'm glad it's not me making such a journey.

We received a telegram advising us to return via Europe instead of taking the shorter trip across the Pacific. We are to report in at Den Hague for a short conference with the office there. So, even though I still have no departure dates or arrival plans for anywhere, at least I know people are thinking about the culmination of our expedition and our return, which is encouraging.

We have a new English couple at the hotel. She is an inveterate traveler and professes to have been in every out-of-the-way spot in the world. She claims to know most of the explorers and hasn't anything good to say about any of them. The second husband seems to tag along to some place where he can wait comfortably while she rushes off to rough it. She had an idea she wanted to go to Kokonor, but we have convinced her it's the wrong time of year for that kind of sport. Her next idea was to cross Turkistan, but we told her that even with all of our political backing we were unable to do it, so she has decided to visit the Chinese Red Army.

Friday the Chinese authorities gave a tea for all the foreigners in Sian in connection with their "Resist the Enemy" and "Peace Week" services. There was a total of twenty-four foreigners in attendance, mostly missionaries, and a funny looking lot they were. The funniest of them all was an Italian Catholic father with a sad, bloodhound face. A small man from the Generalissimo's headquarters made a speech which was translated into English, and one of the missionaries replied for the foreigners. The most interesting part of the whole affair was the tea and cakes

The evening crap game continues to be popular, and Smith is like a circus clown when he has a winning streak. I would think they would tire of it, but they don't, and last night they even had three excitable Chinese playing along with them.

I think we will be leaving here in about a week.

Sian
February 27, 1938

We are still here because Suez seems to be having difficulties engaging our transportation. We have been hard at work until recently, so there is little to report. Today I didn't even get up until after 11:00, which was too late for breakfast. Fred and I ate lunch with Smith, as we often do, and were later joined by Mooser. I like both of these men very much. Smith is friendly and genial while Mooser is outspoken, but his genuine sincerity makes his manner quite acceptable. He despises show and pretense and minces no words in denouncing dishonesty. Dinner was interrupted by a *chin pao*, the third in the last two weeks. The earlier alarms were in error, one because an approaching Chinese plane had been improperly identified. Sian now has a squadron of defense planes which were circling today, steadily climbing until they could barely be seen. We almost broke our necks trying to keep track of them among the thin white wisps of clouds. Either the Jap planes were not bound for Sian or they got scared away for, again, nothing happened.

When the all-clear signal sounded, Mooser asked Fred and me to join him in a drive out to the warm springs, which we did. With us also was one of Mooser's Chinese doctors. Great crowds of people were on the road, and several times Mooser had to tell his chauffeur to drive slower, with greater care. In spite of these warnings, when a small boy dashed out from behind a cart in front of the car, we hit him with a terrible thud. I really believe that the driver could have avoided him easily, but he neither tried to stop nor turn aside. We rushed back to the poor child who was lying in the road with blood pouring from an awful gash in his head. The driver, more concerned with the condition of his front grill, didn't stop to look at the boy and neither did the cart man with whom the child had been traveling. We thought he was dead, but his pulse was still going and presently he began to breathe again. Of course, we turned back to town, and Mooser and I held him in our laps until we got to the mission hospital. I held him in the car while the others went in to get help. They were gone an endless period of time, and I later learned that all sorts of foolish questions had been asked about the boy's religion, etc., before the hospital finally consented to take him in. So ended our little outing.

Several times we have been invited to Rotary Club meetings to hear guest speakers. One of the talks was given by the lady explorer, and she certainly made a mess of it. She is about forty, and her poor husband is in his sixties. I am positive that he would much rather be at home than running around this way, but apparently they were married with the agreement that four months out of every year would be spent traveling in ungodly and forsaken places. She claims she has been in every capital of the world except Lhasa, and has written books with orders for eight more. She is, however, one of the most rattle-brained persons I have ever met, and I fail to see how she gets away with it. She talked endlessly and uninterestingly, reading monotonously from written notes. Mooser, sitting next to me, kept hissing uncomplimentary remarks about her in my ear. She read off a story about traveling in Ethiopia during the war with the Italians and seeing women nursing babies with no heads. That finished Mooser, who snorted and stalked out! If this talk was any example of her writing skills, we decided that we all could write books. She doesn't seem to know what she is doing here or what she wants to see; the only thing of importance is to be somewhere off the beaten track doing something strange. They have just left for a visit to the Chinese Red Army, and we are all relieved to be rid of them. She borrowed a map of China from us and tried to carry it off with her. The night before they left, Fred asked for its return; they had to unpack their trunk to retrieve it.

Another talk was interesting. It was given by Captain Carlson of the U.S. Marines who had just returned from two and a half months marching with the Red Army in its operations in northern Shansi. He has a high regard for this army, composed mostly of very young men with indefatigable spirit who have developed good, effective tactics. The countryside is well organized with a peasant militia made up of men, women, and children banded together in clubs, with training in methods of harassing the enemy. Apparently Japanese control in

Shansi extends only for short distances on either side of the railroad lines, and their territory is interspersed with areas held by the Chinese. It is easy to pass through the Jap lines from one Chinese-held area to another. The Chinese attack by surprise to capture Japanese supplies and ammunition, moving far and fast, informed by the country people of enemy movements. When they leave an area they carry out all the food, which does not allow the Japs the luxury of being able to live off the land. Carlson reports that the Japanese army is not particularly aggressive and that their military machine is grossly overestimated. They are poor close fighters and inferior to the Chinese in strength and toughness. Although they perform under order, they lack the agility to act quickly under unexpected circumstances. He gives them no more than two years before their force breaks down completely.

Youngsters fourteen and fifteen years old act as orderlies and are called "little devils". After a time they become full-fledged soldiers known as "fighters". Officers are called "leaders" and require no special privileges. Both fighters and leaders can attend conferences, and there are no secret plans that are not commonly shared, so before going into action they all know what is to be done and how. They have a high sense of responsibility and do the things they should, not because they are ordered to do them, but because they believe in the action and its consequences. Unlike some other Chinese armies, their wounded are brought in and cared for to the best of their ability. The Red leaders seem to be truly exceptional, extraordinary men anxious to do their best and reluctant to take credit for their successes. Carlson is convinced that with this faction working for her, China will win hands down.

Sian
February 28, 1937

Caton has returned from his money delivery mission, alive and well. He arrived at Fen Yang almost simultaneously with the Japanese troops, so he backed up hastily and returned to Sian as quickly as possible in a freight car with Red soldiers bound for Hankow. They were all young and, although it was cold and they were all uncomfort able, they had the resiliency of youth. Everyone was cheerful as they sang songs about having no money, no clothes, no food, no ammunition but what they had taken from the Japanese. Caton said that most of the students and teachers from the mission school have joined the Red Army and are very enthusiastic about it.

We have had a report from the hospital where we took the boy our car hit yesterday. He is in good shape and, unless complications set in, he will be none the worse except for some bad scars.

Mooser has told me how he happens to be in China. The League of Nations Health Bureau, or whatever it is called, appropriated five million Swiss francs to send fully equipped and manned Red Cross ambulances to China to work with the army. It was practically signed and sealed, when Anthony Eden objected on the basis that the League should not engage in activities that could be construed as unfriendly to Japan; France agreed. As a substitute plan it was proposed that observers be sent out supported by enormous salaries which of course, would be both costly and ineffectual. Mooser got sore and decided to raise a fuss over the issue. He gave a detailed story to the press describing the episode, but not a single Swiss paper printed it, nor would the Associated Press give it coverage. Then he had handbills printed and distributed them on the streets of Geneva. As a result, the sum allotted was vastly reduced, and he was sent here with instructions to devote his attention solely to the civilian population. Now that he is here, however, he says that he will do what he damn pleases, and I think he is ready to send a fully equipped hospital up to the Red Army to care for their seriously injured. He certainly is riding rough-shod over his Chinese doctors and making them toe the line. If anything goes wrong, he pitches into them with no "face saving" allowed. Last week a case of smallpox was discovered in a refugee camp where all persons were supposed to have been vaccinated. He gave the doctor hell and caused him to lose so much face that he had to stay in bed all the next day. He told another of his doctors that since he is probably going to lose face frequently, he had better come to work with a new face every day. Someone else complained that he was working so hard under Mooser he wanted more pay. Mooser called his bluff and fired him. The doctor came back the next day hanging his head, saying he would gladly return to work for half his original salary. He has made himself unpopular around here, but he has also cut the graft that is so characteristic of the Chinese system. If it were Chinese money he was spending he could possibly be coerced into the system, but with foreign money he can get his own way. For a time he was letting his Chinese nurses come to his hotel room to use his bathtub, but had to put a stop to it because they came in droves of ten to twelve at all hours of the day and night.

I gave my talk at the university to the advanced geography class, but I don't think it was very successful. In the first place, I did not have time to prepare it properly, and in the second place, perhaps more personally charitable, I don't think the students knew enough English to follow it well. The university is housed in a large barn-like building several stories high, with rooms opening out onto balconies that circle covered courts. There was no heat, and everyone wore overcoats. At intervals someone came into our court and blew deafening sounds on a bugle so that I had to stop speaking. It was their substitute for an electric class bell, I suppose.

A few days ago Suez received a telegram from Chow reporting that Dr. Koo has had my leave of absence from work extended until next fall. This was news to me, and I can assure you I have no intention of staying around here that long. On the other hand, Suez seems to want to remain in the interior and is doing everything he can to drag out our time here. He acts very funny about it, and I am sure he does not suspect that I am on to his ways. I attempt to combat him in as Oriental a manner as possible in order to play his game and thus far have won most of my major points, although he still bests me in many small delays.

We are pleased with China's recent successes in the air, particularly the fight over Hankow and the raid on Formosa. Carlson told me something interesting about Japanese planes. Rather recently the U.S. developed a device for airplane carburetors that was a guarded military secret. He was surprised, therefore, while examining downed Japanese bombers in the Shanghai area to find that every one of them was equipped with this same device. Apparently the talk about Japanese spies in the U.S. is not all idle chatter.

One of Mooser's Chinese doctors has just returned from Chengchow, which is at the intersection of our railroad here to the Peiping-Hankow line. It was seriously bombed about ten days ago with heavy loss of life. The city had no defense, and the Japs simply had their way. Somewhere in the devastated area lies a general and his cash box, so now sentries guard the place day and night, searching madly about the ruins for the money. The doctor reports that a single Jap plane developed engine trouble and had to land nearby, where country people hauled out the pilot and made mincemeat of him. Notices are being broadcast that if a plane with a foreigner comes down, he must not be harmed. It is also reported that a Cantonese pilot recently landed somewhere near Hankow and, because he did not speak the local dialect, the people thought he was Japanese and killed him. Apparently serious fighting is expected to break out 200-300 miles east of us, and a hospital has been set up to accommodate 25,000 people.

The man with whom Suez has been negotiating for transportation has been stalling him, which has suddenly made Suez very angry. I suspect that now Suez has been thwarted, he will retaliate; probably we will have some action soon.

Sian
March 5, 1938

This is the day we were to have left for Szechuan but we are, as you can see, still here. By this time I have acquired a stoic sense of Oriental patience and never expect anything to be done on time, so my mind was prepared for this latest delay. Suez continues to deal in devious ways, usually working through friends and friends of friends rather than in a straightforward fashion. Arrangements were finally concluded with a man named Chow, and Suez had even paid him $700 in advance. Now we have learned that Chow is also devious and has been lying about the imminent arrival of his trucks. He has now had to rent trucks for our use, which we could have easily done ourselves for half the price. The day before yesterday the vehicles were supposed to have been ready for us, yesterday they were to have been loaded, and this morning we were to have left. However, yesterday Suez did not have the proper permits for our trucks to leave Sian or an endorsement on our passes. Now it is raining and the roads will not be fit for travel.

This past week has been an anxious one because the Japanese started a drive southward through Shansi and are now in the southwestern corner of that province, less than 100 miles away. The governor and commander of Shansi Province, General Yen Si-Shan, is an old man and seems to be playing the same old game that was played so often during the civil wars. His troops simply retired before the enemy without destroying anything behind them. The thought apparently is that sooner or later they will be moving back to the area and anything destroyed will only have to be rebuilt at a loss of money, time, and effort. Therefore, if the general keeps his troops intact and avoids losses from serious fighting, he will eventually be in a strong position and the central government will have to recognize his power. A few days ago it looked as if the Japs would be on our doorstep any minute; however, things appear to be better today. Central Army reinforcements have been sent in, artillery established, and the Jap drive seems to have been stopped where it is. Moreover, the Chinese yesterday made important advances in northern Honan Province, so it appears that if they are quick about it they can cut off the Japanese in Shansi and either starve them out, destroy them, or take them as prisoners.

If the Chinese leaders were all united and working together (as the Red Army seems to function), the Japanese would not have a ghost of a chance. But some of the old-timers are still locally in power and, as long as they can retain their positions, the rest of the country can rot. Patriotism, so entrenched in the minds of Westerners, is not strong here, and many people just sit on the fence waiting to see which way the cat will jump in order to determine personal advantage. Some of them would have no scruples about going over to the Japanese side for their own gain. The Generalissimo has done a giant job of holding things together as well as he can, and I think his influence is spreading and becoming stronger. Anyway, with the Japanese so close we have *chin paos* almost every day, and one day there were two. The day before yesterday a Jap observation plane followed a squadron of Chinese bombers and got past the watch which thought it was just another Chinese plane. It was almost over the city before it was discovered. They have not been bombing cities lately, but I have been a little concerned because our hotel is so close to the railroad station and, should they choose to bomb this area, we might get hit.

The radio in our dining room needs new tubes; that, coupled with Japanese airwave intervention, makes the news broadcasts virtually unintelligible. The electric lights have been going out, so sometimes we have to live by candlelight. This makes the large half-empty dining room an eerie place to spend much time. Nonetheless, the crap game goes on with great hilarity.

I am reading Pearl Buck's *The House Divided.*

Sian
March 8, 1938

When I woke up at 10:00 this morning snow was falling fast and the ground was entirely white. It is a little unusual for it to snow at this time of year, but I am sure that any added moisture in the soil will be welcomed by local farmers.

The morning paper carries good news about the war. Yesterday there was a big battle in Shansi which the Chinese claim killed some 15,000 Japanese. I imagine that this figure is exaggerated, but it is undoubtedly true an important victory was won and that Central Army troops are finally on the scene, opposing the enemy in front of them and tearing up the roads behind. If they can follow up the present advantage, the result may be more favorable than an effective defense would have been. The enemy is learning that it is unwise to extend itself without adequate protection of the rear. If the weather we are having extends into the battle area, it will interfere more with Japanese motorized operations than it will bother the Chinese.

Suez has informed me that the authorities have refused to permit our trucks to go through Szechuan, which on the surface sounds bad. However, just this morning he and Sun have wired Dr. Wong, the director of the Geological Survey and head of the Economic Council, and I feel sure that his positive orders will allow us to proceed as planned.

Caton, Schaberg, and I investigated a kind of circus or group of acrobats that was performing across the way. We passed through a meager bazaar and entered an enclosure about fifty feet in diameter with a canvas wall stretched around it. Admission was two cents. The audience, over half of whom were soldiers, stood around the edge behind a rope while the performers, a man, a woman, a boy, and a small girl, did their tricks, and a musician played a cornet with one hand and beat on two drums with the other. The tune was only a few bars played repeatedly and endlessly without variation. First, the man did a series of tricks with a diabolo, which showed his expertise but did not give evidence of much creativity, until he switched to an earthenware vase. This poorly balanced object, which had a big base with a narrow neck, was spun about and tossed into the air very cleverly with ease of manipulation. Then the boy, who was about ten, stepped out to the center. His face was hideously painted white with spots and a great black mustache, which made it impossible to tell what he really looked like, but his teeth were very white and showed conspicuously below his mustache when he smiled. He could also pop his eyes. Two poles were stuck in the ground with a crossbar about twenty-five feet high, and he clambered up a rope to do his tricks on this trapeze. His clowning and the funny quips he made to the giggling audience were far better than his ability in gymnastics; his antics were quite amusing. The woman, who performed on a slack wire, showed great talent. She was clever, and under different circumstances and with some dressing up, her act would certainly be first rate. The small girl was swung around by her hair at the end of a long rope and went through all kinds of posturing and, although this part of the show did not appeal to me, the audience loved it, for when she finished quite a lot of money in coppers was thrown into the ring. Much was made over one man who tossed in twenty cents. There were some more tricks, the children rolling about on wooden balls and spinning plates at the end of sticks, but we had seen enough and left. We then wandered through the bazaar, a miserable one with tiny booths or stuff spread out on the ground. The items for sale were worthless pieces of junk: piles of broken glass, bent and rusty nails, old padlocks that didn't work, miscellaneous clock bits, etc. We stopped in one of the eating establishments to watch a man operate a hand-driven machine that rolled dough into long thin sheets which were later cut into noodles. Someone asked what kind of people we were and Caton, who speaks reasonably good Chinese, told him that we were Americans. He then wanted to know if we were aviators and Caton said yes, that being the easiest answer, requiring the least explanation.

After we finished lunch the sirens sounded for the first time in five days, but this time the Japanese really came. Chinese planes rose from the field west of the city, circled a couple of times, and flew off to the east. I counted eleven of them as they went overhead. Fifteen minutes later we heard the dull booms of exploding bombs, and shortly afterwards first three and then two more Jap planes flew eastward, and a few minutes later I heard more motors. Glancing to the west toward the airfield I spotted a mass of planes that came out of nowhere. I counted at least thirty of them; they looked like a bunch of gnats circling in close formation. Then there was the noise of machine guns shooting, anti-aircraft batteries snapping, and the sound of more bombs, before the bombers disappeared from sight again. Something had been hit, for a column of gray smoke rose slowly and mushroomed out in the sky, growing larger. Machine gun fire continued, and we could see a dozen more planes swooping and turning at each other. Japanese fighting planes had remained to engage the Chinese while their bombers escaped. This kept up for about half an hour, and then gradually, in twos and threes, the Japanese struck off to the northeast and it was all over. But it was more than adequate excitement for the day.

The military situation does not look good. The Japanese are on the north bank of the Yellow River at T'ung Kuan, only 100 miles to the east of us. Further north they have crossed the river and are now in Shensi Province. Anything might happen; they might even be here in a few days but, personally, I think that Sian will remain safe, at least for a week or two. In the same confident breath, our permits have not yet been issued and our hotel manager appears to hope that they will not come through in time, for when the Japanese arrive he feels that the presence of foreigners in his hotel might save him and his hotel from harm. Needless to say, I hope this experience is not in store for us.

Sian
March 11, 1938

Papers here reported that our *chin pao* on March 8 did no damage to the airfield and that only three people were killed, although many were wounded and some outlying farmhouses were destroyed. Also, a Jap bomber was brought down somewhere to the east of us.

Wednesday morning Sun and I walked through the city to the street where the curio shops used to be. All but one have been closed or moved away, but at the remaining one I bought a set of four scrolls with pictures painted on silk. It was a fine, clear day with the mountains showing to the south of us, and I thoroughly enjoyed the walk and the exercise. That evening Schaberg and Caton invited Mooser, Fred, and me to have dinner with them, so we all piled into Mooser's car and went off to a Cantonese restaurant where we had an excellent meal. It was the cleanest most attractive Chinese restaurant I have yet seen.

The railroad to the east of us is pretty well blocked, and there has been only one train through for several days. After Tuesday's bombing the Chinese have become very panicky, and a number of people in our hotel are desperately trying to get out to Hankow, but are unable to do so. They say that going west, the railroad is swamped with refugees piling up at Pao Chi, the end of the line. That town is so filled with people unable to get transportation out that they are sleeping in the streets. Not only are they unable to get trucks or buses, but the road to the south has been blocked, first by a landslide, and now a heavy snow has stalled more than eighty trucks along it. This is the road we must take so we are prevented from leaving until it has been cleared, even though yesterday we received word that the military office has been ordered to issue our passes to Szechuan.

The ranks of foreigners have swelled. The one train that came through brought an Englishman on his way to Lanchow and a young

German. Last, but certainly not least, our lady explorer is back from the north. According to one of the Chinese doctors, also returning from the Chinese Red Army region, she made such a nuisance of herself, running wildly about getting in everybody's way and snapping pictures right and left, that she was ordered out. Since the Japs had crossed the Yellow River and the situation was growing tense, she herself was not loathe to leave quickly. So, she reported to the doctor that she was pregnant and had to get out as swiftly and comfortably as possible. He was a gentleman and arranged for her to squeeze into his League of Nations car which was returning to Sian with three men, all of their baggage, and cans of gasoline. (This was the same car load that Mooser did not join earlier because there was not an extra inch of space for him.) Everyone was terribly inconvenienced, but she calmly came off leaving her husband, a nice old man over sixty, living up there in a cave. Their trip back was a nightmare, made more difficult because of the snow which necessitated getting out and pushing when they got stuck. Of course this great lady refused to budge from the vehicle or even to walk a few steps when it might have been helpful. When she got to Sian she went crying off to Smith to send a postal truck back for her husband. If it weren't for the old man, I wish they would have been stuck there permanently. I know her tale of pregnancy is untrue because I overheard her this morning trying to wangle her way up to Lanchow in the Englishman's truck. I think Mooser is going to tell her what he thinks of her any minute, and what he thinks of her is not printable.

Yesterday morning a *chin pao* got me out of bed at 8:30, just as I was lying there wondering what to do with my day. You may be sure it made me scramble. We went out and watched the Chinese planes circle the city for about an hour before the all-clear sounded. When we went in for breakfast a second alarm went off. We didn't let it interfere with our meal, and nothing happened.

This morning we had another alarm about 10:30 while I was talking with Sun in his room. I went to my quarters to put on heavy shoes and went out to see what was going on. By that time the second or "urgent" alarm had sounded, and the streets were deserted. For the first time there were no Chinese planes in evidence, and the sky was empty except for a few high thin clouds. At about 11:00 planes began to appear; I counted ten of them. They flew around, and I thought at first they were Chinese as there was no shooting. After a few minutes, however, one dived down low over the airfield, and presently the boom of an exploding bomb announced their nationality and intentions. The anti-aircraft guns cut loose in short bursts of firing, and we could see the shells explode in the sky in small puffs of smoke, but because the marksmanship was poor none of the shots seemed to come even close, and the Japanese planes were almost leisurely in their activities. Periodically one would dive in low and drop a bomb. Altogether, I would say that seven or eight bombs were dropped; they seemed smaller than before and didn't make as much noise, even though the curling smoke indicated some hits. They did not bomb the railroad station close to us, although they certainly had every opportunity to do so, and my mind is relieved that apparently they do not plan to destroy it. After about half an hour the Japs left and Chinese planes appeared. It is possible that the Japs arrived when the Chinese were off raiding somewhere else. In any case, war is beastly business, and airplane bombing seems a cowardly way to fight.

One of Mooser's Swiss assistants is down with typhus fever and is quite ill.

Sian
March 14, 1938

A Japanese broadcast from Tiensin the other evening announced that the recent air battle over Sian netted five Chinese planes shot down and several destroyed on the ground. As there were no Chinese planes here at the time, this preposterous story made us all burst out laughing. Caton laughed so hard that he made us miss the number they claimed to have hit on the ground. The paper here said that there had been eleven Japanese planes in the air, and a man from the field said there were forty-three. Which stories are we to believe? Sunday the Japanese came over again with four planes. They circled the field and left without bombing.

Our raid today was a big one. The first alarm sounded at 11:15, followed shortly by the urgent signal. They came in flying comparatively low, circled the field, and dropped their bombs. Next a group of about six came over and, one at a time, dived, bombed, and then rose to circle the city. Just as we thought it was over, the drone of more engines brought in four heavy bombers from the northeast, which were so enormous that with field glasses we could clearly see the red suns on the undersides of their wings. They went directly to the airfield and dropped their bombs which, judging from the sound of the hits, were big ones, then circled and disappeared. By this time the air was so full of dust and explosions were so numerous that we lost track of what was happening. It appears that each group of attack planes was protected by a group of pursuit planes above them. All during the display we saw only one Chinese plane which came in just skimming the rooftops and disappeared as quickly. The big bombers seemed to go across the sky so very slowly that I would think they would be easy targets for the anti-aircraft guns, and shells exploded in little puffs of gray smoke which then hung stationary in the air as the planes moved on past. We were all praying that one would be struck, but they lumbered by in safety. I wonder what is now left of the airfield. After this last attack, I can't help but think it's been reduced to a bunch of holes in the ground.

The lady explorer's abandoned husband returned safely from Yenan on Saturday. I don't know how he got his ride, but he made the trip in three days via truck. His wife has been in bed with a bad cough and fever most of the time since her return. I wish it were worse.

We still do not have our truck permit. Saturday Suez got Caton to go to the place where our truck has been kept and ride it back to the hotel for safe-keeping. This was necessary because soldiers are commandeering all the trucks they can get their hands on, and the presence of a foreigner seems to keep them away. Then yesterday Suez, the General Motors agent, and I went around to the office of the Military Conmunications Control Department in an effort to step up the action on our permit. I rode in the truck intended for us, and the other two rode in a second truck by which banker Liu wishes to evacuate his family. The office is in a far corner of the city, and we drove there through narrow side streets in an attempt to avoid possible trouble. In spite of our precautions, my truck was stopped by soldiers on the way there and by the police on the way back. I don't know what the driver said to get us by successfully, but I did my part by sitting quietly in the front seat trying to look as much like Buddha as possible. The military officer was very pleasant, but told us that no permits could be issued for places beyond Hanchung, which is only half way to Cheng-tu. When reminded that orders had been sent from Hankow authorizing the issuance of our permit, he said that later military orders stated that no exceptions were to be made. The authorities are, of course, afraid that trucks allowed to leave this province, where they are needed for military transportation, will not be returned or will be seized by the soldiers of neighboring provinces. The General Motors agent gave his personal guarantee that the truck would be returned, and the officer said that he would give our case special consideration. We came away with nothing decided.

Time is going fast, and we are getting nowhere. Not only am I becoming somewhat concerned about the nature of happenings around here, but I also worry whether or not I will have my job waiting for me when I return to the States. It does seem, however, that we are very effectively bottled up here and can do nothing about it. The railroad to Hankow is being shelled by the Japs at several points, and for quite a while now no trains have been able to get through. Even if trains were in operation, I should go that way only as a last resort; it is unquestionably a very dangerous route. Incidentally, we understand that Chinese trains in the northern part of the country run only at night to avoid Japanese bombing, whereas Japanese trains run only by day because Chinese guerrilla bands attack them at night. There is no air service here now, and I think it would be impossible to charter a plane out. Mooser has been trying in vain to fly his assistant, who is sick with typhus, out to the hospital in Hong Kong. It seems that the back door is the only way open to us, and even that is barred without a permit.

The situation in Shensi seems to be a little better, and I think the Chinese are getting the upper hand along the Yellow River. The command here has been taken over by one of the Generalissimo's right-hand men who I understand is very capable. It is said that with him here, Sian is in no real danger of being taken. Nevertheless, everyone who can is leaving. The first group of twenty university professors with their families left this morning on a single crowded truck. They are bound for Hanchung, near which the university will be reestablished. About 1,500 students are due to leave tomorrow for Pao Chi on a special train. From there they will walk the rest of the way, which is only abut 200 miles. Schaberg and Caton are going with them.

Sian
March 16, 1938

Yesterday noon we finally got our truck permit, so I think we will be able to leave tomorrow. Although we feared that we would receive a permit only as far as Hanchung and have to make other arrangements from there, we have the proper papers that will get us all the way to Cheng-tu, in the heart of Szechuan Province. Today ten cases of gasoline are being purchased for the truck's trip down and back, so movement seems imminent. It will take us about a week to reach Cheng-tu if all goes well. We have two mountain ranges to cross, and I expect the road will be rough. The airfield at Hanchung, the half-way city, was severely bombed two days ago, the same day as the big raid here. A letter from Richardson, who went through with our truckload of provisions about six weeks ago, said it was reported that there were thousands of bandits along the road. He got through, though, without any trouble, so it is probably just more of the usual bandit talk we have heard everywhere. Nonetheless, we will inquire along the way and take what precautions we must.

The international population increases and decreases in waves. Recently it has acquired two new Americans: Col. Caldwell, a U.S. military attache, and Jack Belden of the United Press. As erratic service has been resumed by the railway, they both arrived by train and are both on their way to Lanchow. All of this sudden interest in Lanchow suggests that something may be brewing in that direction. Since there is no trouble with the Mohammedans, it would appear that it is a possible push to stop the Japs from cutting the Russian supply road. After we leave, Smith and the League of Nations men will soon be the only ones left, at least until the next wave rolls in.

Japanese planes returned today. They circled the airfield and dived low several times, probably the see what damage had been done the last time around. There was no bombing.

Typhus is rampant here now, and Mooser is treating forty or fifty cases a day. On his train ride, Belden picked up lice from his fellow travelers and has gone around to the delouser. They steamed his clothes, bathed him, and clipped his hair very short. He is a funny looking sight. Etter, Mooser's assistant, is better and over the worst, but still has fever and is very weak. I shall fill my underclothes with pyrethrum powder before leaving and trust that the bugs will stay away. After reaching Szechuan, however, we shall no longer have to worry about that particular disease at least.

The weather has been lovely, with bright warm sunshine during the day. I expect that traveling will be pleasant. I am packed and ready to go, eagerly believing that we are on our way out at long last.

PART VI

Escape from the Interior

Feng Hsien
March 18, 1938

After delays that seemed endless, we got away from Sian yesterday and are well on our way to Szechuan. In the morning our No. 2 boy knocked on our doors a little before 6:00, and shortly afterward Fred and I were having breakfast in the deserted dining room. When we were about halfway through, two young Chinese women and a little girl wearing red knitted tights came in to eat. We later learned that they were to be part of the cargo in the other truck that is accompanying us. Banker Liu had engaged it to send out his immediate family, but Suez informed us that Mrs. Liu is such an opium addict that she decided she could not stand the trip by truck to the next province, so they are staying behind. However, Liu's brother and his family and many other relations are on board; there are over twenty of them.

After breakfast Fred, Sun, and I sat around the hotel lobby ready to go while Suez bustled and clacked, rushing around meeting and greeting his friends and then disappearing for long periods of time to his room to finish last minute correspondence. There seemed to be some trouble with the servants which I later learned principally involved our cook, who was recently arrested by the police at the request of some woman. This new episode had to do with his sheepskin coat which had been stolen during an air raid alarm. The cook claimed that the hotel-keeper took it, and after considerable argument it was agreed to remove $15 from the hotel bill to cover the theft. At the last minute, however, the hotel-keeper disappeared and his assistant would not let the boys remove their baggage until the full bill was paid, so the end result was that the cook lost his coat and has nothing to show for it.

Anyway, we finally got away from the hotel only to stop at the driver's hotel for his bedding, where we had to bodily remove some of his friends from the truck, who were trying to steal a ride. From there we proceeded to the motor office for additional papers and then to the garage to pick up twenty five-gallon cans of gasoline. Eventually we got through the inspection station on the outskirts of town and were actually out on the road by about 10:00. I was afraid all along the way that there would be a *chin pao* and we would be held up even longer.

We are in a blue Chevrolet which is almost new. Fred and I raised such a fuss about the bus we had on our last trip and the fact that we could not see out of it, that Suez has had our current truck fitted with a seat behind the cab and overlooking it. Unfortunately, this seat is so close to the cab and the space so narrow that I cannot possibly sit on it, and since it is also uncomfortable for Fred, I am riding inside with the driver and Fred is on top with the baggage. Suez and Sun have the special seat to themselves.

We left Sian by the west gate, the same way we came in from Lanchow. Just beyond the suburb, we passed the airfield where two large hangars stood. I looked for damage done by Japanese bombs, but could see none; the rows of barracks were all untouched. I was much surprised, for it seemed that enough bombs had been dropped here to wreck the whole place. It just shows how inefficient air bombing is. We crossed the Wei Ho again by the railroad bridge and a little further on turned to the left, away from the Lanchow road.

We followed the river valley all the way, initially along a low terrace with a higher terrace rising precipitously above it which was composed of common drab silt and contained many caves, some inhabited. In places the bluff was so undermined by these diggings it was a wonder it had not caved in. That is what happens, however, whenever an earthquake hits this part of the country, and hundreds and thousands of people have been killed. The countryside looked much more attractive than when we came down from Lanchow; most of the fields are now a delicate green with winter wheat. People were out in the fields weeding on their hands and knees or squatting, while others were cultivating new crops with long-handled, narrow-bladed hoes. Shortly,

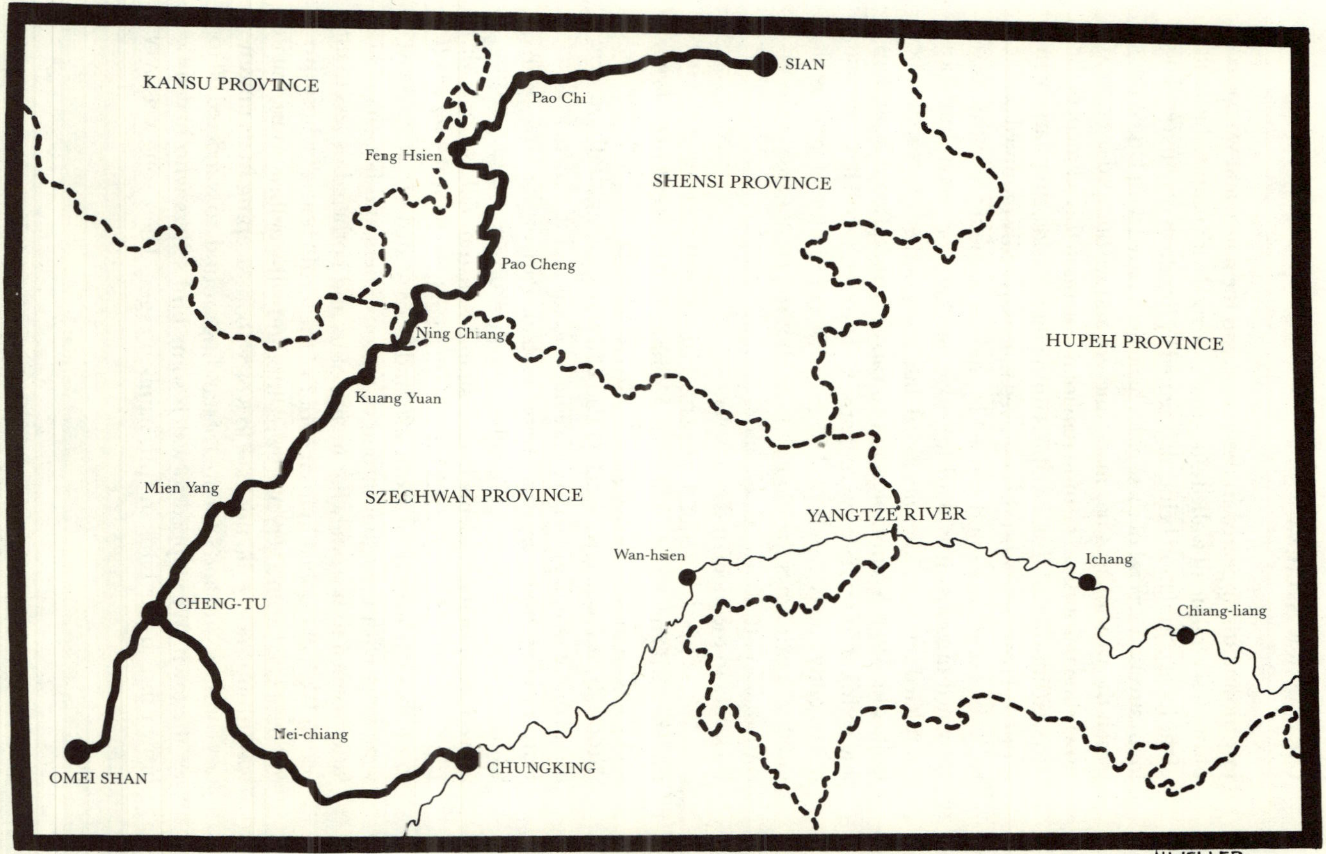

MAP III

Svechwan

HWELLER

low mountains appeared in the hazy sky to the north, and we passed through several small walled cities that swarmed with people, the result of the local population being augmented by hundreds of refugees. The main streets of several of these cities have been paved with large stones which the wear of ages has made uneven, and we bumped over them slowly and painfully. The most remarkable items in this segment of the trip were innumerable stone tablets lining the roadside, singularly or in groups. These were upright engraved tablets, usually mounted on the backs of stone turtles and capped by another stone representing two entwined dragons. It is hard to judge age here for everything once completed is forever after neglected, but many of them appeared to be quite old. More recent tablets have a cap of crossed Republican flags and seem commonplace by comparison. The motor road has been laid out recently and is merely packed dirt with a minimum of grading. It more or less follows the old cart track, but sometimes swerves to the right or left of the track, which causes some of the tablets to present their backsides to the modern-day traveler.

We stopped last night at Feng Hsiang, which means "flying phoenix". (Feng Hsien, where we are now, means "phoenix town", and Pao Chi means "sacred fowl". This seems to be the land of birds.) Although we could have reached Pao Chi easily by nightfall, we were afraid that it would be too full of refugees for us to find a place to sleep. Feng Hsiang, however, was almost as bad. Part of the First Army, which fought so bravely at Shanghai, was there on a recruiting mission, as well as all of the students from a sizable Kansu middle school. Mr. Liu said he could get quarters for us with friends, so he and Suez set off to see about it. We arrived about 4:30, and as we waited by our trucks we were beset with the usual throng of curious idlers and beggars. The latter seemed to be somewhat in awe of us and bothered us less than usual. We had stopped in front of one of the local "hotels" whose tiny rooms opened from a very narrow, damp, and evil-smelling court, but it was full-up and we did not have to worry about sleeping in its unsanitary confines. Sun and I got tired of standing around, so wandered off to see the town. We stopped to watch some bird sellers who had little brown thrush-like birds in split bamboo cages. Their song was very liquid with no really recognizable tune. At another place we observed a beggar family whose children were being offered for sale. I don't know what prices were asked, but there were no takers. A woman and small boy marched back and forth along the street beating a gong and advertising a theatrical performance of some kind, and over on a corner stood a filthy man hawking little toys which swung around on individual strings and made buzzing sounds. It was necessary to keep the string wet, which he did by putting it in his mouth. When some child had one purchased for him by a fond parent, the youngster immediately licked it to keep the string moist. I noticed for the first time an abundance of men in mourning dress. Some men wore all white (the color of mourning), others wore white trousers below their blue jackets, or white jackets over long blue gowns. Still others wore white bands around the edges of their black skull caps. Perhaps these variations mark different degrees of mourning; certainly the large number of these people can be partially explained by the fact that Chinese mourning lasts, I think, for three years.

We met Suez coming back and were soon established as the only paying occupants of an inn in the west suburb. There was one room for Fred and me, which proved to be rather small so I moved my bed out into a half-enclosed place that housed the family flour mill. When I awoke early in the morning I found the mill already in operation—turned by a blindfolded donkey driven by the innkeeper's wife. Asleep beside me on a pile of straw was the mangy family cur.

Today we traveled from Feng Hsiang through Pao Chi to Feng Hsien. We started about 8:00 and, following tributary valleys bordered on the south by high, hazy, snow-capped mountains, reached Pao Chi by mid-morning. Here, in spite of the early hour, our driver and his helper deserted the truck for a lengthy lunch. This gave us a chance to see something of the town, which we could easily do without straying too far afield, as a hustle of humanity swirled around us. This is the end of the railroad, a distinction that Pao Chi will not have for long because the line is being extended and will reach Lanchow in a couple of years, if not sooner. The railroad has already brought modern-style gray brick buildings along the principal street. The crowds of people have occupied all available quarters, and a crowded mat city has sprung up on the outskirts. These little houses are made by hanging mats over shaky stick frameworks, which don't appear to provide much shelter. Many people have brought their businesses with them, so all kinds of junk and second-hand clothing is for sale. The street was also lined with itinerant food sellers. One who established himself near us had some kind of concoction that looked like blanc mange which had been made in a wash basin and turned upside-down on a board. When a customer materialized, the salesman shaved off some noodle-like strings with a tin tool that looked like a cabbage grater and put them in a bowl where they were flavored with various condiments including pepper and oil. He had a single, very dirty, damp rag with which he wiped out the used bowls and chopsticks and also used to moisten his blanc mange. (It is a wonder that there is not more disease in this country.) Hordes of soldiers and civilians, as well as all kinds of conveyances, passed us in every direction. There were carts, rickshaws, baggage and pack animals, coolies with bundles on poles, and small crude sedan chairs, all carrying people and their worldly possessions on the flight west and south. We wondered if Schaberg, Caton, and their students had arrived and, if so, how they were faring, but we saw no sign of them.

We started off again about 10:30, crossed the river over a shaky makeshift bridge, and up a tributary valley coming in from the south. I saw here the first rice paddy fields, now empty save for the stubble of last year's crops. We traveled up this valley, rising about 3,000 feet to a pass through the Chin-ling Shan range, the so-called "backbone of China", dividing the country into the north and south, and from there down the long valley on the other side. This section of the road has had much work done on it, and there are rows upon rows of rocks piled by the roadside to be used to surface it. This impediment, coupled with heavy traffic, makes the roadway so congested that vehicles cannot pass easily, and the road is quite dangerous. Trucks just slam through; no one ever stops at wide places to let others proceed, and often vehicles meet head on where one has to back up, and a long argument ensues. Our driver makes me nervous by his reckless speeding around blind curves and down hills amidst all this activity. It is incredible that there is any motor road at all through these mountains and more amazing that it is so heavily traveled, even during these times. We passed long lines of army carts going south; it was an endless job getting around them. At several places we encountered straggling lines of army conscripts on foot heading north, guarded by a few soldiers so that they could not run away. Each carried a sack of grain that looked like a long white sausage about four inches in diameter—this was his food. The officer in charge usually was last in line, accompanied by his orderly who carried his gear which generally included a large shiny alarm clock. The peasants who were working on the road breaking stones were a wild and raggedy lot. Most of them wore the black Chinese skull cap. In these parts almost every man carries his long slender brass pipe and, when he is not smoking it, sticks it down the back of his neck.

The valley gradually became more rugged, and the low drab silt hills changed to metamorphic and igneous rock. As we rose in elevation the ground became wetter, and the road was muddy and slick. It seemed strange to me that, with rock everywhere, people still prefer to build homes from mud. There is so much rain in this region that flat mud roofs have been replaced by peaked or slanted roofs covered with common gray Chinese tiles or thatching. The journey down the other side of the ridge toward Feng Hsien was much the same, with the valley widening out and forming hills of nearly horizontal cretaceous sandstone.

This village is small with a badly decayed wall. We have stopped at an inn that is a regular station for post office trucks; there were already about ten of them in the large court when we arrived. We are now out of the land of the kang; the beds now are planks laid across two saw horses and covered with pieces of matting.

On the road
March 19-24, 1938

We obtained the very last accommodations left at our inn in Feng Hsien, as five or six more trucks came in the night we were there, and in the morning we found that the additional people all had had to sleep on the ground outside the inn wall.

We got started the morning of the 19th a little before 8:00, but not before excited exclamations from Mr. Liu concerning his belief that bandits had tried to enter his room during the night. He had woken almost everybody and turned out some soldiers, all to no avail. I am sure the problem was imaginary. He is banker Liu's brother, previously employed in the Shensi provincial revenue office, but he has run away, saying that he is afraid of being wounded or crippled by the Japanese. He seems to be an errant coward and a generally useless sort of individual. I am sure the government services are better off without him.

The small city where we spent the night was only half occupied by houses; its western segment was mostly fields. We passed out through a small gate onto a stretch of road under construction and covered with sharp-edged rocks. In spite of the fact that there was a truck approaching us from the south, our driver went right on ahead, and when the two vehicles pulled up eye-to-eye it was impossible to pass. There was a lot of loud talk, obviously mismanaged by our driver as we had to back up all the way to the gate. When we started out again we met a string of military trucks, but we managed to pull off to the side between a pile of rocks and a road roller. This allowed the others to squeeze by, but not without several of them scraping the side of our truck.

We soon turned up a tributary to the left where the road gradually became steeper and snaked back and forth up a slope to our first pass of the day. The elevation was not so high, but the jagged peaks of the nearby ridges were hidden by clouds, and the steep grade was made muddy by a fine rain. We went down into a short valley and turned up toward another pass where differences in vegetation became noticeable. Small evergreen trees were more numerous, and little groves of bamboo started to appear. There were greenish fields of young wheat and stubbled rice paddies. Many of the people we passed wore large bamboo and palm hats, effective against rain as well as protection from the sun. There were small thatched shelters supported on poles in the fields, leading me to think that perhaps crops are sometimes bothered by wild animals and that watchers are stationed there at night to frighten them off.

We climbed again to another pass in the clouds where we became part of a terrible traffic jam. The road was bad, narrow and partly obstructed by piles of rocks, and trucks had worn deep ruts in the mud. Ahead of us, a touring car loaded with passengers and luggage was mired down, and trucks were lining up in front and in back of it. After a delay of over half an hour it was finally pushed to the side of the road, and we were able to proceed.

During the day we passed several columns of troops marching north and some long lines of new recruits. At one point I noticed two men clambering up the mountain in the mist and later, when I heard rifle shots, realized that these were two escaping conscripts. Certainly, if they were able to disappear into the clouds, they would be safe from pursuit. That night Mr. Liu told how their truck, a short distance in front of us, was fired upon by bandits. I knew what had actually happened, but could not convince him of the truth. He certainly has a bad bandit complex; I suspect that he is carrying all of his valuables with him and is terrified of being robbed.

It was still raining when we entered a little valley with a pretty pine forest which we followed the rest of the way into the Hanchung plain. We were moving more into southern country; pussywillows were showing by the side of the road, and trees were light green with bursting buds. Here and there were small trees and shrubs in bloom. Suez said they were wild peach; their abundant white blossoms looked lovely against the brown hillsides. A number of small palms clustered about some of the miniscule farm houses.

The road became better and on a downgrade, so we made good time. The valley was narrow, with steep rocky sides and a river of clear water flowing over its bed of boulders. Here and there, in unexpected places, small temples perched precariously on the mountainsides. At one point beyond a bend we came to an unusual sight—a contemporary iron bridge crossing a canyon, just like one might expect to see in a modern country. At last we emerged through a notch in the Chin-ling Shan and came out into the Hanchung Basin Although the city of Hanchung was to our left, the road to Szechuan veered to the right so we kept on going. Near here we ferried the river on a large wooden barge which was pushed across by half a dozen men with long iron-tipped bamboo poles.

On the other side was the little walled city of Pao Cheng where we spent the night. It was 5:30 when we arrived, but 7:00 before we finally got settled. The motor road skirted the wall of the city to the gates, which were too small for the trucks to enter. The other truck was ahead of us, and when we drew up behind it an angry exchange was in progress. One of the female passengers was creating a stir because the driver could not guarantee the safety of her baggage overnight outside the wall. She was screaming in rage, wildly waving her arms in a most unbecoming manner—but we have seen the same kind of behavior before so the display was nothing new to us. Mr. Liu said that he had made arrangements with the magistrate for our accommodations, but as usual nothing came of it so the four of us went off to find a place for ourselves. There was one very narrow main street with houses crowded on both sides. The only inn we found was full, and the other little rooms we investigated were dark and doubtful places. After walking back and forth several times, someone suggested the school building. We found it in the southwest corner of the city and, after a short delay, the young schoolmaster appeared and warmly welcomed us into one of the large classrooms. Coolies brought our necessities from the truck, and Sun and Suez made up their beds on a couple of desks while Fred and I placed our cots against one of the walls. The accommodations turned out to be much better than at any inn, and we were quite comfortable. Fortunately the next day was Sunday and there was no school. (Most classes start at 6:30 A.M. and, although we intended to get an early start in the morning, we weren't eager for it to be that early.)

On Sunday we ventured west up the Han Valley, which is a fertile agricultural area surrounded by mountains; it is here that most refugees from Sian want to settle. Cut into innumerable little terraced fields, now green with wheat, there are flowering fruit trees and small groves of bamboo surrounding many of the farm houses. Here we saw the first water buffalo which, as we traveled south, began replacing the ox as the most common farm animal. Plows here are different from those in the north, having one handle instead of two and a smaller cast-iron blade.

However, like its northern counterpart, it only stirs up the soil; it does not crumble and turn it over as ours do. The clods have to be manually broken up by men following along with long-handled wooden mallets.

As we went westward the mountains, overhung by clouds, gradually closed in on the river until we were again in a narrow valley bounded by high steep slopes. There was not so much traffic on this stretch of the road which was relatively good but, like so many other things in China, had not been maintained properly. Many bridges had been washed out, necessitating steep and difficult detours. We eventually crossed the river by a makeshift bridge that would certainly be washed out by the first flood of the season, and started up a tributary to the south which led us into an area of small terraced fields, many of them flooded. Every available inch of soil was cultivated; there were fields only a few square yards in extent, and planting ran up among the rocks on incredibly steep hillsides. We climbed steadily along the road which, at one place, made nine hairpin turns up a particularly steep slope. From my seat on the top of the truck I couldn't see the edge of the road or any other evidence of the hillside for hundreds of feet down and, had it not been for the bumping, I might have thought I was flying. We reached the pass and came down the other side to the town of Ning Chiang where we put up for the night.

As usual, it was a crowded place with a main street barely wide enough for our truck. We settled into a small but comparatively attractive hotel where the woodwork had been freshly painted in a variety of vivid colors. We took a group of rooms on the second floor towards the back, which was entered through a circular moon gate. The only drawback was the noise and shouting from the many other occupants. I would say that Chinese are the noisiest people in the world but then, as they quieted down for the night, Fred began snoring, and he can snore louder than anything the Chinese can offer.

It was raining lightly in the morning, and there was talk of staying over a day, but Fred and I prevailed and we set off in mid-morning. I had secretly hoped our companions on the other truck would remain behind because they are a terrible nuisance, but Liu believed he saw bandits the day before and thinks he is safer traveling with us, so they tagged along. We climbed only one pass on this day, and a low one at that, but the road was muddy and one of our back wheels almost slid off the track on a precarious corner. Had that happened we would have been in bad trouble, so the driver and his helper put on chains, and we proceeded from there with greater ease.

After crossing the divide we were in Szechuan, at last.

Our road led westward down a long valley cut in Silurian shale with limestone mountains rising on both sides. At one place the stream flowing down the valley disappeared into a cave in a great limestone ridge. This was one of the most remarkable physiographic features I have ever seen. The road was on the south side of the stream but climbed several hundred feet, passed over the limestone ridge, and came down on the north side of the stream which had reemerged from its underground channel.

Following the valley, we came to a muddy river which flowed in from the north through a narrow gorge and then passed through a wider area cut in the Silurian shale before entering a second gorge cut through an anticline formed by Permian limestone. I had known from geologic reports that this formation was bituminous, but we were surprised to find several places where a little oil had seeped from crevices in the rock. Part of this canyon had sheer perpendicular walls, and for some distance the road had been blasted out of the side, with rock below forming the roadway and rock overhanging it above. To the south were a number of faults and anticlines, and we could see a complete section through the Triasic, Jurassic, and Cretaceous. The last ridge of the Ta-pa Shan is formed by a thick formation of Triasic limestone, and when we passed that we were in the great red Szechuan Basin. The sun came out from behind the clouds, and it was almost warm.

We spent the night at Kuang Yuan, even though our run for the day had been a short one and we arrived there in mid-afternoon. The inn was small, but our rooms at the back were isolated and we were not disturbed by other inhabitants, so I took advantage of the opportunity to strip off my clothes and see what sort of insect populations they contained. Ever since Mooser's talk about typhus, etc., I have felt somewhat crawly. Fortunately, I found nothing.

After dinner we went out for a walk. The city is a small one, situated on the bank of a river where it is joined by a tributary. We went out the south gate through a suburb to a tower erected to the God of Learning. This godlet is represented by a fierce figure with an upraised hand bearing a pen with which he is supposed to mark the name of a man who has achieved great scholarship. Below us in the stream a woman was washing clothes and a couple of men were drawing out water in wooden buckets. We went down to the river bed which was faced with dressed sandstone blocks, the outer walls of the bordering houses rising directly above it. The river was low, with a wide stretch of gray sand and pebbles separating it from the city shore. Tied along the bank were a score or more of large, mat-covered, flat-bottomed boats with whole families living on them. Two new boats were under construction, which we examined with interest. They were made from rough cedar planks held together by hand-wrought headless nails. As it was beginning to get dark, we climbed back up steep stone stairs into the city and returned to our inn. I set up my cot in the open passageway between two courts and went soundly to sleep under the light of a paper covered lantern.

The next day was our longest drive—about 125 miles. We really saw the Szechuan Basin on this part of the trip. Our road led down to the river where we were poled across on a barge with mooring ropes made of twisted palm bark fiber. By the ferry building was a sign warning passengers to dismount from trucks, stating that a truck had overturned last fall, drowning fourteen persons.

The Basin is really a region of hills and valleys some 1,000 feet or more deep; the term "basin" is used only because it is surrounded on all sides by higher mountains. The hills are formed of Cretaceous and Tertiary strata, and a grayish-red color prevails. It is highly cultivated, and the hillsides are terraced from top to bottom, but because the slopes are not as steep as those in Shensi the terracing has a much different appearance. It is attractive countryside, and from high places I could look down the ramifying valleys with their small terraced fields and find reflections of the sky in the flooded paddies intermingling with the muted green patches of delicate wheat buds. In contrast, there were numerous dark green cedar trees on the hillsides between the fields and spots of color where fields of mustard were in full bloom and flowering fruit trees grew in clumps of white and pink near the farmhouses.

The road was a good one and twisted up and down the hills and valleys. In places it was being worked on, and the men scattered at our approach as if their lives depended upon it. They were wise in their flight, for our Chinese driver has little consideration for others. This region seems to lack carts and beasts of burden; all loads were carried or pulled by manpower. The packs men carried on their backs were usually bell-shaped bamboo baskets, and each coolie toted a short crutch-like stick with a large crosspiece at the top on which he supported his load at rest stops. Boxes and bales were mostly transported in old rickshaws retired from human service. This section of the road more or less followed one of the old imperial courier routes, and at places along the side we were able to see the old pathway bordered with centuries-old cedars and paved with flagstones intended for feet, not wheels. More direct than the motor road, in some places it goes straight up and down the hillsides while the new road swings around to provide a gentler grade. We ferried over another stream; this time the ropes that held the barge were made of split and twisted bamboo. They are very strong, but the hands which must hold and manipulate them have to be tough and horny or they would be cut to ribbons.

We stopped for lunch in a small city, but the shaking I have been getting from the truck has caused me to lose interest in food so while Sun and Suez put away good meals, Fred and I restricted ourselves to some hard-boiled eggs and newly baked bread.

We spent last night in Mien Yang. We drove in through a narrow gate where the truck had difficulty making a right-angled turn and proceeded to our hotel behind a very noisy tea house. The rooms had rough wooden bedsteads with posts and curtains of coarse, dirty linen which I was sure housed mosquitoes, but there were none. I set up my bed in a dark hole of a back room with an unsteady floor where the only light came from two holes in the roof. Before dinner Sun and I went out to see the city, which seemed to be a prosperous place, with its shops teeming with people. We walked out the west gate, through the suburb, to a public park with a racetrack but not a blade of grass. Facing it was an imposing but very ugly building of recent construction, sporting a series of neo-Grecian pillars across the front. We were told it was the library. The roof had caved in, and it is now deserted.

Cheng-tu
April 3, 1938

We got off to an early start Wednesday and reached Cheng-tu about noon. The capital city of Szechuan Province, it is located in the midst of a large alluvial area to which it owes its prosperity and importance. The Min Chiang Ho comes down from high mountains in the northwest and enters the lower region of the Red Basin, building up a great, gently sloping fan which has buried all former inequalities of the topography except the tops of the highest hills which now project as rounded knolls and ridges above the alluvium. Although the region enjoys adequate rain, it is intensively irrigated through a series of channels laid out centuries ago by a man still remembered as one of China's greatest engineers and who is now worshipped as a god in temples erected to his memory. The motor road was level and well-graveled, and we made good time in spite of heavy traffic. Here, wheelbarrows are again numerous and much of the time are used for human transportation. Generally the passengers are old women who sit facing forward on special seats constructed above the small wheels. They look very dignified being pushed along, although the way is slow and, I fear, bumpy. Terrible old wrecks of rickshaws, mostly loaded with bales and boxes, are pulled by one coolie between the shafts and pushed from behind by another.

The countryside is cut up into the usual little fields separated by low ridges of earth, all growing healthy-looking crops that are mute evidence of the painstaking care which their cultivators lavish on them. The soil is brown and much more fertile than the red lands that prevail elsewhere in the Basin. This is reflected in a greater density of population. Not only were many farm homesteads scattered among the fields but our dusty road led us through a succession of villages and several walled cities that in the north would have seemed very prestigious places, indeed. As Smith told us it would be, Szechuan is another world, a land of water buffalo, bamboo groves, and water tread mills. Foot binding seems to have gone out of fashion earlier here than in the north, and only the old women have "lily feet". This has changed the status of women to an important degree, for the young ones now, along with the men, share in farm tasks which would have been impossible for their mothers.

We approached Cheng-tu through a series of suburbs as the road was transformed into a narrow street lined on both sides by the usual series of small shops. Suddenly a man sprang out waving and shouting. Our driver came to a sudden screeching halt, and we recognized our No. 1 boy who had left Sian with the first truck load of belongings on February 3. He had gained some weight and was evidently very glad to see us. Under his direction we proceeded by numerous, devious, and very narrow streets to the Ta Chuan Hotel where accommodations had been reserved for us.

The hotel is behind shops on a very modest street, and we entered its brick paved courtyard through a passage that could be closed off by heavy wooden doors. The building is modern, three stories high, with large glass windows of the western type. We went up the front steps, through a passage to the rear, and climbed to the top floor by a stairway very much like the back stairs of an American apartment building. The whole third floor is ours. At each end is a large bedroom; Fred and I have established ourselves in the western one, and Suez has taken possession of the corresponding room to the east. Sun has made himself at home in a smaller room between us, facing north. These are all furnished with nearly new European style furniture of "modern" design. The large room at the head of the stairs has a big round table and many heavily carved chairs and has become our dining room. Small rooms on either side of the stairs have been converted into kitchen, store room, and servants' quarters. We have been told that a year ago an unpopular delegation of Japanese who had tried to obtain important trade concessions in the province had lived here. Trouble broke out and a mob made its way to the hotel, stormed it, smashed windows and much of the furniture, and the Japs had to flee for their lives.

We were greeted and made welcome by Suez's nephew and one of the men from the bank, who appeared shortly after our arrival. An endless conversation in Chinese ensued, punctuated by smiles and innumerable dips and bows. Suez sent out at once for Chinese food, which was our late lunch. The dishes were so hot, with such generous amounts of pepper, that I did not enjoy them much and was hungry again by supper time. When our provisions had been unpacked, Fred and I dined greedily on our own food while Suez and Sun ate out. After lunch, baths were made ready for us in the separate bath house behind the hotel. This is a series of small rooms with enameled iron American bathtubs but no running water. My tub was filled by a servant carrying a bucket, and the water was scalding hot. After it cooled down a little and I had become accustomed to it, I enjoyed a long and pleasant soak. Toilets are located in another small building to one side of the bath house. Inside is a row of stalls with wooden doors; once inside a stall, the only "fixture" is a hole in the floor.

The room Fred and I share is a large one with only one bed. We tossed for it and I won, so he has set up his folding cot in a corner. He is probably more comfortable, for the bedstead has neither springs nor mattress but is tightly laced with unyielding cords of palm fiber over which I have unrolled my sleeping bag. I had been looking forward to catching up with our mail but there were no letters from home for me this time. Suez has received word from Chow, however, that Koo cabled approval of my extended leave from the Illinois Geological Survey to June 1, and I got a batch of developed film from Hankow to study and arrange.

When we awakened on our first morning here, a light rain was falling. We looked out of our windows at the surrounding rooftops and found them partly obscured by delicate green, newly budding leaves on trees growing in the courtyard, which had been invisible from the street. In the afternoon the rain stopped, and we all walked to the Kincheng Bank several blocks away. Like every place of importance, the bank was hidden behind little shops which face the street. A watchful porter admitted us to a long, narrow, dark passageway and the inevitable courtyard beyond, which contained a few small trees. Facing us was the public part of the banking establishment where two or three clerks sat behind high varnished counters open to the weather. (Apparently it never gets very cold here.) We were met there by our acquaintance of yesterday who escorted us to a second court and into a well-appointed room where tea was served. The whole place was charming, and nothing could be less like our American conception of what a bank should be; in fact, it was the perfect setting for a summer tea house. The second court had small trees and vines climbing the pillars along the front of a low porch flanking the surrounding buildings. The doorway through which we entered was bordered with long hanging scrolls of red paper decorated with gilt characters. The large room was carpeted and lit by the usual papered lattice windows. On the walls were a series of glass framed pictures of brilliantly colored and life-like birds embroidered in silk. Cheng-tu is noted for this kind of handicraft.

Once these civilities had been attended to, we were taken to the government offices some blocks away, through a gate guarded by armed soldiers, and into a reception room where again we were served tea. An intelligent looking gentleman in a long gray-blue gown entered, shook hands all around, and carefully examined our passports, which he approved and sent out to be stamped with a new large red chop. He was the Provincial Minister of Economics.

We returned to the hotel leisurely, walking through the city and inspecting a few of the shops. Cheng-tu is probably the best example of a real Chinese city that we have seen. Most of the streets are narrow with virtually non-existent sidewalks, but hard surfaced and quite clean. The buildings solidly line the streets and are generally one story with tile roofs; shop fronts obscure the secluded courtyards of those who live in the back. Few buildings are modern in the Chinese sense, that is, either made of concrete or built several stories high. Although there are several missionary establishments here, I saw no foreigners during our first days here. Of course the streets were thronged with people: pedestrians, peddlers, coolies with their loads swaying from shoulder poles, and rickshaws, but few motorized vehicles and no animal-drawn carts. The shops display a variety of goods; many are stocked with items that could be considered luxury goods. These seemed to be grouped in their own neighborhoods. We stopped at a silversmith's who seemed to enjoy considerable local renown. Behind a high counter facing the street the workmen were busy at their craft; we were led past them into a small, dimly lit back room where the finished products were displayed on cabinet shelves. Much of this shop's business must be with foreigners because many objects were of a kind seldom or never used by Chinese, like salt and pepper shakers which were ornately designed to depict such shapes as tall slender pagodas and human figures. There was also a variety of silver dishes and forks and spoons. I bought several little pickle forks, and Fred acquired an expensive filagree dish.

Mail had arrived at the hotel by the time we returned, including two *Time* magazines, five months old. I have read them avidly, from cover to cover.

That evening we returned to the bank for dinner. It was a large group and several of the men spoke English, but still most of the conversation was in Chinese and of little interest to Fred or me. Although the meal was a good one, it was the final part that was a real delight. Unlike previous occasions, when we rose from the table we did not leave immediately but sat around tea tables while the servants brought bowls of oranges. They were small and seedy, but very sweet, and the first fresh fruit (with the exception of melons) we have tasted since Shanghai. They were a surprising treat. They had been cut into quarters, and we picked up the segments in our fingers to suck them dry, depositing the seeds as gracefully as possible in the nearest spittoon. Servants circulated with much needed hot towels, and at last we left, riding back to our hotel through a gentle rain in shaky rickshaws with their tops up and waterproof sheets pulled over our knees. This latter service cost the princely sum of five Chinese cents.

The next two days were uneventful. One evening we went to the theater. The building was larger than the ones I have been in before; it must have seated about 2,000 people. It had cheap movie house seats, and we sat in the second row. Seats were reserved, and tickets were little flat sticks with Chinese numbers painted on them. Presently a man came in and sat down in the seat directly in front of me. He was restless and squirmed around a great deal, eventually breaking the seat. Then he moved over into the vacant seat next to him. When the man with the ticket for that seat arrived on the scene, the first man refused to give it up to him. They argued loud and long, and the girl usher joined in, later bringing a stool to replace the broken seat. Still the man would not move. All this commotion was, of course, going on during the performance. The manager finally arrived, and the first man was firmly told that he must leave. Having lost both the argument and much face, the first man refused to accept a refund and strutted out in a terrible huff. It was all vastly amusing, both to us and to others within hearing distance, and there was much giggling and pointing. As usual, the house lights were not turned down, and the audience was eating, drinking, smoking, and gossiping. The stage was open. On one side sat musicians with drums and rattles, wearing hats and smoking cigarettes in long slender pipes. On the other side were all the stage tables and chairs and racks of spears and swords. Two doors giving entrance to the stage were covered with gaudy embroidered red silk curtains, and at the back was a drop curtain painted with advertising. Before each act it was raised to reveal painted scenery which seemed to have little to do with the particular scene. Much of it was atrocious European-style interiors with ungraceful figures in niches. Some of the acts seemed to have no relationship to each other, and neither the acting nor the singing was as well done as it was in Lanchow.

On March 25, Sun, our No. 2 boy, and I set off in a hired car for Omei Shan, one of China's sacred mountains. We left Cheng-tu at 2:00 in a very crowded vehicle; the driver and his assistant, both of whom looked like very young boys, and our No. 2 boy occupied the front seat while Sun and I wedged ourselves in the back among our folding cots, bed rolls, and provisions. The car was an old Dodge sedan, and when it got under way the motor sounded none too healthy. The distance to the foot of Omei Shan was not so great, only about 130 kilometers, but our progress was slow, and by 6:00 we had completed only about half of the distance. A misty rain began falling in the afternoon, which became a steady drizzle by evening. The countryside was much like that we saw on our way into Cheng-tu—flat alluvial land all under intense cultivation. The road was graveled and good. We ferried across one stream and crossed smaller ones over stone bridges decorated with dragon heads which faced upstream, pointing their tails downstream over every archway. At one place we passed a group of conscripts being marched off to join the army; some 200 farm boys in worn blue cotton garments formed a ragged column surrounded by a thin rope. Soldiers with rifles and one young officer brought up the rear. The rope was to prevent escapes, and I can only assume it was effective. The most amusing sight was pigs going to market. They were large, well fattened animals, much different from the northwestern Kansu variety. Each one was rolled over on its back in a wheelbarrow and secured with cords. Most of them appeared resigned and lay limply with head and legs wobbling from each jolt of the wheelbarrow. Now and then one would start to kick and squirm and squeal, and the wheelbarrow would stop while the burden was readjusted. I suppose pigs were transported in this undignified fashion on their last journey to conserve their weight for market. It seemed as though pork was more valuable than human flesh, and the farmers showed special consideration to their charges. Early in the afternoon when the sun shone, leafy branches were stretched over the porkers to provide shade, and at the ditches they were frequently sprinkled with water. Such thoughtfulness was purely practical, I am sure, for the pig's position in the wheelbarrow was undoubtedly most uncomfortable, and no attention was paid to the cords binding and rubbing the tender skin under the poor animal's legs.

We spent the night at Mei Hsien. Our car was driven into the back courtyard of the inn through the tea house in front, and Sun and I settled ourselves in a small room with rough wooden bunks covered by straw mats. In the morning the car would not start, and while the driver and his helper tinkered with it Sun and I looked around. We saw for the first time the old Chinese brass cash in circulation. Inquiry revealed that six were equivalent to one large copper, in spite of the fact that the copper was stamped as worth 200 cash and twelve coppers equaled ten cents. That makes cash worth about one-quarter of a cent in our money. Here, also, large coppers are often cut into halves or quarters to make small change.

At last, by pushing it, the car was induced to go, and we repositioned ourselves into cramped quarters and set out about 8:00. Our way continued over alluvium, but the low hills we had seen in the distance yesterday drew closer, and we passed over a few. We crossed several streams on this day; the first we ferried. At the next a bridge was being built, but as it was not yet completed our driver, without hesitating or testing the depth of the water, plunged in at the ford. The stream was broad and its bed rocky, and he drove so fast that the water, which came over the running boards, splashed onto the motor, drowning it out. I had visions of sitting there until we were pulled out, and we did sit there for quite a period of time while the driver and his helper worked at getting us started. We eventually got across and progressed onward once again. Later we came to an important, swiftly flowing river where the ferrymen had devised an ingenious system. A long bamboo rope was anchored to the shore far upstream and made fast to the boat upon which our car was driven. With a sweep, the boat was headed into the river at an angle so that the current carried us farther and farther out into the stream. At the same time and in the same manner, a man in a small boat brought out a cable from the other bank, and in mid-river we were made fast to the other rope and the first one was cast off. We then drifted slowly to the other side, our crossing safely accomplished. The rivers of Szechuan are used extensively for navigation, and the "house-boats" are pointed, flat-bottomed craft with arched mat roofs amidships. They are usually pulled and poled upstream, and we saw lines of men toiling at the ends of long ropes, sometimes waist-deep in the water. When larger boats had masts, the lines were made fast to the mast tops so that, when necessary, the line of one could be slipped over the mast of another and thereby pass it.

As we approached the end of our journey the country became more hilly, and pine trees replaced the cedars which were so prevalent in the Cheng-tu area. We passed mule carts, which we had not previously seen on Szechuan roads. They were two-wheeled and equipped with automobile tires as in the north, but they were quite new and, obviously, a recent innovation here, where the motor road has just been completed. We also saw a company of soldiers dressed in faded blue uniforms, a third of them carrying rifles so ancient I wondered if they could still shoot. Another third carried old long-barrelled flint or match-locks similar to the guns we had seen among the Tibetans. The remainder had only spears. Until now, the central government has seen that few good weapons have reached the armies of the various warlords so as to make sure that they would not be overly dangerous if trouble should arise between them.

The last village we passed through was a paper making center, and the streets were filled with boards on which sheets of coarse, newly made paper were drying. Some of the boards had to be removed from the road to let us through. Beyond us rose lofty hills, their summits disappearing into the clouds. Our road began to rise, and presently we found ourselves in Pao Kuo Ssu, the first of the fifty or more great Buddhist temples of the Omei Shan.

The temple stood on a low ridge and was composed of several buildings with walled courtyards. It was well-kept, and the woodwork of the lower buildings was neatly painted and lacquered. We were greeted by some courteous priests and after lunch, which our No. 2 boy prepared for us, set out on foot for our ascent of the mountain. Our party included two coolies engaged to carry our beds and provisions. They looked like mere boys in their worn blue cotton garments and straw sandals, certainly not strong enough to carry our loads, but they proved to be better climbers than I was and went along at a slow, steady pace. Packs were carried on their backs, lashed to wooden frames which placed the loads high up so the boys could stoop slightly forward to get well under the weight. Each carried a clumsy looking iron-tipped walking stick with a short cross piece at the top. When they stopped for occasional rests their sticks were used to support the pack frames in back, so they were temporarily relieved of most of the weight.

Omei Shan is one of the five holy mountains of China. Its summit, at an elevation of about 10,000 feet, stands some 8,500 feet above the lower country to the east. On that side, the mountain rises in a single sheer precipitous slope. Structurally it is a faulted anticline, owing its existence to thick, massive Permian limestone which is, in turn, overlaid by extrusive basalt. Our business here was to examine the limestone which we had found to be petroliferous along the road northeast of Cheng-tu. In addition to the work aspect, I was glad to make this side trip and see one of the famous holy mountains. We had been told that the trip to the summit would take only two days, one up and the other down. I should have been suspicious and, after making the trip myself, feel quite certain that our Cheng-tu references had never been there. Our way took us along a footpath paved with uneven sandstone flags. The climbing started almost at once, and at first we passed through a dense, almost tropical forest of large trees and thickets of tall bamboo. I went off to the side at several places to examine the small temples we passed, but as the steady climbing continued, my enthusiasm for such excursions diminished along with my breath. Going up at the same time were a couple of dozen Chinese boy scouts, dressed in khaki shorts and shirts and visored caps. They were probably on a day's outing and would return to Pao Kuo Ssu that night.

Soon the trail emerged from the forest, and we began to climb a steep ravine and over a spur of the mountain. The rough stone steps seemed endless, and by the time I reached the top my legs, unaccustomed to such exercise, were on the verge of collapse, and I was puffing like a steam engine. Both Sun and the No. 2 boy were apparently in better condition and didn't seem to mind the exertion. I was beginning to doubt my ability to make the top under my own power and suggested to Sun that we hire carrying chairs for the rest of the trip.

The hillside north of the trail was steep, but it had been cleared and roughly terraced into small fields in which a few peasants were working. Their situation seemed dangerous to me, for a misstep would result in a serious tumble down the hillside. As it was, stones were occasionally dislodged by them and rolled down onto the trail close to us.

After reaching the crest of the spur, our way was level or slightly downhill to the temple of Tao Ssu where, at 3:30, I was glad to call it a day. We turned off the trail, climbed a few steps up some terraces to the temple's entrance, and were welcomed cordially by the priests. After resting half an hour I set out to explore.

Although Buddhist, the temples of Omei Shan are Chinese and in no way comparable to the Tibetan temples. They are built mostly of wood, and all but the most pretentious are innocent of paint. Although they contain both large and small images, these are not as numerous as in Tibetan temples, and the buildings on Omei Shan are entirely without painted panels or hanging silken pictures and other trappings. By comparison, they are plain, empty, and rather uninteresting. This temple, like most of the other large ones, was comprised of several buildings on different levels, separated by walled and paved courts largely filled by stairways leading to the next building. Several of the courts contained blooming bushes that appeared to be double roses from a distance, but on closer inspection proved to be camellias. One had a tree with shiny leaves and waxy purplish-red flowers that looked like some kind of magnolia. Orchids grew in hanging baskets and on the top of an old stone tablet. These were a disappointment, however, for the flowers were dirty greenish yellow, small, and not at all showy. One of the buildings housed some musical instruments unlike any I had seen before; hanging carved logs had been painted to resemble fish and were hollowed out from below so that when beaten with a club they produced a deep resonant bong. I was amused to see in one corner a small rusty cast-iron cook stove with the name "Pansy" on the door of the fire box.

The pine trees below us had given way to firs, and the temple stood in a splendid grove where, among the trees, grave mounds with dressed stone fronts probably encased the earthly remains of some of the important monks who once officiated here. Beyond the grove the land sloped away to the northwest, providing a magnificent view of the other steep and forest covered spurs.

In back of the temple was a grove of bamboo with stalks two or three inches in diameter, standing close to fifty feet high. Sun and I walked through it and came to a series of long narrow terraces among the rocks. Rising at regular intervals from the ground crops were low misshapen trees. At first I took them to be pruned mulberries, which have no leaves at this time of year, but Sun, who had been talking with the farmer, learned that a small worm fed on them and produced a valuable kind of white wax. It suddenly dawned on me that these trees were the source of shellac. I thought it was odd Sun had never heard of such a substance before now, and he became most interested. After more questioning, the farmer explained that every year worms had to be imported from Yunnan Province in the south and placed on the trees because winters here, although mild, are too severe to keep the worms living from year to year.

As dusk approached we established ourselves in a room on the second floor of the main, or lowest, temple building, facing west over the firs. After a supper of bully beef I was more than ready to climb into my sleeping bag and give my legs a well earned rest.

Rain fell during the night, but the next morning was clear when we set out with our party, increased by two carrying chairs (called *wha-gar*) and necessary additional coolies. The chairs were made from two slender bamboo poles ten feet long, lashed about eighteen inches apart. Between the poles hangs a seat of bamboo splints and a foot rest. The poles, with swinging chair, are carried fore and aft upon the shoulders of two coolies. Of our five coolies, two went with Sun's chair and three with mine, since I am much bigger and heavier than Sun, and the extra man spelled the others at intervals. Two of them carried while the third walked unburdened and rested. Riding in the chair was not uncomfortable on level ground, but the seat was high, and I had a precarious feeling as I swung back and forth in rhythum to the coolies' matched steps. Going up the steep steps of the trail, however, was quite another matter. At such times the rider lies back with his feet as high as his head, and in this position I could not help wondering what would happen should one of the coolies miss his footing. The most anxious moments came when one coolie was relieved by the other with a heave and a jolt as the cross piece at the end of the pole was transferred to another pair of shoulders. But no mishaps occurred. All the time I rode my conscience bothered me, for my poor coolies panted and grunted so prodigiously and sweated so profusely that I felt I must be a hardened tyrant to make them labor so hard for my comfort. Although they were well paid for their work, I really didn't have the heart to keep them at it and did more walking than riding. I found that if I stopped for short rests before I was really exhausted I could keep going pretty steadily without discomfort.

At first the trail led us gradually downward for half a mile or so where we turned aside up a valley with a tumbling stream of clear cold water flowing through it. We had not followed it far before we came to a narrow gorge cut through massive limestone which was little more than a slit in the rocks. There was no place for a path, so poles had been set into the walls about ten feet above the rushing water, and across them a rough walk of uneven planks had been built. The construction looked neither too solid nor recent, and I half expected it to give way beneath me at every step, but nothing happened and we passed along safely. Beyond this our climb began again, and at 2:00 P.M. we had gone up about 3,000 feet. We stopped here at the temple of Chu Lao Tung, or the "Nine Old Caves", to spend the night.

Along the way we passed several large temples and a number of small shrines, most of them simply sheds with roofs to protect painted mud figures. Among the human figures (or gods) in some groupings were fierce, unnatural looking tigers. One of them had sharp iron spikes or nails projecting from his muzzle in place of whiskers. We stopped long enough to examine only one of these temples, which was unremarkable except that on the second floor were shelves piled with hundreds of clay Buddhas, each about a foot high. Most of them were exactly alike, gilded and painted; only a few showed important variations. I think they are made by the monks here and purchased by pilgrims who acquire merit in different degrees by the sums of money they contribute.

This temple was in a fir grove near bean fields where a few peasants were working. We soon left these cultivated patches of land behind us and climbed up slopes that were completely forested. Clouds wreathed the mountain above us, and occasionally we passed through swirls of mist. At one place we came into a clear layer where we could look out between two blankets of clouds.

Chu Lao Tung is one of the more prosperous temples, reached by climbing a series of stone steps to a flagged terrace supporting columns that held up the roof. Wooden panels at the front of the building were painted and varnished, and it was roofed with plates of lead. Pasted on the wall was a paper with large characters which read "Destroy the

Communists", a relic of the central government's campaign against the Reds on their "Long March" several years ago.

We were greeted by the head priest and sat talking with him until the coolies arrived with our belongings, after which we settled ourselves in a small back room with rough wooden bedsteads. I explored the temple and its surroundings. A paved path led around one side of the spur on which the temple was situated, past a group of graves, to a place where a lovely view could be enjoyed on a clear day. On this day, unfortunately, the clouds enveloped me in wisps and swirls, and I could see little. The woods were wet with healthy moss hanging on the trees, and between them a thick undergrowth of small bamboo thrived. In a few protected places patches of snow still lay on the ground. On the way back to the temple I glimpsed a shy pheasant with a red head which disappeared into the underbrush almost the minute I spied it. Behind the last temple building a small part of the steep slope had been leveled off to accomodate two monkeys. The priests had put out bean curd for them and the old male was gorging himself, stuffing his mouth until his cheeks were full. The female moved around in the background, but whenever she got too near he fiercely drove her off. They were about two feet high, with long dog-like snouts and short tails. Their fur was dark gray with a fringe sticking out around their faces like a ruff.

As darkness fell we retured to our room for a supper of bully beef (how tired I am of the stuff!) and enjoyed the comfort of a charcoal fire on a round, portable, clay-plastered hearth. My short sheepskin coat that forms a cushion in my *wha-gar* was put to its proper use, and I soon crawled into my sleeping bag for additional warmth.

The sun was shining brightly when we started out in the morning, and it was warm walking. We descended along the foot of a great cliff (probably composed of Jurassic sediments) with outcrops of coal shale in several places. Soon, however, we came to a long series of rough stone steps and began our upward progress, climbing until we were again wreathed in mist. We continued our steady ascent until at last we came to a knife-sharp ridge where we met the trail by which we were to return the next day and where we turned left on a fairly level stretch for a short distance. This part of the journey provided a rather queer sensation because the fog was so thick that we could see the trail only a very few yards ahead and behind us; elsewhere was nothing but fog. It was as if we were out in space with only a patch of solid ground beneath our feet.

Presently we began to climb again, and soon the mist lightened so that we could see about us a little. We passed a troop of monkeys like the two I had seen the day before, scrambling around in the branches, picking and eating buds, not at all frightened by us. We began seeing outcrops of the dark Permian limestone we had come to study. Then, after passing the temple of Ta Chen Ssu, the ground snow became heavier until the trail was covered with it and was slippery and dangerous. It was a perfect winter scene from our north woods, with the dark firs rising out of the white snow. The one thing unlike northern Michigan was the clumps of bamboo which made up the greater part of the undergrowth. Bamboo is not exclusively a tropical plant as most people believe.

All told, we climbed another 3,000 feet during the day. The latter part was less steep, but we were glad to see Chieh Yin Tien, our stopping place, perched upon its exposed ridge above us. We arrived at 1:00 and made ourselves as comfortable as possible in the bleak cold rooms of the temple. This place is about 1,000 feet below the summit of Omei Shan, and we had decided to climb no further. The going had been miserable, with snow and cold making everything wet and clammy. Above us lay only the basalt cap of the mountain, and we had already seen fragments of the rock that had broken loose and tumbled down the steep slopes. The mountain's summit was too exposed to have trees on it, and we were warned that the snow lay thicker above us, the going more dangerous. Obviously this is not the time of year to hope to see much.

The temple was not an attractive place, made of rough wooden planks with numerous cracks, and the drafts made it impossible to keep warm. Even the monks were huddled around a charcoal fire on an open clay hearth. We arrived far ahead of our coolies and provisions, and after five or six hours of strenuous climbing I was very hungry. I saw some of the monks eating peanuts and managed to get some too, which suggested "food" to Sun, who ordered noodles for us. Unfortunately, when they arrived they made the most unappealing meal I have ever faced, like doughy vermicelli, white and absolutely tasteless. The accompanying pepper sauce didn't help much, and the chopsticks looked old and unwashed. However, the food was warming, which was in its favor. I was sorry for our coolies, who were garbed only in sparse cotton clothing. One would have thought they would be frozen solid, but they weren't and seemed unmindful and cheerful.

After our things arrived we set up our beds in a small chamber on the second floor, ate another dinner prepared by our No. 2 boy, and immediately went to bed to keep warm. Sleep was impossible for some time, however, because of a great racket made by boy monks who were apparently doing their lessons, singing and shouting.

I arose early the next morning. Dressing did not take long for I only had to slip on my boots, coat, and hat, and I was out of the temple before sunrise. The clouds had cleared from the upper part of Omei Shan, and the sight which greeted me was one of the most beautiful I have ever seen. Overhead the sky was clear; below me, stretching to infinity, was a sea of clouds. From the island of the mountain, its white billowing surface hid the lower area of Szechuan to the east; to the west other mountain tops rose as dark masses above the clouds becoming smaller and less distinct toward the highlands of Tibet. Northward I could see the ridge where our trail had wound and realized for the first time that we had followed it along the brink of a great perpendicular precipice formed by Permian limestone. The sun appeared, and almost at once wisps of mist began to rise from the clouds like steam from a boiling sea. A gentle wind swept them upward along the steep ravines of the mountainside, and first one and then another part of my view was obscured by moving white veils which became thicker. In less than half an hour I was again lost in fog so thick that I could not see 100 yards in any direction. The magnificent panorama had become a memory of an unreal world.

I returned to the temple for a simple breakfast, and we began our descent. Going down was, of course, less fatiguing than coming up, but in the fog it was necessary to watch each step on the rough uneven stones. My chair coolies had an easy time of it for I rode only on the level stretches. We switched from the trail we had taken up and continued straight along the ridge, climbed over a low knob crowned by another small temple, and resumed our downward passage. We didn't stop at any of the great rambling temples among the firs but paused at a drug store near one for a brief rest. This store was like ones we had seen near several of the other temples and displayed an assortment of dried herbs, roots, stones, fossils, shells, horns, etc., in old cigarette cartons and dusty bottles or hanging in bunches from the beams. Among the drugs were the shells of large modern foraminifers and quartz crystals. Sun said that the latter, powdered, were very good for the eyes. As I examined the shop and its contents, passersby stopped to examine me. Most of them appeared to be mountaineers, dressed in heavier clothing than our coolies, with their feet wrapped in rags and thicker straw sandals, designed to prevent slipping on snow and ice.

We descended 5,000 feet before we came to the bottom layer of clouds. Glimpses of the lower slopes appeared as the mist thinned, until at last we were out in clear air again. It was a relief to rejoin the world of earth and rock and plants, where patches of cultivated fields showed the handiwork of man.

We had planned to spend the night at Wan Mien Ssu, but when we reached the temple it was only a little after noon, and we decided we could make the downward journey easily in one day. We stopped for lunch at a tiny wayside stand; its sanitary conditions were such that my appetite was much diminished by what I saw. Nonetheless there was a tray of steaming dumplings that looked fresh, and I decided that recent cooking had sterilized them adequately, so I ate several. They were actually quite good, made of wheat flour with a center of sweet fruit. Sun lacks a taste for sweet things so he had the cook boil a bowl of noodles. I was thirsty so I asked for tea, but this, apparently, was a luxury the restaurant's patrons could not generally afford. One of the boys went to get some from the nearby temple, soon returning with a dubious looking bowl of scalding tea. In the meantime our coolies enjoyed smacking their lips over bowls of rice with finely chopped pickled vegetables. Only one did not eat, apparently preferring to save his precious coppers and eat his meal at home.

The rest of our way was mostly down a deep V-shaped valley. The slopes were incredibly steep, many of them under cultivation. Scattered about here and there on the hillsides were thatched farmhouses among small groves of bamboo. We went through a number of tiny villages with squalid houses crowded all together. At the edge of one village, under a mat shed, there were several coffins awaiting a propitious time for burial. I guessed from the fragrance of the surrounding atmosphere that their contents were very ripe, but it did not seem to bother the inhabitants.

The valley turned and twisted so that our views were ever-changing. Sometimes the trail was near the bottom, close to the tumbling stream, and at other times we were on a slope hundreds of feet above it. Irrigation canals led off from the stream to wind along the hillsides. At one place the valley narrowed to become a canyon, and we passed high along one side of the rocks. They were probably Jurassic—mainly sandstone. Beneath us the great Permian limestone rose in a large fold. Several enormous springs gushed from the precipitous cliffs, cascading down to the stream a hundred feet below. Beyond the gorge, where the hills lost height, we came to an area of rolling red beds terraced with small fields along the valley and ravines, all flooded for rice. It must have been close to planting time, for men were working knee deep in mud with their buffalo and crude plows. By this time I was very tired; I estimated that we had descended 15,000 irregular steps, and it had been fatiguing. So I clambered into my sedan chair and returned to Pao Kuo Ssu in regal fashion.

After a short rest I set out to explore the local temple and some of the land surrounding it which had been given over to a forest project. When I returned, supper had been prepared by the No. 2 boy.

As dusk gathered I lounged on a porch chair in front of the main temple, eating freshly roasted peanuts and watching the bats flapping across the courtyard. I thought that few more quiet, peaceful places could be found anywhere in the world and, in this mood, retired. Unfortunately, the night brought disillusionment when I was awakened by a terrific racket made by the monks. They chanted, shouted, beat gongs, and rang bells until I thought that Old Buddha himself would be annoyed. Either the commotion died down or I went back to sleep in spite of it, but again I was roused from slumber about 4:00 A.M. by a similar din to which firecrackers had been added. I was quite peeved by this time for I had gone to bed very tired and resented being disturbed twice in one night. After reflection, however, I attempted to alter my feelings because the monks had, after all, been pleasant and hospitable to strangers, and we had no right to object to their religious duties. Sun was also annoyed and, as usual, said, "All priests are useless. They should be killed. They should all be sent to the army."

Our motor trip back to Cheng-tu was uneventful. We followed the same road and saw little that was new. Wonder of wonders, the car actually started-up first thing in the morning and was purring contentedly away at 7:30 A.M. When we came to the bridge previously under construction we found that it had been finished, so there was no need to ford the stream or get stuck again in the same place. In mid-morning we stopped to eat at a place where the Chinese consumed a hearty breakfast and were soon on our way again. Our only mishap was a blowout. While the driver and his helper patched the tire and pumped it up by hand, I investigated a nearby mill. This was flat country, but there was enough water in one of the ditches to turn a combination flour mill and rice huller. Nearby, a farmer was plowing a paddy field with the aid of a water buffalo. The road was almost deserted except for a few passenger wheelbarrows being pushed along.

We reached Cheng-tu about 3:00 P.M., where we were held up by soldiers while I filled out a long printed form before we could enter the city. At our hotel, when I climbed the stairs to our third floor apartment, I realized for the first time how stiff my legs were. It will be several days before I get back to normal again. So, our trip to Omei Shan is over; it had taken six days instead of the three we had been led to expect.

Today is our last day in Cheng-tu, and it has been quiet. My legs are still sore and I didn't feel much like walking, so I read old issues of *Time* magazine. Tomorrow we leave for Chungking.

Nei-chiang
April 4, 1938

I had forgotten to mention why Fred did not go to Omei Shan with us. He had badly strained his back in Sian, and for a few days he could not straighten up and could hardly walk. Although he was better by the time we got to Cheng-tu, he did not feel equal to a mountain-climbing expedition so he stayed in town reading magazines and resting. One day he took a rickshaw out to the Mission University where he saw Richardson, the man who had come down from Sian in our first truck. Fred was impressed with the size and appearance of the school. It was here that he saw several full-sized pandas which had been captured and were owned by a man who claims rights to the pandas that were earlier delivered to the U.S. He wouldn't let anyone take pictures for fear the photos would be sold to news agencies, causing him to lose shekles and publicity for himself. Fred reports that they are really very stupid animals, probably as useless as South American sloths, and he didn't think it would be much of a job to catch one. Another day Fred had a call from some German Eurasia pilots, one of whom we had met in Sian. (This was the one who caused such a stir by having to circle the airfield in order to land.) They tried to pump Fred for information about Russian aid from the northwest, but Fred suspected they were probably official German observers and told them nothing. They reported that the German who had flown into Sian on his way to Hankow while we were there had attempted to return westward to Germany on horseback, but had become lost in the mountains with frost-bitten feet and has had to have his legs amputated. This was the same man who created the spy scare in Suchow by taking pictures of the airfield. It's a small world here in the backwaters of civilization.

On the 4th we all left Cheng-tu as scheduled, with the exception of our No. 1 boy who took a job in the shop where he had sold our extra provisions for us. He decided not to return to Shanghai because he did not think he could easily get work there. The shopkeeper wanted someone to guarantee the boy's honesty; Suez refused to do this for some reason, but we gladly paid his back wages, amounting to several hundred dollars, so he could put up security for himself, and our relationship ended well.

Our baggage truck has been fitted with a gas generator to burn charcoal instead of gasoline. It carries a couple of tanks beside the cab which look like hot water containers, and it gives the truck an amusing appearance. It had to stop several times during the day for more charcoal, but ran very well. The servants sit up on top of the load on back, and we four occupy the same Dodge motor car that Sun and I took to Omei Shan. We are much more comfortable, however, because our No. 2 driver and bed rolls are all on the truck. I am doubtful about the running ability of the car and considered riding on the truck also, to be near my bedding and our food supply, but the truck is very full and the driver has assured me that the car is all fixed up. I guess I will live out my days with faith.

Our first twenty kilometers were over the flat alluvial land I have described before. All along the way we met wheelbarrows carrying great blocks of red sandstone into the city from a quarry in the hills to the southeast. Sandstone ledges stuck out of the hillside in many places, but most of the area was terraced and farmed. Even low ridges between the individual fields were planted in beans and wheat. Groves of small orange trees were set out in rows across some of the fields, and their glossy foliage contrasted sharply with the more delicate green tones of the crops growing beneath them. Tung oil trees were in bloom and looked very pretty. Their leaves are shaped like those on our catalpa trees but smaller, with spikes of large white flowers touched in the center with mauve. One of the curious roadside sights is the water buffaloes wearing straw sandals. I guess that they work in the flooded paddy fields for such long periods of time that their hooves become soft, and the footwear is designed to prevent injury from the pebbles on the road.

By 7:00 P.M. we had traveled 210 kilometers and reached this place, called Nei-chiang, a small inland city boasting electric lights but without other modern conveniences. Our hotel is dirty and crowded. Only two rooms were vacant, both too small for our cots, so we shall have to sleep on the matted curtained bedsteads that are our only furnishings.

Nei-chiang
April 5, 1938

We did not go on to Chungking today. Instead Fred, Sun, and I motored south to see the salt wells of the Tzu-liu-ching District. This is the most famous salt locality in Szechuan and has been studied by both Chinese and foreign geologists. These salt wells, some over 2,000 feet deep, are drilled near the crest of a large well-formed anticline, and some of them get a little oil and gas.

We went along our road back about two kilometers and then turned on a motor road built by the Salt Revenue Department. The country is just like that through which we have been traveling—red beds with occasional sandstone forming subdued terraces and mesa topography where every patch of ground is farmed. As we approached Ta-feng-pao we saw the first of the wells. They were some distance from the road, so we did not stop there but drove into the small city where the wells were more easily accessible. We left the car in the center of town and found a man who could show us around.

The wells have been drilled by man power, using the most primitive sort of equipment. I was sorry not to see any being put down because it must be an interesting process. Anyway, the wells are deep and cased with stones only near the top. The Chinese have no pipes in which to pump up the brine, so it has to be bailed out. Originally this was done by man or animal power, but the more important wells are now outfitted with steam hoists and bailers made of sheet iron about eight inches in diameter and 100 feet long. They are raised via a derrick made of many poles lashed together with ropes, and although they are clumsy looking, they seem effective. They are so old, however, that when the bailer is hoisted the whole structure wobbles and shakes in a dismaying fashion. When the bailer is finally up, a man releases a valve at the bottom and water foams out into great vats. Thus the brine is collected. To make salt, it must be evaporated. The brine is then brought from receiving vats to the evaporating plant either by coolies carrying it in large wooden buckets at each end of shoulder poles, or it is piped through large sections of bamboo. To make these pipes, the joint partitions are knocked out and the great stalks are wound tightly together with strips of split bamboo. The small end of one piece is fitted into the large end of another, and by this arrangement pretty good pipes are made. If the salt well is located above the evaporating plant, the brine simply travels down the pipe by gravity; otherwise it has to be pumped up high enough so that it will. This is done by naked coolies pedaling the same sort of machine that farmers use to pump water from one field into the next. They seem tireless at their monotonous and exhausting work, but I did not see one of them slack off. (We were told that the workers around here are paid ten to fifteen Chinese cents a day and given their food.)

The brine is evaporated in shallow cast-iron pans about four feet in diameter. They are arranged in pairs on big mud stoves, where one is the evaporating and the other the crystallizing pan. The brine is boiled in the evaporating pan until it is saturated, then transferred to the crystallizing pan where bean juice is added, and it is covered with a wooden lid. Here, natural gas was being used for fuel, but there are other well areas where I think they use coal. The coarse salt crystals are packed into deep round mat baskets and go off to the salt merchants or warehouses where they are weighed and graded. The larger cakes are usually sawed into quarters; two of these quarters are a coolie's load. The government tax is about 70 or 80 percent of the selling price.

We returned to Nei-chiang in the early afternoon. As it was too late to start out for Chungking, we just sat around here for the rest of the day.

Chungking
April 8, 1938

I was bitten lavishly by bed bugs during the night. Also, there was quite a storm, complete with thunder, lightning, and rain, but by morning the skies were clear. We started early, expecting to reach Chungking by mid-afternoon, but motor trouble resulted in our spending most of the day broken down on the road. Our truck passed us by and went on ahead. The trouble was with the gasoline pump, but the driver tore almost everything else apart before he found what was wrong. A couple of times he managed to get us going but the problem continued, so he finally left us at the edge of a tiny village while he walked twenty li back to a larger town for the necessary piece of leather for repairs. We were, of course, surrounded by a curious throng who stood staring with their mouths open. Among them was a tiny girl who looked about three, but must have been at least five. Dirty and unkempt, she wore only a tattered jacket which showed her to be mere skin and bones. She was the first of the abandoned children I have seen. Someone gave her a piece of sugar cane which she tore into and chewed like a little animal. When the cane was gone she began picking up peanut shells we had thrown on the road, but after eating several found them unsatisfactory, so she sat down in the road and started to cry. It was easy to see that she was starving, but nobody paid any attention to her except other children, who mimicked her and laughed. Fred gave her a handful of peanuts, which quieted her down, and she eventually wandered off uncertainly down the road. We began to notice other older children in the same condition, begging by the side of the road or sleeping under overhanging ledges where they appeared to live. We saw other beggars along the way, some with terrible open sores, probably syphilitic, and in several places men lay by the road who seemed to have dropped from exhaustion. We passed one man covered with blood, lying on a piece of matting on a bridge. Without a doubt, life here is cheap and full of uncertainty.

As a result of our delay we did not reach Chungking, and I wished I had trusted my intuition and gone with the truck. We stopped after dark at Lai-feng-yi where we went into an ordinary restaurant with an uneven earth floor and two barefoot waiters. The food was unappetizing so I filled up on something like an omelette and rice. It is unthinkable to travel at night, so we found a place to sleep in a big bare room over the restaurant where we had a couple of doors taken off their hinges and placed on benches off the floor. Over these went straw mats and quilts, which I was afraid to examine too carefully. Going to bed consisted solely of removing my shoes and lying gently down on top with my sheepskin coat folded up for a pillow. I'll have to admit that I slept very well.

We got an early start in the morning and went off without breakfast. Just outside of Chungking the car broke down again, so we did not enter the city until mid-morning. We didn't know where the truck had stopped, so we went first to the bank and then to the insurance company. After these two visits it was noon, and we were taken to a nearby delicatessen and bakery for a combination breakfast and lunch of rolls and coffee; the rolls were really good with plenty of butter that came in by airmail from Hong Kong. It was a real treat. The bank made tentative arrangements for Fred and me to put up at the Canadian Mission, but we decided to stay with Sun and Suez at a Chinese hotel called, for some unknown reason, the Sullivan. It is a dilapidated place, but the rooms are big and have baths, so we are quite comfortable.

Our truck and its provisions had not yet been located when we had to check in with the Provincial Geological Survey, so we were forced to go without being able to clean up—and me with four or five days of whiskers. We didn't know the way so took rickshaws and were let out at the entrance to a very narrow and odiferous alleyway. To my surprise, this led to a series of buildings with glossy black woodwork, surrounding two courtyards. There we met the director and another man from Nanking and formerly on the National Survey, both friends of Sun's. I got the information I wanted and have decided that the trip I had planned out of Chungking will be unnecessary. We walked back to the hotel where our belongings had been delivered and, after bathing, shaving, changing clothes, and having dinner, Fred and I went to the movies. The picture was nothing special, and the news reel showed Edward, as Prince of Wales, inspecting German war veterans; it must have been years old.

Chungking
April 11, 1938

Our stay in Chungking has been uneventful. The city, located on the Yangtze River where one of its principal tributaries joins it from the north, is confined to the point of land between these two streams. The main streets either follow the contour of the slope or angle up it gently.

They are faced with mostly modern buildings of reinforced concrete, primarily three stories high, on narrow streets and alleys that go up and down the hills via stairways. Chungking looks a lot like Hong Kong except that it does not have imposing buildings. Most of the local Europeans live on the other side of the river, so we did not see many of them out on the streets. Busy and prosperous, this is the shipping point for most of Szechuan's products, but although the river is navigable for some distance higher, steamers do not ordinarily progress any farther up it. There are many American cars on the streets, but of course most people ride rickshaws. Going up hill, the pullers have a hard job of it and move painstakingly, but coming down, they run. I expected to see them tripping, tumbling, and colliding, because once underway I do not see how they can stop, expert though they must be. The great crowds of pedestrians cooperate by sidestepping these wayward flights quickly, albeit at the last possible moment. There are also many light sedan chairs in use, with seats in roofed-over boxes which look ungainly fastened between the two long poles well forward of the middle; I suppose this is to achieve balance and weight distribution for going uphill.

We have been invited to two dinners and one luncheon. The first dinner was given by the bank and was a foreign style meal; per usual, it was not as good as native Chinese fare. The second dinner was given by the Survey director. The luncheon was compliments of the insurance men. We also took occasion to visit the British and French consulates to get the visas we will need in Europe. The consulates are in the upper part of the city in large buildings surrounded by nice gardens and lovely views. At the British Consulate we were greeted by a huge hound which jumped all over us; the French Consulate's waiting room was a veritable museum of Chinese curios.

One day there was much excitement caused by the visit of the British Ambassador; another day there was a celebration with firecrackers because of a Chinese victory in the north. The worst feature of our stay was the very noisy street outside our hotel windows. Although it was a short dead-end street, it was constantly filled with hawkers shouting their wares, and everyone else was hollering. Each night there was at least one fight. Chinese fighting is not very physical but it is noisy, with shrieks of anger and indignation as they push at one another. When I first saw a street fight I laughed, and Sun asked me why I found it so amusing—didn't Americans fight? I showed him how Americans fight by balling my right hand into a fist and lightly popping him on the chin. He stepped back with a look of horror and said, "Oh, but that would hurt!" Here they shout and shove, and eventually someone is knocked off his balance and sits down hard on the ground, but I have never seen a bloody nose.

I write this aboard the little river steamer on which we will start our journey down the Yangtze, through the famous gorges. We boarded this afternoon because she pulls out very early tomorrow. Our hand baggage was brought by two sedan chairs while we walked the length of the main street and down a great flight of steps to the river bank, where we got into a sampan and were rowed about half a mile downstream to our boat. From a distance she seemed small and dingy, but accommodations on the upper, first class deck, are clean, although hardly commodious. There are only six first class staterooms, but since there is only one other passenger we have each claimed a room for ourselves. The boat's name is *Kangting*. She is about 650 gross or 350 net tons and belongs to the China English Navigation Company. There are three English officers: the captain, first officer, and first engineer.

We are on our way home at last.

Ichang
April 14, 1938

Dinner on board our steamer was good, and the food has continued to be so. I know that the bed I am sleeping in is the very best I have occupied since Shanghai. The other passenger boarded early on the 12th just before we cast off, an Englishman, one of the company's agents.

I awoke this morning shortly after the boat got underway and before it was light. I dressed and rushed out so as not to miss any scenery as our journey down the fabled Yangtze began. The water was slightly reddish in color but was not as muddy as the Yellow River, even though one could still not see below the surface. The level of the river stood at about the ten foot stage, still low water; during the summer rains it rises ninety feet or more at Chungking. The record rise occurred in one of the gorges where they once reported 273 feet. Navigation of the upper portion of the river is both difficult and dangerous. Nowhere does the river have a flood plain, and its steep hills rise abruptly from both sides. The rocks are folded into a series of anticlines and sineclines trending northeast-southwest, and the river flows mostly parallel to that structure. In places, however, it turns and passes across the strike, and it is in these areas that the dangerous places are. The more resistant sandstone ledges stick up along the river bank into the middle of the stream, greatly restricting its navigable channel. The boats all carry Chinese pilots who have spent their entire lives on the river and know the position of every rock and reef and exactly how much water there must be to clear them. At places along the bank there are scales painted on rocks so the pilots can gauge the depth of the river. The current is often very swift, and there are many whirlpools and inequities on the bottom that shoot the water up to the surface so that in places the river almost seems to boil. Every year there are accidents, and our own steamer scraped the rocks last year, stoving in some of her bottom plates. It is not uncommon to see the residue of past accidents in the gorges, and we have thus far seen several wrecked steamers. In spite of it, there is much traffic. In two days we have passed dozens of steamers and innumerable junks of every size and appearance; each district apparently has its own type. Going upriver they are propelled by oars, sweeps, sails, poles, and human trackers, or any combination of these. Some of them have as many as twelve rowers standing up to their oars or twelve trackers bent double, pulling on a bamboo rope made fast to the mast. It takes them six weeks to go from Ichang up to Chungking against the current whereas westbound steamers make the trip in three or four days. Downstream, they float with the current and hurry themselves along a bit by rowing. Although junks are supposed to keep to the sides of the river out of the steamers' way, they are so numerous that it must be difficult to avoid hitting them, and we saw the wrecks of many of them washed up along the shoreline. Those that are heavily laden are in danger of being swamped by the wash raised by passing steamers, and at many places our power was shut off and we drifted past them to avoid this. Steamers passing each other are generally advised of an approach by a series of red and white signal stations, and sometimes the channel is marked by buoys in the shape of small covered sampans. In other places banks and rocks are marked by small trees fastened upright on them. It is assumed, I suppose, that when these trees are not visible or have been washed away the place is no longer shallow.

Most of the time I have been sitting topside on a roof over the bridge where the view is good. This area, enclosed by a rope railing, is called, with a flair of pomposity, the "sun deck". Right behind me is the siren which warns junks out of the way, and when it blows it not only showers me with a bath of steam and water, but nearly bursts my ear drums. Early on I learned to stop up my ears with my fingers at the first sign of a blast. There is a big red, white, and blue Union Jack painted on the floor of the deck up here to warn off Jap bombers with destructive ideas.

The Chinese seem to hold some animosity against the British boats along the river; the captain told me that they are fired upon almost every trip. Our boat has two bullet holes through the funnel, and one drilled clean through an iron stanchion, a stateroom door, and out the other side. I am not aware that we have been shot at during this trip, although Fred says he saw two bullets hit the water near us.

Travel on the river is too dangerous to be undertaken at night, so we anchored opposite a small city named Wan-hsien for our first night and were off again the second day before dawn.

Along the way we passed a rather attractive temple built on a small but high and precipitous hill. There is a legend that long ago enough rice ran out from a crack in the rock to feed all the priests who lived there, until one avaricious old priest tried to increase the supply by enlarging the hole. It broke the spell, and no more rice was ever seen. Every culture and every language seems to have this moral tale in one form or another.

At about 10:00 we came to the first of the three big gorges caused by the exposure of a great limestone formation along the crest of an anticlinal fold, which here runs about four and a half miles. The river narrows, and much of the way is confined between sheer cliffs rising some 3,000 feet straight up from the water's edge. In the upper part of a great crack in one of the rock faces, in an area that appears to be totally inaccessible, are what look like three large box bellows; the place is named appropriately "Wind Box Gorge". It is said that long ago an army was trapped in this gorge by enemies. Their general ordered junks to be broken up and the timbers stuck into holes cut in the rock to form a stairway by which the army escaped up the cliffside. The holes are supposed to be still visible, but although I looked carefully I did not see them.

Emerging from this gorge into a short narrow valley through red beds, we came upon the second gorge, known as the Wushan Gorge, the longest one along the river — twenty-five miles. A whole great anticlinal mountain range is cut through by the river, which causes it to constrict and flow between two sheer cliffs so close together that it seemed I could easily reach out and touch both sides at the same time. Once out of this gorge we were in Hupeh Province, a step further east on our outward journey. We steamed through a considerable stretch of red bed country and at last reached the Ichang Gorge, which is really a double gorge for the granite brought up in the core of this anticline has been worn down into comparatively low rolling country between two mountains whose crests are marked by high limestone cliffs and crags. After fourteen miles in this gorge the anticline is crossed, the river broadens out, and the hills sharply decrease in height.

I have been watching fishermen along the river banks sweeping the water with small nets on the ends of bamboo poles but, until today, I never saw anyone catch anything. I had come to the conclusion that this is a pretty hopeless business; I am sure that one successful fisherman knows joy unbounded. Other men fished with large dip nets hung on poles hinged to the front of their boats so the nets could be raised or lowered. Some of the gravel banks along the river were being dug, sieved, and washed for gold, though precious little gold is found in these parts. I have read that the poverty level of a district can be judged by the amount of gold it produces, for only desperation drives men to turn to this method of trying to earn a living.

Just above the gorges we passed a small low island of mat houses from which smoke and steam rose in great clouds. There are salt springs here, and there is an important salt industry in progress during low water. With all this life and work along the river there must be many drownings; indeed, during just these two days I have seen three corpses floating face down in the water. One had been at the surface only a very short time for the junk men had not yet removed its clothing. The others were bloated and decomposing, and a big black crow was perched on one, making a hearty meal.

Ichang is not far to the east of the Ichang Gorge, nestled on the river's left bank where the country is low and flat. On the other side are small hills of red beds but, unlike Szechuan Province, these are not terraced or cultivated, and the fields are confined to little valleys. Ichang is the head of navigation for the larger river boats, and we will change here to the *Changsha* which will take us on to Hankow. We came in late in the afternoon and anchored close to our next vessel.

Chiang-ling
April 17, 1938

We transshipped from the *Kangting* to the *Changsha* almost at once on the 13th and found ourselves in much better surroundings. This boat is about 2,500 gross, 1,500 net tons. The first class cabins are on the upper deck; they are larger and there are more of them. There is a nice deck and comfortable chairs from which to survey the passing scenery. The only incident of our transfer concerned Suez. Opium is raised in Szechuan but not downriver, and there is a lively trade in illicit smuggling. I saw several packages thrown off the *Kangting* to waiting sampans just outside of Ichang, which I imagine was part of the local drug traffic. Someone must have tipped off the authorities that Suez was a smoker because a man from the Opium Bureau came aboard and thoroughly searched his baggage for contraband.

All the next day we remained anchored in the river at Ichang, part of the time taking on a load of tung oil which is the principal and most valued export of western China. We did not go ashore because there seemed nothing particularly interesting to see; British and French flags flew from several buildings which were probably mercantile and shipping offices. An English gun boat, looking very trim, was anchored a short distance upriver from us, and a shabby, dirty French one was below us. There were also a lot of other ships including a Japanese river boat that obviously had been seized by the Chinese.

The Ichang airfield has been raided several times by Japanese bombers, without much damage. Most of that day a Chinese plane circled and maneuvered over the city, dragging a target after it, and we heard occasional bursts of fire from the Chinese getting practice in anticipation of the next Jap attack.

Our ship carries four British officers. We were joined by another passenger, a Lt. Martin of the U.S. Navy who is being transferred to a submarine tender in Manila. He is hoping to catch the S.S. *Potsdam* out of Hong Kong, just as we are.

We got off at daybreak on the 15th and resumed our voyage. About a mile down the river and opposite some Standard Oil tanks we passed two sleek American gun boats looking very ship-shape with light gray paint and gleaming brass work. Here the Yangtze is a wide river flowing through alluvial land with very low banks. Much of the adjacent land is subject to flooding and is therefore not farmed. Instead, these areas are covered with coarse green grass or a lush growth of reeds. We saw a few huts built of these reeds, and here and there people were cutting and loading them on small boats for transport. There were low levees and small clusters of farmhouses surrounded by trees, but for the most part the country seemed deserted—at least along the river. About midday we stopped at a town to take on bales of cotton. A large group of either young soldiers or older school boys were ushered on board and given a tour and lecture. After they disembarked we continued down the river until we anchored at dusk. It was a quiet and relatively boring day.

Another early start yesterday. About 8:30 A.M. we came to a steamer, the *Kiang Wo*, belonging to another British line. It was grounded on a shoal at the head of an island, broadside to the current, and had been stuck there for two days. Had we caught the earlier steamer out of Chungking as I had hoped, we would most probably have been aboard her, pacing back and forth in frustration. We passed, turned in a very narrow channel and, with our bow upstream, went to her rescue. Our captain maneuvered, taking careful soundings, and finally anchored. A rope was rowed from our ship to the *Kiang Wo* and with it a steel cable was pulled across. On the first try we were a bit too far apart and the cable would not reach, so we swung in a little and tried again. Actually, we got so close that I was afraid we would go aground ourselves;, later the engineer told me that we had only six inches of clearance under us. The rope and cable were eventually made fast and both ships steamed up, churning the water for all they were worth, to no avail. About this time one of the American gun boats from Ichang, the *Guam*, came by, and as the Lieutenant thought he might miss his ship in Hong Kong because of this delay, he transferred over to her by launch to make a quicker trip of it. The *Guam* left us and we cast off, went back up river, turned around again (which took fully an hour), and returned to the *Kiang Wo* for another try. We hitched onto the stranded steamer once more and pulled steadily for at least an hour before she finally began to move. Gradually she came off the shoal and at long last was freed. We dropped the cable, maneuvered up river to turn around, and were back on our way, the rescue completed. We left her anchored in the river, cleaning the mud out of her pumps. This means that we will be a day late in reaching Hankow. However, I am not yet concerned and feel fairly certain that our Hong Kong departure date can still be met.

We continued downriver until it was pitch black and then anchored in a lonely place with not a light in sight along the shore, only the stars and the moon above. This morning we steamed onward to the mouth of a large tributary which joins the Yangtze from the south and are anchored here at the small city of Chiang-ling, where we are loading more boiled tung oil. It is packed in small barrels which seem to come endlessly out of a junk moored along side of us. A coolie brings out a barrel, and as each cask is passed over to the steamer the tally man hands out a pointed bamboo stick by which the count is kept. The junk is covered, and the junk master's wife is perched on top watching cabbage and fish drying in the sun. A little before noon a group of young Chinese came aboard and had a special meal served foreign-style in the first class salon. I think it was a party given by the second officer, who is a nice-looking Chinese youth, quite natty in his blue uniform with brass buttons and his white cap. They all seemed to have a good time.

Below deck we carry a lot of Chinese in second and third class. Second class has beds, third does not. This part of the boating business is sublet to a man who employs "tea boys" to minister to passengers' needs. They are paid no wages but make their living off tips the passengers give them. Sometimes tea boys outnumber passengers, and the captain has tried to cut down their number without much success. Whenever we stop, small boats swarm along side to sell various kinds of questionable looking food to the second and third class passengers, passing it up in baskets tied to long bamboo poles. All sorts of activities go on below decks; there has been a loud Mah-Jong game under my cabin every night, and I often catch a strong whiff of opium.

Hankow
April 20, 1938

Chiang-ling, where we anchored for a load on the 17th, is a small city on low reddish clay hills with a few European-style buildings on its outskirts. In the distance a tall slender pagoda rose from the top of a knoll. A number of junks and steamers were anchored and tied up along her shoreline, including two Chinese gunboats whose principal function is to fight river pirates. In the early afternoon the *Kiang Wo*, the steamer we pulled from the mud bank, came in, none the worse for wear, and at about this same time we raised anchor and started off down the Yangtze again. Not far out of Chiang-ling we came upon a small Chinese steamer that had also run aground. She must have been going full bore when she hit for she had slid up partly out of the water, and no amount of pulling could possibly dislodge her. She will have to stay there until the river rises sufficiently to float her off.

From here to Hankow the river changes course from southeast to somewhat east of north. Although the land is mostly flat and alluvial, there are ridges and hills at intervals rising above the river which in places somewhat constrict it. Geologically, these are tops of old mountains whose lower parts are buried by the alluvium. For the rest of our journey they were never completely out of sight, nor were the small temples that stood upon some of the crests. This part of the valley was more populated, and we passed a number of small farming villages. There was more traffic on the river, with hundreds of junks sailing downstream, while occasional tugboats towed bunches of them up in the opposite direction. Fred said he saw a large fish jump out of the river so I began watching carefully, and just as dusk began to settle I saw a lot of them. They were not fish, but dolphins. I wouldn't have guessed they swam so far upriver away from the sea.

The channel must be wider and safer along this stretch because we did not anchor at dark as we have done previously, but continued on until about 10:00. It was so dark I could barely make out the river bank and thought there might be a danger of our running down smaller boats. By watching the position of the stars I recognized that we steamed around a big meander in the river and finally stopped at the neck of a sharp bend.

The ship was underway when I awoke in the morning, and we reached Hankow about 8:00 A.M. on the 18th. We were met by men from the Kincheng Bank as well as from the Ministry of Public Health, for whom Suez will be working. His brother-in-law, Dr. Yen (another one), who is the head of it has made an attractive deal for him here. Hankow is very crowded (the population has jumped from 1,200,000 to 3,000,000 people since the war started) and is, at present, the administrative center of the country—Chungking being the provincial capital. Accommodations for Fred and me have been arranged at a hotel on the Bund; Sun and Suez are staying in an apartment at the bank. Directly after leaving my things at the hotel, Sun and I went to call on Dr. Wong, the Minister of Economics and Director of the Geological Survey. At his office over the Canton Bank we were advised that he was home ill, but when our arrival was announced to him by telephone he insisted that we come around to see him. Since his apartment is just around the corner from the bank, we were there in minutes and found him with his head bandaged behind his right ear. He said he had been running a fever, but also that he was feeling better and expected to return to work in a few days. We had a friendly talk about our work and his trip to Europe, when he went to the coronation with the Chinese delegation last spring.

We returned to the bank where Fred joined us for a rather simple Chinese dinner. Arrangements have been made for us to fly to Hong Kong tomorrow. We have more baggage than the fifteen kilos weight allowance, so that afternoon we took our excess to the Eurasia office so it could be flown out on an earlier flight. All went well until the customs examiner came to the maps we had made. We couldn't convince him that they had little military value, so we all had to go to the Customs House for an official ruling on them. After waiting around and seeing several people, we were told to obtain a permit from Dr. Wong's Ministry; this would allow us to take them out of the country. The whole affair took most of our afternoon. Sun joined us for dinner, and we were having some not very good ice cream at a soda fountain afterwards when we thought we heard the air raid siren. Sun jumped into a rickshaw and rushed back to the bank. Later we found that we had only imagined it. The Japanese have apparently lost so many planes raiding Hankow that now they come only at night. The moon is a little past full, and the night before we arrived there were three raids, resulting in little damage. They have not been back since.

Yesterday morning Sun and I paid another call on Dr. Wong and explained our problem with the maps. He gave us a note to the Ministry on the back of one of his cards which we took there and waited an endless time for someone in authority, who finally arrived and telephoned the Finance Ministry to contact the Customs House. I hoped that something would be done before we got further embroiled in more Chinese red tape; it all seems so involved.

At noon Sun gave the four of us a farewell dinner in a famous Szechuan restaurant. The place smelled like a Chinese laundry, and I was none too hopeful. We ate in a room on the second floor with large French windows opening onto the street, and the meal proved to be OK. (I hoped it would be our last Chinese dinner but, unfortunately, the invitations keep coming.) Sun and I went back to the Economics Office where our pass was being made out, and eventually a most formidable looking document on thick paper about two feet square with enormous red seals was processed. It required my photo, and of course I didn't have one with me. Fortunately, I had given a small picture of myself to Sun the other day, which he returned. We pasted it on the proper spot, paid twenty cents in revenue stamps which were stuck in the right places, and I returned to the hotel about 5:00 with all the required papers.

Meanwhile, Fred had gone to the American Consulate to give reports on ourselves and the Americans we had met in Sian. While there, he met Col. Stillwell, who had also been in Sian. Stillwell reported that our lady explorer, against all advice, had gone up to Lanchow and Sining, and he hoped he would never see her again. (Apparently she continues to make "friends" wherever she goes.) Last night Fred visited the American gun boat, *Luzon,* with the intention of asking to buy some U.S. cigarettes from the canteen, but the captain was so nice, treating him to chocolate cake, that he didn't have the nerve.

We are shipping our heavier baggage directly to the United States from here. We took it to the China Travel Service yesterday morning, signed a lot of papers, paid $300, and left it to be sent on. I sincerely hope I see it again.

The city of Hankow is referred to as the "Chicago of China", just as Shanghai is called China's "New York". It is located on the north side of the Yangtze at the mouth of the Han River. On the other side of the Han there is another city, and a third city is situated on the south side of the Yangtze at this same point. As we approached the city coming down river, we first saw tall buildings sending up fumes of black smoke, and as we sailed in closer we were almost overwhelmed by the large number of ships moored and anchored along the Bund. The heart of the city is the French Concession, which we have hardly left during our stay here. The river is so low now that a wide expanse of sloping sand separates it from the Bund, which is dominated by the Customs House. Beyond are large brick and stone European-style buildings and, except for the junks, Hankow seen from the river presents little that is Oriental. Although crowded, there is not the congestion so typical of Shanghai, and in the Concession, at least, there are no teeming Chinese alleys opening directly on to the main streets. The banking and business section of the city sits well back from the river, its imposing structures mostly dominated by great Grecian columns, which seem to me to be an unhappy choice of architectural design for a Chinese city. The most remarkable building is the Kincheng Bank, in a triangular area between two converging streets. The apex of the triangle is a garden which one must enter through a great iron gate to reach the front entrance. The effect, however, is somewhat spoiled by the slightly shabby shops that border the other two sides.

Although everything is orderly it is easy to see that Hankow is not in its normal state at present. Windows on the first and second floors of many of the larger buildings are blocked by sand bags, and concrete machine gun shelters have been built at many of the street intersections. At intervals in the Concession there are heavy wooden gates covered with barbed wire that can be closed at a moment's notice, and in numerous other places timbers strung with barbed wire are piled by the side of the street, ready to be made into instant barricades. There are, of course, many soldiers. Foreign buildings all fly their national flags and also have them painted on their doors and gates. Sailors from the gun boats as well as several companies of French marines are in evidence, especially at night when they parade the streets in groups, singing so loudly one might conclude that they are not entirely sober. Street life is like that of Shanghai, with coolies carrying great bundles to and from the ships. Rickshaws abound. There are few taxis, but there are open carriages drawn by incredibly small horses.

Our hotel is near the end of the French Bund next to the Russian Embassy, which is an enormous old brick residence flying its red flags with the star, hammer, and sickle. Our hotel also used to be a residence, but is now run by a German woman who has lived in China for some thirty-seven years. The most conspicuous person here is a very fat, over-enamelled barmaid who looks as though she has retired, by necessity, from the world's oldest profession. Our third floor room is large but shabbily furnished. The plumbing in the bathroom is defective because the water pressure is often too low to reach us. In order to reserve this room for us the bank had to pay six days in advance of our arrival, which makes it rather expensive for our short stay. It is undoubtedly the stingiest place I have ever been in; we have to fight to get a towel apiece, and the meals, included in the price, are very skimpy. Sometimes we get jam for breakfast, but there is never any butter. The tablecloths and napkins all have holes in them. Off the dining room is a bank vault where the previous owner probably stored valuables and where the current proprietress now keeps her small supply of cans and bottles, which she doles out carefully one by one.

We have had some last minute callers: Captain Carlson and Peter Fleming, who wrote the book, *News from Tartary*. He is a young fellow with a clipped British air, but quite pleasant. He was very interested in our travels, and we had a nice, though brief, visit. We heard that Belden, the American reporter we met in Sian, went on up to Lanchow and, when last heard of, was in jail for taking pictures of the airfield. One would have thought he would have known better—I would certainly hate to be confined in a Chinese jail.

After this visit, Fred and I hastily washed up and took a rickshaw to the bank for **another** farewell dinner party for us. The only other European there was Dr. Buck, Pearl Buck's divorced husband. He had been a professor at Nanking University, I think in agricultural economics, but since 1934 has been a representative of the U.S. Treasury Department here in Hankow. He was an interesting man and I enjoyed talking with him.

We leave tomorrow for Hong Kong.

Section from a letter to Dr. Yen:

April 22, 1938

After Kansu we turned our attentions to the oil possibilities of Shensi and Szechuan Provinces. This involved no field work in Shensi and only a rapid trip across Szechuan. Familiarity with the general geologic conditions was gained, however, by a study of the reports made to the Standard Oil Company in 1914 and 1915 and more recent Chinese Geological Survey publications. The areas which appear to possess oil possibilities are much larger in each of these provinces than in Kansu and are certainly worthy of additional study by experienced geologists.

Structurally, Szechuan appears to be a more attractive area than Shensi because of many well-formed anticlines. Some oil has been found in the salt wells, but not in important amounts. No oil has previously been known from this formation, and none of the salt wells have been drilled deep enough to reach it. It seems that drilling to this formation might be justified at one or more favorable locations unless more detailed field work should disclose unfavorable conditions that we know nothing about at present. At any rate, further work should be done in this province.

Hong Kong
April 24, 1938

We flew out of Hankow on April 21 as planned. Eurasia planes make a round trip between the two cities every day. Ordinarily their base is Hankow, and they would leave early in the morning to return in the afternoon. With the recent Japanese night raids, however, it seemed safer to reverse the schedule so that planes do not risk being damaged on the ground by remaining in Hankow overnight. We were informed that our plane would leave at 11:00 A.M. and were instructed to be at the airfield by 10:00 to pass inspection. To get there we had to ferry upstream across the river and then motor several miles out into the country. At the last minute Suez accompanied us because he had to go east on personal as well as Public Health business and, as he is terrified of plane travel, he thought being with us might take some of the fear out of it. We arrived at the field a little later than expected but were still the first passengers to check in. Fred's bags were searched carefully and his photographs scrutinized, while my bag was not opened at all and no one asked about my pictures. I carried the maps, which had been made into a roll, in my hand; they went unnoticed.

I do not know exactly how our passages on this flight were obtained on such short notice, for all seats are said to be reserved months in advance. Apparently we are important enough that others were made to give up their seats to us. Later, the other passengers drifted in (about half European and half Chinese) and the plane finally came in about noon. The two pilots disembarked, a table was set up in the hanger for them, and a boy brought them dinner which they ate while the plane was being refueled. They were the same two Germans that Fred had talked with in Cheng-tu. Half an hour later we clambered on board, the doors were shut, we taxied, and were soon off the ground on our last stage out of China.

The flight was uninteresting because the atmosphere was very hazy, with so many clouds that visibility was poor. First we flew over a portion of the Yangtze alluvial plain where much of the land was flooded to form irregular lakes, and the rest was divided into little fields, green with crops or brown with the muddy water of rice paddies. Low hills appeared as we flew into a ragged cloud front, and we dodged in and out between the billowing masses of white vapor. Sometimes we were below them, sometimes blustering right through them, and at other times we were on top. Clouds look very different seen from above—more alive, somehow—perhaps because we got so close to them that we could see their writhings and twistings. As we went through these clouds, rising and falling air currents caused the plane to roll and pitch considerably, and rough stretches made some of the Chinese very sick. I expected to be, but surprised myself and even enjoyed a cup of hot coffee and cookies served by the steward, which was all the lunch we had.

Between the clouds we caught glimpses of barren mountain sides intersected by lines of tiny fields marking the valleys and, here and there, little toy villages. In the afternoon the clouds became more dense and dark and finally joined to become a continuous layer with the tops of the mountains projecting through it. We flew close beneath the surface, winding in and out among the hills, and were near enough to distinguish individual farms, some with tall square towers plastered white, which looked strangely Italian. We came to a broader valley with a muddy river meandering through it which we followed until suddenly the sea appeared before us with an occasional junk sailing over its roughed-up surface.

The Chinese coast is very irregular, with low mountains rising directly from the water which is dotted with numerous small islands. The plane descended until we were at an elevation of only a few hundred feet. It skimmed the top of the water, over some islands and promontories, steamships appeared and grew bigger beneath us, and finally the island city came into view. We passed over it and went a few miles beyond to the airfield on the mainland, just outside of Kowloon. Within a few minutes we were on the ground. The trip had taken five hours.

Just before reaching Hong Kong we flew over part of the railway which carries munitions into the interior. There were also sections of excellent surfaced road which the Japanese have been bombing systematically for more than eight months now, sometimes several times a day. One of their principal targets has been a large railway bridge here. It is only recently, however, that they have been successful in hitting it; it was repaired immediately. I have heard that, in spite of thousands of bombs dropped on it, railroad service has been interrupted for only three days. From the ground it looks easy to hit a target from the air, but after looking down from our plane at the little dots that are buildings and the pieces of string that are roads, I can see that it is not as easy as I had imagined. I do not think the Chinese are very much afraid of air raids anymore. They say that in Canton, where there are alarms every day, the only people who stop work are those who are in others' employ.

Our plane stopped before the hangar and we all piled out, passing through a very perfunctory customs examination. We were met by the bank manager and Suez's oldest son, were driven into Kowloon where we caught a ferry to the main city of Hong Kong on the island, and checked into the Hong Kong Hotel. (This is the same hotel where I stayed on my way home from India fifteen years ago!) Fred, Sun, and I took the last three remaining rooms, so Suez went around the corner to a Chinese hotel. We had a few drinks and went to the bank where I was given a letter from Yen who is back in Shanghai. I was also handed a package containing two exquisitely carved pieces of camphor wood which at first I understood were presents for us but, after admiring them, learned that I was being asked to deliver them to Mr. Hussey who is now in Paris. We had dinner at the Golden Dragon, a "high class" joint where there is opium smoking, gambling, and plenty of sing-song girls. They knew no English, of course, and our little bits of Chinese were not of the Cantonese dialect, so communication was null and void. Nonetheless, they insisted on doing everything for us, almost to the extent of putting the food in our mouths, which really got to be quite a nuisance. The food was good and fortunately not over abundant. When we got back to our hotel rooms our trunks from Shanghai had been brought up.

The next day was a busy one. Among other things, I went to the bank to get money for our trip to Europe, took the needed things from my trunk, repacked it, and arranged to have it shipped to Chicago and Urbana, bought a smaller trunk as well as a bathing suit to use on the boat, got steamship tickets at the American Express, learned that I must have a vaccination certificate, and went to a doctor for the shot and papers. The doctor told me Hong Kong was in the midst of the worst small pox epidemic he had ever known. In the evening I met Fred in the cocktail lounge where he was chatting with Etter. (He is the League of Nations man who was so sick with typhus in Sian. He traveled down to Hankow by train and flew into Hong Kong the day before we did. He is recuperating and looks quite well.) He joined us for dinner and, luxury of luxuries, we all went to a good movie in an air-conditioned theater, after which we ended up in the roof garden, drinking beer until nearly 1:00.

Yesterday was not nearly so hectic. I went back to the American Express to sign papers for my trunk and bought some marks for the boat. In the afternoon we again went to the movies, and I spent the evening reading *Time* and *The Saturday Evening Post.* Although the day was nice with sunshine and we could have gone sightseeing, we didn't. Neither of us felt much like it.

Today is Sunday, and it is raining. This morning I went to Suez's hotel to give him some papers and invited him to the ship for a drink tonight before she sails. I finished packing, got the baggage sent aboard, and paid the bills. The rain hadn't stopped by the time we had to leave for the ship, so we took a rickshaw to the ferry. After crossing to the mainland we made a dash for the boat, which was docked close by, and are now established on the S.S. *Potsdam*. One more stage of our adventure has ended.

I think that Hong Kong is the nicest of the Oriental cities, but I am not sorry to leave it behind. The weather is bad this time of year; it is rainy with a high humidity, and one is almost always uncomfortable. Although the public lobby of our hotel was attractive, it was always crowded, and the individual rooms somehow looked old and shabby. The roof garden band plays until 2:00 every morning and has constantly kept me awake. The city is full of soldiers and sailors, mostly English, although there must be an American ship in port because the party in the roof garden last night sounded like it. The band kept playing American pieces like the Navy's "Annapolis Song", "The Maine Drinking Song", "The Stars and Stripes Forever", etc., with much singing, yelling, and stomping overhead. I am glad to be away from it all. I am also glad to be out of China. We have had an interesting adventure and I don't regret any of it, but in the same breath I am glad that its time and effort is in the past.

I will not write again because I shall probably beat my letters home. Besides, I shall have little to say other than that I am counting the days.

Epilogue

Epilogue

The areas controlled by Japanese military forces in the spring of 1938 made it impossible for my father to return to Shanghai from the interior as he had originally planned. He was thus unable to conclude his geologic interpretations of the expedition with Chinese authorities in the manner intended. By November of that year, both Canton and Hankow had fallen into Japanese hands. Because of this situation, it was not possible for Standard Vacuum Oil Company to proceed as they must have hoped to assist in the development of the oil structures indicated by the exploration. However, continuing correspondence between my father and the company gives evidence that Standard maintained its requirement that the trip be treated with extreme confidentiality, and he was not to publish anything technical or scientific about his experiences in China without their expressed approval. Although a complete set of geological reports and maps was turned over at the end of the trip to the Chinese syndicate, Dr. Koo in Paris, and Standard Vacumun Oil Company in New York, I am unsure as to whether or not Standard ever gained anything very positive from its involvement with the expedition. It is obvious, however, from correspondence in my father's files that China, desperately in need of oil for its war effort, went right to work on the Shih Yu Ho anticline near Yu Men. The syndicate released its mineral rights in the provinces, the Chinese National Geological Survey sent Mr. Sun back to Kansu, and under his supervision in February 1939 the first well was drilled on the gravel terrace near the oil seepage described in the reports. Before 1937, Chinese oil production was measured in quarts and, in its crude condition, was used solely as a lubricant. This first well, developed under the most primitive of conditions and with relatively untrained personnel, began to produce over twenty barrels of oil a day. In time, with equipment brought in from Szechuan and elsewhere and the development of several distillation plants, nine more wells were drilled in the immediate area. A letter from my father to T.E. Mobley of Standard Vacuum in June 1942 states that Mr. Sun, in the U.S. for extensive oil field geology training, reported that the Yu Men wells then had a capacity of about 1,000 barrels of oil and 10,000 gallons of gasoline a day, except in winter when cold weather caused the oil to congeal. This was the first major oil field in China. In 1956 a rail link was built to Lanchow; until then, the oil was transported out by truck. A pipeline was constructed in 1957. The Yu Men refinery was enlarged and modernized, and by the late 1960s it was reported that production from that area was "about two million tons".

Also in 1942, both the Board of Economic Warfare and the Office of Land-Lease Administration contacted my father for information about the oil and gas situation in China. They were particularly interested in the Yu Men area as the location was far in the Chinese interior, relatively safe from Japanese attack.

My father's spasmodic correspondence with Standard Vacuum, relative to seeking permission to publish various articles on oil in China as requested, continued until 1944.